THE FIERCE URGENCY OF NOW

THE
FIERCE
URGENCY
=== OF ===
NOW

LYNDON JOHNSON, CONGRESS,

AND THE BATTLE FOR THE GREAT SOCIETY

JULIAN E. ZELIZER

PENGUIN PRESS

NEW YORK

2015

PENGUIN PRESS
Published by the Penguin Group
Penguin Group (USA) LLC
375 Hudson Street
New York, New York 10014

USA · Canada · UK · Ireland · Australia
New Zealand · India · South Africa · China
penguin.com

A Penguin Random House Company

First published by Penguin Press, a member of Penguin Group (USA) LLC, 2015

Photograph credits appear on pages 355–356.

ISBN 978-1-59420-434-0

Printed in the United States of America
1   3   5   7   9   10   8   6   4   2

Designed by Gretchen Achilles

For Meg

We have also come to this hallowed spot to remind America of the fierce urgency of now. This is no time to engage in the luxury of cooling off or to take the tranquilizing drug of gradualism. Now is the time to make real the promises of democracy.

—MARTIN LUTHER KING JR.,
August 28, 1963, at the Lincoln Memorial, Washington, D.C.

CONTENTS

THE FIERCE URGENCY OF NOW

THE CHALLENGES OF
A LIBERAL PRESIDENCY

Lyndon Johnson hated being vice president. He was at heart a legislator who had been relegated to the sidelines of legislation. For almost three years he had watched John F. Kennedy fumble most of the big domestic issues of the day, either because the president was unwilling to take on the toughest challenges of the moment, or because he was too afraid of the political fallout, or because he knew he lacked the ability to win the legislative battles he faced on Capitol Hill. At the time of Kennedy's death, most of his major domestic initiatives—including civil rights, a tax cut, federal assistance for education, and hospital insurance for the elderly—were stalled in Congress or had not yet been introduced there. Kennedy and his advisers had made a conscious decision to keep Lyndon Johnson out of their inner circle, despite his extensive experience on Capitol Hill, for fear that his well-known thirst for power would cause problems for the president.[1]

At 4:00 a.m. on November 23, 1963, the day after Kennedy's assassination gave him the presidency, Johnson reclined on his bed, his top advisers arrayed around him for an impromptu meeting. He mapped out a grand vision for his team. The new president told Jack

Valenti, Bill Moyers, and Cliff Carter, with "relish and resolve," according to Valenti, "I'm going to get Kennedy's tax cut out of the Senate Finance Committee, and we're going to get this economy humming again. Then I'm going to pass Kennedy's civil rights bill, which has been hung up too long in the Congress. And I'm going to pass it without changing a single comma or a word. After that we'll pass legislation that allows everyone anywhere in this country to vote, with all the barriers down. And that's not all. We're going to get a law that says every boy and girl in this country, no matter how poor, or the color of their skin, or the region they come from, is going to be able to get all the education they can take by loan, scholarship, or grant, right from the federal government." After pausing to catch his breath, almost as if exhausted by his own ambitions, the president concluded, "And I aim to pass Harry Truman's medical insurance bill that got nowhere before."[2]

Jack Valenti's recollection of that moment perfectly portrays the Lyndon Johnson who had suddenly become the nation's leader. He was a creature of Congress, a legislator by character and long experience, who was determined to push through a transformative body of laws that would constitute nothing less than a second New Deal.

Though many liberals had long doubted that Johnson was anything but a southern racist conservative who sometimes pretended to be one of them, he was, when he became president of the United States, truly determined to expand the role of the federal government in domestic life far beyond what his hero Franklin Roosevelt had accomplished. Johnson had started in politics as a New Deal liberal, and over the years he had grown ever more determined to deal with issues FDR had ignored and on which Johnson himself had been ambivalent at best during his own political career, most notably civil rights and health care. He wanted to use the presidency to build legislative majorities behind the ideas that liberals had been discussing and deliberating—but not enacting into law—for more than a decade.

Lyndon Johnson's vision of a presidency that would spearhead major liberal legislation faced enormous obstacles, however. Historians have often failed to understand how the Great Society—President Johnson's agenda of big domestic programs—was enacted, because they have accepted two myths about the nature of the political challenges the Great Society had to face.

The first myth presents the 1960s as the apex of modern American liberalism, the culmination of those forces that arose in the Progressive Era at the turn of the twentieth century when the federal government came to be seen as a positive good, when social movements leaned toward the left, and when conservatives were marginal and irrelevant.

A recent generation of historians has shattered this portrait of the liberal era in politics. They have rediscovered the enormous influence of conservative activists, philanthropists, organizations, and politicians in the decades that directly followed the New Deal. Shifting attention away from the White House and toward the U.S. Congress is one of the most effective ways to gain a very different perspective on the dynamics of American politics before the age of Reagan. Though many of the nation's presidents had embraced liberal ideas, Congress was a powerful institution dominated by a conservative coalition of southern Democrats and Republicans who rejected liberalism. During the 1930s, as the political scientist Ira Katznelson has shown, FDR was already forced to compromise his New Deal to appease southern Democrats and Republicans by agreeing to federal legislation that protected the racial order of Dixie and made it difficult for organized labor to gain a foothold in that low-wage nonunion region.[3]

After the 1930s, Congress was a graveyard of liberal legislation.

At the time of President Kennedy's death, the record for liberal reform was meager. The spirit of the New Deal seemed a distant memory. It had been two and a half decades since any significant social legislation had been passed. President Truman lacked the skills of his predecessor, and he spent much of his political capital advancing the nation's involvement in the cold war. Congressional conservatives killed most of his marquee domestic proposals, including national health care, and even turned back one of the hallmark achievements of the New Deal, the Wagner Act, which had guaranteed the right of workers to organize into unions and created the National Labor Relations Board to supervise union elections, by passing the 1947 Taft-Hartley Act, which allowed states to enact "right to work" laws that made it more difficult for unions to organize workers. The Republican president Dwight Eisenhower, though he accepted the permanence of the New Deal, had limited domestic policy aims and spent much of his second term pushing back against liberal Democrats in Congress who were demanding that the government do more, and spend more, to tackle social problems. President Kennedy, a hard-nosed pragmatist who continually rebuffed liberals who he believed had unrealistic expectations of what could be accomplished through legislation, saw his fears confirmed when he was soundly throttled by the conservatives in Congress on a number of proposals. As Kennedy pointed out in an interview in 1962, "I think the Congress looks more powerful sitting here than it did when I was there in the Congress."

Many of the southern Democratic committee chairmen, who, with their Republican allies, dominated Congress, opposed the changes Johnson hoped to pursue. These long-serving southern Democrats were dead set against racial integration in public accommodations and believed that a proposal to provide insurance to cover the hospital stays of the elderly was socialized medicine. They believed in the right to vote in principle but didn't support giving the

4

attorney general any power to ensure that African Americans could exercise that right. These conservatives vehemently opposed the idea that the federal government would provide financial assistance to the schools that educated the nation's children, and they claimed that communists were pulling the strings of all the grassroots movements that were seeking racial equality and economic justice.

The committee chairmen were shocked but not moved by Kennedy's assassination. When Johnson called on the nation to fulfill Kennedy's agenda in order to honor the life of the martyred leader, congressional conservatives responded with stolid indifference. When Johnson took office, liberalism was in bad shape, fragile and ineffective, beset on all sides by powerful enemies. If Johnson was going to persuade Congress to pass his policy wish list, he would have to change the power structure that reinforced the conservative stranglehold on the legislative process.

Despite the nostalgia many feel today for the Congress of the 1960s—wishful memories of an institution where it was easier to pass legislation—the truth is that until 1964 Congress was seen as a dysfunctional branch of government, where southern Democrats and Republicans regularly brought the legislative process to a complete standstill.[4] The short period in which Congress enacted most of the Great Society programs was more an aberration than the norm in those years.

The second myth about the 1960s has to do with presidential power. Much of the history written about the Great Society in this period presents it as the product of Lyndon Johnson's brilliant legislative prowess—how he wielded the power of the presidency to force legislators to vote for legislation they had long vehemently opposed. "Johnson left huge footprints wherever he stepped," wrote the historian Bruce Schulman, "overwhelming nearly everyone who crossed his path and achieving more than nearly any other American politician."[5]

The central image of the myth is Johnson as practitioner of "the Treatment"—this imposing man, six feet four and whose fluctuating weight crept up to 240 pounds, literally leaning on his colleagues, physically and verbally bullying, cajoling, lobbying, and threatening until they had no way out but to give him what he wanted. In photographs of the Treatment we see Johnson, having barged into the personal space of his target, putting his hands on the man's shoulders or inching his nose right up to his face as he bends the man to his will. "The Treatment," wrote the columnists Rowland Evans and Robert Novak, was "an almost hypnotic experience and rendered the target stunned and helpless."[6] Although the physical dimension was gone when Johnson tried to convince over the phone, he used the same bullying techniques to win people over with his voice. The Treatment could be seductive or terrifying, or usually a little of both.

Yet Johnson did have an uncanny command of the legislative process, which he had perfected as Senate majority leader in the 1950s. He employed powerful strategies for scheduling debates, manipulating arcane parliamentary rules, learning the background and personality of every legislator and using all this information to his advantage, conducting votes on legislation, and using pork barrel politics to build voting alliances on the floor. His mastery of all these tactics has been used to explain how, as president of the United States, Johnson changed the way Americans lived their lives.

Johnson remains a central figure in the debate about the triumph of presidential power in these decades of the twentieth century—the so-called rise of the "imperial presidency." In this context, Johnson is the essential clue to how presidents can make Congress work by handling legislators and the legislative process in the right way.

When health-care and financial regulation bills were stuck in Congress in late 2009 and early 2010, Democratic senators were reading Robert Caro's most recent volume about the Senate majority leader Lyndon Johnson to figure out how President Obama could get his troubled bill through an obstructionist Congress. "A few of us joked that we should just get Robert Caro's book on Lyndon Johnson, highlight a few pages, and leave it on the president's desk," one White House aide recalled. "Sometimes a president just needs to knock heads. It's kind of what the combatants secretly want. [Johnson] twisted their arm, they had no choice—he was going [to] defund them, ruin 'em, support their opponent, whatever the fuck—and the deal was cut. It lets them off the hook. They had no choice. I mean, for fuck's sake, he's the goddamn president."[7]

But all the political savvy in the world has never been enough to move a Congress where the legislators who controlled the chambers fundamentally opposed the proposals that were coming from the White House. The veneration of the Treatment obscures how politics works; it overemphasizes the capacity of "great men" to effect legislation by force of personality and undervalues the more complicated and significant effects of the political environment in which a president must operate—congressional coalitions, interest groups, social movements, and voting constituencies. In 1963, Johnson understood this better than most, given his extensive experience on Capitol Hill. Political scientists correctly remind us that the institutional rules and procedures of Congress play a huge role in determining what kinds of opportunities presidents have in office because they structure the incentives and behavior of legislators on Capitol Hill.[8]

This was as true for Johnson as it has been for all other presidents. In November 1963, the committee process defined Congress. Johnson knew that the conservative committee leaders in the House and the Senate had the power to set the congressional agenda, to put certain issues on the front burner and ignore others, regardless of what opinion polls or grassroots activists were saying the American people wanted, to say nothing of what the president of the United States wanted. Senior committee chairmen could prevent bills from being debated or voted on; they could attach rules to legislation that would make floor debates unmanageable and susceptible to tricks and tactics that would subvert legislation. The secretive nature of Congress in this period, when television cameras were still prohibited from the chambers and when most hearings were conducted behind closed doors, gave elected officials the liberty to subvert legislation without being subject to public scrutiny. Senators had the right to engage in filibusters, speeches of unlimited length on any topic that stopped the normal progress toward a vote and could not be ended except by a virtually impossible supermajority of sixty-seven senators.

Johnson often complained of the limits of his power and scoffed at the perception that he had extraordinary human skills that enabled him to move his colleagues. Indeed, he had lost some of his ability to directly shape this process as he wanted when he moved from Capitol Hill to the White House. As president, he had to rely on legislators to do for him much of the legislative work he had once done for himself. About his power, President Johnson once complained, "The only power I've got is nuclear . . . and I can't use that."[9]

The key to the success of the Great Society had less to do with the overwhelming popularity of liberalism or the presidential power of Johnson than with the specific changes between the summer of 1964 and the November elections that created unusually good conditions in Congress for passing domestic bills. In other words, we need a less Johnson-centric view to understand how this historic burst of liberal domestic legislation happened. We need to ask not only what Lyndon Johnson did that was so special but what legislative conditions existed that allowed someone with Johnson's skills to succeed.

During this critical period, the power of the conservative coalition was diminished, first by the actions of the civil rights movement, which in 1963 and 1964 placed immense pressure on legislators in both parties to pass laws that would benefit African Americans, and subsequently by the 1964 elections, which gave liberals the huge majorities they needed to prevent conservative committee chairmen from thwarting their domestic policy aims in Congress. Not only did liberal Democrats have the votes necessary to pass bills and kill filibusters, but Republican moderates, a sizable force in their party, were running as fast as they could from all positions that might allow Democrats to brand them as right-wing extremists in the wake of the ultraconservative senator Barry Goldwater's landslide loss in the presidential election.

Johnson deserves his share of credit, but less for being an especially skilled politician who could steamroll a recalcitrant Congress than for taking advantage of extremely good legislative conditions when they emerged. Moreover, Johnson's success with domestic programs resulted from a risky political maneuver he undertook in 1964 and 1965 to maintain momentum for his legislation. Resisting all the opposition he faced from White House advisers and legislators, including hawks like the Georgia senator Richard Russell, Johnson escalated American involvement in the war in Vietnam. There were many reasons why he ended up listening to the hawks and embarking on a disastrous war in Southeast Asia, including his general agreement with the domino theory of communism, but one of the most important was a political calculation that a liberal Democratic president had to be hawkish on foreign policy in order to be successful. Otherwise, Johnson believed, he would give conservatives—who had thrived on foreign and domestic anticommunist crusades in the early 1950s—too much ammunition with which to attack his administration as weak on defense.

Johnson was forced to deal with the consequences of this decision when legislative conditions deteriorated after the 1966 midterm elections. The ability of Republicans to play on concerns about inflation and Vietnam, and a brewing racial backlash among northern Democratic constituencies in response to urban riots and the black power movement, significantly reduced the size of the Democratic congressional majority. The conservative coalition rebounded after its losses in 1964, and when Johnson once again had to face a strong conservative coalition, all the Treatment and parliamentary tricks in the world had little practical effect on Congress. Johnson spent his final two years as president contending with the politics of austerity as he pushed for a desperately needed tax hike and congressional conservatives pushed back for steep cuts in domestic spending, all of which, combined with the protests over Vietnam, virtually crippled his ability to secure more big legislation.

Although this period of liberalism was much more fragile, contested, and transitory than we have usually remembered, the programs that came out of it have endured. One of the most remarkable aspects of the Great Society is how much still lives with us today, fifty years later, so much so that most Americans regard its programs as essential manifestations of the national government's responsibility to its citizens.

This is a book about how the work of grassroots activists and changes in the power structure of Congress enabled a liberal president to fulfill his grand legislative ambition—the creation of a second New Deal that would complete the work of Franklin Roosevelt, expand the welfare state, and extend the full rights of citizenship to African Americans and the poor. The conditions in which these achievements were possible existed only for a short time. When those conditions changed, the great period of liberal legislation was ended by a resurgent opposition, but the achievements of the period were never overturned and have remained irrevocable.

CHAPTER TWO

DEADLOCKED DEMOCRACY

When John F. Kennedy delivered his inaugural address on January 20, 1961, over twenty thousand Americans gathered in bitter-cold weather at the east front of the U.S. Capitol to watch the new leader take over from his Republican predecessor, Dwight Eisenhower, a military hero who had been extremely popular throughout his two terms in office, times of relative peace and prosperity. Though Kennedy had barely defeated Vice President Richard Nixon, those who voted for the Massachusetts senator were delighted with their choice. He had had a thoroughly mediocre record in Congress, but his enthusiasm, his charisma, and his youthful energy, all of which had been emphasized by television, led many Democrats to believe that Kennedy could be a transformative president.

In his speech, Kennedy offered tough words for the Soviet Union. He warned that the United States would "pay any price, bear any burden, meet any hardship, support any friend, oppose any foe to assure the survival and the success of liberty." But the words that inspired liberals were his challenge to "my fellow Americans" to "ask not what your country can do for you, ask what you can do for your country." In this phrase liberals heard a president demanding that citizens take action to improve conditions in their country. They were desperate to see in Kennedy a leader who would move their domestic agenda forward after two long terms of standpat Republican rule in the White House. The inauguration also offered at least one symbol that confirmed liberal hopes about the true intentions of this cold warrior from Massachusetts. Kennedy had invited Marian Anderson, the African American singer who had once been barred by the Daughters of the American Revolution from singing at Constitution Hall, to sing the national anthem, a choice that displeased southern Democrats opposed to civil rights. Here Kennedy, the centrist Democrat, who during his eight years in the Senate had been tepid toward organized labor and a tough anticommunist, gave a hint that some observers took to mean that things could be different for African Americans during his presidency. The editors of the *New York Times* went so far as to say that "President Kennedy's Administration opens a new chapter in the history of the American people."[1]

Yet even if the president turned out to be on their side, the chances of success were not great for liberals whose outlook and aspirations had been tempered by the events of the post–World War II era. Despite the expansion of presidential power that had taken place since the early twentieth century, most political veterans understood that the shift from one administration to the next frequently produced more limited results than voters expected at the height of the campaign. This was because of the immense power of a legislative branch in which conservative southern Democrats still ruled by virtue of their tight hold on most of the major committees and their voting alliance with the GOP.

For years, Congress had been the chief obstacle to liberalism. While congressional conservatives didn't have enough power to dismantle the New Deal, much of which their constituencies supported, they were able to prevent liberals from expanding the domestic role of government any further. When liberals had proposed measures to expand FDR's New Deal—legislation to deal with racial discrimination, workers' rights, housing conditions, or health care—conservatives had always struck them down. The brief grace period to come would be defined by Kennedy's efforts to navigate the growing tensions between the ambitions and demands of postwar liberals and the determination of a powerful and entrenched conservative coalition to prevent them from achieving any progress whatsoever.

Liberals, who had been shut down for years by the conservative coalition, were hoping in January 1961 that this time things would be different. They anticipated, without much justification other than what they had observed on the campaign trail and a few signals during the inauguration ceremony, that they would get energy and support from Kennedy. They hoped that the charismatic young Democratic president would have the ability to deliver legislation and get their agenda moving in a Democratic Congress.

CONGRESSIONAL CONSERVATISM

Though conservatism had many sources of support in the decades prior to 1960—including business leaders who funded anti–New Deal Republicans and grassroots activists who railed against Franklin Roosevelt's liberalism—the primary base of power for the Right was Congress, dominated by a coalition of powerful southern Democratic and midwestern Republican representatives and senators. The southern Democrats represented primarily rural constituencies of farmers, agribusiness, poor whites, poor African Americans, and individuals involved in military contracting. Most of the Republicans in the coalition represented rural interests, fiscally conservative small-town voters, and small- and midsize-business leaders. Members of this coalition were not united on everything, but they were united in opposing most legislative proposals that could benefit

African Americans, immigrants, organized labor, and other disadvantaged groups and in supporting benefits for farmers, small businesses, poor whites, and military contractors.

The conservative coalition had taken form in 1937 in reaction to President Roosevelt's landslide reelection victory, which seemed at first to have cemented a productive future for New Deal liberalism. FDR had trounced his Republican opponent, Alf Landon, and Democrats had gained huge majorities, but in the year after the election Roosevelt overreached. He had been deeply frustrated in 1935 and 1936 when the Supreme Court declared the National Industrial Recovery Act and the Agricultural Adjustment Act unconstitutional. So now, without consulting any legislators, he proposed adding up to six new justices to the Court, in a transparent effort to dilute judicial opposition to his policies. There was furious opposition to this proposal. Conservatives said it would destroy the constitutional separation of powers, and they compared FDR to certain European dictators. Many liberals and moderates, who had been totally unprepared for FDR's request, were publicly critical of the president as well. They worried that expanding the Supreme Court would set a precedent that some future conservative president might use against them and their interests. Roosevelt aggravated the situation by proposing a reorganization of the executive branch that conservatives saw as a further attempt to usurp congressional power. They defeated the court-packing plan and watered down the executive branch reorganization bill. During the 1938 Democratic primaries, a defiant Roosevelt campaigned against five congressional opponents in his own party. Unfortunately for Roosevelt, four of the candidates won and returned to Capitol Hill to oppose him in 1939.[2]

FDR died in 1945, but the conservative coalition lived on. President Truman watched helplessly as the coalition stripped away everything it could of FDR's achievements, notably the price controls that had been put in place during World War II and a federal commission to combat racial discrimination in wartime employment. When Truman called on Congress to pass national health insurance in 1949 and 1950, the coalition, allied with the American Medical Association, labeled the plan "socialized medicine" and made sure the bill was defeated. The coalition was also a driving force behind anticommunist legislation in the 1950s; its members insisted that the government use the most stringent measures possible in pursuing alleged communists. While anticommunism had a powerful hold on politicians of both parties in this period, the conservative wing of each party generally wanted to take ever more aggressive steps in hunting alleged communists, in making allegations about who might be a fellow traveler or sympathizer, and in flouting civil liberties protections. Whenever President Eisenhower veered to the center on polices aimed at rooting out communists at home, the coalition pushed him back toward the right.

The conservative coalition was able to maintain its power in Congress because each of the major parties was fractured. Unlike today's parties, which are ideologically united with virtually no overlap at their extremes—no Republican is more liberal than the most conservative Democrat; no Democrat is more conservative than the most liberal Republican—then there was notable cross-party overlap and frequent breaking off of factions from each side of the aisle. Democrats were divided between a conservative southern and a liberal northern faction at odds over civil rights and unionization, Republicans between midwestern conservatives who wanted to constrain the government on most economic matters and liberal northeasterners who were sometimes more progressive—on civil rights, for example—than many Democrats.

The coalition's operations were informal and ad hoc. Conservative Democrats met in one building and conservative Republicans in another. Each group would send one member to the other group as a liaison. Representative Joseph Martin of Massachusetts, who was the leader of the House Republicans from 1939 to 1958, later explained that "when an issue of spending or of new powers for the President came along, I would go to Representative Howard Smith of Virginia, for example, and say, 'Howard, see if you can't get me a few Democratic votes here.' Or I would seek out Representative Eugene Cox of Georgia, and ask, 'Gene, why don't you and John Rankin [of Mississippi] and some of your men get me some votes on this?'"[3]

The practice of organizing and sharing votes was important, but the coalition exercised its power primarily through members who held key positions in the congressional hierarchies.[4] All members of Congress served on committees that debated proposals and drafted bills to be sent to the House or Senate floor for general debate and a vote; each committee focused on legislation in its assigned policy areas. The House Ways and Means Committee, for example, handled taxation, trade, and Social Security and unemployment compensation. In 1960, conservative southern Democrats chaired almost half the major committees in the House and the Senate, including Ways and Means. The committees determined what bills would reach the House and Senate floors—no bills could make it there without a majority vote of one committee or more—and the committee chairmen exercised total control over their committees. After a committee passed a bill in the House, the bill also had to make it through the House Rules Committee, which determined the schedule and rules for debate on the floor, before it could be voted on by the entire chamber.

In the early twentieth century, as a result of reforms that decentralized power in response to a series of ruthless House Speakers and a strong desire to spread the workload in Congress as the government grew in size, formal rules were established and informal rules evolved that gave committee chairmen significant autonomy from the Speaker of the House, the Senate majority leader, and other party leaders. Chairmen controlled the agendas for their committees, they decided which bills would be discussed and which would be ignored, and they managed the bills—they planned the strategy and the rounding up of votes necessary to pass the bills—after their committees sent them to the floor.

A large number of the major committee chairmen, who by the rules had a virtual veto on all legislation, were southern members of the conservative coalition. This was because promotion on committees depended entirely on seniority, rather than on any assessment of ability, knowledge, or even party loyalty. When a member entered Congress, the party assigned him or her to one or more committees. Naturally, a legislator would ask to be assigned to a committee where he could implement benefits to his constituents—or, in common Washington parlance, deliver pork. A legislator elected by a largely urban constituency would have little interest in being placed on the Agriculture Committee.

A member well positioned to provide benefits to his constituents was likely to win reelection, move up in committee rank by virtue of his accumulated seniority, and in time reach a position of leadership—chairman, if his party was in the majority, or ranking minority member. The longer a member stayed in office, the higher he rose in rank, whether or not he voted as the president or his party leadership wanted him to. Theoretically, party leaders could make new committee assignments at the start of each Congress, but in the 1950s and 1960s the parties followed the norm of seniority as if it were law. Committee members were never punished for disloyalty or disobedience. When each new Congress began, the party caucuses in the House and the Senate automatically voted to approve the most senior committee members of the majority party as chairmen. To amass enormous power, a legislator had only to be reelected by his constituents and remain conscious some of the time at committee meetings. Senator James Murray of Montana, who became senile in the 1950s, continued nonetheless to chair the Interior Committee, while the more junior Washington senator Henry "Scoop" Jackson ran things behind the scenes. Between 1946, when legislative reorganization consolidated the committee system, and the late 1960s, the norm of seniority advancement was violated only on rare occasions.[5] One was in 1953, when the Oregon senator Wayne Morse switched parties.

Southern Democrats did notably well in the seniority-based committee system because their districts were not competitive. From the end of Reconstruction until the 1970s, the South was a one-party town; Republicans were virtually nonexistent there. Most elected Democrats held on to their offices for many terms; they were usually able to defeat primary challengers who were less well-known, less well funded, and helpless to deliver congressional pork to their districts and states. Unfairly apportioned districts favored sparsely populated rural communities over urban centers. State legislative bodies in the South, which were biased toward conservative rural populations, drew up districts that granted far less representation to residents of the cities, where most African Americans lived. Even when there were big population shifts—African Americans moving into cities—the apportionment of districts stayed the same. Thinly populated rural white districts had the same number of representatives as densely populated urban areas.

Even when the number of northern liberals increased in the House and the Senate during the 1950s, committee chairmen could push back against their demands for legislation. A measure required a majority vote on a committee to send it to the floor of the House or the Senate for action by the full body. The conservative coalition could usually provide enough Republicans to secure a conservative majority, but Democratic chairmen always had the ultimate power on their committees—to do nothing at all. The Mississippi senator James Eastland, an ardent racist who took over as chairman of the Senate Judiciary Committee in 1956, liked to joke that as chairman of the Subcommittee on Civil Rights he was always a roadblock to legislation. "Why, for the three years I was chairman," he said, "that committee didn't hold a meeting. I had special pockets in my pants, and for years I carried those bills everywhere I went and every one of them was defeated."[6] Of course, the bills were never actually defeated; they were simply never deliberated or voted on by the committee. If the Senate leadership had been motivated, they could have freed those pocketed civil rights bills from captivity in Eastland's committee by adding the contents of the bills as amendments to other bills or by taking advantage of rules that allowed senators to forcefully discharge legislation from the hands of a recalcitrant chairman. The House leadership had similar tactics available to its members. But representatives and senators were usually reluctant to violate any aspect of the committee process, because each member benefited from it in those areas most important to his political career; if a member stayed long enough in Congress, he might even capture a chairmanship and its powers for himself. Any challenge to a committee chairman would become a precedent that could ultimately limit any representative's prerogatives. Liberals were well aware that there were already a few senior liberals—like Emanuel Celler on the House Judiciary Committee—who used their powers as chairmen to move liberal bills to the floor.

Southern chairmen were powerful also because of the importance of their region to the Democratic Party when it came to picking presidents. No Democrat could win the White House without winning the South, which therefore remained the electoral base of the party. Between Reconstruction and 1952, no Republican presidential candidate had won any state from the Old Confederacy. Liberal Democrats became even more cautious about angering southern leaders after the 1952 election, when the Republican Dwight Eisenhower won in Virginia, Florida, Tennessee, and Texas. In 1956 he added Louisiana to the tally.

On those occasions when one of the more liberal committees—House Education and Labor, for example, or House Judiciary—reported out a bill, the conservative coalition could still count on its voting power to defeat the bill on the floor. Even as the number of northern liberals increased in the House and the Senate during the late 1950s, southern Democrats had enough votes, along with their Republican allies, to kill most bills. In 1957 and 1958, southern Democrats and midwestern Republicans controlled 311 out of 435 seats in the House, and they held 71 out of 96 seats in the Senate. Even after the midterm elections of 1958, which increased the number of northern liberals in both chambers, the conservative coalition retained a ninety-two-vote majority in the House and an eighteen-vote majority in the Senate. John F. Kennedy didn't have any coattails; in 1960, Democrats lost twenty-two seats in the House, among them a substantial number of liberals.[7]

In the Senate, which the journalist William White called "the South's unending revenge upon the North for Gettysburg," members of the conservative coalition had an additional tool at their disposal: the filibuster.[8] It was first used in 1837, when a minority took advantage of the ambiguity in the chamber's rules regarding extended debate. A group of Democrats held the floor to demand that the Senate expunge from the record a censure of Andrew Jackson that had passed in 1834 after the president withdrew deposits from the Bank of the United States. After loading up on cold hams, turkey, and coffee, the senators only had to give speeches for a few hours before the rest of the Senate gave in and passed the resolution they were demanding.[9] This event became the precedent for future sessions; the Senate held on to the notion that the majority could not limit debate but a minority of one or two or several senators could extend debate to intolerable lengths and to the exclusion of any other Senate business.[10] The rules and traditions that developed around the practice of the filibuster permitted any member of the Senate to prevent a bill from being voted on as long as he stayed on the floor and kept talking—about almost anything. In the 1950s and 1960s, senators, or small groups of senators, regularly used this tactic to prevent civil rights legislation from reaching a vote. The filibuster was the ultimate reason why liberal senators chose not to take the risk of violating committee rules, procedures, and traditions to pull civil rights bills out of committees run by racist southern chairmen: they knew from experience that any civil rights bill that made it to the Senate floor would surely die there by filibuster.

In 1917, senators had provided a mechanism for ending filibusters. Frustrated by a Republican filibuster against arming merchant ships in the middle of World War I, Democrats, with the support of President Woodrow Wilson, passed "Rule 22," which allowed senators to shut down a filibuster by voting for "cloture." According to the original rule, a filibuster could be stopped only with the support of two-thirds of the chamber, which by 1961 comprised sixty-seven votes. Unless there were enough votes for cloture, a filibuster could continue until a bill died and was buried under unlimited talk. In 1938, southern senators—among them Louisiana's Allen Ellender, who said, "I believe in white supremacy, and as long as I am in the Senate I expect to fight for white supremacy"—killed an antilynching bill by mounting a six-week filibuster.[11] Southern Democrats did the same against anti–poll tax legislation in 1942, 1944, 1946, and 1948. In 1946 and in 1950, the southerners filibustered a proposal to make the Fair Employment Practices Commission, which had been established during World War II to maintain racial calm at wartime production plants, a permanent institution to combat racial discrimination in the workplace. Liberals sometimes used filibusters too. In 1953, Senator Wayne Morse filibustered for twenty-two hours and twenty-six minutes against legislation to allow states the right to control natural resources in certain offshore lands.

These committee arrangements and Senate rules were the structural barriers Congress presented to President Kennedy when he entered the White House in January 1961. To those liberals who hoped that Kennedy would emerge as an effective liberal president, Congress presented a daunting challenge.

A NEW GENERATION OF LIBERALS
WANTS MORE

Liberal politicians who entered Congress in the late 1950s and early 1960s knew that Congress itself was the main roadblock to their agenda. These liberals, primarily northerners, were part of a generation that had been inspired by FDR and his New Deal. They were committed to protecting and expanding Roosevelt's domestic record, though they were keenly aware of the other formidable obstacles they faced, among them the prevailing cold war mentality, which made political activity perilous for anyone whom conservative opponents could label a socialist or a communist. These liberals believed that the best way to separate themselves from the far left was to demonstrate their commitment to a muscular policy against the Soviet Union. The liberals were also well aware that they had been unable to advance their domestic agenda under Eisenhower, who balanced the federal budget by reducing spending and enjoyed close to 60 percent approval ratings throughout most of his two terms in the White House.

The postwar liberal movement was driven by the actions of legislators, interest groups, and grassroots activists. All of them believed the New Deal had been enormously successful in easing the pain of the Great Depression and enacting domestic policies to create a more just capitalist economy. The economy was now expanding at a rapid clip. Unemployment was low, inflation was contained, and the gross national product was getting bigger every year. More and more people were enjoying the economic security that came with being part of the American middle class. The liberals' goals in the postwar period were to create programs that would help more Americans enter the middle class and to tackle structural problems that existed in good times and bad—racial inequality, inadequate health-care coverage, underfunded education, urban decay, and chronic poverty— but could best be addressed when the economy was producing economic rewards for a majority of the workforce.

Starting in the 1948 election and continuing with each election through the 1958 midterms, the liberal bloc in the House and the Senate had gradually expanded. The spread of organized labor in northern states, the influx of African Americans into the North, and the growth of urban areas, which tended to be more liberal politically, had resulted in the election of more legislators who supported the New Deal and wanted the federal government to do more. In traditionally Republican areas of some states—California and Ohio, for example—organized labor was providing pivotal support in getting liberal Democrats elected.

Younger senators, among them Paul Douglas of Illinois, Clair Engle of California, Vance Hartke of Indiana, Herbert Lehman of New York, Ed Muskie of Maine, and Harrison Williams of New Jersey, were itching to challenge the southern Democrats.[12] They didn't want to follow the advice Speaker Sam Rayburn had given a newly elected congressman named Lyndon Johnson and others of their predecessors that they should "go along" to "get along." They didn't want to cooperate if it meant accepting that their principled aims would continue to be thwarted; they wanted to marshal their resources, use the advantages they had in Congress, and win.

An archetype of this generation was the Minnesota senator Hubert Humphrey. Raised in South Dakota, Humphrey was a product of prairie populism who idolized William Jennings Bryan and Franklin Roosevelt. The politics of the 1930s captivated him; he wrote a master's thesis at Louisiana State University, where he graduated in 1940, about the philosophy of the New Deal. "Democracy and socialism," Humphrey wrote, "are alike motivated by the desire to free the individual from oppression and to guarantee to each an opportunity for personal happiness, for self-realization, for practical liberty and spiritual freedom."[13] When he moved back to the University of Minnesota to pursue a doctoral degree in political science, he studied parliamentary procedure and learned how conservatives used congressional rules to block liberal legislation. He also served in the Minnesota branch of the federal War Production Board and as assistant director of the War Manpower Progress Commission. After a stint as a professor at Macalester College in 1943 and 1944, during which he worked as the manager for FDR's campaign in Minnesota, Humphrey decided to enter politics rather than just teach about it. He was active in the Democratic Party and in the Minnesota Democratic-Farmer-Labor Party, which he and other local Democrats created in a 1944 merger with Minnesota's relatively successful left-wing Farmer-Labor Party. He continued to endear himself to liberal organizations. In 1945, organized labor helped him win election as mayor of Minneapolis by rallying working-class Democrats to his side. His administration created the first Fair Employment Practices Commission in municipal government. Three years later, he ran for the Senate. In the middle of his campaign, he drew national attention during the Democratic convention in Philadelphia when he called on all Democrats to endorse a stronger civil rights plank in the party platform than most, including President Truman, were willing to accept. He declared, "To those who say that this bill of rights program is an infringement of states' rights, I say this: the time has arrived in America for the Democratic party to get out of the shadow of states' rights and walk forthrightly into the bright sunshine of human rights."[14] The Mississippi and half of the Alabama delegations stormed out of the convention hall and lined up soon afterward behind the States' Rights Democratic Party and the candidacy of South Carolina's segregationist governor Strom Thurmond.

After his election to the Senate in 1948, Humphrey continued to rattle conservative cages. He launched his senatorial career with a speech on the Senate floor in which he called the filibuster "a violation of the principle of majority rule on which our democracy is based." He also delivered a speech in which he proposed the elimination of the Joint Committee on Reduction of Nonessential Federal Expenditures, a committee chaired by the Virginia senator Harry Byrd, one of the giants of Capitol Hill. Humphrey, who was already persona non grata among southerners for his support of civil rights, accused Byrd's committee, which was responsible for eliminating waste and extravagance, of being wasteful and extravagant. Notwithstanding his gracious demeanor, Byrd was not a man who took criticism lightly. He was known among his colleagues for being quick-tempered. Six days after Humphrey's speech, Byrd offered a rebuttal, in which he corrected "misstatements" Humphrey had made. Senior members of the Senate then stood up to denounce Humphrey, one by one, for four hours straight. When the Minnesotan, who slouched in his chair throughout the verbal beating, stood up to offer his response, his colleagues left the chamber. In the hallways of the Senate, senior members whispered derogatory statements about Humphrey within earshot.[15]

Over his years in the Senate, Humphrey learned to moderate his tone and to accept compromise. Doing so allowed him to serve as the informal liaison between the Senate majority leader, Lyndon Johnson, and the liberal wing of the Democratic Party. Johnson, who felt he could use Humphrey to control and contain the liberals, had convinced the Minnesota senator that he had to be more pragmatic if he didn't want to "suffer the fate of those crazies, those bomb-thrower types like Paul Douglas, Wayne Morse, Herbert Lehman. You'll be ignored, and get nothing accomplished you want."[16] Humphrey took Johnson's advice and moderated his style but always with the clear objective of securing a place for liberals at the legislative bargaining table.

In 1959, younger liberal members of the House, frustrated with the power of the southern Democrats and their Republican allies, formed a caucus they called the Democratic Study Group (DSG). The caucus included about eighty members from twenty-one states, so it had the potential to be a substantial force in the House. It had grown out of an informal network of liberals, elected in 1954 and 1956, who had signed the "Liberal Manifesto" circulated by the Minnesota representative Eugene McCarthy, which outlined the goals of the more urban and liberal members of the chamber. The goals of the DSG were to lobby congressional leaders for liberal legislation and for procedural reforms that would weaken southern conservative committee chairmen and to help the growing body of new liberal members gain seats on important committees. The DSG employed a talented staffer named William Phillips to do research—on the powers of committee chairmen and other issues—intended to assist caucus members in devising successful legislative strategies.

Senator Humphrey, the members of the DSG, and other liberal legislators were not working alone as they prepared their challenge to the conservative coalition in Congress. They could count on a number of interest groups that were formed in the late 1940s and the 1950s to fight for their agenda. One was the Americans for Democratic Action (ADA), created in 1949 by professors, policy makers, and activists committed to pursuing tough anticommunist policies along with a progressive domestic agenda that included federal government actions to secure civil rights for African Americans. In 1955, the two major wings of organized labor, the American Federation of Labor and the Congress of Industrial Organizations, merged to form the AFL-CIO, which represented almost fifteen million workers. The AFL-CIO constituted a powerful counterforce in Washington to the Chamber of Commerce and other business groups and provided local union affiliates with a national lobbying operation. The AFL-CIO's president, George Meany, and Walter Reuther, who headed the United Automobile Workers, enjoyed a level of direct access to presidents that labor could never have imagined decades earlier.[17] The AFL-CIO and all the groups devoted to civil rights, including the ADA, participated in the Leadership Conference on Civil Rights, which coordinated communication and lobbying among more than fifty civil rights organizations.

These liberal interest groups and others used various tactics to push Congress to pass bills that would strengthen unions, protect civil rights, offer assistance to the cities, provide health insurance to the elderly, and more. They distributed to their members and to journalists compilations of how congressmen and senators voted on important issues and grouped them—liberal, moderate, or conservative—so that constituents would be aware of where their representatives stood. At election times, these organizations provided campaign assistance and advice to candidates they supported. The AFL-CIO's Committee on Political Education worked with the political departments of state and local chapters to endorse certain candidates, to distribute campaign material, and to conduct voter registration drives. The union leaders had the ability to persuade a large portion of their fifteen-million-person membership, which was heavily concentrated in northern states, to campaign for, and vote for, AFL-CIO-backed candidates.[18] Most of these organizations also hired talented lobbyists; two were Andrew Biemiller, who worked for the AFL-CIO, and Clarence Mitchell of the Leadership Conference on Civil Rights. Both men had spent their careers in liberal networks, knew how Congress worked, and became permanent fixtures in the Capitol. Biemiller was a former Wisconsin congressman who had been involved in socialist politics in the 1930s. Mitchell was a longtime political operative, primarily as a lobbyist for the NAACP. Both men believed that passing legislation was the best way to achieve social justice. "When you have a law," Mitchell said, "you have an instrument that will work for you permanently. But when you branch out on a separate line of direct action, you may wind up with nothing."[19] These lobbyists constantly tried to pressure legislators to vote for liberal measures by presenting arguments in favor of a bill and by mobilizing or threatening to mobilize union members to create political pressure in a legislator's constituency. In an era when no cameras were allowed on the floors of Congress and most legislative deliberations were closed to the public, the lobbyists and their staffs informed their constituencies about what their representatives in Congress were doing on their behalf.

While liberal congressmen and lobbyists worked Washington, grassroots activists stumped for liberal legislation everywhere around the nation. They pressured local, state, and federal government officials, and they pressured President Kennedy to throw the weight of the presidency behind the legislation they wanted to pass. Foremost among the liberal activist organizations was the civil rights movement.

THE PRESSURE INCREASES
FOR CIVIL RIGHTS

Liberal Democrats in Congress believed that President Kennedy would use the bully pulpit to promote legislation on better health care and aid to education, both core issues in his campaign, but they were skeptical about how hard he would be willing to fight for legislation to achieve racial equality, and they were pessimistic about the results, even if he did push. Civil rights leaders were unwilling to assume that the president, or any other politician in Washington, would push hard enough for civil rights, and they were determined to force the issue with grassroots protests and massive lobbying in Washington to build pressure on Congress.

By the early 1960s, the civil rights movement had been gaining strength for many decades. The National Association for the Advancement of Colored People was formed in 1909, in response to a wave of lynching and segregationist laws in the South. The organization focused primarily on getting judicial remedies for racial injustice; an example was the 1936 case that resulted in the desegregation of the University of Maryland's Law School. During World War II, it was the demands of African American leaders that impelled the federal government to create the Fair Employment Practices Commission to prevent employers from discriminating based on race when hiring factory workers for wartime production. Many of the 125,000 African American soldiers who returned from World War II became involved in local protests. These men, who had fought for democracy in segregated units against the Nazis and the Japanese, were in no mood to tolerate discriminatory practices at home.

In the 1950s, the NAACP mounted court challenges to laws that upheld segregation, and it secured its biggest victory in 1954, when the Supreme Court, in *Brown v. Board of Education,* ruled that school segregation was illegal. State Department officials also pressured the executive branch to be more proactive on civil rights in light of the Soviet Union's use of stories about racial conflict in the United States as part of its cold war propaganda. The horrible treatment of African diplomats near Washington, D.C., had long been an embarrassment to the U.S. government.[20] At the local level, activists were starting to mobilize protesters. The 1955–1956 bus boycott in Montgomery, Alabama, was launched after the NAACP member Rosa Parks refused to give up her seat to a white passenger. The boycott brought the city to a standstill and captured international attention. In 1957, white resistance to the integration of Little Rock Central High School in Arkansas forced President Eisenhower to send federal troops into the state to protect black students. That same year, the charismatic preacher Martin Luther King Jr. formed the Southern Christian Leadership Conference (SCLC), which organized against segregation at the local level and pressured Congress to enact national legislation. While the national NAACP was reluctant to embrace street action and mostly focused on fighting Jim Crow through the courts, some local affiliates worked throughout the 1950s to encourage the use of sit-ins to protest racial segregation. They organized networks of southern African Americans and trained them to conduct civil disobedience and political protest. After four students from North Carolina Agricultural and Technical State University started a sit-in to resist their treatment at a segregated lunch counter in the Woolworth's department store in Greensboro in 1960, the protests spread throughout colleges in the South, resulting in the formation of the Student Nonviolent Coordinating Committee (SNCC).

During the early 1960s, dramatic acts of civil disobedience rocked the South, catapulting civil rights to the forefront of the national consciousness and moving non-southern legislators in Congress to support civil rights with greater force and conviction.

On May 4, 1961, just four months after Kennedy's inauguration, the Congress of Racial Equality (CORE), under the leadership of James Farmer, dispatched interracial teams of young activists south from Washington, D.C., on Greyhound and Trailways buses. The first wave of these Freedom Riders passed through North Carolina and Virginia in an ominous calm, but in Alabama they encountered violent responses. Approximately six miles outside of Anniston, a white southerner tossed a firebomb onto a bus. The mob attacked the passengers as they escaped the flaming bus. In Birmingham, Alabama, the police, under the leadership of the commissioner of public safety, Eugene "Bull" Connor, refused to protect the riders as they were beaten with baseball bats, tire chains, and iron pipes by a mob of Klansmen.[21] "Negroes and whites will not segregate together," declared the man who controlled the police and who, as one of only three elected officials in Birmingham, had the authority to appoint temporary justices who controlled the court system. Connor was the law in Birmingham.

The FBI was not helpful to the protesters. Its director, J. Edgar Hoover, had little sympathy for the civil rights cause. His main concern was finding out how many communists were working in the movement's leadership circles. The FBI director also depended on his connections with local southern law enforcement authorities to work on other sorts of crimes. He did little to force local police authorities to take any actions they didn't want to take. The protesters were standing alone.

The White House kept the movement at arm's length during Kennedy's first few months in office. The president believed the Freedom Riders were aggravating tensions in the South to a level that would be unproductive; he did not want to be pressured into pushing for legislation he did not believe he could get passed; and he worried about a backlash against civil rights if some supporters in Congress believed the violence in the South was being provoked by grassroots activism rather than by racists determined to stop any progress toward ending Jim Crow. Kennedy asked his adviser Harris Wofford, an early supporter of civil rights and a friend of Martin Luther King Jr.'s, "Can't you get your goddamned friends off those buses? Tell them to call it off! Stop them!"[22]

Kennedy's concern about racial injustice was genuine, but it was profoundly attenuated by political considerations. He was disgusted by the savage police attacks and sympathetic toward demands that the racial status quo had to change, but he was willing to take only small steps to address conditions that were now being seen on television news reports in the homes of more Americans every day. Kennedy had made gestures of support toward the movement in the past; shortly before his election he had called Coretta Scott King when her husband, who had been arrested in Georgia after a protest, was in prison. The call, which many of his advisers had strongly discouraged for fear it would cost him crucial southern votes, won Kennedy some respect among African American leaders who heard about it, and from King himself, who appreciated that the senator had taken the risk to reach out to him. In the White House, Kennedy was sometimes willing to take small steps toward promoting racial equality. He issued an executive order in March 1961 that created the Committee on Equal Employment Opportunity to investigate discriminatory practices in employment by businesses receiving federal funds and to encourage better practices. Vice President Johnson was put in charge of the committee, which had little actual power. It was soon clear that these presidential actions were not responsive to the magnitude of the racial crisis that was boiling up in the South.

Some of Kennedy's reasons for restraint in addressing racial issues could be found in his view of the history of civil rights on Capitol Hill. When he looked there, he saw only discouraging prospects for the present and the future. Between the end of Reconstruction and 1956, every single civil rights bill had been killed in a congressional committee or by a filibuster.

When Congress finally started to pass bills, they were deemed unsatisfactory by all parties. In 1957, the violent confrontation over school desegregation in Little Rock, Arkansas, had persuaded President Eisenhower to propose civil rights legislation. Many congressional Republicans supported him; they felt that supporting civil rights was the moral thing to do, and they also believed it would be good politics; if they seized the initiative on civil rights, they could win African American votes in swing states. As Robert Caro has recounted, Lyndon Johnson, who believed the government would sooner or later have to address the problem of racial inequality and who felt that the Senate needed to respond to its growing liberal bloc, devoted all his tremendous energy to brokering deals and forming voting coalitions to pass the bill.[23]

The senior Georgia senator, Richard Russell, who was known as the most powerful man in the upper chamber at that time, was a masterful, soft-spoken parliamentary tactician and the person with the most sway over the Democratic caucus. He believed Lyndon Johnson was the only southerner who had a chance of becoming president, but only if he could get some credibility with northerners on civil rights. Russell was willing therefore to give Johnson some leeway to pass a bill as long as it was sufficiently weak to satisfy southerners. Leeway didn't mean Russell would support such a bill; it only meant he wouldn't go all out in his opposition if Johnson could find the votes to defeat a filibuster. To show Russell that he could put together support for such a bill, Johnson cut a deal with a group of western Democratic senators who had been seeking federal funds for the construction of a hydroelectric dam in Hells Canyon, on the Oregon-Idaho border. Johnson persuaded his southern colleagues, who had been adamantly opposed to sending federal money west, to vote in favor of the dam. In exchange, the western Democrats agreed to join with the southerners in voting against certain provisions of the civil rights bill that would be too radical for southerners to support.[24]

The primary intent of the 1957 legislation was to fortify the voting rights of African Americans. Only about 20 percent of eligible African Americans in the South were registered to vote at the time. The bill Johnson carved out of the original proposal assigned to local juries the job of deciding whether there had been violations of the law against depriving African Americans of voting rights. The fact that in the South blacks were never permitted to serve on juries virtually ensured there would be no convictions. Johnson also blocked a proposal, which liberals thought was essential, that would have given the attorney general the power to initiate suits to combat discrimination rather than requiring him to wait for private actors to bring suits. The provision would have freed African Americans from the responsibility—and personal risk—of pursuing redress on their own and placed that burden on the Department of Justice. But Republicans, including those who were supportive of civil rights legislation, and southern Democrats would not allow such a dramatic extension of federal power. At each stage in the deliberations, Johnson depended on the ad hoc coalition he had built around the Hells Canyon deal to extract concessions from liberals; they would have to go along, or there would be no bill at all.

The severely watered-down compromise bill, which southerners forced northerners to accept through the filibuster, created prohibitions against the denial of voting rights and established the six-person federal Civil Rights Commission to investigate voting rights abuses and make reports to the president. The attorney general could seek court injunctions against violations of voting rights, though not against other kinds of racial discrimination. Federal judges could hear cases based on violations, though local juries would decide the cases. In short, Johnson and the southerners had rendered the bill toothless; the law that was passed gave the federal government very little power to enforce its provisions. The most important aspect of the legislation was that it was the first civil rights measure passed by Congress since Reconstruction and cleared the way, or so Johnson promised, for stronger legislation in the future. "We've shown that we can do it. We'll do it again, in a couple of years," Johnson promised reporters.[25]

Liberals complained that the measure would have little effect. "I am fed up with the argument that the civil rights bill the Congress passed is better than no bill at all," the Oregon senator Wayne Morse said. "I deny that premise."[26] Southerners of course complained that the bill did too much, that even this empty shell of prohibitions against voting discrimination established a reprehensible intervention by the federal government into matters that were constitutionally the business of individual states. The same dynamic recurred in 1960 when Congress moved to strengthen the 1957 voting provisions by giving the federal government more power to monitor voting practices at the local level. The legislation achieved only a small improvement in the law; it allowed federal referees, under the supervision of the Justice Department, to investigate local voting rolls.

Enforcement of provisions that prohibited the restriction of voting rights would still be minimal under the bill; African Americans would still be prevented from voting, but the 1960 legislation, as mild as it was, passed only after a filibuster that lasted 125 hours and 16 minutes—until civil rights proponents agreed to a major compromise in the legislation. The photographs in newspapers of senators sleeping on cots during this filibuster, when Johnson insisted on keeping the Senate in round-the-clock sessions, vividly conveyed the efforts southern senators were willing to exert to prevent African Americans from enjoying their basic right to vote.

The lessons from 1957 and 1960 were clear to President Kennedy, who had been in the Senate during both of these debates. Even mild civil rights proposals were guaranteed to encounter fierce political opposition from southern Democrats, who remained a potent and effective force. Battles over civil rights squeezed other important legislation off the congressional agenda. Proponents rarely obtained what they wanted, leaving liberals frustrated with continuing racial injustice protected by the filibuster and southerners enraged by the infinitesimal ground they had surrendered to civil rights.

With all this history in mind, Kennedy didn't want to put civil rights anywhere near the top of his legislative agenda for 1961 or 1962. He agreed with a memo Harris Wofford had written during the transition period, in which his adviser had argued that the only real possibility for achieving progress on civil rights was by working through the judiciary and executive branches. Unless there was a reform of the filibuster rule to make it easier to achieve cloture in the Senate, Wofford had written, southern opponents would be able to block any meaningful civil rights measure that reached the Senate floor. If Democrats sought filibuster reform in 1961, Wofford added, "the Southern fight against this would inflict a serious wound to your other legislative prospects."[27] The history of civil rights and these ominous predictions at the outset of the term had a profound effect on Kennedy's strategic thinking. Most civil rights activists believed it was essential to solve the racial crisis through congressional action, because only legislation forged out of national debate with bipartisan support could provide durable solutions to such massive social problems. Kennedy, for his part, didn't think he could get this done, nor was he willing to try. Instead, he decided to do what he could through executive action, though this was a limited solution and a fragile one; it could easily be reversed by the next president.

The president's other concern was that if he tried and failed to legislate civil rights in his first year as president, he would have reduced his capacity to get Congress to pass what he saw as higher-priority legislation. His primary objective in 1961 was to pass a temporary, across-the-board tax cut that would boost demand and accelerate economic growth. He also wanted legislation that would provide health insurance to senior citizens. He expected that the conservative coalition would try to block all his domestic initiatives, but he hoped that by avoiding civil rights, at least early in his term, he would improve his chances of passing the rest of his proposals.

The president was also worried about his prospects for reelection in 1964. Like all Democratic candidates, Kennedy was dependent on southern votes, but after 1952 the South was not as solidly Democratic as it had once been. In 1960, Kennedy had barely defeated Vice President Richard Nixon in one of the closest elections in U.S. history, and his decision to select Lyndon Johnson as his running mate, a move that infuriated liberal Democrats who saw the Senate majority leader as a pillar of the conservative establishment, had been essential to Kennedy's victory in Texas and in several other southern states. The president understood that his support in the region remained soft. After all, he had won only about 51 percent of the vote in Texas; many southerners didn't trust him; and despite his moderate record in the Senate, conservatives still feared he was secretly more liberal than he admitted.

Kennedy was sympathetic to those who were fighting against racial injustice, but he possessed neither the moral determination nor the political tenacity to go all out for a civil rights bill. He pushed back against the pressure many officials were putting on him to respond to the violence against the Freedom Riders with legislation. Kennedy's brother Attorney General Robert Kennedy displayed very little sensitivity when he told the NAACP's Thurgood Marshall, the lawyer who argued the *Brown v. Board of Education* case, "That's the problem with you people. You want too much too fast."[28]

What civil rights activists wanted was legislation, and they wanted it now. They rejected Kennedy's pragmatic logic, which had been used since Reconstruction as an excuse for federal inaction. The president was capable of vigorous efforts; they had seen him make them for other controversial domestic issues—health care for the elderly, for example, where he authorized a strong public relations strategy to pressure Congress. The perception that there would be no commitment from Kennedy only intensified the belief of civil rights activists that their program of protests and confrontations was the only way to get action from Congress.

The relationship between Kennedy and civil rights leaders grew increasingly tense. James Forman of SNCC called the president a "quick-talking [and] double-dealing" politician.[29] "The Kennedy civil rights strategy," recalled Arthur Schlesinger Jr., who chronicled these events, "however appropriate to the congressional mood of 1961, miscalculated the dynamism of a revolutionary movement."[30]

Martin Luther King Jr. believed it was imperative for Congress to pass legislation that would outlaw racial segregation and protect the voting rights of African Americans. Kennedy, for his part, feared that if the public perceived him as being too close to King, he would be hamstrung politically. Initially, the administration refused to invite King to meet with the president in the White House.

When a meeting finally took place, on October 16, 1961, it only served to widen the divisions between the White House and the movement. King's invitation was conditioned on his keeping the meeting totally confidential. Before King saw the president, Kennedy's adviser Harris Wofford informed the minister that one of his top associates, Stanley Levison, was an active operative in a Soviet spy network. Levison had been a Communist Party member until he quit in 1956, before he started to work with King, but the accusation that a Soviet agent had infiltrated the movement and the further implication that it would harm King's credibility were clear attempts by the administration to use cold war hysteria to intimidate King. When, after a pleasant lunch with Kennedy and his wife, Jacqueline, King pressed Kennedy to fulfill his campaign promise to ban racial segregation, the president responded that he lacked sufficient congressional support to take such action.[31]

The violence against the Freedom Riders in Alabama was just the beginning. There was violence in other southern states too, much of it in reaction to Department of Justice efforts to integrate public universities. Kennedy's use of executive action to support court-ordered integration of specific universities had stirred extreme resentment in the South. The president's handling of these crises during the summer of 1962 was in stark contrast to his handling of the Cuban missile crisis in late October, when he stood up to the Soviets. These dramatic events, watched around the world, resulted in an apparent victory for the United States and displayed to Americans a resolve that was missing from Kennedy's dealings with the civil rights crisis. He had stood up to Khrushchev, but now he seemed to be standing by and allowing demonstrators to be brutally beaten when they asked for basic rights. Many Americans were appalled by the contradiction. Nor was Kennedy having success with his priority domestic legislation: health care for the elderly, a tax cut, and federal assistance for education were all bottled up in Congress.

Nothing was getting done.

But, largely in response to the demonstration and lobbying by the civil rights movement, the legislative environment had begun to change. With Kennedy's agenda frozen and violence spreading in the southern states, Congress was feeling rapidly mounting pressure for civil rights legislation. There was a partisan dimension to this new wave of pressure. The competition to be the party of civil rights heated up in the House, where Republicans publicly accused the president of failing to keep his promises on racial equality. Most House Republicans were philosophically open to civil rights legislation and didn't have to face a southern wing of their party that was dead set against such legislation. For more than a decade, Republicans had cultivated the idea that they were still the party of Lincoln and could gain partisan advantage by working for civil rights legislation while Democrats remained divided on the issue. The threat to Kennedy was that Republicans would ally with liberal Democrats, as they had done in 1956 and 1957, and get a bill to the floor. This would humiliate the president, disprove his analysis of the political realities, and allow Republicans to claim credit for any progress on civil rights.

On January 31, 1963, nine Republicans on the House Judiciary Committee, with the support of sixteen other Republicans in the chamber, introduced a civil rights bill.[32] The bill would make the Civil Rights Commission permanent and grant it more power to investigate voting rights abuses. The attorney general would have the power to initiate suits on behalf of individuals denied admission to segregated schools. The bill would create a permanent commission to investigate job discrimination by businesses receiving contracts from the federal government. The Republicans also proposed that states not be able to use literacy tests for people who had at least a sixth-grade education. Finally, the bill instructed the Census Bureau to gather statistics on how many people voted in each state, to be used to determine where discrimination was taking place.

Republicans criticized Kennedy for failing to make real the promises of equality that had been offered in the 1960 Democratic platform. The New York Republican John Lindsay said, "Despite the elaborate promises of 1960, the Democrats have not lifted a finger to give the country a meaningful civil rights bill." Republicans closed ranks behind the proposal. It had the support of the ranking Republican on the House Judiciary Committee, William McCulloch; the House Republican leader, Charles Halleck, an Indiana congressman who liked to describe himself as a "gut fighter"; and the House Republican Conference chairman, Gerald Ford. New York's governor, Nelson Rockefeller, who was the voice of liberal northeastern Republicanism and a probable presidential candidate for 1964, accused Kennedy of having "abdicated virtually all leadership toward achieving necessary civil rights legislation."[33] The Republican National Committee used the traditional Lincoln Day celebration to make a direct appeal to African American voters who were frustrated with Kennedy's lack of vigorous commitment.[34] In the Senate, the Kentucky Republican John Sherman Cooper teamed up with the Connecticut Democrat Thomas Dodd to sponsor legislation similar to the House bill.

The civil rights movement, with its conscious strategy of creating a crisis in the South, by broadcasting the brutality of southern segregation across the country and accelerating the partisan competition over civil rights, was doing what the liberal Democrats in Congress had failed to accomplish: it was pushing Kennedy, albeit slowly, toward legislation. Though the movement had yet to shake southern Democrats, its impact on northern and midwestern Republicans had changed legislative conditions and improved the chances that some kind of bill could emerge from the House Judiciary Committee. In response to the mounting criticism from Republicans, the president finally, on February 28, appeared on television to announce that he was proposing a civil rights bill. Displaying his characteristically cool

TV demeanor, Kennedy said that racial equality was a right, and he called voting discrimination the biggest problem the government had to address. "Therefore, let it be clear," Kennedy proclaimed, "in our own hearts and minds, that it is not merely because of the Cold War, and not merely because of the economic waste of discrimination, that we are committed to achieving true equality of opportunity. The basic reason is because it is right."

The president followed his dramatic declaration with several extremely modest proposals aimed more toward easing political tensions than addressing the serious problems at hand. One provision of the bill was to strengthen the voting rights laws by imposing tighter restrictions on the use of literacy tests in the South. Another provision would require temporary federal referees to make sure that African Americans could vote in states where there were pending legal claims by African Americans that their rights had been violated. Another provision would require the courts to expedite voting suits. There was also a minor measure to provide financial and technical assistance to local school districts that were still desegregating in response to the Supreme Court's 1954 *Brown v. Board of Education* decision. Finally, Kennedy recommended extending the Civil Rights Commission, which gathered information on civil rights abuses, for another four years.

The one measure that Kennedy did not propose was a prohibition on segregation in public accommodations. Kennedy feared that such a proposal would certainly torpedo any civil rights bill in the Senate. Besides southern Democratic opposition, Everett Dirksen, the Senate minority leader from Illinois, had supported a number of civil rights measures since the 1940s but opposed a ban on segregation because it would threaten property rights and business.[35]

Two days later, Republicans on the House Judiciary Committee released a statement welcoming Kennedy's "belated" announcement but were "disappointed" with the "timid and almost reluctant proposals" that had come from the White House. They pointed out that the bill did not empower the attorney general to bring civil actions against racial discrimination and would do almost nothing about discrimination in employment. McCulloch reminded reporters that the only civil rights bills to have passed Congress had done so under a Republican president and that most of Kennedy's proposals were already in the bill Republicans had proposed a month earlier.[36] Governor Rockefeller told a rally organized by the New York State Conference of the NAACP that the proposals came "two years too late" and didn't achieve much of what had been promised in the 1960 Democratic platform.[37] The Republican senators Jacob Javits and Kenneth Keating of New York, along with six other Republicans, were bolder. The liberal Republicans proposed prohibiting discrimination in hotels and lodging facilities that were involved in interstate commerce, doing more to prevent voting discrimination, and creating a permanent federal commission to combat employment discrimination.[38] The sponsors called on Democrats to support their proposal and work with them to pass bolder measures than the ones Kennedy had endorsed.[39]

Although they publicly praised the president, civil rights leaders were even angrier than before. They too thought Kennedy's proposed legislation was meager and inadequate; it didn't deal with racial segregation, nor did it truly protect voting rights. They had suffered through too much bloodshed to be satisfied with the president's empty words and proposals. The Republicans were putting forward much bolder ideas. "The administration is missing the boat," said CORE's director, James Farmer. "Many Negroes are becoming disenchanted with the administration and will be inclined to vote for the Republican in the next election."[40] The White House offered what had become its rote response—that the president's proposal was its best shot, given the current political situation in Congress. Southern Democrats were not likely to allow even this bill to succeed, according to Kennedy, and they certainly would not go for anything more, as the historical record proved. "We go up there with that," Kennedy told his advisers, referring to a bolder bill that would have targeted racial segregation, "and they'll piss all over us."[41]

Liberal Democrats were caught in a bind. They felt they needed to stand behind the president's bill, even though Republicans were offering a much more attractive package. Yet the White House put very little effort into pushing its own bill forward, so both bills languished for the time being.

Though Kennedy's weak proposals had divided civil rights supporters and halted momentum for passage of a bill, Martin Luther King sensed that sentiment in Congress was becoming more favorable to his aims. He concluded that he needed to keep the struggle alive in the streets. King was as much a politician as an activist, and he was confident that direct protests could promote legislative action. He understood that confrontations with police and white racist citizens were the most effective way to generate the media attention and public sympathy he believed would be necessary to force legislation through Congress. His goal was not to sway officials in the southern states, who he did not believe would overcome their racism anytime soon, but to promote federal legislation that would guarantee African Americans their rights in the region. Civil rights demonstrations were his way of lobbying for votes in Congress.

King moved now to orchestrate a series of bold and dramatic protests, which he named Project C, in Birmingham. He chose Birmingham because it was known as the most segregated city in the country. Department stores, schools, and almost all institutions were legally segregated by race. City officials had closed the public parks when a federal court ordered them to be integrated. African Americans could only expect to get the worst-paying jobs in the city.[42] Birmingham was also the site of extreme racial violence against African Americans. Fifty bombings of homes in recent years had earned the city the name "Bombingham." The police, under the control of Bull Connor, had a long history of brutality against African Americans. Now Connor promised an aggressive response against any civil rights protesters, whom he characterized as outsiders invading his city to cause trouble.

King's frank purpose for Project C—C for "confrontation"—was to get images into the national media. The nightly news shows of the three networks had been covering the civil rights movement throughout the early 1960s, broadcasting shocking film and pictures at a time when more and more Americans were buying television sets, which had become available only in the late 1940s. Newly developed portable cameras were allowing reporters to capture vivid photographs and film of the clashes in the streets as they happened.[43]

The local civil rights leadership, under the direction of the pugnacious pastor Fred Shuttlesworth, who had escaped in 1956 when his house had been dynamited, was having trouble finding activists willing to engage in civil disobedience under the very dangerous conditions that existed in Birmingham. Although many were willing to be imprisoned for the cause, fewer were prepared to undergo the massive brutality they expected from counterdemonstrators wielding lead pipes and baseball bats and police swinging batons and powerful fire hoses.[44]

King turned himself in to the police for having violated an order against staging a protest. While he was in jail, he wrote a letter about his belief that the moral law necessitated civil disobedience: "One has not only a legal but a moral responsibility to obey just laws. Conversely, one has a moral responsibility to disobey unjust laws." King pointedly turned the conventional political wisdom in Washington about pragmatism and incrementalism on its head. With Kennedy in mind, King warned that moderates posed a greater threat to racial progress than did white racist extremists. White moderates, King argued, continually insisted on a slow timetable when they were the very people who had the capacity to win the support of large majorities. "For years now I have heard the word 'Wait!'" King wrote. "It rings in the ear of every Negro with piercing familiarity. This 'Wait' has almost always meant 'Never.'" The letter was circulated among preachers and protesters involved in the movement, but the press, at least initially, didn't pay much attention to it.[45]

After he was released from jail, King decided to stage higher-stakes protests to continue bringing attention to Project C. He wanted to show the nation once and for all what conditions were like in the South; he believed it would take the most brutal images of oppression to move public opinion against the procedural power of the southern congressmen and fundamentally change the dynamics in Congress.

On May 3, King and hundreds of activists, including school-children, congregated at the Sixteenth Street Baptist Church for a march to downtown Birmingham. Connor had instructed his forces to make sure the protesters didn't create trouble in the business district. When the children attempted to do so, the police sprayed them with fire hoses and attacked them with police dogs. The images, broadcast on television and printed in newspapers, were horrifying.

President Kennedy told members of the Americans for Democratic Action that the photographs of children being attacked had made him "sick." King was unrelenting. The images he was projecting on television and in newspapers could not be edited by local or national political leaders. Standing before reporters, he said, "I am not criticizing the President, but we are going to have to help him. The hour has come for the Federal government to take a forthright stand on segregation in the United States."[46]

There was little hope that the governor of Alabama would protect the demonstrators. George Wallace, one of the most important figures in southern politics, had built his early career around progressive economic policies but had been elected governor in November 1962 on a promise to protect racial segregation. He had become adept at channeling white anger to his political advantage, and he had no sympathy for Martin Luther King.

Kennedy wanted to secure some kind of arrangement that would minimize tensions and violence in Birmingham. He sent Burke Marshall, the head of the Justice Department's Civil Rights Division, to meet with local government officials, local businessmen, and civil rights leaders. Marshall was a former antitrust lawyer whose low-key approach to negotiations had worked well in previous tense situations. The president hoped that mediated discussions could end the crisis. He was encouraged when Marshall struck a tentative agreement between the civil rights leaders and the business and government leaders that provided for Birmingham to desegregate washrooms and certain other public facilities.

Within days, however, all hope for the voluntary agreement went up in smoke. On May 11, white racists firebombed the home of Martin Luther King's brother, the Reverend A. D. King, and a motel King frequently used as his headquarters. Riots erupted in Birmingham's African American neighborhoods. On May 13, Kennedy was ready to federalize the Alabama National Guard and prepared army troops to enter the city if necessary to restore order. But it was King who calmed the situation by persuading local residents to stop the rioting. Tensions in Alabama smoldered, just one inevitable event away from bursting into flames again.

KENNEDY FINALLY PROPOSES A STRONG CIVIL RIGHTS BILL

After two years of violent clashes, imprisonments, and deaths, President Kennedy met with his advisers on May 20 and 21 to consider proposing a new civil rights law to decisively end segregation in the

South. The president had considered the Senate Republicans' March proposal in light of the situation in Alabama and concluded that if he didn't propose a stronger bill, the protests would escalate and the response from white southerners would become more dangerous. Republicans would again seek support among liberal Democrats for their own bill, which might well succeed in the wake of the spreading violence. It seemed likely that if he didn't act, Congress would move forward without him. The civil rights movement had generated enough pressure for action from congressional liberals in both parties and from a growing number of moderates, including the party leadership. The president still didn't believe he could get the Senate to pass a bill, but he and his advisers were convinced that by proposing some adequate legislation, they might get King and the other leaders to stop the demonstrations, ease the pressure, and end the violence. Given that the GOP had made proposals, it seemed possible that a bill could move through the House.

On June 3, the congressional pressure for legislation became even more intense when a group of House Republicans introduced a revised bill that included everything they had proposed in January plus a provision that outlawed segregation in public accommodations, including stores, restaurants, and theaters. The Republicans were willing to propose the measure that President Kennedy had thus far avoided.

The chairman of the House Judiciary Committee was the New York congressman Emanuel Celler, one of the few powerful senior liberals in the chamber. His committee had jurisdiction over law enforcement agencies and the administration of justice, and this included civil rights legislation. The bill would also have to survive the Rules Committee to get to the floor of the House. If it did get there, the bill would have to be bipartisan. "If this is not warfare, I don't know what is," Lyndon Johnson told Kennedy's speechwriter Theodore Sorensen. "They're arresting them by the thousands;

they're killing them by the dozens." The president, he said, needed to get "Republicans in on this thing" if they were going to pass a bill in the House and eventually the Senate.[47]

As the legislative process moved deliberately forward, there was another confrontation in Alabama. On June 11, Governor George Wallace stood on the steps of the Foster Auditorium of the University of Alabama and blocked two African Americans, Vivian Malone and James Hood, from entering the building to register, despite a court order based on *Brown v. Board of Education* that prohibited the university from denying admission to African Americans. Earlier in the day, President Kennedy had federalized several units of the Alabama National Guard. Malone and Hood, escorted by guardsmen, returned to the auditorium, were allowed to enter, and were registered.

On the same day, in Washington, D.C., President Kennedy met with the Senate minority leader, Everett Dirksen, and the House minority leader, Charles Halleck. He told them that the situation in Alabama confirmed the need to pass civil rights legislation. If African Americans did not get legislation that guaranteed their rights, the protests would continue to provoke still more violent responses from white southerners until the entire situation escalated beyond control.[48] If Congress passed legislation and abolished legally sanctioned segregation, southerners would have no choice but to comply, and civil rights activists would be able to draw down their protests, or so Kennedy hoped. He also hoped he could get the Republican leaders, who were seeing support for legislation growing within their caucus, to work with him on a bill that would satisfy liberals and moderates in both parties.

At 8:00 p.m, just hours after the Republicans had gone, Kennedy introduced to the nation the new proposal he would soon send to Congress.[49] Americans watching their televisions could see that his demeanor was quite different now from what it had been when he had presented his weak bill at the end of February. Gone was the cool and dispassionate president so many Americans had become accustomed to seeing. They saw instead a leader bursting with emotion and determination. Kennedy said, "We are confronted primarily with a moral issue. It is as old as the Scriptures and is as clear as the American Constitution." He warned that "redress is sought in the street." In the final moments of the thirteen-minute speech, Kennedy looked up from his text and seemed to be speaking impromptu. With passion in his voice, he reminded the nation, "Today there are Negroes unemployed, two or three times as many compared to whites, inadequate education, moving into the large cities, unable to find work, young people particularly out of work, without hope, denied equal rights, denied the opportunity to eat at a restaurant or a lunch counter, or go to a movie theater, denied the right to a decent education, denied—almost today—the right to attend a state university even though qualified."

Despite the passion in Kennedy's speech, Vice President Johnson didn't think the president had done enough to maximize the chances for passing a civil rights bill. He had not lobbied Congress prior to the public announcement; he had left Johnson out of all the internal deliberations about the proposal; and he had never asked his vice president, a longtime leader in Congress, to be a liaison there on behalf of the bill.[50]

On June 19, Kennedy sent his proposal to Congress. It was by far the boldest civil rights legislation yet proposed by a president in the twentieth century. The legislation prohibited imposing a literacy test in any federal election on any American with a sixth-grade education. It also allowed the attorney general to file suits to desegregate schools. The most significant part of the proposal prohibited discrimination on the basis of race in public accommodations, including restaurants, recreational areas, hotels, motels, and all other retail businesses. The legislation would also cut federal funding to programs that discriminated based on race.

The constitutional grounding for the law was the Fourteenth Amendment's guarantee of equal protection under the law to all citizens. Burke Marshall, the head of the Justice Department's Civil Rights Division, had persuaded Kennedy that the interstate commerce clause of the Constitution, which had already been used to outlaw child labor and enact minimum wage laws, should also be cited as support for the legislation because it would give the government a stronger legal position from which to defend the law when southerners opposed it, as inevitably they would, by claiming it violated states' rights.

Though civil rights groups had demanded the creation of a permanent federal employment commission, Kennedy felt that such an action would cost the bill too much support from key elements of the coalition whose support was necessary for passage. Moderate Republicans had strongly opposed any measure that allowed the government to intervene in the affairs of business. Southern Democrats had adamantly protected their racially segregated labor market since the New Deal days, when they forced FDR to exclude key parts of the southern workforce from Social Security and other benefits. Realizing they might very well lose on the issue of segregation, southerners were desperate to block any federal disruptions of the economic foundation of their region, which relied on cheap African American labor.

As Congress considered the legislation, Kennedy asked civil rights protesters to agree to a moratorium on "unruly tactics or pressures" that could diminish support for the bill in Congress, but civil rights leaders refused the president's request to cool it. Bayard Rustin, a well-known proponent of nonviolent civil disobedience and a key ally of King's in the Southern Christian Leadership Conference, and A. Philip Randolph, a labor leader who in World War II had persuaded FDR to issue an executive order banning discrimination in the defense industries by threatening a march on Washington, along with representatives from the AFL-CIO, the Southern Christian Leadership Conference, the National Council of Churches, and other civil rights, religious, and labor groups, revived an old tactic. A march on Washington would be a "living petition" that would "place the national human rights problem squarely on the doorstep" of the federal government. Despite some worries that protests would become violent and undermine progress toward legislation, the march, which took place on August 28, was a peaceful gathering of 200,000 people, who heard a series of stirring speeches in front of the Lincoln Memorial. Martin Luther King proclaimed, "I have a dream that one day on the red hills of Georgia the sons of former slaves and the sons of former slave-owners will be able to sit together at the table of brotherhood."

After the rally concluded, President Kennedy met with the top civil rights leaders—Dr. King, A. Philip Randolph, Whitney Young, and Roy Wilkins—and labor's Walter Reuther at the White House. Kennedy had scheduled the meeting after the rally rather than before, so it could be canceled if the march turned violent. Because the march had gone so well, the civil rights leaders were beaming with confidence as they walked into the White House. When they entered the Oval Office, Wilkins said, "We think today's demonstration, if it did nothing else, . . . showed that people back home, from the small towns, big cities, the working people, men who gave up two days' pay, three days' pay, . . . who flew from Los Angeles at $300 round-trip to come here. It means that they and not Martin Luther King or Roy Wilkins or Whitney Young or Walter Reuther have dreamed up this civil rights business." Emboldened by the display of solidarity they had just presented to America, they urged the president to allow the House Judiciary Committee to broaden the legislation. In particular, they suggested that he support the creation of a permanent federal employment commission and a grant of greater powers to the Justice Department to fight racial discrimination.

Walter Reuther said that through this march, "We've put together the broadest working legislative coalition we've ever had. And we're going to work, not only on the Hill, but we're going to be able to mobilize the grassroots support back home in critical congressional districts where a fellow has to be persuaded."

Once again, Kennedy treated his visitors to a review of the legislative realities he believed the White House was facing. He walked them through the state delegations in the House and counted votes to prove that the bill had only between 158 and 160 Democratic votes. He explained that they would need 60 Republican votes in the House and 20 to 25 Republican votes in the Senate or they could not pass the bill. When Randolph heard the president's analysis, he replied, "It's going to take nothing less than a crusade to win approval for these civil rights measures." He suggested that only Kennedy would be able to lead such a crusade. Kennedy said that the measure would have a better chance if it was coming from the grass roots and congressional pressure. If it came from the president, opponents would be able to make Kennedy the issue, which would be easier for them than arguing against civil rights. The president told the leaders that they, and congressional Democrats, would have to lead the effort to rally support for the bill. Even at this point, Kennedy was hedging his commitment to civil rights legislation.[51]

CHAIRMAN CELLER'S MOVE

The civil rights movement had pushed Kennedy into proposing legislation, and movement leaders would continue to organize pressure on legislators who were deliberating the bill, but liberals understood that the legislative process confronted them with several crucial points at which conservative opponents could kill the legislation or severely water it down. First the House Judiciary Committee had to draft and report a bill to the House Rules Committee, which then, if it voted to put the bill on the calendar, would determine the rules for the floor debate. If the bill survived the Rules Committee process, then the House would have to pass the bill subject to amendments. If passed, the bill would be delivered to the Senate, where the Judiciary Committee would debate the measure and decide whether to report it to the floor. Finally, the full Senate would debate the bill and vote on it, but only if civil rights proponents could gather the sixty-seven votes they needed to end the inevitable filibuster. If there were major discrepancies between the House bill and the one the Senate passed, the legislation would go to a conference committee—a panel of representatives from the House and the Senate—who would try to find a compromise between the two versions of the bill that their respective chambers would then have to vote to approve.

It appeared that the first stage of the process would be the easiest for civil rights proponents. The House Judiciary Committee was one of the few committees that comprised a sizable group of liberal to moderate legislators and a truly liberal chairman. But even here the administration would need bipartisan support. The Judiciary Committee had thirty-five members—twenty-one Democrats and fourteen Republicans—but because eight of the Democrats were southerners who supported the Jim Crow status quo, only thirteen Democrats could be counted on to support the bill in the committee. Chairman Celler and the other liberals would need five Republicans to join them for a majority to report out the bill.

Congressman Celler was a longtime proponent of civil rights. Although he was much older than the postwar liberals—the Brooklyn-born German Jew had been elected to Congress before FDR became president—he was a leader and mentor to them. He had become chairman of the House Judiciary Committee in 1949 and had handled the 1957 and 1960 civil rights legislation in the House. The bill that Kennedy had sent to his desk in June was one he had been waiting to push for many decades. The modest and diminutive chairman did not physically intimidate people, but when it came to legislating, no one was tougher or more skilled at using the procedures of the House to pursue his objectives and outsmart his opponents. He would be more than comfortable limiting, or completely blocking, the participation of his conservative opponents on the committee and punishing any legislators who caused him problems by withholding his support for measures they might need his support to get passed.

All the liberals on Judiciary took their committee work seriously, but Chairman Celler had been around long enough to know that nothing—except perhaps the filibuster on civil rights—was inevitable when it came to congressional politics. At a minimum, they all wanted to draft Kennedy's proposal in the strongest language possible so that when the bill reached the tougher stages of the process, they would have staked out the best possible position from which to negotiate. They worried that President Kennedy and his brother would undercut them by signaling to conservative Democrats who opposed civil rights that the president was willing to compromise too much of what was most important in the legislation.

President Kennedy was in fact willing to compromise; he knew he needed bipartisan support, starting in the Judiciary Committee. Without informing anyone, the administration had already privately secured the support of the ranking Republican on the committee. Over the July 4 holiday, Kennedy's man Burke Marshall had traveled to Piqua, Ohio, where William McCulloch maintained his home and district office. McCulloch, whom one reporter described as a "wispy little man from small town Ohio," was a solid midwestern fiscal conservative with a safe House seat. As the ranking Republican on Judiciary, he possessed substantial institutional power to reward Republicans who were loyal to him and therefore could deliver a significant bloc of votes on civil rights. Conservatives greatly respected him, because on most issues he stood to the right. He opposed most federal programs, including aid to education, and was a staunch defender of gun rights and school prayer. He was known in Washington for his insistence on discipline in spending; he was one of the rare legislators who didn't always try to get pork for his district.[52]

The most important thing about McCulloch was that he had a long record of pushing for strong legislation to end racial injustice. He had become sympathetic to the civil rights cause while practicing law in Jacksonville, Florida, where he represented a predominantly African American clientele and saw firsthand the consequences of racial discrimination. After serving in World War II, he had returned to Piqua, where he participated in a campaign by the NAACP to end segregation in local restaurants, a brave move for a lawyer who hoped to succeed in politics in a strongly conservative district. Though only about 2.7 percent of his constituents were African Americans, the congressman believed federal legislation was necessary to protect voting rights and achieve racial integration.[53] In 1956, nine years after his election to the House, he had supported the bill that culminated in the 1957 Civil Rights Act, although his version had been much stronger than what Johnson and the Senate ultimately passed. McCulloch was also working with a sympathetic House Republican caucus, as the multiple bills introduced between January and March demonstrated. Kennedy and Marshall knew that McCulloch could bring them the Republican votes they needed on the Judiciary Committee.

When Marshall arrived for his meeting with McCulloch, the congressman made him wait for much of the morning to "cool his heels for a while." Marshall was not pleased about the delay, but he couldn't afford to insult the congressman. When they finally met, McCulloch made several demands. The first was that the administration promise to protect the bill from being picked apart in the Senate. In 1957 and 1960, McCulloch and other congressmen had been embarrassed after they had gone out on a limb to sponsor the legislation in the

House. They had teamed up with liberal Democrats, to the chagrin of many of their fellow Republicans, and then had to watch the Senate remove relatively strong civil rights provisions they had taken big political risks to support. McCulloch's second demand was that the administration assure him that the president would give Republicans full credit for House passage of the bill. McCulloch's third demand was that Republicans not be asked to support an equal employment practices commission that had the power to regulate, rather than to investigate, civil rights violations by private employers, because Republicans would face a backlash from their business constituency if they did so. Finally, McCulloch didn't want the administration to talk about their deal in public, so Kennedy would have to push for a bipartisan bill without being able to say publicly that the GOP had already agreed to go along with him. Marshall agreed to all of McCulloch's demands.[54]

The immediate outcome of Kennedy's secret deal with McCulloch was that the president made public statements in which he talked about the importance of bipartisanship. This reference gave Celler a whiff of some kind of compromise in the offing, which confirmed his determination to push the legislative debate as far to the left as possible. This strategy would then force the administration to hold the center by defending its original proposal against both extremes. It was even possible, Celler calculated, that he would be able to liberalize the bill and still get enough Republicans on board.

The process began in a Judiciary subcommittee stacked with liberals from both parties and chaired by Celler himself, so he would have absolute control of the panel. The subcommittee held public hearings in July and early August and began executive sessions in late September. The chairman allowed various committee members to propose amendments that liberalized the measure to such an extent that their final draft dramatically transformed the president's proposal. It extended the prohibitions on the use of the poll tax to include state and local elections. It created an equal employment opportunity commission with the power to order private companies found to be practicing discriminatory hiring to cease and desist such practices. It also empowered the attorney general to investigate and prosecute any cases where an individual claimed his civil rights had been violated; the attorney general could do this even if no civil suit had been filed, and he could do it in cases where the claim was that equal protection had been denied for any reason, not just on the basis of "race, color, religion or national origin." Finally, the subcommittee extended the prohibitions on segregation to any establishment that received permission or a license from the state; this would have the effect of broadening the scope of the legislation to cover medical facilities and private schools.

When he learned what was happening in Celler's subcommittee, McCulloch grew furious. He announced publicly that the amendments were "so severe" that they imperiled the "passage of civil rights legislation" on the floor of the House.[55] Kennedy's response to the liberal amendments the subcommittee had made to his cautious proposal was to yell at his brother, "What the hell is this? Can the NAACP deliver sixty Republican votes on the floor? Can they? McCulloch can deliver sixty Republican votes."[56] Minority Leader Halleck duly added his warning that Republicans would not support the amended legislation.[57]

Civil rights activists naturally praised Chairman Celler's work. The Leadership Conference on Civil Rights applauded the liberal subcommittee for finally taking the necessary steps toward engaging the federal government in aggressive enforcement of laws against all kinds of discrimination, but while the activists were celebrating, the administration was scrambling to hold its deal with the Republicans together. Celler's plan had succeeded; his subcommittee had shifted the debate toward the left; the administration was defending its original proposal as the conservative alternative to the liberal subcommittee version, rather than watering it down any further to satisfy conservatives.

Kennedy had other reasons to worry about the liberalization of the bill. After all his confrontations with southern governors, his support in the South was slipping fast, and a stronger civil rights bill would not increase his popularity there. The Democratic National Committee reported in September that he would lose in Georgia, Louisiana, Arkansas, North Carolina, and South Carolina if the election took place at that time. Without victories in those southern states, Kennedy would have lost in 1960. If the Republicans nominated an anti-civil-rights candidate to run against him, Gallup reported, most of the South would vote for that opponent.[58]

Now the administration met with Congressman McCulloch to figure out how to undo the damage Celler had done. McCulloch said he still supported the original deal, as did Halleck, but the administration would have to remove the amendments Celler's subcommittee had added. The GOP didn't want to take the heat from civil rights activists for weakening the proposal. To this end, Robert Kennedy appeared before the Judiciary Committee on October 15 and requested that the provisions the subcommittee had added to the bill be removed. After his testimony, Kennedy explained to reporters, "What I want is a bill, not an issue." Civil rights organizations were deflated. "There is no reason for this kind of sellout," said James Farmer, complaining that President Kennedy "thinks he has the Negro vote in the bag and . . . can back out on civil rights."[59]

Celler agreed to allow the full Judiciary Committee to vote on two bills—the liberal subcommittee version and a substitute bill that consisted of the administration's original proposals, plus some new measures adapted from the liberal amendments made in subcommittee, including an equal employment opportunity commission that could not order discrimination to stop but could investigate cases and make recommendations to the Justice Department for possible prosecution.

Kennedy met with the leaders of the Republican and Democratic parties on October 23, before the Judiciary Committee voted on the two alternatives, and made it clear that he supported the bipartisan administration version of the bill and not the more liberal subcommittee version. McCulloch promised to support and protect the administration version on the House floor. "I want to get a bill that's good, help in the situation, and assure a lot more rights to the colored people and the other people," Halleck said, "but it's got to be one that can pass." He complained that Celler's subcommittee "blew this thing up to be hell, that the whole purpose of that was to put the Republicans in the position of emasculating the bill." Kennedy reminded the legislators that he and the attorney general were "getting the opprobrium for having diluted" the bill.[60] Kennedy pressed Halleck and McCulloch, in front of Celler, to agree that they would support a compromise that looked like the original proposal if the administration and enough Democrats joined them. After some back-and-forth, Halleck finally agreed that the GOP would push for the compromise.[61] Celler watched the discussions unfold just as he had planned. The original proposals were to be preserved, but with an equal employment opportunity commission added, and the administration and the Republicans had agreed to stand firmly behind the legislation.

On October 29 the House Judiciary Committee rejected the subcommittee proposal by a vote of 19 to 15. Five northern Democrats and 3 northern Republicans were on the losing side, along with the 7 southerners (5 Democrats and 2 Republicans) who voted for the version they were certain would never make it through the House. The substitute bill, which contained the administration's proposals, passed 23 to 11. Eight southerners and 3 northern Republicans voted against the final legislation. Nine Republicans joined 14 Democrats to make sure the bill succeeded. "In my judgment," the attorney general said, making sure to give Republicans their due in public, "if it had not been for their support and effort, the possibility of civil rights legislation in this Congress would have been remote."[62]

The final bill the Judiciary Committee sent to the Rules Committee severely limited the use of literacy tests in federal elections. The bill also prohibited discrimination in all public accommodations. The Equal Employment Opportunity Commission (EEOC) would have five members and could investigate charges of discrimination, but the bill gave the attorney general the power to act only after private persons complained that they had been denied equal protection "on account of race, color, religion, or national origin." The Leadership Conference on Civil Rights "deplored" the president's decision to defeat the subcommittee bill, but most, including King, still praised the legislation and promised that their organizations would mobilize support for it.

The future of the legislation was still in doubt. It would have to survive the House Rules Committee, which was controlled by its racist chairman, Howard Smith of Virginia, then win the support of a majority of the House, and then make it through the Senate filibuster. Kennedy admitted he had no strategy for dealing with the Senate, where it was unclear whether the public accommodations measures would even win a majority. "We don't see how we can get a two-thirds vote for cloture, almost for any bill," Kennedy said.[63] As he headed to San Antonio, Texas, on November 21, with the hope of shoring up support among conservative southern voters for his reelection campaign in 1964, civil rights activists were left wondering how much determination Kennedy really had to keep the bill moving through the legislative process.

CHAPTER THREE

NEW PRESIDENT,
SAME OLD CONGRESS

W hat happened in Dallas on November 22 was horrific. The entire nation was stunned.

It happened at a low point in Lyndon Johnson's career. In the 1950s he had ambitions of becoming president; now he felt like a ghost in the White House. One of FDR's vice presidents, John Nance Garner, famously said the office "wasn't worth a bucket of warm piss," and Johnson knew this firsthand. He had been forced to watch these historic years of racial turmoil from the sidelines. He had not been included in most major White House decisions; in fact, he had barely been in touch with the president. The president's inner circle of advisers didn't like or trust him. Indeed, they were openly disdainful of him; they ridiculed him as a crass bumpkin. Johnson could never put aside his own resentment of the president, who he felt didn't deserve his position, and his brother Robert, who he believed was arrogant and ineffective.

The hours that followed the assassination were a whirlwind for everyone who had been in the motorcade. Johnson, at first isolated in the hospital and unaware of what was going on, was finally placed in an unmarked police car and escorted to the Dallas/Fort Worth airport, Love Field, where Air Force One awaited him. As Johnson made his way onto the plane, the nation was just learning what had occurred in Texas. Sixty-eight percent of Americans heard about the shooting within thirty minutes. "From Dallas, Texas," Walter Cronkite, holding back tears, said on CBS News at 2:37 p.m., "the flash, apparently official. President Kennedy died at 1:00 P.M. Central Standard Time, two o'clock Eastern Standard Time."

At that moment, Lyndon Johnson feared that the assassination had been an effort by the Soviets to destabilize the U.S. government. In the middle of the cold war, he knew his first responsibility was to show the world that the government was still functioning. He looked confident as he walked into the stateroom of Air Force One. At 2:40 p.m., with his wife, Lady Bird, on one side and Jacqueline Kennedy on the other, Johnson took the oath. As soon as the ceremony was over, the plane took off and carried the new president from Texas to Washington, D.C.[1]

Lyndon Johnson was very different from his predecessor. He was fundamentally more liberal and more committed to the New Deal than Kennedy had been. Despite his southern background and his conflicts with liberals over political compromises he had made as Senate majority leader, Johnson was fiercely determined to expand on Franklin Roosevelt's domestic accomplishments. He was a product of Congress who believed in and revered the institution, where he had worked for more than two decades. He knew how the place operated, and he had developed close relationships with almost everyone in each chamber. While Kennedy, who had served thirteen years in Congress but never in a leadership position, spent much of his presidency fearing what Congress could do to him, Johnson was willing to take the political risks he knew were necessary to produce legislation in the House and the Senate. Johnson recognized that the moment for another New Deal had arrived, driven by the energy, ambitions, and anger of the civil rights movement. Johnson had never believed that Kennedy possessed the political skills or the courage to extract legislation from the opportunities that had fallen to him. Now, ironically, with Kennedy's death, Johnson had an additional tool, the unfulfilled legacy of his slain predecessor. He was determined to break the impasse that had halted liberal progress when Kennedy was president.

Johnson spent the evening of November 22 in several hours of meetings at the White House with legislative leaders and his new advisers. His aim was to figure out what he could accomplish on Capitol Hill over the next several years: How much time would he have to pass legislation? When would the opposition gain enough strength to block him? What items should he push for and in what order? A few months later, when the speechwriter and longtime adviser Bill Moyers met with Johnson in the Yellow Oval Room, the president, a masterful analyst of political reality, made it clear how little time they had to get anything done. Moyers recalled that Johnson clutched a notepad on which he had written a truncated schedule: "'November 22, 1963,' and then a column of months that went to January 19, 1965, and then another from January 20, 1965 to January 19, 1969, and from January 20, 1969, to January 19, 1973 . . . Out to the side there was a scrawl which said '1964, win,' '1965, P&P'—that means propose and pass . . . and then for 1967 it said 'hold gains.'" Looking up at his fellow Texan, Johnson explained the calendar: "Bill, I've just been figuring out how much time we would have to do what we want to do. I really intend to finish Franklin Roosevelt's revolution . . . In an ideal world . . . we would have about 110 months to his 144 months . . . I'll never make it that far, of course, so let's assume that we have to do it all in 1965 and 1966, and probably in 1966 we'll lose our big margin in the Congress. That means in 1967 and 1968 there will be a hell of a fight."[2]

Exhausted from the day's events following the assassination, LBJ returned at a little before 9:30 p.m. to his home, a three-story mansion, the Elms, in the elegant northwestern section of the city, where he was joined in the living room by a group of close friends. At one point, Johnson lifted his glass of orange soda and, staring at the portrait of his mentor, the late House Speaker Sam Rayburn, that hung over his television set, said, "Oh, Mr. Sam, I wish you were here now. How I need you."[3]

After spending several hours watching the TV news, Johnson finally retired to his bedroom. But he was not done for the day. He asked his adviser and friend Horace "Buzz" Busby to join him. Johnson sat on the edge of his king-size bed as Busby pulled up a chair beside him. Lady Bird, also worn out, lay next to her husband and tried to sleep while the two men spoke. Lady Bird had no trouble with this ritual, as she was accustomed to her husband's late-night conversations with advisers in their most intimate of spaces. Johnson rattled off all the legislation that he wanted to pass, much of which had been bottled up since the 1930s. "You know, almost all the issues now are just about the same as they were when I came here in Congress nearly thirty years ago," Johnson said to Busby.[4] Finally, he allowed his confidant to leave the room and moved on to his next meeting. His excitement, his ambitions, and his concerns were too great for him to rest. He called in Jack Valenti, Bill Moyers, and Cliff Carter and told them that he wanted to pass every piece of legislation that had stalled under Kennedy, and more.

JOHNSON'S AMERICA

Lyndon Johnson reached personal and political maturity during the presidency of Franklin Roosevelt and became a New Deal man—a man deeply committed to the principles of modern liberalism—for the rest of his life. He believed the federal government should provide economic assistance to those who were unable to work. He believed there should be a social safety net for workers and their families. He believed the federal government should open doors to more Americans to enter the middle class by giving them the tools they needed to become economically self-sufficient. He believed the government should strive to ameliorate social tensions that restricted access of certain groups to a decent life in a prosperous nation.

His political views were shaped in a much different world from the one in which John F. Kennedy, as the well-educated scion of a wealthy and prominent Massachusetts family, was raised. Johnson was born in 1908 (he was nine years older than Kennedy) in a rural Texas community where, though his family was in relatively good shape during much of his childhood, he witnessed economic hardship firsthand.

Lyndon's father, Samuel Ealy Johnson Jr., was a farmer and an investor in cotton futures; his wife, Rebekah, was a graduate of Baylor University. Lyndon was the first of their five children. Sam also served in the Texas state legislature, where he became known as a populist who railed against the power of corporations and defended the needs of workers. Lyndon saw his father fight for an eight-hour day in the railroad industry and push for the regulation of utilities. Sam Johnson even challenged the Ku Klux Klan, which he saw as an un-American organization and a blight on the state. During his time in the legislature, Sam's farm and his investments prospered; when Lyndon was five, Sam and Rebekah moved their family to a nicer home close to Johnson City, which had 323 residents. Though the home was a big step up, the new neighborhood still didn't have electricity or paved roads, and most homes lacked indoor plumbing.

Johnson was an intelligent young man but not a disciplined student. He frequently missed classes and struggled to keep up with his schoolwork; he was more interested in following politics and playing with the neighborhood boys. His fondest memories were of accompanying his father to Austin and watching firsthand the exciting life of legislative politics. Then, in the 1920s, after having both prospered financially and enjoyed a long period of professional respect, Sam lost much of his money when drought and the boll weevil ravaged the cotton crop; cotton prices plummeted, and with them the value of Sam Johnson's investments. When Sam retired from the state legislature in 1924, he was so deep in debt that he was forced to take such low-paying jobs as working on road construction crews. By the time Lyndon finished school, the Johnsons were living in poverty.

Defying his parents, who wanted him to continue with his education, Johnson traveled to California, where he worked a number of makeshift jobs. After a few months on the road, he returned to Texas, where he found construction stints near Johnson City. One was dragging gravel on the highway for a road construction crew, a job that was physically brutal and emotionally unsatisfying. He didn't earn much money and hated the job. "I'm tired of working just with my hands, and I'm ready to start working with my brain," he told his mother.[5] He took the college entrance exams in 1927 and passed. Lyndon enrolled in the Southwest Texas State Teachers College, an institution of higher learning intended for students who were planning to go into teaching as a vocation.

The Johnson family could offer him little financial support, so Lyndon had to work his way through college. For a time he worked as a janitor to pay for his books, room, and board. He was not a star student at Southwest Texas State, though his classmates recognized his native intelligence and charisma. He took part in campus politics and did some reporting for the college newspaper.

Short of money again, he left school and took a teaching job in a south Texas town called Cotulla. His students were the children of dirt-poor Mexican American farmworkers who couldn't afford to send them to school with lunch. The town was rigidly segregated. Johnson saw a group of Mexican Americans desperately searching through piles of garbage in hopes of finding grapefruit rinds to eat.[6]

The white Texans in town, he recalled, treated the Mexicans "worse than you'd treat a dog."[7] Johnson threw himself into his teaching; he was highly effective in the classroom and went out of his way to offer extracurricular help to his students. After he returned to college and finished his degree in 1930, he worked at several other teaching jobs.

The lure of politics was strong. Congressman Richard Kleberg, who was elected in 1931, hired Johnson as his secretary in Washington. The position proved to be an exceptional opportunity; the wealthy Kleberg was profoundly uninterested in the job of legislating and spent little time in his office. Johnson seized the opportunity; he took over as much responsibility as possible and developed contacts throughout the House. Acting like a party leader, he organized a "Little Congress" of staffers who met regularly, plotted strategy, and gained the attention of key members of the Texas delegation, which included the populists Maury Maverick and Wright Patman, and also Sam Rayburn, who would become Speaker of the House in 1940. Johnson had an affinity for the New Deal; he saw the federal government embracing the same ideals his father had promoted as a politician back in Texas and addressing the same chronic economic problems he had confronted as a child, a teacher, and a worker. Johnson lobbied Kleberg to vote in favor of the Agricultural Adjustment Act even though the congressman was predisposed to vote against such federal interventions in local affairs. When Johnson was offered a highly paid position as a lobbyist for General Electric, he turned it down; he committed himself instead to the pursuit of higher political office.

In 1935, Sam Rayburn, who was then a rising congressman in the House Democratic caucus, recommended Johnson to President Roosevelt to serve as director of the National Youth Administration (NYA) in Texas. Roosevelt had created the NYA by executive order that year to provide unemployed young Americans with education and vocational training. The program offered young men and women public jobs that paid about $30 a month. Johnson quickly earned a reputation in Washington and Texas as an effective administrator with shrewd political skills. The head of the NYA, Aubrey Williams, informed the president that Johnson was running the best of all the state operations. Johnson displayed intense compassion for the impoverished communities that the NYA was assisting. He worked hard to bring federal assistance to Mexican American children who lived under the same conditions as those he had once taught, and to African American children too. He created an informal advisory council of African Americans to make sure assistance money was reaching young African Americans, and he also boosted the level of financial assistance that went to African American college students for their tuition. He went so far as to stay overnight at African American colleges, at a time when public accommodations were strictly segregated throughout the South, in order to monitor firsthand how his programs were working.[8]

In 1937, the same year Roosevelt was under attack from conservatives in Congress over his effort to pack the Supreme Court, Johnson won a special election to represent the Tenth District of Texas in the House of Representatives. As a congressman, he dutifully followed the wishes of the president and the party leadership. When disaffected southern Democrats joined with Republicans in a conservative voting bloc, Johnson remained a strong defender of the national party agenda—federal development programs for farmers, rural electrification, and federal jobs. Fully committed to the overall vision of the New Deal, Johnson worked tirelessly to bring funds back to his district. He was loyal to FDR and voted in favor of all his New Deal legislation, even when his southern colleagues broke with the president on such controversial measures as the establishment of a federal minimum wage and the reorganization of the executive branch. One of FDR's most influential assistants said that the Texan had proven to be a "perfect Roosevelt man."[9]

Sam Rayburn thought so highly of Johnson that when he became

Speaker of the House in 1940, he invited him to participate in his "Board of Education," a group of Democrats who were invited to join the Speaker in a twelve-by-twelve-foot room on the ground floor of the Capitol where "board" members regularly drank bourbon, played cards, and plotted political strategy and tactics. As a member of this elite inner circle, Johnson learned Rayburn's political philosophy, including such famous axioms as "You cannot be a leader, and ask other people to follow you, unless you are willing to follow too," and "Any jackass can kick down a barn, but it takes a good carpenter to build one." The sayings were simple, but they guided many legislators in making sound political decisions.

In 1941, Johnson ran for a vacant Texas Senate seat. His campaign emphasized his commitment to New Deal liberalism, particularly the programs that benefited farmers and the unemployed, but he also emphasized the intensity of his opposition to legislation that supported unions and civil rights—a shift away from his previous support for the minimum wage and other legislation that helped organized labor. He was hoping to appeal to the great majority of voters in his state who opposed civil rights and unions, but the shift to the right didn't work. Johnson was devastated when he lost to the brutal and corrupt campaign of a thoroughly conservative opponent, but he had learned a great deal about the underside of electoral politics.

A frustrated Johnson vowed that he would never again allow himself to be defeated by vote manipulation and fraud. He had been a liberal with sympathy for the disadvantaged, but now he was also determined to be a ruthless politician. He would do whatever he thought was necessary to win higher office. In that spirit, he volunteered to serve in the war, well aware that the experience would become a vital part of his portfolio in his next electoral run. His service mainly consisted of fact-finding missions for General MacArthur in the Pacific. When he volunteered for a bombing mission and his plane came under fire, he was awarded a Silver Star, even though others on the mission, who had much greater responsibilities, received nothing. MacArthur knew Johnson was close to the president; he even suspected Johnson of spying on him for FDR.

In 1942, when FDR asked legislators who had been serving in the military to resume their political jobs, Johnson eagerly returned to Washington, where he faced a challenge from a right-wing Democrat in the 1944 election. Major victories in the European war bolstered popular support for all of Roosevelt's political allies, and Johnson won reelection to the House.

After the war's end and Roosevelt's death, Johnson took aim at the unions, in an effort to improve his right-wing credentials. In 1947, he voted in favor of the Taft-Hartley Act, which undercut the ability of workers to unionize. The legislation allowed states to enact right-to-work laws, which meant that workers did not have to pay union dues in those states but could work in a unionized plant and benefit from wages and other terms negotiated by a union without paying to support the union. The opposition to unions in the South was as intense as the animosity toward civil rights. Many southerners feared that unionization would destroy the one competitive advantage their economically underdeveloped region had over northern industry—cheap labor, much of which came from the African American community. Because of such opposition, unions had largely failed in their efforts to organize southern workers. The white South also hated the Congress of Industrial Organizations for its racially diverse vision of industrial unionism. No southern legislator, including Johnson, believed he could survive politically if he supported organized labor.

Johnson's next opportunity to advance came in 1948, when the incumbent senator Lee "Pappy" O'Daniel announced he would not run for reelection. This time Johnson mounted a ruthless campaign and defeated Texas's former governor Coke Stevenson, a staunch opponent of racial equality and critic of America's growing role overseas. The tactics on both sides were controversial, as was the vote count; the key to Johnson's victory was a town in south Texas where adjusted ballots gave him a statewide victory by an unlikely eighty-seven-vote margin. Stevenson decided not to challenge the results in state court because a full investigation would have revealed that his campaign had also tampered with ballots. A federal court granted Stevenson an injunction that would prevent Johnson's name from appearing on the ballot in the general election. Desperate to reverse what could be a devastating decision for his candidacy, Johnson sought the assistance of the brilliant lawyer Abe Fortas, who directly petitioned the Supreme Court associate justice Hugo Black to end the injunction. Black ruled in Johnson's favor. Though Johnson won the election, his opponents, and some supporters, always believed that Johnson had stolen the election, and he was forever after derided by his Texas political enemies as "Landslide Lyndon."

Johnson thrived in the Senate. He loved the wheeling and dealing that took place there, and he earned the respect of the Georgia senator Richard Russell and other senior southern leaders. Johnson was loyal to these powerful men; he worked Russell's will on civil rights, though he was allowed to remain publicly neutral on the issue to burnish his acceptability as a potential candidate for national office, and he defended powerful Texas oil interests against proposed federal regulations. In 1953, Russell orchestrated Johnson's election as Senate minority leader after Republicans retook control of the White House and Congress in a devastating election for his party. When Democrats won back control in the midterm elections of 1954, they elected Johnson as their majority leader, making him one of the most powerful people in Washington.

As majority leader, Johnson struggled to balance the demands of the growing cohort of liberal Democrats and the southern committee chairmen who controlled the chamber. His strategy was to find issues where Senate Democrats could ally with the Eisenhower administration against factions of the GOP that opposed the president. Hence, Johnson led Democrats to embrace a strong internationalist stance, support tough policies against the Soviet Union, and tag Eisenhower's Republican opponents, primarily the Ohio senator Robert Taft and Indiana's senator Homer Capehart, as isolationists. He defended many federal programs against conservative attacks, both older New Deal programs and newer ones—funding for scientific research at universities, for the space program, and for interstate highway construction. He moved bills through the Senate that raised the federal minimum wage and provided federal support for housing; these liberal initiatives had been dormant in the upper chamber until the majority leader threw his weight behind them. Johnson earned the respect of liberal legislators, among them Senator Humphrey, who agreed to work as a liaison between the majority leader and northern Democrats, who still didn't fully trust him.

The most difficult issue for Johnson was civil rights. Like other southern liberals and moderates, he was visibly conflicted. In his private conversations and correspondence, he regularly expressed the racist beliefs common in Texas that African Americans were intellectually and physically inferior to whites. At the same time, though almost no politician anywhere in the South could support civil rights legislation and get reelected, he displayed genuine concern about racial injustice and expressed support for alleviating the terrible conditions under which African Americans suffered in the United States. He said of his time teaching Mexican American kids in south Texas, "I could never forget seeing the disappointment in their eyes and seeing the quizzical expression on their faces—all the time they seemed to be asking me, 'Why don't people like me? Why do they hate me because I am brown?'"[10] His work at the NYA and his support for the minimum wage and public housing were early evidence of his support for policies that indirectly alleviated racial inequality.

Like many Americans, he was moved by the bold actions of civil rights protesters. He believed that chronic racial tensions in the South undermined the national position and prerogatives of southern politicians and regional business leaders. Senator Russell's mentoring of Johnson and acceptance of his relatively moderate position on racial issues were calculated to get Johnson into the White House, where, presumably, he would hold the line against any extreme concessions on civil rights, or so Richard Russell believed, and he would defend government policies that benefited the region—primarily high levels of defense spending and generous farm subsidies. In 1956, Johnson was one of only three southern legislators who did not sign the "Southern Manifesto," a virulent denunciation of the Supreme Court's *Brown v. Board of Education* decision.

Though he personally expressed racist sentiments, Johnson had a genuine belief, born out of his father's work in Texas politics and the New Deal and out of his own, that the government had a responsibility to alleviate social problems. He knew poverty and its effects from his own experience, and he had genuine sympathy for the poor, regardless of the color of their skin; he identified with them personally, and it was this that gradually moved him toward supporting major federal civil rights legislation, including the 1957 bill.[11] The legislation offered a modicum of protection for the voting rights of African Americans but was so weak that it actually protected southern political and economic institutions. Johnson's work on the bill, along with his support for anti-union legislation, did little to dispel abiding liberal suspicions that he was a conservative southern wolf in ill-fitting sheep's clothing.

In 1960, Johnson was furious when John Kennedy, who was younger and less experienced, won the Democratic presidential nomination, but he agreed to be Kennedy's running mate because he believed it might improve his chances of succeeding Kennedy in 1964 or 1968. Their victory awarded Johnson the job worth less than a bucket of warm piss and took him from being a powerful figure in the Senate to being the butt of vice presidential jokes.

Despite his ambivalence about civil rights and unions, the man who became President Johnson on November 22, 1963, was and had always been a New Deal liberal. He was hesitant and sometimes fearful of the demands the younger liberals were making on Washington, but he was and had always been sympathetic to the concerns that drove them. He had grudgingly and cautiously moved toward supporting civil rights legislation, and by the time he became president, he sensed that the time had come to move decisively for civil rights. He was prepared to take big steps in that direction, but first he had to deal with another piece of President Kennedy's unfinished business.

STARTING THE GREAT SOCIETY
WITH BUDGET CUTS

Like so much of Kennedy's agenda, his tax bill, first proposed in his 1963 State of the Union address, was stalled in Congress. In September, the House had passed a version of the legislation that lowered individual and corporate taxes by about $13 billion, but the issue of spending was left unresolved. A number of southern Democrats voted for the bill after Wilbur Mills, the chairman of the House Ways and Means Committee, assured them the Senate would secure an agreement for a stringent budget. Now the bill was lying inert in the Senate Finance Committee, chaired by the deficit hawk Senator Harry Byrd of Virginia.

Johnson knew he would face the same obstacles as Kennedy had faced if he tried to move the bill. To get it passed, he would have to make a deal with Byrd that would include the serious budget cuts he and the other conservatives were demanding. It was not an auspicious way to begin a drive to pass the massive amounts of social welfare legislation Johnson had in mind, but he figured he could turn the situation to his advantage if he handled it right. He could ask for more money for programs later.

Johnson believed lower taxes would help the economy and also help Democrats in the 1964 election. According to the White House economists, led by the Keynesian chairman of the Council of Economic Advisers, Walter Heller, a tax cut for wage earners would boost demand and stimulate growth. The GNP was growing—it increased by $100 billion between 1961 and 1964—while unemployment hovered at 5.5 percent. Corporate profits were up, personal income was rising, and overall the nation's economy was thriving. On the day after Kennedy was assassinated, the Council of Economic Advisers had produced a memorandum that the tax reduction would increase GNP by another $12 billion in 1964 and $30 billion annually starting in 1965.[12]

The U.S. economy had performed well throughout the post–World War II years, but Johnson's liberal Keynesian economists believed it had not reached its full potential and could do even better. The tax cut, they argued, would help to stimulate the economy, and there was enough room for growth that it would not cause inflation. The economists believed that short-term deficits in good economic times were a sound investment in healthy growth.

Johnson had political reasons too for wanting Congress to pass the tax cut. If it could be passed by the early months of 1964, the economy would get a boost before the next presidential election, and Americans would be walking into voting booths with more secure jobs and fatter wallets. Bill Moyers told the speechwriter Ted Sorensen, a holdover from the Kennedy administration, "These fellows all tell him the tax bill now will mean an immediate upsurge in the economy, which ought not to be delayed until next April, May, June."[13]

The problem for Johnson was that while fiscal conservatives, including Wilbur Mills and Harry Byrd, the chairman of the Senate Finance Committee, had hesitantly accepted the argument that a tax cut could stimulate more economic growth, they insisted that Congress pass, and Johnson accept, big spending cuts to limit the size of the federal budget deficit. They shared a belief that the government's budget should be balanced. In their view, balanced budgets were proof that the federal government had control over its finances. A commitment from Johnson to a tight budget would give them some evidence that the White House would not allow the deficit to spiral out of control. They argued that large deficits, by putting too much money into circulation, would inevitably cause inflation. It was also their belief, shared with the financial community on Wall Street, the Chamber of Commerce, and the National Association of Manufacturers, that federal deficits raised interest rates and discouraged private investment.

Senator Byrd let it be known that he would not allow a tax bill to leave his committee unless the president agreed to a federal budget of $100 billion or less, no more than $2 billion above the previous year's budget. The Appropriations committees in both the House and the Senate controlled the spending side of the budget, and Byrd also wanted Johnson's promise that he would keep his request from the House committee within the same $100 billion limit. The chairman could count on nine of the seventeen members of his committee to support him on the tax bill, including the ranking Republican on the committee, Delaware's senator John Williams, who was known to be a zealot for balanced budgets and entirely unsympathetic to the views of Walter Heller and the other liberal Keynesian economists. If Johnson didn't say yes to the budget figure, Byrd's committee would say no to the tax cut.

Byrd's demands were a direct challenge to Johnson's advisers, who wanted him to propose a budget closer to $108 billion, which they believed was the bare minimum necessary to pay for existing programs and have some resources available for new programs.

Johnson's experience in Congress had taught him to show deference to the southern committee chairmen who held the purse strings. He was also feeling intense pressure to have Congress pass a tax cut soon so that southerners wouldn't be able to hold it hostage during a filibuster over civil rights. If the White House got the legislative sequence right, so that Congress passed the tax cut soon, the Senate would have no other urgent business before the summer, and the Democrats would be better able to outlast a filibuster and force Dixie to allow for a vote on civil rights.

At a meeting with his economic advisers, Johnson told Walter Heller that liberals would have to swallow hard and accept a budget that was closer to $100 billion than $108 billion. The budget bureau director, Kermit Gordon, responded that the only way they could render the budget acceptable to Byrd would be to make severe cuts in popular programs, and he chose as an example the rural electrification program, which Johnson had long cherished for the benefits it had brought to his poor Texas constituents when he was in Congress.[14] Heller complained that the president should stick with their $108 billion budget as an "irreducible minimum," but Johnson pushed back. He said, "Unless you get that budget down around $100 billion, you won't pee one drop."[15] Johnson displayed to the group a memo Heller had written in which he outlined how deeper spending cuts would harm domestic programs. He said he agreed with Heller but needed to make very practical choices: "You have to give something to buy off Byrd."[16]

Two days later, on November 27, Johnson delivered his first presidential address to a joint session of Congress. His purpose was to restore confidence that the nation would get through the crisis of the assassination and that Lyndon Johnson was up to his new job. Speaking from a black loose-leaf notebook filled with typewritten text and some handwritten notes he had jotted down at the last minute, the president emphatically connected his administration to that of his deceased predecessor. "Let us continue," he said, and proceeded to highlight his intention to get the civil rights legislation and the tax cut through Congress. He focused on the tax cut and devoted most of the speech to explaining what it would accomplish. "No act of ours could more fittingly continue the work of President Kennedy than the early passage of the tax bill for which he fought all this long year. This is a bill designed to increase our national income and Federal revenues, and to provide insurance against recession. That bill, if passed without delay, means more security for those now working, more jobs for those now without them, and more incentive for our economy."

In December, in an effort to accelerate the deliberations in the Appropriations Committee, Johnson invited Senator Byrd to the White House for lunch to talk over the numbers. When he got the call, Byrd told a journalist with whom he happened to be meeting at the time, "He wants to work on me a little bit." Before they dined, Johnson gave the chairman a personal tour of different rooms in the White House, including the "little room where he gets his rub," the senator reported later. As they started in on dessert—vanilla ice cream—Johnson asked Byrd if he would accept a budget that came in under $107 billion. Byrd quickly replied, "Too big, Mr. President, too big." Johnson offered a lower figure. Byrd said nothing. Johnson said, "Just suppose I could get the budget somewhere under $100 billion. What would you say then?" Byrd said that if the president could reach that number, he would still not be able to support the bill publicly. As one of the most fiscally conservative members of the Senate, he could not openly sign on to the deficit that would come even with a budget as low as $100 billion, nor did he want to back down from earlier statements that using taxes to manage the economy was the wrong way to go. He would, however, allow the bill to come to a vote in the committee and would signal to his colleagues that they could vote in favor of it without incurring his wrath.[17]

By the time the New Year started, Johnson's staff had been able to reduce the size of the federal budget, through actual program cuts and some accounting trickery, to under $100 billion. Kermit Gordon had worked hard to trim the budgets of agencies or reduce the size of individual programs to get to the total $100 billion figure Johnson needed. Gordon also estimated some expenditures at levels that would add up to the desired numbers, even when there was every reason to believe the numbers would actually be much higher. When Heller suggested to Johnson that they confirm the figures with Secretary of the Treasury Douglas Dillon, the president dismissed the idea. "Dillon is down vacationing on Hobe Sound," Johnson said, "and if he wants to have his rest or his leisure on Hobe Sound he can have it, we're going ahead."[18] With this kind of manipulation, which Johnson continued to employ throughout his presidency, his staff came up with a budget so frugal that it fundamentally contradicted his bold promises about fulfilling Kennedy's agenda, not to mention creating a second New Deal. But Johnson figured that when he got the tax cut he wanted, and when he harvested the political benefits of that, he would win the presidency on his own merits and plunge ahead with his big legislative plans.

On January 7, the day before his State of the Union address, Johnson called key members of Congress to inform them that his budget proposal would be $97.9 billion, just slightly higher than the federal budget when Eisenhower left office in 1961.

Johnson's decisions about federal spending created some tension over the dramatic State of the Union address he delivered on January 8, 1964. He acknowledged that his administration would have to stick to a tight budget, then proceeded to outline the domestic programs he envisioned. Speaking about an "unconditional war on poverty," Johnson said, "It will not be a short or easy struggle, no single weapon or strategy will suffice, but we shall not rest until that war is won. The richest Nation on earth can afford to win it. We cannot afford to lose it." He also named hospital insurance for the elderly, federal funding for schools, food stamps, and several other programs he intended to pursue in the coming year. But, in a nod to Byrd and his allies, Johnson promised that his agenda could be accomplished on the cheap: "It can be done with an actual reduction in federal expenditures and federal employment." He pledged a "progressive administration which is efficient, and honest and frugal." Most of the reductions in his budget would take place in Defense (through base closings), the Atomic Energy Commission, the Post Office Department, and the Agriculture Department. The president had already instructed all federal agencies to slow down hiring and find additional ways to trim their budgets.

Senator Barry Goldwater, who was preparing to run for the Republican nomination in 1964, didn't believe the president's budget promises. He asked how Johnson could propose such grandiose programs and still reduce the budget. "Republicans are ugly as hell," Johnson said to the House majority leader, Carl Albert. "I thought that they could approve of a reduction like that."[19]

Some liberals too expressed disappointment, albeit for different reasons. Many liberals were already unhappy that Johnson was starting his term with a tax cut. They understood the promise of giving workers more money to spend on the goods they needed and strengthening the economy in the process, but they also realized tax cuts were hard to reverse and could leave the government with less money for domestic initiatives in the next few years. As Tennessee's senator Al Gore Sr. warned, "Once taxes are cut, they are not likely to be re-imposed . . . Congress will always be ready to cut taxes, never ready to raise them."[20] One of the most powerful labor leaders in the AFL-CIO, James Carey, said that Johnson's promise to support a frugal budget contradicted the aims of the promises he was making on domestic policies.[21] In the *Wall Street Journal,* the reporter Alan Otten concluded, "President Johnson's November election strategy is emerging ever more clearly: To keep the nation's conservatives happy without sending his labor-liberal cohorts off sulking into their tents."[22]

Though it was clear to all that there was a gap between potential costs of the programs the president was calling for and the fiscal message he presented before Congress, the overall size of the budget he promised had its intended political effect. Byrd called Johnson to say, "That was an eloquent speech you made. You've made a good start."[23] Byrd would tell reporters in no uncertain terms that he would not obstruct the bill "in any way."[24]

Now that Johnson had agreed to spending levels that satisfied the chairmen of the tax-writing committees, Byrd and Mills allowed the tax bill to move forward. In the middle of February, the House and the Senate passed the Revenue Act of 1964, which cut tax revenues by a total of about $11 billion by reducing high and low rates from 91 and 20 percent in 1963, to 77 and 16 percent in 1964, and to 70 and 14 percent in 1965 (the rates would continue to fall from there, with the high rate reaching 44.6 percent by 2013). Corporate tax rates were lowered from 52 percent in 1963 to 48 percent in 1965. In a nationally televised speech, Johnson called the bill "the single most important step that we have taken to strengthen our economy since World War II." The bill, he promised, would raise the income of millions of Americans and "encourage the growth and the prosperity of this land that we love." Congress would also pass spending bills to fund Johnson's programs at the low levels the president requested.

THE CHALLENGES TO COME

The first two months of Johnson's presidency had changed the attitude and atmosphere of the White House. Gone were the diffidence and trepidation of the Kennedy period. Anyone who knew Johnson understood that he had determination and tenacity that were rare in Washington; he was serious about a second New Deal, even if he would have to wait a little while before he could get it started.

But had Congress changed? The conservative coalition that had stifled Kennedy remained as powerful as ever, and even the dynamic, motivated, and seasoned legislator who was now president wouldn't be able to compel legislators to do what he wanted. "I've watched the Congress from either the inside or the outside, man and boy, for more than forty years," Johnson said, "and I've never seen a Congress that didn't eventually take the measure of the President it was dealing with."[25] To get his stimulus tax cut, he had surrendered to Harry Byrd's budget demands, and he would have very little money for new programs in the next year—an inauspicious position for a president who aimed to launch a second New Deal. He had downplayed the costs of what he was hoping to accomplish; he had no idea of how massive—and expensive—the Vietnam War would become; and he had created expectations in the public and Congress based on these underestimations of the sacrifices his actions would ultimately require.

The only area of policy where Johnson believed things could be different was civil rights. Over nine decades, Congress had passed only inconsequential civil rights bills, but recently lobbying and grassroots pressure by the civil rights movement had dramatically altered the political situation; a sizable number of congressmen in both parties were demanding the passage of Kennedy's civil rights bill, and they were willing to challenge the southern Democrats to get the job done.

Johnson too wanted the civil rights bill to pass. He believed that segregation should end, and he agreed with the basic objectives of civil rights leaders. He thought that the measure that Kennedy had proposed would be good for the country and could be the foundation for more legislation to address voting rights and employment discrimination.

The civil rights debate in Congress would determine not only what Johnson could do for civil rights but what he would be able to do for the rest of his term. If he failed to get the civil rights bill through Congress, his presidency could be ravaged by racial conflict in the months leading up to the 1964 election; a civil rights bill stalled in the House or the Senate could stall every other piece of legislation he wanted to pass. But if he got a significant civil rights bill passed—and it now appeared there was a pretty good chance that he would—and then won the election, he would have a clear road ahead of him for the grand policy agenda he wanted to drive forward. Knowing exactly what was at stake, he set out to test just how much Martin Luther King, Clarence Mitchell, and other civil rights activists had changed the situation on Capitol Hill.

CHAPTER FOUR

LEGISLATING CIVIL RIGHTS

S enator Richard Russell, the dean of the southern Democrats, privately acknowledged that Lyndon Johnson was likely to succeed in getting substantive civil rights legislation through Congress. The civil rights movement had taken hold, and the Georgian could see that his side was fighting a last-ditch effort with depleted forces. Russell was even uncertain whether some younger southern colleagues, such as Al Gore Sr. of Tennessee and William Fulbright of Arkansas, would stick with the southern caucus, because they were not as invested in protecting racial segregation as they were in promoting the economic vitality of their region.[1] Publically, Russell said, "Despite overwhelming odds, those of us who are opposed to the bill are neither frightened nor dismayed."[2] Russell was also well aware that elected officials who spoke too vehemently against the civil rights bill in this debate would risk alienating African American voters who were growing in numbers, despite the laws designed to perpetuate their disenfranchisement. "I realize there is a group in the South and in some places in Georgia that is yielding to overwhelming force even if they don't like the trend," Russell said.[3]

Russell's only hope was that if southerners could use the two procedural weapons that remained at their disposal—the House Rules Committee and the Senate filibuster—the civil rights coalition in Congress would agree to amendments that significantly weakened the final legislation. "Bear in mind," warned the columnist Roscoe Drummond, "that no filibuster on civil rights legislation has ever been broken before its principal purposes were achieved."[4]

BEATING JUDGE SMITH

The House Judiciary Committee had passed the civil rights bill at the end of October 1963, but in December the bill was still stuck in the Rules Committee, the hostage of the committee's chairman, Howard Smith. Born and raised in a plantation home built by slaves in the Shenandoah Valley, Smith, a former judge, was hostile toward almost everything liberal. When it came to civil rights, he was still fighting the Civil War. The tall and lanky Smith was a courtly gentleman who could charm you over a mint julep and then destroy you in committee a few hours later. He had once prevented the Rules Committee from reviewing a civil rights bill by leaving Washington to assess fire damage to one of his barns back in Virginia. "I knew Howard Smith would do anything to block a civil rights bill," Speaker Sam Rayburn had quipped, "but I never suspected he'd resort to arson."[5]

Chairing the Rules Committee gave Smith immense power. The committee, often referred to as the "legislative gatekeeper," controlled the agenda for the House. The committee held hearings to determine the rules that would govern how the bill was debated on the floor and what the time limit on debate would be. These decisions were enormously consequential; the scheduling of the debate and the rules attached to a bill would create or limit opportunities for opponents to amend legislation in ways intended to sink it.

Since taking over as the chairman of the Rules Committee in

1955, Smith had skillfully used procedural tactics to defeat many liberal bills. He had been supported in his efforts by his alliance with the Mississippi Democrat William Colmer and the five Republicans on the committee. The ranking Republican, Ohio's Clarence Brown, a man with little tolerance for experiments in domestic policy, had been a staunch opponent of Franklin Roosevelt and Harry Truman and was Smith's reliable ally on most issues, though not on civil rights. Smith also had the full support of the House Republican leader, Charles Halleck from Indiana. Halleck liked to call himself "100 percent Republican" and was known for lines like "Once you are in a war the only thing to do is win it." He didn't like the government to spend too much money on the disadvantaged and had little respect for politicians who tried to solve the nation's social and economic problems.[6]

The Democratic Study Group had challenged Howard Smith's power in 1961 by pushing a reform through the House that expanded the size of the Rules Committee from twelve to fifteen—the new members were two liberal Democrats and one moderate—but the reform didn't do liberals much good. Most members of the Rules Committee still refused to cross their intimidating chairman, and the committee had stifled thirty-four of Kennedy's proposals the year after the reform was enacted.[7]

Civil rights bills were always at the top of Smith's hit list. He did not believe in racial equality, and he had no intention of acceding to any demands to expand the rights of African Americans. Congressional proponents of civil rights would have to force a bill out of Smith's committee. They believed the best method for doing so was House Rule 57, one of several procedural reforms adopted in 1910 (and revised in 1931). According to this rule, a simple majority of House members could bring any legislation directly to the floor if they signed on to a "discharge petition" that had been submitted to the clerk of the House, who would keep secret the names of the signers.

Traditionally, legislators were cautious about using discharge petitions. Members of the majority party did not want to embarrass the Speaker by joining a rebellion against a committee chairman the party had officially appointed, and no member of either party wanted to do anything that might undermine the committee system through which any member might someday gain a chairmanship. Of 331 discharge petitions filed with the clerk between 1931 and 1962, only three of them accumulated enough signatures to force a bill to the floor.[8] Lyndon Johnson remembered one of those cases from May 1938, when he had just entered the House. Presidents traditionally kept out of procedural matters inside the other branches of the government, but when Franklin Roosevelt threw his active support behind a discharge petition to move a wages and hours bill to the floor of the House, the discharge petition got all the necessary signatures in just two hours and twenty-two minutes.[9] In the days immediately after he became president, Johnson told liberals that a discharge petition would be essential. "We've got to petition it out," the president told the head of the United Steelworkers, David McDonald.[10]

On December 9, Congressman Celler filed a petition with the clerk of the House to discharge the civil rights bill from the Rules Committee to the floor. Northern Democrats literally ran to line up in the aisles to sign the petition, even before Speaker John McCormack called the House to order at noon. A hundred thirty-one members, including twenty-four Republicans, had signed by 7:14 p.m. After the initial burst of enthusiasm, the line trailed off, and liberals still needed more signatures.[11]

The driving force behind the discharge petition was the Missouri Democrat Richard Bolling and his colleagues in the Democratic Study Group. Bolling, who had first been elected to the House in 1948, was a highly intelligent liberal who had studied the minutiae of the legislative process and was cognizant of how important the skillful use of legislative procedure had been to the success of southern Democrats. Now DSG members, 125 or so, lobbied their colleagues to sign the petition. They emphasized to colleagues that signing would be a critical statement of where a member stood on the issue of civil rights and the power of the senior southern Democrats. Getting enough signatures was an uphill battle; about 100 members of the Democratic caucus were southerners, and big-city Democrats, who had enough clout in the existing system to make them hesitant to endorse the petition, numbered 60.[12] By December 13, Democrats had gathered about 150 total signatures for the discharge petition. If they got 10 more Democrats, as Richard Bolling expected they would, plus 40 to 50 more Republicans favorable to civil rights, they would be very close to the 218 votes they needed.

At this point, Judge Smith was getting the message that the petition *could* succeed, which would be a humiliating defeat for the Rules Committee chairman. He was getting pressure from inside the Rules Committee too, particularly from the ranking member, Clarence Brown. Though Brown was a staunch conservative, he was one of the midwestern members of his party who remained proud of the antislavery tradition of the GOP; he often boasted that the main line of the Underground Railroad, on which slaves had escaped from the South to Canada, ran directly through his district. He had been motivated by the civil rights movement and believed that most of his midwestern colleagues were as well. Now he wanted the chairman to allow his party colleagues on the committee to vote to send the bill to the House floor.

Johnson, fearing that delay would be Smith's most effective tactic, sent clear signals to Democrats that he expected them to sign the petition.[13] He told his close political confidant Robert Anderson, who had been Eisenhower's Treasury secretary, that Smith intended to "run it over until January. And then January, they'll be late coming back, and he'll piddle along and get into February, and then maybe they won't get it out until March. And then in March, the Senate [will] be able to filibuster it until it goes home, and there'll be nothing done." Johnson would not accept delay, and he didn't want extended debate. "This country is not in any condition to take that kind of stuff . . . and that's going to hurt our section, and it's going to hurt our people. And it's going to hurt the conservatives."[14] Johnson wanted action, and he wanted it now.

In an effort to spread this message through the news media, the president implored Katharine Graham, the owner of the *Washington Post*, to publicize the delays in the House in a way that would make clear they amounted to obstruction. He told Graham that every House member who refused to sign the discharge petition should be considered "as being anti–civil rights, because he is even against a hearing."[15] On December 6, four days after Johnson's phone call to Graham, the *Post* published an editorial titled "Tyrant in the House," which reported to readers that "the tyrant who heads that Committee [Rules], Howard Smith of Virginia, has held up an imperious hand forbidding the House to act on civil rights legislation which, if it came to the floor, would certainly be endorsed by a majority of the members."[16]

Over the Christmas weekend, civil rights activists, working through the Leadership Conference on Civil Rights, traveled to the districts of undecided representatives to generate constituent pressure on them to support the discharge petition. "Our efforts during the next two weeks," said Arnold Aronson, one of the top officials in the Leadership Conference on Civil Rights, "when most members of Congress will be home for the holidays must be directed toward getting them committed to this goal." The National Council of Churches passed a resolution calling upon church members to write their legislators urging them to sign the petition.[17] An unofficial moratorium on demonstrations that had been in effect since Kennedy's assassination ended with civil rights protests in five southern cities. In Columbia, South Carolina, more than a hundred college students marched through the downtown area carrying signs that read, "We Want Fair Employment Practices Now" and "We Want Restaurant Desegregation Now." There were 126 people arrested for disorderly conduct. In New Orleans, an interracial group of about four hundred protesters attended a memorial service for Kennedy and then marched to a post office where they mailed letters to the Louisiana congressional delegation urging them to vote for the civil rights bill. In Chapel Hill, North Carolina, nine people, including a retired eighty-year-old minister, conducted a sit-in at a local restaurant until the police carried them away. In Atlanta, Georgia, Martin Luther King led a demonstration in the downtown area. "The cancer of segregation," he told everyone in attendance, "cannot be cured by the Vaseline of gradualism or the sedative of tokenism."[18]

Back in Washington, Clarence Brown met with Judge Smith to tell him that he was putting Republicans in an extremely awkward spot by pressuring them not to sign the petition and in effect place themselves on the side of those who opposed civil rights.[19] Brown's comments increased the pressure on Smith by demonstrating that the DSG could gain the backing of Republicans in its discharge efforts.

In an effort to stall the petition, Smith had announced back in early December that the Rules Committee would hold hearings sometime in January. The move worked; there were 165 signatures on the petition, but Bolling was unable to obtain any more after Smith scheduled hearings. Nevertheless, the DSG considered its lobby a success. It had forced the stubborn chairman to conduct hearings, and it had the 165 signatures, which were a clear threat to Smith that if he went back on his word, more representatives would sign on and the bill would likely be discharged.

The House Rules Committee opened hearings on the civil rights bill on January 9, 1964, in the committee's regular meeting room in the Capitol—a cramped Victorian parlor with mahogany walls, red velvet drapes, and an ornate chandelier—where members usually deliberated on nothing more than the time limit and the rules for debate on a bill. This time Smith planned to conduct formal hearings, including discussion of the substance of the bill; his aim was to use the hearings as a platform from which to attack the legislation and delay the floor vote as long as possible. About a dozen reporters squeezed into the room, shoulder to shoulder. Committee members sat in black swivel chairs around a green baize table. A bust of George Washington hung over the nonworking fireplace.[20]

Smith had realized he could not kill the bill in his committee. The liberals had forced his hand with the discharge petition, and the civil rights movement had created irresistible pressure on members of Congress. Public opinion had shifted so drastically as a result of the protests that Smith was now standing against a massive tide of public and congressional opinion. Public support for civil rights had risen from 49 percent in June 1963 to 61 percent in January 1964. In the South, most white respondents conceded that congressional passage of the legislation to end segregation was virtually inevitable, even if they weren't eager to live with the results.[21] But though Smith knew he couldn't kill the bill, he believed he could still wound it.

The chairman "opened the proceedings by taking his long cigar from his mouth, raising his bushy eyebrows and saying benignly to the witness, 75-year-old Emanuel Celler of Brooklyn . . . 'It's rumored around here that you want to get a rule on H.R. 7152.'" Smith had called Celler as a witness in an attempt to challenge the legitimacy of the Judiciary Committee's vote on the bill by criticizing how its chairman had handled his hearings. It was a futile stab. Celler, who knew that Smith would extend his hearings for as long as he could, warned, "Patience is finite. Is it small wonder that the Negro's patience and forbearing are at an end . . . But the die is cast. The movement for civil rights cannot be stayed."[22]

On January 18, while the Rules Committee hearings were in progress, Lyndon Johnson met with Martin Luther King Jr., James Farmer, Roy Wilkins, and Whitney Young at the White House. The president's guests anticipated a discouraging lecture from Johnson about the math in the Senate, much the same as what they had heard from Kennedy after their march on Washington.

Johnson surprised them. He sat with the civil rights leaders in a circle of chairs beside a fireplace in the Oval Office. As he spoke, the leaders leaned forward in their seats, attentive to his every word. Johnson wanted to demonstrate to them just how broad his commitment was to a transformation of race relations and to assure them that he would fight tooth and nail for the civil rights bill once it passed the House Rules Committee. In the first part of the conversation, the president described a poverty proposal his staff was working on and explained why he believed fighting poverty was an essential part of the civil rights struggle. He wanted to approach the problem of race relations from a broader perspective, he told the men; he wanted to resolve not only segregation but the multiple factors that perpetuated racial inequality. He explained his views as having evolved from his own upbringing and work in Texas, where he had seen the impact of poverty on Mexican Americans and African Americans who were struggling to survive.

The president then focused on civil rights legislation. He promised the leaders he would push for the bill without "a word or comma changed." As he was speaking, the president picked up the phone to make an apparently spontaneous call to the legislative liaison Lawrence "Larry" O'Brien, which had actually been prearranged before the meeting started. Johnson asked O'Brien how many signatures they now had on the discharge petition. O'Brien reported that they now had 178 signatures. Johnson asked O'Brien to bring him the names of twenty-five Republicans and fifteen Democrats who could still be persuaded to sign. After hanging up the phone, he turned back to King and his colleagues and told them he would need their help in pressuring these members to sign.[23] He also told them that he wanted the House to vote on the bill before Lincoln's Birthday on February 12, a day on which Republicans usually returned to their districts; the president didn't want these legislators to face any constituents who might have been mobilized by opponents of the bill to demonstrate against civil rights.

The civil rights leaders were pleased with what they heard from Johnson. Each in turn expressed his agreement with the president, particularly on the economic dimensions of racial inequality. The unemployment rate among African Americans, Whitney Young said, was a "national disgrace." Martin Luther King, who had for years been thinking and talking about the connections between racial and economic inequality,[24] called poverty a "real catastrophe" for the African American community.

It was the first time these men felt they were talking to a president who was listening to them. In their press conference, King called the meeting a success. Young told reporters, "One out of four Negroes is unemployed. One of every six Negro families lives in a house classified as substandard. Five hundred thousand Negro youths between the ages of 16 and 21 are out of work and out of school. We regard this as not a mild recession for the Negro but a catastrophic situation, a national disgrace." King noted that the president had not asked them to compromise on the civil rights bill and that they had no intention of doing so. African Americans would reject "any watering down," of the bill, King said.[25] The following day, many of the major newspapers carried stories about the meeting and some included photographs of Johnson sitting with the African American leaders in his office. The stories sent a strong signal to Smith and other southern legislators that there was common cause between the president of the United States and the civil rights leaders.

Although in public they continued to condemn the legislation, privately Smith and his conservative allies were angling for surrender in the committee on the best possible terms—so they could fight on the most favorable terrain on the House floor.[26] One southerner told the *Wall Street Journal,* "We can talk ourselves blue in the face about the evils in this bill and nobody's going to listen. If we can't find more outside help pretty soon, I'm afraid the cause is hopeless."[27]

On January 30, after nine days of hearings, during which Smith had forced his panel to review every single word in the bill and offered southerners yet another platform to deliver speeches attacking civil rights, the Rules Committee, by a vote of 11 to 4, reported the legislation to the entire House. Five Republicans joined 6 Democrats to vote in favor of the bill; the 4 southern Democrats voted against it. Judge Smith had been able to obtain support in the committee for an "open rule," which meant that in the course of debate on the House floor members could propose amendments that could be added to the bill by the vote of a majority of the House. The civil rights bill would thus be vulnerable to amendments that would weaken it and also to "poison pills," amendments containing provisions designed to make the bill unacceptable to members who would otherwise have voted for it. According to the rules attached to the bill, the House would consider the legislation by the committee of the whole, which meant that the vote of each member would not be recorded, thereby giving legislators considerable room to hide their ultimate decision from constituents and the press unless observers in the galleries could figure out what they had said to the teller who was keeping tabs. Civil rights supporters were still confident, however, that they could block any poison pills that southern conservatives might propose on the floor.

DEBATING RACIAL JUSTICE
ON THE HOUSE FLOOR

On the opening day of debate in the House of Representatives, eager visitors lined up in the corridors to wait for any seats that became available upstairs in the galleries. Tourists were having trouble getting seats, because the Leadership Conference on Civil Rights had organized its members to watch the proceedings and monitor how every legislator voted on proposed amendments. In an era when television cameras were not permitted in the chamber and many votes were unrecorded, the physical presence of civil rights activists—opponents called them "gallery vultures"—was also intended to exert pressure on representatives involved in the debate.[28]

Civil rights groups, unions, and religious organizations were still working all around Washington to secure votes. Jane O'Grady, a lobbyist for the Amalgamated Clothing Workers, escorted union leaders from around the country to the Longworth and Cannon office buildings to meet with congressmen and secure their votes. Outside of Washington, religious organizations were focused on pressuring Republican representatives from midwestern congressional districts. The churches educated local congregants in Nebraska, Ohio, Iowa, Minnesota, and other midwestern states on how to pressure members. In Indiana, the campus minister of Purdue University, Ernest Reuter, organized a statewide campaign to pressure Charles Halleck. Presbyterian ministers frequently met with Halleck to tell him of their "deep concern with the unequal and often unjust treatment of our Negro brothers in our free society."[29]

Civil rights activists had obtained commitments to support the legislation from 220 legislators, but they could not be certain that all of them would keep their word. Movement leaders focused on holding these legislators to their promises, not just to vote for the bill, but also to be stalwart in voting against amendments that would damage it. Joseph Rauh, a founder of the ADA and a prominent civil rights and labor lawyer, and Clarence Mitchell launched an "all-out lobbying effort with their congressmen friends." Rauh and others from the Leadership Conference on Civil Rights told their members to come to Washington as soon as possible.[30] Members of the Democratic Study Group met daily in the office of the New Jersey Democrat Frank Thompson to count votes, devise strategy, and make sure there was constant pressure on moderate Democrats to live by promises they had made to move the bill intact to a favorable vote.

Johnson was also at work for the bill. He told James Webb, the administrator of the National Aeronautics and Space Administration, that Charles Halleck was asking what the White House could do for him. Halleck had raised the issue of a grant for Purdue University, a major research institution that was located in his district. Webb agreed to talk to Halleck directly and to award Purdue over $700,000 to construct a building as well as some research grants. "The net effect, Mr. President," Webb said, "is that if you tell him that you're willing to follow this policy as long as he cooperates with you, I can implement it on an installment basis. In other words, the minute he kicks over the traces, we stop the installment." Johnson was pleased.[31] When he wanted to, Halleck could be a ruthless leader who was known for threatening to withdraw financial or other party support from any member who defied him on a bill. With Halleck firmly on his side, the president was in a much stronger position to count on Republican votes. As a consequence of his receipt of presidential pork, Halleck did keep Republicans relatively united in an alliance with northern Democrats to defeat a number of amendments, mostly from southerners, that aimed to undermine political support for the legislation.

Once Halleck's support had been secured, Congressman McCulloch remained the key player in the GOP. He had staked his reputation on this bill when he helped move it through Judiciary, and he had no intention of watching it be dismantled on the floor. On February 7, the Arkansas Democrat Oren Harris tried to weaken the bill with an amendment that removed the section that authorized the federal government to cut off funds to state and local programs that were practicing racial discrimination, a provision that had originally been pushed by New York's congressman Adam Clayton Powell Jr. Republicans immediately cried foul. McCulloch announced that if this change was made to the legislation, he would withdraw his personal support from the bill, which would surely trigger an exodus of Republicans who looked to McCulloch as their touchstone for what was acceptable when it came to changes in the legislation. McCulloch's opposition was enough to kill Harris's amendment.[32]

Civil rights proponents beat back every amendment the conservative coalition proposed until, on February 8, Howard Smith proposed an amendment that added the word "sex" to Title VII, the provision of the bill that prohibited workplace discrimination on the basis of race, national origin, ethnicity, and religion. Looking slyly over the rims of his glasses, he offered his House colleagues a discussion of gender equality. He referred to a letter from a constituent who complained about an "imbalance" between the number of women and the number of men living in the United States. He read letters from women upset about gender discrimination, including a Nebraskan who complained about the "surplus of spinsters" and the fact that the government had "killed off a large number of eligible males" in wars.[33]

Though cynically conceived, Smith's amendment didn't come out of left field. A skillful network of female lobbyists had been fighting for decades to broaden support for their amendment on Capitol Hill. The judge had been a longtime supporter of the Equal Rights Amendment to the Constitution. Many other conservatives also supported equal rights for women; it was an issue that commanded strong support from upper-class, privileged, educated white women in the South. Some politicians, including Smith, hoped that by appealing to women, they could gain their support in the fight to maintain racial segregation in the region and create a buffer constituency against the votes of new immigrants who had come to American cities at the turn of the century. The amendment would also negate protective labor laws that had been established to specifically protect female industrial workers.[34]

Gender equality was also a liberal issue. Feminists in the labor movement had been lobbying for the federal government to take steps to prohibit gender discrimination in hiring. A report of the President's Commission on the Status of Women, released in 1963, emphasized the need to open opportunities for women in the marketplace through executive action and legislation.[35]

Of course, Howard Smith's aim in offering his amendment wasn't really gender equality. His proposal was an ingenious poison pill that would expand the power of a federal agency, the Equal Employment Opportunity Commission, far beyond what the administration or the House Judiciary Committee had proposed. Smith expected that this expansion would be unacceptable to moderate Republicans and Democrats in both the House and the Senate, who would choke on the pill and either back away from their support of the entire legislation or, at a minimum, insist on the excision of the section that would establish the EEOC.

The amendment had natural momentum. Ten out of eleven female members of the House rose to support it. "We outlast you," said the New York Republican Katharine St. George. "We outlive you. We nag you to death. So why should we want special privileges? We want this crumb of equality." Without the inclusion of Smith's amendment, said the Michigan Democrat Martha Griffiths, "white women would be at the bottom of the list in hiring . . . It would be incredible to me that white men would be willing to place white women at such a disadvantage."[36]

Understanding the complex politics at hand, the Oregon Democrat Edith Green, an ardent supporter of women's rights who had for a long time been fighting for a law that would mandate equal pay for equal work, made the tough choice to direct the administration's campaign against the amendment. One colleague later recalled, "She was probably the most powerful woman ever to serve in the Congress. On any important legislation, such as women's rights or education or dealing with minorities or poor people, she could switch people's votes on the floor through the power of her intellect and her ability to persuade."[37] Green had concluded that the gender equality amendment could jeopardize civil rights. She told her colleagues she knew she would be "called an 'Uncle Tom,' or perhaps 'Aunt Jane'" for her vote but that, while there was terrible discrimination against women, "there has been ten times, maybe a hundred times, as much humiliation for the Negro woman, for the Negro man and the Negro child, yes, and for the Negro baby who is born into a world of discrimination."[38]

Despite Green's opposition, the amendment survived. Southern Democrats were joined by Republican opponents of the EEOC and a few liberal Democrats in supporting Smith's amendment, which carried by a vote of 168 to 133. The final language in the bill prohibited discrimination in hiring on the basis of race, color, religion, national origin, or "sex."

The House had swallowed the pill, but the bill still didn't die. Both the administration and Howard Smith had miscalculated the political impact the amendment would have. Liberal Democrats who had opposed inclusion of the amendment for fear it would hurt the bill finally supported the legislation with "sex" added to Title VII. Most moderate Republicans were ultimately unwilling to vote against a civil rights bill whose time had come. They also assumed that Senator Dirksen, who opposed the creation of a federal commission with strong power to deal with employment discrimination, would insist on severely weakening, if not eliminating, the EEOC as part of any final deal with Johnson. As a result, a prohibition on sex discrimination became part of the bill.

On February 10, 1964, two days before Lincoln's 155th birthday and slightly more than a century after he issued the Emancipation Proclamation, the House passed the civil rights bill by 290 to 130. The bill received the support of 152 Democrats and 136 Republicans. The main source of opposition was predictable. Ninety-one Democrats voted against the bill, 88 of whom were from states in the Old Confederacy, and 35 Republicans joined them in opposition, 10 of whom were the rare breed of southern Republican.

The supporters of the bill burst into applause after the final vote and surrounded Emanuel Celler to congratulate him. Understanding that Republicans would be pivotal in the Senate, Celler quickly reminded his colleagues to thank Congressman McCulloch for all his work.

But proponents of civil rights understood that victory celebrations were premature. The big test for civil rights had never been the House; it would come in the Senate, where the odds were far less favorable. The southerners in the Senate had the filibuster.

THE FILIBUSTER BEGINS

Normal Senate procedure was for the bill to be reported to the Judiciary Committee, where the chairman was James Eastland, another of the southern segregationists. Of the 120 measures related to civil rights that had been sent to the Judiciary Committee over the past ten years, only the 1957 bill reached the floor, because Johnson and Dirksen had agreed to circumvent the committee.[39] It was always within the power of the majority leader to send a bill directly to the floor rather than to a committee, but it was rarely done. The majority leader was always a long-serving senator who had benefited from the rules of seniority that gave committee chairmen their power and was invested in supporting the traditional way the Senate did business. In this case, however, Johnson was able to persuade Majority Leader Mike Mansfield to make an exception to the usual practice because the civil rights bill was so important. Mansfield received support in doing this from a bipartisan coalition of thirty-four Democrats and twenty Republicans who voted to support the move.

As soon as the bill reached the Senate floor, Johnson tried to make sure that time was on the side of civil rights proponents. He announced to the Democratic and Republican leadership that he wouldn't care if the Senate conducted no business other than the civil rights bill until the end of the year. The message to southern senators was that they would be unable to force his hand on compromises simply because the White House wanted the Senate to move on to other business. Southerners knew that Johnson had an ambitious agenda he planned to send to Congress, but he had already pushed through the one bill he urgently needed Congress to pass before the election—the tax cut—and now he had made it clear he was willing to wait on the rest.

The strategy of the members of the southern caucus was to delay a vote on the civil rights bill as long as possible; there was always a chance that something would break their way. For the time being, they had enough votes (nineteen)—along with the minimum of fifteen Republicans they assumed would join them—to sustain a filibuster. The wild card in obtaining cloture would be twenty to twenty-five conservative and moderate Republicans whose votes were needed to reach sixty-seven. Until civil rights proponents secured their sixty-seven votes for cloture, there were things that could happen that would put pressure on them to agree to major compromises to the legislation. Violent civil rights protests could start to turn public opinion away from the cause of racial justice.

Non-southern Democrats might begin to see the movement as a threat rather than a moral crusade. An international crisis, like the Cuban missile crisis in 1962, could quickly divert public attention away from the civil rights legislation. President Johnson, despite his grandiose rhetoric, might become restless that Congress could do nothing to move forward with other items on his legislative wish list. Southerners would be making speeches constantly during their filibuster; perhaps they would say something that would change some Republican votes from for the bill to against it. All these possibilities imperiled the legislation.

The Senate debate over civil rights began on March 30, 1964. "You can almost hear the roll of the drums at Bull Run, Gettysburg and Appomattox as the Senate wheels into line for a civil rights engagement 100 years overdue," wrote Robert Albright in the *Washington Post*.[40] The galleries were packed with civil rights advocates who had gathered as the self-appointed eyes and ears of the nation. One network, CBS, had assigned a reporter, Roger Mudd, to stand in a Capitol corridor, receive reports from staffers inside the Senate chamber, and transmit special reports throughout the day via CBS TV and radio and on the *Evening News*.[41]

Hubert Humphrey kicked off the deliberations with a stirring three-and-a-half-hour speech in which he depicted the debate about civil rights as the great moral struggle of the era. He evoked the African Americans and white Americans who had been physically beaten by southern police as they risked their lives trying to force the nation to confront the racial injustice at the heart of American democracy. He noted that there were many hotels in Charleston, South Carolina, that allowed guests to bring in dogs but prohibited African Americans, and he reported that, according to government data, an African American college graduate could expect to earn less than half the salary of a college-educated white American.[42] "The time has come for America to wash its dirty face and cleanse its countenance of this evil [racial discrimination] . . . The Negro no longer can be told, 'There is your place, and stay here.' They won't take it anymore and they shouldn't. They are sick of it."

The southerners who opposed the bill also saw civil rights as a moral· cause, but they had entirely different criteria of right and wrong. In their minds, civil rights advocates were radical agitators who wanted to destroy wholesome southern communities, where white Americans and African Americans lived separate from each other, as ordained by God. Southern senators believed they were the last defense against a world where African Americans and white Americans in Georgia and Alabama and South Carolina would be compelled by federal law to eat in the same restaurants, sleep in the same hotels, and get haircuts from the same barbers, against the wishes of all moral people of both races.

In support of his vision, Russell had organized his small, fierce army of eighteen southerners and one Republican—the Texas senator John Tower, who had won the seat Johnson had vacated in 1960— into three "platoons," each of which would be on watch, holding the floor and debating a particular section of the legislation, for a ten-hour period. Mansfield had decided not to keep the Senate in continuous session (it would adjourn every evening at 10:00 p.m.); each platoon member would have to filibuster for about four hours a day without a break.[43] The senator who was speaking could not leave the chamber, even to go to the bathroom, during his term, or the filibuster would officially come to a close. Russell assigned a trusted senator to serve as a captain for each platoon: Lister Hill of Alabama, Allen Ellender of Louisiana, and John Stennis of Mississippi. "We intend to fight this bill with all the vigor at our command," Russell told a group of reporters after leaving a forty-five-minute closed-door meeting with his army.[44]

On most days, a filibuster was not fun to watch. A speaker would address a sparsely populated chamber and read a speech written for him by aides, or perhaps some marginally relevant published material. On one afternoon, Richard Russell demonstrated how ridiculous the discourse could become when he came to the defense of the African American boxer Cassius Clay, who had changed his name to Muhammad Ali after joining the Nation of Islam. Clay had been forced to vacate his heavyweight title by the World Boxing Association for agreeing to a rematch with Sonny Liston without the permission of association officials. Russell said that the boxing officials were guilty of practicing the same intolerance that was the subject of the civil rights agitation.[45] Government attempts to regulate discrimination were, in Russell's view, a "slippery slope" that would inevitably lead to regulations to protect African American boxers who changed their names.

The chamber usually looked like an ornate ghost town. Although Mansfield had called off all committee business while the debate over the civil rights bill was taking place, so that senators would have no excuse if they were absent, most of them didn't make it anyway. There wasn't even a quorum present during much of the first week of debate. On one afternoon, a senator slept in the front row as one of the civil rights captains responded to some of the southern attacks in a voice that was barely audible.[46]

The only energy in the chamber was in the inflammatory rhetoric of the southerners, filled with dire warnings about how the legislation would destroy the constitutional fabric of the nation. In previous debates, southerners had emphasized the dangers of miscegenation and the likely degradation of the white race, but now they stuck mainly to constitutional arguments, which they believed might win them broader support than the arguments based on racist ideology they had employed in the past.[47] They also warned that the legislation would restrict freedom of choice in personal association and infringe on the rights of persons to do as they wished with their private property. Senator Eastland predicted that the bill would bring the nation back to "Stalin, Khrushchev, Nasser, Hitler, and a dictatorship." Senator Hill discussed dining arrangements. If "Mr. Jones wishes to go out to dinner with people of another race he is free to do so . . . If Mr. Smith wishes to go to dinner with people of the same race he likewise may do so free of any official restraint and may select an eating place for that purpose . . . This bill, however, would deprive Mr. Smith of his present freedom; it would do this by forbidding any eating place from serving clientele of one race only."[48]

Conservative senators also aimed to arouse opposition to the bill on the part of working-class northern Democrats by warning that the legislation would result in racial quotas in the workplace. They called attention to a ruling by the Illinois Fair Employment Practices Commission that ordered the Motorola Corporation to hire an African American man who had failed an employment test the commission decided was unfair, on the grounds that it disfavored "culturally deprived and disadvantaged groups." Businesses throughout Illinois had protested the decision, and the *New York Times* columnist Arthur Krock had written that Title VII of the civil rights bill would make this the law of the land. "If Congress approves the pending measure," he wrote, "with Title VII included, and the constitutionality of this section is affirmed by the Supreme Court . . . [t]hen a Federal bureaucracy would be legislated into senior partnership with private business, with the power to dictate the standards by which employers reach their judgments of the capabilities of applicants for jobs, and the quality of performance after employment, whenever the issue of 'discrimination' is raised."[49] Liberal Democrats responded that the bill would not require businesses to hire a certain number of African Americans. "Contrary to the allegations of some opponents of this title, there is nothing in it that will give any power to the Commission or to any court to require hiring, firing, or promotion of employees in order to meet a racial 'quota' or to achieve a certain racial balance," Humphrey said. "That bugaboo has been brought up a dozen times; but it is nonexistent."[50]

Civil rights supporters were still worried about whether these kinds of arguments would scare off undecided senators, particularly as they watched George Wallace campaign in the 1964 Democratic primaries. On April 7, Wallace surprised many observers by winning over 260,000 votes in the Wisconsin primary. The outcome made it clear that the racial tensions of the South were also swirling around in some northern constituencies at the time that Democratic leaders were lobbying for Senate votes on the civil rights bill. Administration officials dismissed Wallace's showing as insignificant, but Senator Dirksen captured the sentiment of others when he noted that "it is an interesting commentary on the depth of feeling the people must have on civil rights when a candidate from the old Confederacy can invade a northern state" and win this number of votes.[51]

ORGANIZING LIBERALS, OUTFLANKING CONSERVATIVES

The Montana senator Mike Mansfield had worked as a young man in the copper mines of Butte, taught history at the University of Montana, entered the House of Representatives in 1942, and succeeded Lyndon Johnson as Senate majority leader in 1961. He handled his caucus in a laid-back manner, as it had been done before Johnson centralized operations under the majority leadership. Rather than strong-arming his members, Mansfield liked to collect as much input as possible from them and then try to craft bills that would win broad support. His strategy had not worked very well when Kennedy was in the White House, and Johnson believed it made the civil rights bill more vulnerable to the aggressive tactics of the southerners.

With Johnson sidelined in the White House and Mansfield

proving to be a weak leader, the liberal legislators, still smarting from previous losses on civil rights, had committed themselves to good organization and coordination with the liberal interest groups. They wanted physically and emotionally to wear down the southerners who were engaged in the filibuster, to force each of them to spend a maximum number of hours speaking on the floor, and to increase the pressure on uncommitted Republican senators to vote in favor of cloture. The liberals would be in constant contact with every senator to make sure that no side deals were cut that involved endorsing revisions that would weaken the bill. While southerners publicized their arguments against civil rights to the media, liberals reminded reporters what King and his allies had been fighting for.

Senator Humphrey's teams were called the Civil Rights Corporals' Guard. Each team was responsible for handling any negotiations that took place about specific parts of the bill and for responding to southern attacks on the Senate floor about particular issues. The leaders of the civil rights teams were Warren Magnuson of Washington for public accommodations; Philip Hart of Michigan on voting rights; Joseph Clark of Pennsylvania on the equal employment commission; Paul Douglas of Illinois on school desegregation; Edward Long of Missouri on the Civil Rights Commission; John Pastore of Rhode Island on proposed restrictions on federal funds to segregated programs; and Thomas Dodd of Connecticut on some additional minor provisions. Senator Dirksen assigned Minority Whip Thomas Kuchel to head the GOP effort on the Senate floor. Kuchel was a liberal Californian who had come under vicious attack from the far-right John Birch Society for his moderate views on race. The Republican captains, all the senior liberal wing of the party from the Northeast, were Jacob Javits and Kenneth Keating of New York, Clifford Case of New Jersey, and Hugh Scott of Pennsylvania.

Humphrey and Kuchel made certain there was a clear line of communication between the White House and Congress. Every morning the liberal leaders met with the administration officials Larry O'Brien and Mike Manatos from the Office of Legislative Liaison to coordinate the responses they would offer to opponents' speeches on substantive issues and thus shape public opinion through press reports on the "debate" in the chamber. The meetings were also preparation for any negotiations that might arise among senators—about issues, for example, like the federal employment commission—where deals could be made that would commit senators to support cloture. Finally, the meetings were the central processing mechanism for vote counting—where each senator stood on cloture and strategies for identifying colleagues who might be persuaded by a personal call from the president or a visit from representatives in the civil rights movement.

Once or twice a week, Clarence Mitchell, Joseph Rauh, and Andrew Biemiller joined the morning meetings. Attorney General Robert Kennedy became the main public voice for the legislation; even though he and Johnson hated each other, the president hoped the move to include liberals would insulate him from attacks by northern Democrats. Deputy Attorney General Nicholas Katzenbach and Assistant Attorney General for Civil Rights Burke Marshall represented the Justice Department in the daily operations. Katzenbach was the key man for the administration.[52]

Responding to quorum calls was one of the procedures by which southerners and liberals tried to wear each other down every day; it was the dry stuff of the legislative process that mattered greatly on Capitol Hill. According to the Constitution, the Senate needed a quorum to conduct all its business—in 1964, fifty-one senators—but this requirement was more honored in the breach. There were rarely that many senators in the chamber, even during this filibuster debate, but if any senator requested a quorum call, fifty-one members had to be in the chamber by the time the roll call finished, or the official business day came to an end. Otherwise, the official day continued until the chamber had disposed of the issue at hand. This mattered during a filibuster because by rule every senator was permitted to make no more than two speeches in one official day. If the official day did not end, southerners had to extend their filibuster speeches to compensate for their small numbers. To force the southerners to do as much exhausting speechifying as possible—especially because Mansfield had decided to let the senators take a break at night—it was incumbent on the liberals to be ready to scramble into the chamber in force at very short notice.

When, in the fifth week of the filibuster, liberals failed to muster a quorum, Humphrey quickly moved to make sure it didn't happen again. He created a phone list that would enable him to instantly contact a sufficient number of senators who had agreed to be on call. Liberal organizations also helped make sure their allies responded to each southern trick. On April 13, a group of U.S. senators from both parties went to the Washington Senators' home opener with President Johnson, who threw out the first pitch. Between the third and the fourth innings, at around 2:20 p.m., there was an unusual public address announcement: "All U.S. Senators are requested to return to the chamber." The legislators were caught off guard; they thought there had been an informal agreement that southerners would not call for a quorum during the game. Senator Humphrey, who was becoming increasingly frustrated with the filibuster, jumped up from his seat.[53] With so many politicians piling out of the stadium to get back to the Capitol, one fan joked, "It's a good thing they didn't ask for the Representatives too, or the stadium would be half empty."[54] The only person not surprised by the announcement was Senator Russell. He remained comfortably in his seat as the game resumed.

Most of the other senators in attendance ran out of the gates and directly into the four limousines that the Leadership Conference on Civil Rights had sent to the stadium as a precaution against the precise trick the conservatives were trying to pull. The baseball fans made the mile drive in a little more than eight minutes. "We have returned!" boasted Humphrey to his colleagues. The supporters of civil rights made the quorum call just after 2:30.[55] It was a win for the liberals in the Senate, but without a quorum of senators rooting them on at the ballpark, the Senators lost 4–0 to the Los Angeles Angels.

During these months, civil rights supporters continued to drum up constituent pressure on uncommitted senators to vote for cloture. Simply the threat of a civil rights protest at home could be a powerful influence on a senator in the context of what had been going on in 1963 and 1964. It was evident to all how extreme the positions of the southerners were; no moderate senator wanted to be publicly associated with them. The Congress of Racial Equality talked about mobilizing its supporters in Illinois, the home state of Everett Dirksen. As the minority leader, Dirksen was the only senator who could deliver enough Republican votes to obtain cloture. Although he had made public statements in support of a bill, most legislators and civil rights activists believed that the minority leader was doing little or nothing to stop the filibuster in March or April. James Farmer said his organization would bring marchers directly to the post offices so they could mail letters to Dirksen in support of the bill. He also said that protesters would set up shop right outside the senator's home in Buena Vista to shine the media spotlight on how he was obstructing progress in the Senate by passively supporting the filibuster. Though CORE did not follow through outside his home, which was primarily occupied by his elderly mother-in-law, it did hold demonstrations in Chicago and other parts of the state. Dirksen warned that he would not be intimidated. "If the day ever comes," he said, "when under pressure of picketing or other devices I shall be pushed from the rock where I stand to render a judgment against my convictions, my justification in public life will have come to an end."[56] Despite his bluster, the Senate minority leader was affected by the commotion that the protesters were generating within his electorate. He came to accept the necessity and inevitability of legislation that would prohibit racial segregation.

There were protests all over the country; in some places it wasn't about influencing particular senators but about bringing ever more widespread media attention to the cause. In Tulsa, Oklahoma, CORE activists organized a sit-in at a segregated restaurant; more than fifty people, black and white, were dragged out by the police and sent to police headquarters. Thirty-five thousand people, the biggest integrated crowd in the history of the state, walked to Legion Field in Birmingham, Alabama, to hear the evangelical preacher Billy Graham, who had been a longtime opponent of segregation, on Easter Sunday. In St. Augustine, Florida, three hundred civil rights protesters, including Mary Parkman Peabody, the seventy-two-year-old mother of Governor Endicott Peabody of Massachusetts, conducted sit-ins at segregated movie theaters, hotels, and restaurants. After the police arrested Peabody for trespassing and conspiracy at the Ponce de León hotel, she refused to pay the bond and remained in jail for two nights. Because of her participation, the national media reported the story. "We are down here because as Christians," Peabody explained, "we believe in the dignity and worth of every human being. Civil rights is the number one problem in this country. It is a problem in the North as well as the South."[57]

Martin Luther King issued public warnings to the Senate that further delay in invoking cloture would mean bigger protests and possibly another march on Washington. He and other civil rights leaders brought their supporters to the city, to "dramatize this blatant use of legislative power" to block civil rights.[58] The protests would make Dirksen, who understood that public opinion was now in favor of a bill, look like the main source of obstruction to racial justice.

Religious groups aligned with the civil rights movement were instrumental in keeping up pressure on the uncommitted senators to vote for cloture. In some of these constituencies, where there were few African American voters and legislators might have felt the issue with less urgency, religious leaders and institutions used their moral influence to press for equal rights. Religious institutions played a huge role in these communities. Congregants listened to their preachers, and legislators paid attention when spoken to. When these groups started to press midwestern Republicans to support the civil rights cause, the pleading had great effect. "The most important force at work today on behalf of civil rights is the churches—Catholic, Protestant and Jewish," observed Senator Humphrey.[59] The Commission on Religion and Race was an umbrella organization that coordinated religious pro-civil-rights protests. "The secret of passing the bill is the prayer groups," Humphrey told Rauh and Mitchell. Humphrey told a reporter, "Just wait until [senators] start hearing from the church people."[60] In Iowa, the national Jewish organization B'nai B'rith convened a meeting of local Christian religious leaders with Senator Bourke Hickenlooper—an archconservative who thought of the civil rights bill as a dangerous aggrandizement of federal power that violated states' rights—during which they persuaded him to support a vote for cloture so that the civil rights bill could at least be voted on. A Quaker did the same with the Kentucky senators, John Sherman Cooper and Thruston Morton.[61] A phone call to the South Dakota Republican Karl Mundt from a priest and a bishop, one of whom had been his high school classmate, was important in persuading him to support cloture. "I hope that satisfied those two goddamned bishops [sic] that called me last night," he said.[62] The religious organizations also conducted letter-writing campaigns and organized events to raise awareness in many states. Clergy coordinated sermons on specific weekends to sell their message. Every week, religious organizations mailed information to church and synagogue congregants, urging them to write or call their senators. Ministers asked prominent local congregants to speak personally with their state's senators.[63] Senate staffers became accustomed to the huge volume of letters that would pour in on Tuesdays and Wednesdays from midwestern congregants who had heard their preachers speak over the weekend about the issue.[64]

They also came to Washington. On a rainy April 19, a group of Jewish, Protestant, and Catholic seminarians held a vigil at the Lincoln Memorial. They huddled together under umbrellas to talk about civil rights and to pray. They were the first contingent of a large group from seventy-five seminaries. Each contingent planned to spend twenty-four hours at a time at the memorial, during which the members would pray for two three-hour periods. They slept on air mattresses at the Church of the Holy Comforter and received food from various women's organizations. They promised to stay in Washington until the Senate passed the House bill.[65]

Ministers and rabbis joined representatives from the Leadership Conference on Civil Rights in the Senate galleries to remind senators that they, and God, were listening to every word the legislators said. "You couldn't turn around where there wasn't a clerical collar next to you," Joseph Rauh recalled.[66]

The southerners were losing the public relations war. On April 27, the pollster Louis Harris reported that Americans, including southerners, favored cloture by a margin of three to one and civil rights by two to one. The public accommodations section of the bill, which was the heart of the measure, received the strongest support from the public, a result of the moral and political pressure applied by the civil rights movement and the strong support from organized labor, religious organizations, and the news media. Public support for the bill had increased in the course of the civil rights filibuster, from 63 percent of the nation favorable in November 1963, to 68 percent in February 1964, to 70 percent in April 1964.[67] According to the polls, only 21 percent opposed Johnson's position on civil rights, a notable decline from 30 percent in February 1964 and 50 percent in the fall of 1963.[68]

Lyndon Johnson applies "the Treatment" to Louis Martin, a journalist, civil rights activist, and trusted presidential adviser, on April 20, 1966, during a reception for Democratic National Committee delegates. The president's one-on-one powers of intimidation and persuasion are memorialized as being essential to advancing his domestic agenda even during a period when liberals dominated both houses of Congress.

In the early 1960s, Congress was ruled by a conservative coalition of southern Democratic committee chairmen and senior midwestern Republicans. In this photograph, the Connecticut senator Prescott Bush sleeps in his office during a twenty-four-hour filibuster against civil rights legislation in 1960. Scenes like this inspired one Democratic senator to call Congress the "Sapless Branch" of government.

The House Rules Committee chairman, Howard "Judge" Smith (left), was one of the most notorious leaders of the conservative coalition.

The legislative logjam finally started to break when grassroots activists galvanized public support for civil rights legislation. Images of children being confronted and arrested by police in Birmingham, Alabama, shocked the world.

The ranking Republican on the House Judiciary Committee,
William McCulloch of Ohio, reached a secret deal with Kennedy
administration officials over the July 4 holiday of 1963. He agreed
to support Kennedy's civil rights proposal as long as Kennedy
gave credit to the GOP and prevented southern Democrats from
watering down the bill.

When Kennedy sent a civil rights bill to the House in June 1963, the
House Judiciary Committee chairman, Emanuel Celler of New York,
the most senior liberal in the House, used the power of the chairmanship
to push aggressively for passage of the bill.

Lobbyists for the major liberal advocacy organizations laid out a strategy to make sure the well-organized southerners did not succeed in stalling the bill by using their familiar legislative tricks. Left to right: Joseph Rauh (ADA), Clarence Mitchell (NAACP), and Roy Wilkins (NAACP) at a meeting on August 23, 1963, in Washington.

The AFL-CIO was an integral part of the liberal lobby for civil rights. The lobbyist for the organization, Andrew Biemiller, had immediate access to all of the most powerful politicians of the day.

Civil rights supporters marched on Washington on August 28, 1963, to demand that Congress pass civil rights legislation.

Martin Luther King Jr. and his colleagues were disappointed when, despite the success of the march, President Kennedy expressed to them his pessimistic assessment of the bill's legislative prospects.

At the time of Kennedy's assassination on November 22, 1963, very little of his domestic agenda had made it through Congress. Johnson was determined to persuade legislators to pass transformative programs. On November 28, he prepared to deliver his first televised address as president of the United States.

Johnson inherited the same conservative Congress that had stifled Kennedy's initiatives. At this meeting on December 7, 1963, Georgia's conservative senator Richard Russell, Johnson's mentor, seems not at all intimidated by the new president's aggressive style.

President Johnson meets with his top advisers. Left to right, facing the president: Pierre Salinger, Bill Moyers, Ted Sorensen, and Jack Valenti.

President Johnson hoped to ride the momentum created by the civil rights movement. During this meeting with civil rights leaders on January 18, 1964, he promised he would fight for the Civil Rights Act and make no compromises with the opposition. Left to right: Martin Luther King Jr., President Johnson, Whitney Young, and James Farmer.

The opposition to civil rights was fierce. These protesters picketed Representative William McCulloch after the Ohio Republican voted with the majority when the House of Representatives passed the Civil Rights Act on February 10, 1964.

These three southern Democrats met on March 21, 1964, to plan strategy against the civil rights bill in the Senate. Left to right: Senators Harry Byrd of Virginia, Allen Ellender of Louisiana, and James Eastland of Mississippi.

Martin Luther King Jr. (left) and Malcolm X (right) meeting in the halls of Congress on March 26, 1964. They threatened to mobilize massive grassroots protests against any senator who continued to support the filibuster.

The civil rights filibuster consumed Washington for months. Here, on April 13, 1964, opening day of the Washington Senators' baseball season, Lyndon Johnson shares some of his popcorn with Speaker of the House John McCormack (to the president's immediate right) and Majority Whip Hale Boggs. The game would be punctuated by an announcement that all senators should return to Capitol Hill for a quorum call.

Nicholas Katzenbach, who served as deputy attorney general and attorney general under Presidents Kennedy and Johnson, was the administration's point man in negotiations with the Senate over civil rights.

Senate minority leader Everett Dirksen, known as the Wizard of Ooze for his melodramatic orations, sits cross-legged on top of a desk in the Senate press gallery on April 7, 1964—his favorite position in which to talk with reporters during these weeks—outlining the amendments he planned to make to the civil rights bill that had passed in the House. In the end, Dirksen delivered enough Republican votes to end the civil rights filibuster. Dirksen was able to do that only because the civil rights movement had convinced many midwestern Republicans to support the bill.

With victory in sight for the Civil Rights Act of 1964, Johnson was
already campaigning for his War on Poverty.

President Johnson persuaded Sargent Shriver (left), who had headed
the Peace Corps, to run the War on Poverty. Shriver's boundless energy
helped build strong legislative support for the initiative.

Johnson made his liberalism a central theme in the campaign. Robert Kennedy was running for a Senate seat in New York.

With the Gulf of Tonkin Resolution, Johnson shored up his credentials as a cold war hawk. The Senate Foreign Relations Committee chairman, William Fulbright, helped the White House find support for the resolution, which granted the president broad authority to conduct military operations in Vietnam

A billboard for Senator Barry Goldwater's 1964 presidential campaign in Atlantic City, with a comment by his opponents appended.

Johnson watches the 1964 election returns as reported by the three broadcast television networks.

PRESIDENTIAL VOTE

JOHNSON LEADING
GOLDWATER LEADING

The 1964 presidential election created the perception that there was a mandate for Lyndon Johnson and made liberals a dominant force on Capitol Hill. Johnson won 486 electoral votes and 61 percent of the popular vote. Democrats gained huge majorities in the House (295–140) and the Senate (68–32). Here is how the presidential election looked at 1:30 a.m. EST, November 4, 1964, as returns showed the proportions of the Democratic landslide.

A dejected Barry Goldwater during a news conference at Camelback Inn near Phoenix, Arizona, after he lost the presidential election. Republicans were thenceforth afraid to be associated with the extreme conservatism Goldwater represented.

Lyndon Johnson admiring a portrait of Franklin Roosevelt. In 1965, Johnson hoped to complete the work FDR had started when he created the New Deal.

Lawrence O'Brien, legislative liaison for Presidents Kennedy and Johnson, understood the immense possibilities that had resulted from the election. Left to right: Lyndon Johnson, Lawrence O'Brien, and Bill Moyers.

The House majority leader, Carl Albert, would serve as the president's point man in the House of Representatives during the Eighty-ninth Congress throughout the debates over most of the major domestic bills.

The Missouri congressman Richard Bolling, a founder of the Democratic Study Group, entered the Eighty-ninth Congress with grand expectations about moving forward with the liberal domestic agenda and congressional reforms that would permanently weaken southern conservative chairmen.

President Johnson tried to stay out of the public eye—he didn't want to give opponents the chance to make the debate be about him rather than about racial equality—but he was nonetheless a gigantic presence behind the scenes. He frequently leaned on Humphrey and Mansfield to keep the pressure on uncommitted senators. He spent a lot of time literally counting votes, a job most presidents had left to staffers. Joseph Califano recalled that "Johnson would make call after call, hold meetings into the night, and count congressional heads." He would ask Larry O'Brien to repeat to him exactly what senators had said so he could figure out for himself how firm their positions were.[69]

Johnson distributed all the pork he could get his hands on to win votes in the Senate. He had Secretary of the Interior Stewart Udall personally promise the Arizona senator Carl Hayden that the White House would offer assistance to the Central Arizona Project, a huge public project to move water from the Colorado River into Arizona, in return for Hayden's promise to support cloture. Hayden was not a strong supporter of civil rights—in 1957 he had joined southern Democrats to delay the civil rights bill—but water was something Arizona desperately needed, so he made the deal.[70]

Yet there were clear limits to what Johnson could do. For every phone call in which he was able to cajole a senator into supporting cloture, there were others who refused to budge no matter how intense the Treatment became. When Johnson leaned in heavily on the West Virginia Democrat Robert Byrd, virtually begging him to support the administration in an election year, Byrd responded in an equally aggressive fashion: "I hope to hell we beat it. We're going to do all we can for Lyndon Johnson. We don't need that bill. You know, you know I'll carry the weight where it's needed . . . But not on this."[71]

Johnson publicly campaigned for the civil rights bill only as one component of the campaign-style barnstorming trip he took in late April to promote his antipoverty program. On the trip, which was known as the Poverty Tour, Johnson delivered more than thirty speeches in under a month to ten states; he traveled most of the time by airplane and covered more than ten thousand miles.[72] In the course of his pitch for the poverty program, the president talked frequently about the connection between poverty and race.[73] Huge crowds greeted him everywhere. In Pittsburgh, he assured an audience of steelworkers that he would get a civil rights bill through the Senate "if it takes all summer" and that "we don't want any Democratic label on it. We want it to be an American bill."[74] In Georgia, addressing the state legislature, with the racist senator Herman Talmadge and his wife sitting behind him, he urged the assembly to support civil rights. When he returned to the White House, Johnson could barely contain his excitement. He told Larry O'Brien, "I made sixteen speeches and we had a million people. That's a minimum . . . Old Herman Talmadge got up after I made two civil rights speeches that he was present at, and said, 'I just want to say that I have never seen as many people anywhere.'"[75]

NEGOTIATING WITH DIRKSEN

The final breakthrough in the civil rights struggle occurred behind closed doors, when Johnson turned to the Republican minority leader, Everett Dirksen, to deliver the votes he needed for cloture. It could have been a lot worse. Dirksen firmly believed that the job of a legislator was to make the compromises necessary to pass bills. Like so many others in this period of insider politics, when legislators stayed in office for long periods of time and devoted their careers to the institution of Congress, Johnson and Dirksen knew each other well, liked each other, and believed in working together. "They were old pros," Johnson's adviser Jack Valenti recalled. "They understood the ground rules and played by them, and never allowed combat in the press to obscure a hospitable regard for each other."[76]

Johnson was confident he could make a deal with Dirksen. Though he was a midwestern conservative known primarily for his attacks on government spending and his opposition to federal regulations on business, Dirksen had supported several civil rights measures in the past, including the 1957 bill. The Illinois Republican was fully aware of how public opinion had shifted as a result of the civil rights protests in Alabama and Mississippi.

Johnson was hoping to take advantage of Dirksen's concern for his legacy. Like Johnson, Dirksen measured his worth by the legislation he was able to move through Congress. At the moment, the senator was in terrible health—he had emphysema, from smoking three packs a day, and a peptic ulcer.[77] The president felt that if the Democrats gave Dirksen something he wanted in the final bill, he would seize the opportunity to have his name on a truly significant piece of legislation. Letting Dirksen play a role in shaping the final legislation did carry some significant political risks; it would surely draw fire from liberals whose support Johnson needed on this and other issues.

"You've got to play to Ev Dirksen," Johnson told Hubert Humphrey. "You've got to let him have a piece of the action. He's got to look good all the time."[78] Though this was a bitter pill for a devoted civil rights advocate to swallow, Humphrey had become enough of a legislative operator to recognize that they would have to let Dirksen claim a measure of credit for passing the civil rights bill. Humphrey later said he "would have kissed Dirksen's ass on the Capitol steps."[79]

Though characteristically elusive, Dirksen gave numerous indications that he could support the civil rights bill as long as certain changes were made. The events of the past few months had brought him to the side of the civil rights activists in terms of prohibiting segregation in public accommodations. The part of the bill that now troubled him most was Title VII, which established the Equal Employment Opportunity Commission. Dirksen thought the commission, as constituted in the bill, represented an excessive and dangerous expansion of federal power. He had always been an opponent of federal regulations on business, and he thought the EEOC would have too much authority over a firm's hiring decisions. If the House bill were passed, the EEOC would have more authority than some agencies for equal employment opportunity already established by some states, including Illinois. Dirksen warned this would create a jurisdictional mess, with federal and state authorities competing over policy and businesses uncertain about which rules to follow.[80] He also believed the measure could result in the establishment of racial quotas, which would compel the employment of certain groups at the expense of individual rights.

Dirksen recognized that to round up enough votes for cloture, he needed a compromise that would placate conservative Republicans who were adamantly opposed to the EEOC. The chairman of the Republican Policy Committee, Bourke Hickenlooper of Iowa, who didn't like Dirksen and wanted to challenge him as minority leader, wasn't on board with the deal Republicans had worked out in the House. In fact, he objected to the entire Civil Rights Act on the grounds that it would give bureaucrats too much power to intervene in the personal lives of Americans. The Iowan's influence on the most conservative members of the Republican caucus could cause Dirksen trouble.

While the filibuster was well under way, Johnson, Mansfield, Kennedy, and Humphrey entered into top-secret negotiations with Dirksen. They were prepared to compromise on the EEOC as long as they could protect the section of the bill that prohibited segregation in public accommodations. In their minds, this had been the focus of the civil rights protests over the past few years, and there would be outrage among activists and liberal politicians if it didn't pass. They had also looked at the polls and seen that public support for the desegregation of public accommodations was stronger than ever before. Although many liberals believed that ending racial discrimination in hiring was equally important to achieving civil rights, they also understood that Dirksen was not alone. A strong EEOC had substantial opposition among Republicans whose support they needed, and it would bring business interests into a debate they were otherwise happy to sit out. The civil rights movement had focused on ending segregation in schools and public accommodations and had turned congressional opinion on the issue, but it had not yet done the same on employment discrimination. When it came time to begin serious talks with Dirksen, President Johnson intended to stand firm on desegregation but give some ground on the structure of the employment commission.

The president relied on Burke Marshall of the Civil Rights Division and Deputy Attorney General Nicholas Katzenbach to make the deal with Dirksen. Attorney General Robert Kennedy would continue to serve as the administration's spokesperson on the bill. On May 5, the Justice Department officials met with the Senate Democratic and Republican leaders to begin discussions on the civil rights bill. Humphrey, remembering Johnson's instructions to flatter the minority leader, insisted that the talks take place in Dirksen's large office.

When Katzenbach and Marshall entered Dirksen's office for the first meeting, they couldn't help but notice the portrait of Abraham Lincoln looking at them over the minority leader's shoulder. An elaborate collection of elephant figurines grazed on Dirksen's desk, under the sunny bipartisan brilliance of fresh marigolds in an elegant vase.

Dirksen's legal staff had brought with them bundles of research and notated drafts of the bill,[81] which were soon spread out over the large rectangular wooden conference table where the men sat and slowly reviewed the content of the bill, section by section.

As word of the negotiations spread through Washington and the civil rights community, some liberal organizations were displeased with Dirksen's prominence in the debate. Demands expressed by brave African Americans and white college youth were now to be answered by a white, antigovernment midwestern conservative. Conservatives who blocked legislation for years were then allowed to take credit for bills they were finally forced to accept. Humphrey recalled that some of his liberal allies told him, "You're the manager of the bill. We're the majority party. Why don't you call Dirksen to your office?"[82]

These reactions were what Johnson had expected, but he didn't believe he had any other option, given the politics of the Senate. Dirksen held the balance of power to stop the filibuster. Everything depended on what happened in his office. Every morning, the group around the conference table included Senators Dirksen, Mansfield, Humphrey, Kuchel, Magnuson, and Hickenlooper and from Justice Katzenbach and Marshall. Dirksen and Katzenbach sat next to each other at the head of the table. In the evening, the group was smaller, only Katzenbach, Marshall, Dirksen, and their legal staffs, who combed the language of the bill, line by line, looking for points of disagreement and compromises to resolve them. The group was often joined by Nebraska senator Roman Hruska, who was invited to represent the conservative wing of the GOP. The drinking and smoking that accompanied the negotiations lubricated the process at all hours of the day. Evenings usually saw the crystal ashtrays on the table filled with cigarette butts and all the participants gathered around the "Twilight Lodge," Dirksen's private bar that was fully stocked with bourbon, whiskey, and gin. "The process took time, and we were lucky to get one provision agreed to every two days or so," Katzenbach recalled. "In those meetings Burke and I discovered three important facts: first, Dirksen wanted to be sure the provision [on employment discrimination] did not affect his state of Illinois in any significant way; second, he obviously wanted the bill rewritten, to appear different, even if there were no substantive changes, so that he could explain to all his colleagues all the 'changes' he had negotiated; and third, it behooved us to get agreement before too much bourbon had dulled the senator's recollection of what he had okayed."[83]

The administration invited lobbyists from the Leadership Conference on Civil Rights to attend the meetings on Tuesdays and Thursdays. Their role was to give a strong presentation of what the bill had to do to satisfy the movement; their participation was meant to bolster their confidence that the Senate would actually reach agreement on a good bill and to make them feel invested in the legislative deliberations. On the other hand, the participation of the civil rights lobbyists was limited, because the Justice Department felt that ultimately there would have to be certain concessions made to Dirksen that the civil rights representatives would not want to agree to.[84]

During the fifth day of deliberations, the negotiators reached the crucial section on the equal employment commission. If a deal wasn't struck, the filibuster would be much likelier to continue. Dirksen suggested turning the EEOC into an investigative body with limited enforcement power. State commissions would have the primary authority to handle employment discrimination. The federal commission could investigate, however, if a state commission failed to implement remedies or if a state had no commission. Because there were no state commissions in southern states, whereas several northern states (including Illinois) had commissions, the compromise would protect much of the North from intervention by a federal commission but still allow the government to take action in most of the South. Humphrey and the White House could live with this. The administration also agreed to strip away some of the power the House bill granted to the EEOC, namely the power to file suits. Under

Dirksen's compromise, the EEOC could only investigate problems and make recommendations to the Department of Justice, whose attorneys could then take action.

The following morning, the staff reviewed the proposed language on the EEOC. Humphrey brought Joseph Clark to the meeting. The Pennsylvania senator was one of the most liberal members of the Democratic caucus, a passionate civil rights advocate, and a reformer who had just recently published a book lambasting the way the conservative coalition had made Congress dysfunctional. Clark walked into Dirksen's office with a script in his head about how the next few minutes would unfold. He had spent most of his time as one of Humphrey's floor corporals pushing back against southern misinformation and making the case for a civil rights bill that addressed inequality in the workplace. Dirksen, aiming to get himself more support from conservative Republicans and the business community, wanted to see if he could squeeze out a better deal on the EEOC than the one he had agreed to the previous day. As he slowly walked through the language of the section and explained his remaining concerns, Dirksen kept an eye on Clark, who made quite visible his unhappiness with what the minority leader was saying. When Dirksen came out and asked directly if they could agree to make the EEOC even weaker, all the participants in the room turned immediately to see Clark's reaction. They were not disappointed. The senator pushed his chair back from the table, stood up, and, without even looking at Dirksen, stormed out of the room. "It's a goddamn sell-out!" he shouted as he walked through the door. Humphrey turned to Dirksen and said, "See what pressure I'm up against?" Dirksen acknowledged that he understood and brought the negotiations on the EEOC to a close. Humphrey and Clark had planned the walkout in advance.[85]

At 4:05 in the afternoon on May 13, Johnson's team and Dirksen finalized their deal. Attorney General Kennedy, who had been present at the last meeting, called Johnson to let him know: "We had a meeting all day today, with Senator Dirksen on the civil rights bill . . . And [it would] appear that we have an agreement." Kennedy said that Dirksen was "hopeful" they could get the votes on cloture.[86] Johnson immediately called the minority leader. "I saw your exhibit at the World's Fair," Johnson told him, "and it said, 'The Land of Lincoln,' so you're worthy of the 'Land of Lincoln.' And the man from Illinois is going to pass the bill, and I'll see that you get proper attention and credit."[87]

Predictably, the civil rights groups were upset about the weakening of the EEOC. Andrew Biemiller, according to Humphrey, shook his head and said, "This is awful," but most of the liberals had suspected that in the end the president and the leadership would agree to a compromise along these lines, and they knew they were walking away with a bill that enacted a historic transformation in race relations, with bipartisan support, by ending de jure segregation.[88] The very liberal Philip Hart, known as the conscience of the Senate, advised his Democratic colleagues to leave behind any concerns and support the bill.[89]

They would now have enough votes for cloture, but Johnson still wanted as much Republican support as he could get on civil rights as possible; he believed bipartisan support would be essential to help protect the legislation over the long term. Johnson had told Humphrey that there was the potential for a "real revolution in this country" once the bill went into effect, a reasonable fear given southerners' violent response to Martin Luther King's protests. The more emphatically Republicans expressed their support for the legislation at the start, the better the odds would be that the law could withstand the challenges Johnson expected it to face in its early years if southerners refused to abide by the law, responded with violence, or challenged it in court. "So we've got to make this an American bill and not just a Democratic bill," Johnson said.[90]

On May 26, Senator Dirksen introduced an omnibus amendment to the civil rights bill that included all the changes that had been agreed to with Humphrey and the administration. Despite the significant compromise on the EEOC, this was not a repeat of 1957, when civil rights supporters had seen their dreams go up in legislative smoke; the rest of the bill had survived the backroom negotiations remarkably intact. Dirksen had taken more of a bite out of the bill than many civil rights proponents were hoping for, but in exchange he had thrown his full support behind provisions that were far stronger than anything that had been done since Reconstruction; it was a bill that would have seemed impossible just one year earlier. The civil rights movement had spent an enormous amount of blood and energy fighting to desegregate the institutions of the South, and this legislation would put the weight of the federal government behind the final accomplishment of the task.

The final vote on cloture had to wait a few more days because the Republicans faced an added complication. Most in the GOP expected that their vote on civil rights, and that of the Democrats, would play a significant role in the November election. The bill was being debated in the middle of the presidential primary season. The front-runner for the Republican nomination was the Arizona senator Barry Goldwater, who represented the right wing of the party and was part of a campaign to purge the GOP of the centrists who had played a large role in the party, notably in their support of civil rights. Goldwater, who was well liked personally on both sides of the aisle, focused on his strident anticommunism and defense of free-market principles. He had made a name for himself by attacking organized labor and charging that Democrats were weak on defense. He also openly opposed the civil rights bill as a dangerous extension of government power, though he did not defend racial inequality; he argued that the role of the federal government had to be limited even in this matter. Senate Republicans agreed that they would not allow the vote on cloture to happen until after June 2, the day of the California Republican primary, for fear of embarrassing Goldwater.

So the vote was delayed. This only heightened the tension between what Republicans were doing in the Senate and what Goldwater was saying on the campaign trail. Nevertheless, Goldwater won the California primary, and some northern Democrats fretted that his victory would encourage conservative Republicans to break ranks with Dirksen out of fear that their constituents would punish them for supporting the liberals' bill.

A VOTE ON CLOTURE, FOLLOWED BY A VOTE ON CIVIL RIGHTS

Before the longest filibuster in Senate history—sixty days—was finally choked off, West Virginia's senator Robert Byrd delivered one final speech. With the end in sight, he started speaking at 7:38 p.m. on June 9 and finished the next morning at 9:51. The speech had lasted fourteen hours and thirteen minutes. More than 150 people, including former senators and House members, stood along the walls of the chamber to witness this crucial step toward racial equality and justice in America—the final defeat of the southern filibuster against civil rights. It was standing room only in the press gallery.[91]

Preceding the cloture vote, all eyes turned to the senator from Illinois, who wanted to make a speech. Despite having spent a relaxed morning on his Virginia farm, during which he ate a light breakfast and picked flowers from his garden to bring to his office, Dirksen was worn down from the sixteen-hour days he had spent working on the compromise bill. A Senate page handed the senator two pills before he started to talk. The speech he held in his frail hands was twelve pages long.[92]

There was near-total silence in the chamber as everyone leaned forward to hear what Dirksen said. The senator, known by many as the Wizard of Ooze, got right to the point. He held nothing back in defending the legislation that would now be a major part of his legacy. He called civil rights a "moral" issue that "must be resolved. It will not go away. Its time has come." To make his point clear, Dirksen quoted Victor Hugo's words: "Stronger than all the armies is an idea whose time has come."

At 11:00 a.m., after the bell rang to call senators to the chamber, the roll call began. "Mr. Aiken," called the clerk. "Aye," the Vermont Republican responded.[93] The senators, according to one reporter, "bent over their desks, like schoolboys doing their sums, recording the votes of their colleagues."[94] They scribbled down each man's vote beside his name, and vote by vote got closer to sixty-seven. The administration's plan seemed to have worked. Dirksen, and the pressure from religious organizations, had persuaded Hickenlooper to vote for cloture, though the Iowa senator still planned to vote against civil rights. The next to vote was the New Hampshire Republican Norris Cotton, who had insisted to Republican leaders that he would not vote for cloture unless the Senate adopted his amendment to limit the employment commission to dealing with companies of a hundred workers or more. The amendment had failed, but Dirksen had gotten to Cotton. The senator voted aye. As the roll call proceeded, Roger Mudd stood outside the Capitol and reported on the votes as they were relayed to him. A scoreboard tracked the cumulative totals. A little later, all eyes turned to the Nebraskan Carl Curtis, a stalwart Republican and ardent Goldwater supporter, who had said for months he would vote against cloture. When the clerk called his name, he voted aye. It was an acknowledgment of how much times had changed.

The most dramatic event in the roll call occurred when the clerk reached California's senator Clair Engle, a liberal who had recently been through two operations for a brain tumor and was unable to speak. Engle was a strong civil rights supporter who was often called Congressman Fireball for his boundless energy. On this historic day, the senator had come to the Capitol in an ambulance and was rolled into the chamber in a wheelchair. The sight of Engle, slouched in his wheelchair with his arm in a sling and a visible hairpiece covering the two surgical scars on his head, was a shock to his fellow senators.[95] The senator lifted his quivering hand and motioned toward his right eye to express his approval of the cloture motion.

Fifteen minutes after the vote began, Senator John Williams, who had focused most of his efforts in Congress on fighting corruption and cutting federal spending, offered the decisive sixty-seventh vote. One senator yelled out, "That's it!" Carl Hayden, who had remained in the cloakroom to await the moment when he might have to keep his promise to Johnson and vote for cloture, breathed a sigh of relief. When the voting was finished, Humphrey put his tally sheet in his mouth so he could wave both hands in the air in celebration. Mansfield's body seemed to sag with relief. Richard Russell kept his tearing eyes down on a yellow piece of paper, on which he seemed to be scribbling.[96] Most of the southerners were somber.

The vote for ending the civil rights filibuster was decisive, 71 in favor of cloture and 29 against. Twenty-seven Republicans had joined 44 Democrats in favor of ending the filibuster. Only 6 Republicans, including Goldwater (the others were Wallace Bennett of Utah, E. L. Mechem of New Mexico, Milward Simpson of Wyoming, John Tower of Texas, and Milton Young of North Dakota), had voted against cloture, along with 23 Democrats, mostly southerners, a few from border states, and a few westerners. Nine of Goldwater's most ardent Republican supporters voted for cloture.

Lyndon Johnson was on the stage at the College of the Holy Cross in Worcester, Massachusetts, about to give a commencement speech to twenty thousand students and their families, when an aide scrambled onto the platform and whispered to him. The president smiled broadly. "We are going ahead in our country to bring an end to poverty and racial injustice," Johnson said to the students a few minutes later, with a strong emphasis on the final two words of the sentence. "In the last 10 minutes we made progress. The Senate voted 71 to 29 for cloture." The crowd erupted into applause.[97]

On June 19, a year after Kennedy had introduced his civil rights proposal to Congress, the Senate was ready to vote on a bill. Before the vote, Dirksen made another dramatic speech, this one aimed not at history but at Barry Goldwater, whose nomination Dirksen believed would lead his beloved Republican Party down a path of extremism and reaction. The Illinois senator said that the federal government had adopted a number of laws over the century, including food safety regulation and prohibitions on child labor, that had once been called radical but were now viewed as reasonable enforcement of constitutional purposes. He reiterated his view of civil rights as a "moral force" that would "not be denied, it will not be stayed." Goldwater stared straight ahead as his colleague indirectly castigated him. Dirksen then read the names of twenty governors who had written to him in support of the bill; he emphasized the name of the Arizona governor.

At 7:49 p.m. on the eighty-third day after debate had begun, the Senate passed the civil rights bill in a nine-minute vote, 73 to 27, with 46 Democrats and 27 Republicans voting in favor. The southern senators stood firm in their opposition. After the vote was tallied, the African Americans and clergy sitting in the galleries couldn't help violating the rules of the Senate. They applauded. "We have fought the good fight," Senator Russell said, "until we were overwhelmed and gagged."[98]

On the evening of July 2, the beginning of the long Independence Day weekend, Johnson signed the Civil Rights Act of 1964 at 7:00 p.m. in the East Room of the White House. The law ended segregation in public accommodations, strengthened the federal government's power to investigate and report employment discrimination, prohibited the distribution of federal money to government programs that practiced segregation, and banned gender discrimination in employment.

After signing the bill, Johnson proclaimed, "We believe that all men are created equal. Yet many are denied equal treatment. We believe that all men have certain unalienable rights. Yet many Americans do not enjoy those rights. We believe that all men are entitled to the blessings of liberty. Yet millions are being deprived of those blessings—not because of their own failures, but because of the color of their skin . . . But it cannot continue. Our Constitution, the foundation of our Republic, forbids it . . . Morality forbids it. And the law I will sign tonight forbids it." Martin Luther King called the passage of the civil rights bill "the dawning of new hope."[99]

But beneath the euphoria, there were concerns in the White House. While passing civil rights instantly placed Johnson's presidency in the history books, the short-term political consequences of this successful outcome were not immediately clear. Johnson had always known going into this battle that the electoral costs to him and his party could be very great.

On the night the president signed the legislation, Bill Moyers walked into his boss's bedroom and found him looking forlorn. Surprised that Johnson would be sad after such a historic victory, Moyers asked him what was wrong. "I think we have just delivered the South to the Republican Party for a long time to come," Johnson said. While the president could also imagine the benefits that would accrue to him and to his party from greater support among African Americans and liberals, the loss of the South—the longtime electoral base of the Democratic Party—to Republicans would have disastrous consequences.

The future of the rest of Johnson's agenda remained in doubt. While the victory over the Senate filibuster meant the end of the legislative veto the conservative coalition had held over domestic policy since FDR's second term, the progress was limited to one very specific area; there was no pressure available in other areas comparable to what the civil rights movement had exerted on Congress.

The next question would be whether Johnson could use the momentum from the civil rights victory to break the back of the conservative coalition on other issues—health care, education, poverty—where the numbers on the floor still didn't add up. Without the social pressure from outside the political system, it seemed unlikely. This was why the upcoming election would be so important; Johnson hoped that Democrats could claim a majority that would allow him to move major legislation in the absence of a social movement as strong as the one that had made civil rights possible.

CHAPTER FIVE

HOW BARRY GOLDWATER
BUILT THE GREAT SOCIETY

President Johnson hoped that his victory over congressional resistance to civil rights had positioned him for more legislative successes. While he was signing the Civil Rights Act, his staff, at his behest, was frenetically developing new proposals for the "Creative Period" he envisioned, during which the federal government would solve many of the biggest problems that faced the nation.[1] He had assembled thirteen task forces, staffed by some of the most brilliant experts from government, universities, and think tanks, to develop proposals he would introduce to Congress after the election. They focused on a broad range of issues—education, health care, the preservation of the country's natural beauty, income maintenance, among others.

Johnson knew that his success of the moment didn't guarantee more victories. His power was not unchallenged, and he wouldn't have the fervor of the civil rights movement to create the same level of pressure for every ambitious piece of liberal legislation he wanted to pass through Congress. He would need a decisive electoral mandate in the upcoming November election to establish liberal

Democratic dominance over Republicans and southern Democrats in Congress.

A DEFINING WAR ON POVERTY

The first big effect of the election came well before November 3, as Johnson looked forward to creating an issue that would distinguish him from his Republican opponent, who was expected to be Senator Barry Goldwater, and show liberals that he was truly devoted to New Deal principles. He was also looking backward. As an accidental president, Johnson wanted to distinguish himself from his predecessor and legitimate himself and his presidency. Because he believed the true measure of a president was his legislative record, looking ahead to November, he wanted to embellish his record for the day when voters would evaluate him as the nation's leader. Shortly after taking over the presidency, he had told two of his friends, "I have a very difficult problem. I feel a moral obligation to finish the things that JFK proposed. But I also have to find issues I can take on as my own . . . I have to get reelected in a year and a half, so I have to have something of my own."[2]

The something of his own was the War on Poverty.

The idea had grown out of policy research and discussions conducted by the economist Walter Heller for John Kennedy. Heller and other liberals were frustrated with the inadequacy of existing programs to help Americans who were living in poverty. The federal government had been providing assistance to the poor throughout much of the twentieth century, as Washington took a stronger role over state and local governments and charitable institutions.[3] But it had become clear in the 1950s that Aid to Dependent Children, which had been created in 1935, and other federal programs for the poor were not working. With almost forty million Americans living in poverty in the best economic times, there seemed to be an urgent need for more robust government action. The same liberal legislators who were pushing for civil rights and health care—the Illinois senator Paul Douglas and others—had been calling for legislation to address the problem. Campaigning in the 1960 West Virginia primary, Kennedy had been struck by the severity of the economic hardship he encountered. In 1962, Michael Harrington published *The Other America*, in which he analyzed the two nations he said coexisted in the United States, the affluent America and the "other America."

No one was satisfied with how the problem of poverty was being addressed. For liberals, the issue was that existing benefits were inadequate, primarily because federal bureaucrats didn't know what services the poor really needed. For conservatives, it was that the poor were becoming dependent on welfare programs. In 1962, Kennedy had proposed and Congress had passed the Public Welfare Amendments, which funded "rehabilitative services" to help the unemployed enter the job market and provided more money for training social workers. For liberals, it was a good start; for conservatives, it was more of the same problem.

Heller had briefed Johnson about the poverty issue and the programs Heller and his interagency working group had come up with to deal with it. Johnson liked what he heard. Heller told him that his team had rejected expensive plans to create public jobs and instead settled on a more modest proposal that would allocate federal money to local governments and citizen-run organizations so they could design plans they believed would best help their impoverished communities. Heller's group had also discussed a work-training program for young men.

Heller's approach to a war on poverty made sense to Johnson. The programs would tackle a social problem that had concerned him since he was a young man in Texas. "That's my kind of program," Johnson told Heller. "I'll find money for it one way or another."[4]

Johnson sent a proposal for the Economic Opportunity Act (EOA) to the House of Representatives in April, while southerners were still filibustering civil rights. The proposed legislation comprised assistance for those living below the poverty level and for those who were not self-sufficient. Rather than placing the poverty program under the control of the Department of Health, Education, and Welfare or another existing government agency, Johnson proposed creating the Office of Economic Opportunity (OEO) to administer and coordinate the various pieces of the policy. The idea was that establishing an independent agency would allow the director of the program to be more aggressive when launching new initiatives, because he would not be working for a cabinet official who was responsible for handling many other programs as well, and would centralize decision making under one administrative body so that the programs could be coordinated. Johnson selected John Kennedy's brother-in-law Sargent Shriver, the energetic and charismatic director of the Peace Corps, to head the OEO. Although Shriver initially resisted on the grounds that he preferred to stay with the Peace Corps, he succumbed to Johnson's intense personal pressure.

The central program in the War on Poverty would be the Community Action Program (CAP), which was based on experimental grants similar to those President Kennedy had authorized to combat juvenile delinquency. The CAP would rely on local Community Action Agencies (CAAs) that would be established by local communities and staffed by local officials and local activists to direct the allocation of federal antipoverty funds. The OEO would provide financial and technical support to the CAAs that put forth the best comprehensive plans to coordinate the funds from federal, state, and local agencies to target poverty. The CAAs would also use funds from the OEO to promote local government reforms to improve the responsiveness of the government to the poor.

The idea of community action was rooted in the cutting-edge

social science of the period—the principle of "maximum feasible participation"—that poor people should be empowered to participate in designing the programs that would assist their communities rather than having anonymous bureaucrats do this for them. Funds would be spent most effectively if individuals who had firsthand knowledge of the problems in specific communities had a role in deciding how the money would be used. The principle was a response to a concern on the part of younger liberals that federal bureaucracies had not appropriately served the interests of the poor.[5]

The proposed legislation also included the Jobs Corps—a work-training program primarily for people between sixteen and twenty-one years of age from dysfunctional living environments to spend time in camps, where they would receive education and vocational training. The program would also provide loans to poor rural families and small businesses. There would also be a domestic Peace Corps—Volunteers in Service to America, or VISTA—that would train young people and send them around the country to work on projects to improve living conditions in poor communities.

The election was an impetus for Johnson to move as quickly as possible on the Economic Opportunity Act. He made it clear to every member of Congress that he considered this to be *his* bill and that its success, or failure, would be seen as a measure of his skill as president. "This is a party measure. This is party responsibility. If I lose this," Johnson told George Mahon of Texas, chairman of the House Appropriations Committee, "it's telegraphed around the world that, by gosh, the Republicans roll me and roll me good on the key measure, the only single Johnson measure that was sent up. Everything else was Kennedy."[6]

Johnson's political and electoral motivations meshed with his sincere policy beliefs. Fighting against poverty had been central to what the Democratic Party had been doing since the 1930s. He believed the War on Poverty would help the communities of poor Americans whom he had been surrounded by as a youth. This really was his kind of program.

A Democrat who launched a war against poverty would offer a stark contrast, in Johnson's mind, to the man the Republicans selected as their nominee at their convention in the middle of July. When, during his acceptance speech at the convention on July 16, Goldwater issued his steely declaration "Extremism in the defense of liberty is no vice . . . Moderation in the pursuit of justice is no virtue," one reporter quipped, "My God, he's going to run as Barry Goldwater."[7] The party was being driven to the right, pedal to the metal, by its resolute nominee, aided by a burgeoning network of conservative activists inspired by anticommunism, hatred for liberal Supreme Court rulings, and opposition to an expanded role of the federal government in domestic policy. Goldwater's supporters had been working assiduously since 1960 to win the backing of grassroots organizations and party operatives by persuading them to take a chance on Goldwater rather than choose a centrist Republican who simply mimicked the Democrats and would have little chance of defeating the incumbent.[8] Governor Nelson Rockefeller of New York, Governor William Scranton of Pennsylvania, and Ambassador to South Vietnam Henry Cabot Lodge, the voices of moderation in the party, had helped Goldwater win by viciously attacking one another in the primaries. Goldwater's highly controversial vote against the Civil Rights Act in July had positioned him in clear opposition to the expanding role of government under Johnson.

Johnson wanted to depict himself as a president who cared about average Americans and would use the federal government to help them. His civil rights achievement and his programs to end poverty demonstrated that he was a "President of all the people," as he described himself throughout the spring and summer. As one reporter for the *Washington Post* noted, Johnson's antipoverty proposal would allow him to "project to the voters an 'image' of his party as the friend of the little man and the underprivileged—the party with *more heart, with the most concern* for human values. It is an image that the Democrats as a party have put forward successfully for the most part, especially since the great depression of the 1930s."[9] Declaring war on poverty was also a declaration of war on Goldwater and his conservatism.

From the moment he announced the plan to the House and the Senate, Republicans came down hard on the proposal, and their attacks became stronger after their party convention. Republicans claimed that the legislation would have no salutary social effects. Despite the small budget Johnson had attached to the plan, they said it would result in an excessive and costly expansion of government power. They characterized the proposal as a political ploy designed to provide the White House with money for vote buying before the election. Goldwater labeled the program a "Madison Avenue" scheme with the "single objective of securing votes."[10] The New Jersey representative Peter Frelinghuysen, a moderate Republican, charged that Sargent Shriver would become a "poverty czar" and that the money would "stir up a nightmare of trouble" when Shriver dispensed it to militant activist organizations in New York.[11] The former president Dwight Eisenhower dismissed "catchily labeled panaceas—like 'war on poverty'—which usually turn out to be new channels by which even more power is siphoned into the federal government."[12] Minority Leader Charles Halleck poured an enormous amount of his energy into blocking the legislation. In his individual meetings with Republicans, Halleck insisted that members commit not to vote for it and warned that he would no longer consider anyone who supported the bill to be part of the Republican Party. The implicit threat was to withhold campaign money and other kinds of assistance.[13]

Johnson believed the antipoverty program had a chance of passing before the election despite Republican opposition because it was essentially a revival of New Deal jobs programs—the National Youth

Administration, which Johnson had run in Texas, and the Civilian Conservation Corps—and because local party officials would have a major role in deciding how to distribute it. What could be better going into an election? As Johnson had told Chicago's mayor, Richard Daley, the embodiment of the machine mentality, "Get your planning and development people busy right now to see what you can do for the crummiest place in town, the lowest, the bottom thing, and see what we can do about it. We'll get our dough, and then you can have your plan ready, and we'll move."[14] The part of the program that would end up becoming the most controversial—the inclusion of nongovernmental organizations in the decision-making process of the CAAs—had not yet surfaced as a concern for most officials who would be voting on the bill.

Because the legislation would be cheap to implement—only $500 million for the new War on Poverty programs and about $400 million in additional funds for existing programs that dealt with poverty—Johnson would not have to go back to Harry Byrd or any of the other congressional budget guardians.[15] Johnson's budgetary request was in fact far below what most experts believed would be necessary to make a serious dent in chronic poverty.

The War on Poverty was also sold as a fundamentally conservative program.[16] When Johnson phoned undecided legislators to win their votes, he stressed that his collection of programs would help the poor become self-sufficient and alleviate the conditions that had recently led to urban riots. Of the people who lived in the Harlem neighborhood of New York City, where there had been a riot shortly after the Republican National Convention, Johnson said, "They've got no jobs, they can't do anything, they're just raising hell."[17]

Johnson's major theme was that the program would not provide government handouts. He told Congressman Mahon that the initiative would teach the poor "some discipline" and give them skills so they could drive a truck for a living instead of sitting "around a poolroom."[18]

At the time of the legislative debate, the Job Corps caused more controversy than any other program in the EOA, because southerners assumed that in the wake of the passage of the Civil Rights Act the camps would be integrated, though not all southern Democrats opposed the program on these grounds. The opposition of most southerners to federal programs had largely been based on fears of racial integration, which was now going to happen anyway. While some southerners grumbled about any distribution of funds to African Americans, they were happy to see federal money go to the poor whites who were their constituent base. The highest rates of dependency on Aid to Families with Dependent Children were in the South (2.2 percent of the population in the South; in the West and the North it was 1.5 percent, and it was 1.7 percent on the Pacific coast),[19] and most of the program's recipients would be white.[20] Most poor Americans in 1964 lived in rural areas and small towns.[21] African Americans in the South would get a little money, but whites would get by far the most.

The bill moved swiftly through the Senate, which finished its work on the bill before the House did. A few weeks after the long filibuster against civil rights ended, the Michigan senator Pat McNamara introduced the bill. The Labor and Public Welfare Committee, on which McNamara was the senior ranking Democrat, conducted hearings on the legislation and sent it to the floor by a vote of thirteen for the bill with only the Republicans Barry Goldwater and John Tower against it. "We oppose this poorly constructed and misbegotten legislation," announced the man who was now the official Republican nominee to the national media.[22]

During the floor debate, some southern senators, Richard Russell for one, ritualistically grumbled that the legislation would trample on states' rights. Sargent Shriver approached Georgia's senator Herman Talmadge, a segregationist who had been a strong supporter of programs for the rural poor, and asked him for advice on how to deal with southern concerns. He told Talmadge, "This is the problem, Senator. We can't allow all this money to become bogged down in the state and local government apparatus, and we cannot allow a system to be established whereby the purposes of the legislation can be frustrated totally by the clique that might be hanging around a particular governor." Talmadge listened closely. The senator would not be able to vote for this legislation, because, in his mind, it was too closely connected to civil rights and could cause him problems in his state. But he was sympathetic to the basic objectives of the program and would be open to Georgia's receiving the funds if they became available. He decided to give Shriver advice about how to win the vote. After puffing on his cigar and tapping the ashes into his spittoon, he proposed that the legislation allow governors to veto War on Poverty programs they didn't like. The plan was safe, he explained to Shriver: "They're not going to disapprove of many of them, because the governors all want to have the money come into their states . . . the governor politically doesn't want to be in the position of being the person who is preventing a certain program from taking place in his state." Shriver was impressed and persuaded. Here was a way to please Richard Russell with an amendment that would never be used. It gave each state governor the authority to veto any project that the OEO proposed for his state.[23] The amendment was attached to the bill, and the Senate passed the legislation on July 23, just a week after the Republicans ended their convention, by a vote of 61 to 34, with 11 southern Democrats in favor and 11 against.

In the House, the legislation was first considered in the liberal Education and Labor Committee. Its chairman was Adam Clayton Powell Jr., who also served as minister of Harlem's Abyssinian Baptist

Church and had been a controversial figure from the moment he first entered the House in 1945 and angered colleagues by sitting in the "wrong" sections of the segregated House dining room and barbershop. He had repeatedly antagonized southerners in the late 1940s and throughout the 1950s by proposing amendments to appropriations bills that would have prohibited federal funds from going to racially segregated institutions. One such amendment had become Title VI of the Civil Rights Act of 1964.

As chairman, since 1961, Powell had been very effective in moving liberal bills through the committee. He displayed sound parliamentary acumen and an ideological boldness that frustrated southerners who still didn't believe African Americans should be allowed to drink from the same water fountains they used, let alone run important congressional committees. His flamboyant personality and the color of his skin had caused him trouble in public life. His 1960 trial for tax evasion had ended in a hung jury. Three years later, his refusal to pay a $211,500 slander judgment fine for accusing a Harlem woman of being a "bag woman" for corrupt police in New York City meant he risked arrest anytime he set foot in his own district. Later, a congressional investigation for using government funds to pay for personal travel and expenditures resulted in sanctions against him and the loss of his chairmanship.

Powell used the same strong-arm tactics to move the Economic Opportunity Act swiftly through his committee as southerners had used against civil rights. He prevented Republicans from offering amendments to the bill. He blocked their participation in markups. He did not allow objections. He scheduled meetings at odd hours and on Mondays, Fridays, and weekends, when legislators traditionally wanted to be back in their districts mingling with constituents, an important activity in the summer of an election year, when members desperately wanted as much interaction with voters as possible. When

Republicans did manage to get to committee meetings, Powell gave each minority member just five minutes to cross-examine witnesses.[24]

On May 26, Powell's committee sent the bill, by a party-line vote of 19 to 11, to the more conservative Rules Committee, where Howard Smith would sit on it until after the Senate passed the bill. Then the 1961 reform that had expanded the Rules Committee from twelve to fifteen members finally paid off, along with the prudent inclination of moderate Democrats not to vote against the president's signature bill in an election year. The committee passed the bill on July 28 by a vote of 8 to 7, with all the Republicans and two southern Democrats, Smith and Colmer, voting with the opposition, but even with the bill out of the Rules Committee the White House was still worried. Larry O'Brien's vote counts indicated that the administration had somewhere between 200 and 210 House votes for the bill, at least 8 votes fewer than the 218 it needed. Republicans were steadfast in their opposition. Halleck believed the program to be wasteful, and he had no intention of handing Johnson another legislative victory to run on in 1964.

The key to the vote on the floor would be to make sure that enough southern Democrats could put aside their concerns about civil rights and vote for the bill. To this end, the president had asked for help from the conservative Georgia congressman Phil Landrum, a segregationist who, in the 1950s, had earned the enmity of organized labor for championing legislation to weaken unions but who, like many southerners, supported public works projects and area redevelopment programs that helped the white constituents in his impoverished Appalachian Mountains district. Larry O'Brien believed that Landrum would do a "whale of a job" in winning support for the bill from fellow southern Democrats,[25] and Landrum enthusiastically accepted the job. "I want it clearly understood here," he told his colleagues, "that it is a source of pride to me to have my name on this bill."[26] Landrum was a southern legislator who had accepted the fact that southern life would change with the end of Jim Crow, and now he believed that there should be poverty programs to help everyone in need, black or white. He worked furiously behind the scenes to win his colleagues' votes for the bill. He reiterated to them that even if certain parts of the program, the Job Corps, for example, would be integrated, there wasn't much they could do about it, given that the Civil Rights Act had made integration the law of the land, so they might as well accept the federal money. Most legislators understood this without Landrum's detailing the logic for them, but southern and moderate Democrats felt more politically secure with a solid southern conservative like Landrum publicly in favor of the legislation. If Phil Landrum could say yes to Lyndon Johnson, so could they.

Feeling the pressure to get the bill passed before legislators left Washington for the Democratic National Convention in August, Johnson cut a series of additional deals to fortify southern Democratic support before the final vote on the floor. To get Russell Tuten's support, he agreed to have the chief of the Corps of Engineers approve a project in the congressman's Georgia district (Tuten voted yes). He told Alabama's Robert Jones that he would talk to the editor of a local newspaper that had endorsed Goldwater and persuade him to endorse Jones in the election (Jones voted yes).[27] The Texas Democrat Olin Teague told Johnson he couldn't vote for the bill because if he did, conservatives in his district would attack him as too liberal, but he promised he would work privately to expand support among other southern members. The president assured him that the program would bring a lot of money into his district, which included Texas A&M University: "By god they'll be calling it Olin Teague College."[28] With Johnson's approval, Larry O'Brien even tried to break Republican unanimity by calling on union leaders to pressure liberal Republicans in Pennsylvania. O'Brien also asked railroad owners in the state, who had just received federal assistance as a result of mass transportation legislation, to lobby liberal

Republicans (six Pennsylvania Republicans ended up voting in favor of the bill).[29]

A problem arose when members of the North Carolina delegation, headed by Congressman Harold Cooley, informed the administration they would not support the bill unless they were guaranteed that Adam Yarmolinsky would not have a role in running the program.[30]

"Who the hell is Adam Yarmolinsky?" Johnson asked.

Yarmolinsky was Sargent Shriver's top aide, an organized and efficient administrator whom Shriver relied upon in developing the poverty program; Shriver intended to appoint him as his deputy.

Yarmolinsky's parents were leftists who had been active in numerous political causes. He had worked at the Defense Department, where he was one of Robert McNamara's "whiz kids." When McNamara said that he wanted to hire Yarmolinsky at Defense, Sargent Shriver suggested the secretary should take a look at his FBI file first. When McNamara received the file from J. Edgar Hoover, he was alarmed to learn that it was "as thick as a Manhattan phonebook." But that wasn't the main reason Harold Cooley wanted young Yarmolinsky excluded from working on the poverty program. The main reason was that when he was working at Defense, Yarmolinsky had worked to desegregate southern military bases, including one in North Carolina.[31]

Without the votes of the North Carolina delegation, the bill would be in trouble, especially if other southerners followed their lead.[32] In an effort to hold North Carolina, House Speaker McCormack convened a meeting in his office with Shriver, Cooley, and South Carolina congressman Mendel Rivers. A number of Democratic whips joined them to hear the discussion. Cooley repeated his demand. Either the administration promised that Yarmolinsky would not work in the program, or the entire North Carolina Democratic delegation would vote no. In a prearranged move, Congressman Rivers announced that he and his fellow South Carolina Democrats would also vote against the bill. It was clear to McCormack that the bleeding could get worse.

Shriver told the congressmen that he did not have the authority to determine who would be appointed to the agency, but he also defended Yarmolinsky as an outstanding public servant. He emphasized that top-level staffing was entirely in the president's hands. Cooley claimed that Shriver had previously said that he *did* have control over who would be appointed. Shriver and Cooley went back and forth; the discussion grew increasingly heated. The Democrats in the room sat uncomfortably, staring down at the floor. When Louisiana's Hale Boggs vouched for Yarmolinsky, Cooley demanded to hear from the president about his intentions. Desperate to establish some calm, well aware of how furious the president would be if he saw this measure go down to defeat, Speaker McCormack walked with Shriver into a small adjoining room and called Johnson on the phone.

In response to Johnson's first question, Shriver described Yarmolinsky's work under McNamara and the conversation that had just taken place. Johnson thought for a minute, then told Shriver to let the Carolinians know that Yarmolinsky would not be appointed. "We've just thrown you to the wolves," Shriver later told his friend, "and this is the worst day of my life."[33]

The Economic Opportunity Act passed in the House on August 8 by a vote of 226 to 184. Though only 22 Republicans voted for the bill, Larry O'Brien's vote counts proved to have been too conservative; the final measure got much stronger support than the president had expected from southern Democrats, with 60 of them voting yes. At the end of August, Johnson signed the bill into law. The passage of the Economic Opportunity Act was a campaign promise fulfilled in advance; it was Lyndon Johnson's proof that he could deliver legislation to benefit everyone.

SHIFTING RIGHT INTO VIETNAM

If the Economic Opportunity Act gave Johnson a bill to help define his presidency to American voters, his decisions about Vietnam in early August were intended to insulate him from Republican attacks that he was weak on defense. It was no surprise to anyone that Senator Goldwater was emphasizing national security issues in his campaign. Johnson was not tough enough on communism, Goldwater said, repeating a mantra Republicans had used since early in the cold war, when they charged that President Truman had "lost" China to "the Reds." Johnson, who had seen Democrats lose control of the White House and Congress in 1952, when Republicans used the stalemate in Korea against them, accepted as a truism that he would have to protect his foreign policy flank in the upcoming election battle, so he began to take a more hawkish line in Vietnam.

Southeast Asia, and Vietnam in particular, had preoccupied U.S. policy makers since 1954, when the French pulled out of their Indochinese colony and left it divided into a communist North and an anticommunist South. President Eisenhower decided to send limited assistance to the South. "You have a row of dominoes set up and you knock over the first one," he said, "and what will happen to the last one is the certainty that it will go over very quickly . . . The loss of Indochina will cause the fall of Southeast Asia like a set of dominoes." Though Kennedy expanded the U.S. commitment by sending thirteen thousand military advisers to help train the South Vietnamese forces, he was reluctant to commit ground troops. He knew that the South Vietnamese government, run by Ngo Dinh Diem, was corrupt and unreliable. In the summer of 1963, Diem's crackdown on Buddhists who were protesting persecution by his government led to widespread unrest and the belief that he wasn't strong enough to withstand the opposition in his own part of the country. On November 2, he was killed in a CIA-backed coup.

Throughout the early months of 1964, Democrats in Washington agonized over what to do about Vietnam. Many senior legislators, including conservative Democrats who were generally extremely hawkish on fighting communism everywhere else, counseled President Johnson against expanding America's role in Southeast Asia. Senator Russell, one of the biggest hawks of the Democratic Party, who had been a strong supporter of the cold war buildup since the late 1940s and tended to call for the United States to take tough stands against the Soviet Union, as he had done during the Cuban missile crisis in 1962, bluntly told the president that Vietnam was not essential to U.S. national interests, the conflict would bog down American troops in a deadly quagmire, and there was a real danger the Chinese would enter the war.

Johnson understood these arguments, but his advisers, later referred to by the journalist David Halberstam ironically as "the best and the brightest," were pressuring him to increase America's presence in the region to prevent North Vietnam's leader, Ho Chi Minh, from unifying the country under communist rule. They argued that if South Vietnam fell to communism, other countries in Southeast Asia would soon fall too, like Eisenhower's dominoes. Johnson believed them.

He also believed that any Democratic president, in order to be effective in his legislative efforts, would need to embrace a national security policy that was firmly opposed to communism. He told Russell that in certain states, including Georgia, voters would "forgive you for everything except being weak."[34]

During July, Goldwater had warned that the new leader of the Soviet Union, Leonid Brezhnev, was more dangerous and aggressive than his predecessors had been, and he accused Johnson of refusing to stand firm against communism throughout the world. He predicted that Johnson was preparing to fight a halfhearted ground war against the communists in Vietnam and that he would be too timid to use America's arsenal of bombs and airpower. Goldwater had caused quite a stir back in May, before he was the official nominee, when he said he would be willing to consider the "defoliation of the forests by low-yield atomic weapons" to gut the supply routes being used by the communists in Vietnam. At the Republican convention, Goldwater had promised to institute a "win policy": military commanders would have the authority to do what was necessary, and President Goldwater would not stand in their way.

In July, Johnson, goaded by Goldwater, ordered the navy to intensify its operations off the coast of North Vietnam. The administration intended the presence of U.S. destroyers as a show of force to the North Vietnamese and to Republicans at home who were calling him weak. On August 2, Washington received reports of an attack on navy ships in the Gulf of Tonkin. The evidence that this was a concerted effort by the North Vietnamese to hit U.S. forces was sketchy at best. Johnson decided to downplay the incident. He made it clear to his advisers that there would be no response, and when the North Vietnamese remained silent about the incident, he concluded that there was no need for any U.S. action.[35]

Johnson understood the political stakes of the situation and decided to wait. Goldwater, who was vacationing in Newport Beach, California, was asking in the media if the presence of U.S. destroyers in the Gulf of Tonkin meant that the president was planning on using ground forces in the battle and if there was a change in foreign policy ahead.[36] On August 3, Johnson told Secretary McNamara they needed to be "firm as hell" without making any dangerous statements that could escalate America's involvement into a full-scale war. Johnson said that he had spoken to a banker in New York and a friend in Texas, both of whom praised how the navy had handled the situation until now, but both of whom wanted to "be damned sure I don't pull 'em out and run, and they want to be damned sure that we're firm. That's what all the country wants because Goldwater's raising so much hell about how he's gonna blow 'em off the moon, and they say that we oughtn't to do anything that the national interest doesn't require. But we sure oughta always leave the impression that if you shoot at us, you're going to get hit."[37]

In the morning of August 4, there were reports of a second attack in the Gulf of Tonkin. Once again, little intelligence was available, and some of what was available suggested that the attack, if it took place, had been provoked by actions taken by the U.S. destroyers. Johnson told one aide, "Hell, those dumb, stupid sailors were just shooting at flying fish"—and the White House concluded the attack had been a mistake or a decision by a low-level commander.[38] A leak from the administration to the press created a public impression that there had been an unprovoked attack and that policy makers saw this as a key moment for the United States to prove how serious it was in the fight against communism in Southeast Asia.[39] When Johnson met with legislative leaders to tell them what had happened, the Republicans in the room supported passage of a congressional resolution authorizing the use of force. At a subsequent meeting, Johnson and Kennedy's top adviser, Kenneth O'Donnell, agreed that any failure to forcefully respond would provide conservative Republicans with a huge opening to attack the administration for being weak on defense.[40] Johnson agreed with O'Donnell that he was being "tested" and that he needed to have a tough response for the North Vietnamese and for the Republicans. After reviewing the intelligence one more time, Secretary McNamara and the Joint Chiefs of Staff concluded that an attack had taken place. It would later be revealed that the intelligence was based on inaccurate information provided by officials at the National Security Agency.[41]

Regardless of the doubts prevalent among high-level officials,

Johnson embraced the argument that there had been an unprovoked attack. He asked Congress to pass a resolution that granted him the authority to expand military operations in the region if necessary. Johnson asked Goldwater to support him, and Goldwater immediately agreed that the war should not be an issue in the campaign. After meeting with Johnson at the White House, he made a public statement in which he expressed his support for Johnson's overall strategy.

Many congressional Democrats were uncomfortable granting so much power to the president to expand American involvement in a war. Johnson asked Arkansas's senator William Fulbright, chairman of the Senate Foreign Relations Committee, to lobby Democrats and give them the president's assurance that if he decided to send troops to Vietnam beyond responding specifically to the alleged incidents in the Gulf of Tonkin, he would return to Congress to request the power to do that. Congress had passed a number of similar resolutions in recent years—on Formosa, the Middle East, Berlin, and Cuba— none of which had resulted in war, so few in the House and the Senate saw the resolution as leading inevitably to wider war. "I took Fulbright's word at face value," Senator Mansfield recalled.[42] It was just as important to everyone involved that a demonstration of force was essential to blunting Republican attacks on Johnson's national security policies. Liberal and moderate first-term senators elected in 1958 were worried about winning reelection, and many agreed to vote in favor of the resolution; no Democrat wanted to defend softness on communism in a tough political campaign against any Republican hawk.[43]

The Senate passed the Gulf of Tonkin Resolution on August 7 with only two dissenting votes: Oregon's Wayne Morse and the Alaska Democrat Ernest Gruening. The House took less than forty minutes to pass the measure unanimously. The resolution authorized the president to take "all necessary measures to repel any armed attacks against the forces of the United States and to prevent further aggression." The resolution was extraordinarily vague and broad—Johnson later said it was "like grandma's night shirt, it covered everything"— even though he, and Fulbright, had promised Democrats that the resolution would apply only to the current circumstances in the Gulf of Tonkin.

The Gulf of Tonkin Resolution, just weeks before the Democratic National Convention, sent a message to the North Vietnamese—and to American voters—that the United States would take a tough stand against communist aggression. The resolution was as much a battle in the war against Republicans as it was against communism. Though the implications of the alleged attacks on U.S. destroyers were far from clear, Johnson believed he had to send a strong signal to the electorate that he would take a tough stand against communism.

Johnson's first strike in the campaign against Barry Goldwater was the passage of the War on Poverty; it embodied his distinct presidential vision; it was his own thing. The Gulf of Tonkin Resolution was a second strike in the campaign; Johnson believed his best defense against Goldwater was a good offensive stand against the North Vietnamese. He was pleased when his poll numbers rose immediately in response to the resolution. Its dire consequences to the United States, to the Vietnamese, and to Johnson's presidency would not become evident until several years after he won the election.

A CAMPAIGN ABOUT LIBERALISM
VERSUS CONSERVATISM

Johnson and Goldwater both campaigned to create the perception that the election was a choice between right-wing conservatism and Great Society liberalism. While each candidate targeted the character of the other—Goldwater questioned Johnson's ethics, and Johnson portrayed Goldwater as psychologically unstable—policy issues were front and center in both campaigns.

When the Republicans had nominated Goldwater in San Francisco in July, the proceedings had conveyed the clear message that the party was making a choice to stand behind conservative principles rather than lining up behind another centrist Republican who might have broader electoral appeal. Choosing Goldwater meant taking a stand against the expansion of the federal government that had been occurring since the 1930s.

The Democrats met in Atlantic City, once the jewel of Atlantic coast beach resorts, now becoming a seedy, crime-ridden eyesore. They offered a ringing endorsement of liberalism, but liberalism didn't have it easy at the convention.

The Mississippi Freedom Democratic Party (MFDP) was a group of African American Democrats who had been selected by African Americans in the state to represent their interests at the convention. They arrived in Atlantic City to protest the abuse of voting rights in the South and demanded to be seated in place of the official state delegation, which they reminded Democrats came from a state whose politicians were elected almost exclusively by white voters—only around 5 percent of the African Americans in the state were registered to vote—and which was led by a well-known and outspoken racist. The MFDP challenge to the party threatened to raise questions about Johnson's commitment to liberal goals, to diminish the electoral benefits of the civil rights and poverty legislation Congress had just passed, and to trigger an internal party battle that would give Goldwater a shot at winning more southern states. Governor John Connally of Texas told the president, "If you seat those black jigaboos, the whole South will walk out." Johnson pleaded with civil rights leaders to think about the long term. He promised them that if they acceded to the seating of the official delegation and he was elected, he would deliver more historic legislation to secure full civil rights for all African Americans.

During credentials committee hearings to decide the fate of the MFDP, television news broadcast dramatic testimony about the violence and abuse the delegates had confronted in their struggle for voting rights. The activist Fannie Lou Hamer provided riveting testimony about the violence she had endured throughout her career as an activist. Toward the end, she asked, "Is this America, the land of the free and the home of the brave, where we have to sleep with our telephones off the hooks because our lives be threatened daily, because we want to live as human beings, in America?" President Johnson, fearful of how Americans would be swayed by this moving speech, convened an impromptu press conference so that the television stations would turn their attention to him rather than cover the end of her appearance.

Initially, liberals on the committee sought a compromise whereby the MFDP would obtain half of the seats, but Johnson feared that this arrangement would provoke a civil war among Democrats at the convention; southern Democrats had formed a third party in 1948 over civil rights, and they could do it again. Instead, the president sent Hubert Humphrey to Atlantic City to broker an alternative compromise by which the members of the regular delegation would be seated after they took an oath to support the ticket and agreed that future delegations would not be selected by racially discriminatory procedures. While Humphrey was negotiating, Johnson and the FBI kept tabs on the civil rights activists through a wiretap. In the end, the MFDP received two at-large seats—and votes—at the convention, but the white official delegates would still cast all the votes for Mississippi. The liberals on the credentials committee had agreed to the compromise under pressure from the White House. Most civil rights activists were furious at what they saw as a betrayal. "We didn't come all this way for no two seats," Hamer said.[44]

The convention began, and Democrats focused once again on selling Johnson and his legislative achievements. Rhode Island's senator John Pastore delivered a blistering keynote speech on the opening night of the convention. With the delegates on their feet, cheering and clapping, the senator, a brilliant orator, lashed out against the GOP. In characteristic fashion, he waved his arms and jabbed his fingers in the air as if berating Goldwater himself. He extolled Johnson's "nine miracle months" of productivity, during which civil rights, the tax cut, and the Economic Opportunity Act were passed. Pastore told the delegates that LBJ had accomplished more than any other president had ever done in such a short time. While Kennedy had dreamed of civil rights, Pastore said, "it was brought to fulfillment by President Johnson." He castigated Goldwater and the rest of the Republican Party for seeking to weaken the Social Security program, repeal the minimum wage law, and dismantle other crucial strands of the social safety net. The Republican National Convention, Pastore thundered, had been captured by "reactionaries and extremists . . . lock, stock and barrel."[45] Throughout the hot New Jersey days and into the nights, convention speakers blasted the extreme policies of the GOP and contrasted them with their party's remarkable legislative output under Lyndon Johnson.

Hubert Humphrey, selected by Johnson as his running mate, gave a barn burner of a speech on the closing night of the convention that centered on domestic policy. "Most Democrats and most Republicans in the United States Senate voted last year for an expanded medical education program," Humphrey said. "But not Senator Goldwater. Most Democrats and most Republicans in the United States Senate voted for education legislation. But not Senator Goldwater." The delegates chanted the refrain "But not Senator Goldwater" every time Humphrey repeated the phrase. Humphrey emphasized the theme of the convention and the Johnson campaign: the Republicans had become the party of "stridency, of unrestrained passion, of extreme and radical language." He appealed not only to Democrats but to moderate Republicans.

Though Johnson did not deliver a very thrilling acceptance speech on his fifty-sixth birthday, he did offer an unabashed defense of his domestic record. He promised that the Democratic Party would "continue to extend the hand of compassion and the hand of affection and love to the old and the sick and the hungry." Building on Humphrey's popular refrain, Johnson worked his way through a list of issues that mattered to the country, essentially asking for a mandate from voters: "Most Americans want medical care for older citizens. And so do I. Most Americans want fair and stable prices and decent incomes for our farmers. And so do I. Most Americans want a decent home in a decent neighborhood for all. And so do I. Most Americans want an education for every child to the limit of his ability. And so do I . . . Most Americans want victory in our war against poverty. And so do I." Johnson told the delegates that the nation, "in this hour, has man's first chance to build the Great Society—a place where the meaning of man's life matches the marvels of man's labor."

On the final day of the convention, Johnson also spoke to Democratic leaders in a private meeting to inform them of a theme he was planning to make central for the remainder of the campaign. The idea was that a "frontlash," which would move Republican voters away from their right-wing candidate, would be more significant than any backlash among Democrats against civil rights. Johnson cited opinion polls that showed Goldwater was receiving less support from Republican and independent voters than Richard Nixon had in 1960. "We are finding that one out of every three Republicans stated they are part of the frontlash and will not vote Republican," Johnson said. "We'll gain two to three times as many as we lose."[46] He asked his advisers to spread this message to the press.[47]

Johnson had ample reason to feel good about his prospects. National polls showed that he had a formidable lead over his opponent throughout the country. In the Republican state of Maine, support for Johnson over Goldwater was running seven to one. In Maryland, where Governor George Wallace of Alabama had scared some Democrats by doing relatively well in the Democratic primaries with a campaign attacking civil rights, Johnson received 60 percent approval ratings. In Wisconsin, the other state where Wallace had done well, Johnson led Goldwater 53 percent to 35 percent. Gallup reported in early September that Johnson was right about the "frontlash." More Republicans were planning to defect from their party than in any of the last seven presidential election cycles.[48]

During the campaign, the Democratic National Committee made unprecedented use of television spots to convey the message that the president was a productive leader and Goldwater was a dangerous extremist "who would ruin this country and our future," as Jack Valenti put it.[49] The DNC had signed a contract with the advertising firm Doyle Dane Bernbach, which had created many famous campaigns, among them "Think Small" for Volkswagen. The Johnson campaign spent a lot of money on television advertising and broadcast, according to one study, more negative spots than any campaign until that time.[50]

There were also many television spots that emphasized the positive achievements of the Democratic administration (a strong economy with a booming GNP and low rates of unemployment) and the progressive legislation (the Civil Rights Act and the Economic Opportunity Act) that Johnson had already pushed through Congress.

One ad, called "Accomplishments," reviewed the tragic circumstances under which Johnson took office, then went on to explain how Johnson passed a number of historic bills, including the tax cut and civil rights, within a few months. "John Kennedy's death commands what his life conveyed: that America must move forward," Johnson was seen saying. "And now the ideas and the ideals which he so nobly represented must and will be translated into effective action." The narrator then said, "The promises made that November day were strong promises. One by one, they have been kept," and listed Johnson's legislative achievements and also his firm stance against communism after the Gulf of Tonkin attacks.

The president's campaign also released a blistering series of negative television ads designed to eviscerate Goldwater in the eyes of Democrats, independents, and nervous Republicans. The most famous of these ads went on the air on September 7, 1964. It began with a girl picking the petals off a daisy. Viewers watched her counting the petals to ten; then they heard a male voice counting down from ten to one. The camera zoomed in on one of the girl's eyes, and a nuclear explosion filled the screen. President Johnson, in voice-over, said, "These are the stakes—to make a world in which all of God's children can live, or to go into the dark. We must either love each other, or we must die."[51] Another male voice said, "Vote for President Johnson on November 3. The stakes are too high for you to stay home."

The "Daisy" spot, though it aired only once, remains the most famous of the campaign, but there were other tough-minded ads that conveyed the perception that Goldwater's domestic policy ideas were just as radical and dangerous as his foreign policies. "Keep fear of Goldwater as unstable, impulsive, reckless in public's mind," Jack Valenti had advised Johnson. "This is our strongest asset. Don't let up on the possibility of Goldwater dismantling Federal government—specific hits on Social Security, TVA, farm subsidies."[52] In one ad, viewers watched Ku Klux Klan members marching in their regalia, burning crosses. The narrator said, "'We represent the majority of the people in Alabama who hate niggerism, Catholicism, Judaism, and all the *isms* of the whole world.' So said Robert Creel of the Alabama Ku Klux Klan. He also said, 'I like Barry Goldwater. He needs our help.'"[53]

Another ad reviewed a series of statements Goldwater had made about Social Security. The camera focused on a Social Security card, the iconic image of New Deal liberalism, and viewers were told, "On at least seven different occasions, Barry Goldwater has said that he would drastically change the social security system . . . even his running mate, William Miller, admits that Barry Goldwater's voluntary plan would wreck your social security." The camera then zoomed in on a pair of hands ripping the card apart, followed by a video of Lyndon Johnson delivering a speech in which he warned, "Too many have worked too long and too hard to see this threatened now by policies which promise to undo all that we have done together over all these years." The narrator concluded, "For over thirty years, President Johnson worked to strengthen Social Security. Vote for him on November 3."

The rest of the campaign emphasized the same themes. In a speech broadcast on national television, Johnson, without mentioning Goldwater, said, "We are now told that we the people acting through Government should withdraw from education, from public power, from agriculture, from urban renewal, and from a host of other vital programs. We are now told that we should end Social Security as we know it, sell T.V.A., strip labor unions of many of their gains and terminate all farm subsidies. We are told that the object of leadership is not to pass laws but to repeal them." During a southern campaign swing, Johnson defended his civil rights record and told his audience they should expect more. In Louisville, Kentucky, he told a large crowd gathered near the courthouse square, "We are going to wipe out poverty in this region, in the rural mining areas, as well as in the cities of Kentucky."[54]

Goldwater's campaign was poorly organized, and his advertising was not nearly as effective as Johnson's. The Arizona senator also tended to play the part the Democrats had assigned to him. During a visit to Appalachia, one of the most economically depressed regions in the country, Goldwater told a cheering crowd of about six thousand people, "The theorists of the much-advertised 'Great Society' have redefined the luxuries of yesterday as the necessities of today, and those who fall behind in this race constitute the new class of 'the poor.'" The senator dismissed the War on Poverty as outdated "gimmicks" from the Great Depression era that would stifle economic growth.[55] He ripped into the Medicare proposal in a speech to a group of retirees in Florida.

Goldwater's campaign was also wrongheaded and poorly executed. As he became more desperate, he attacked the morality of Johnson's administration rather than its public policies. A lot of Goldwater's time and energy was devoted to showing that he was neither extreme nor crazy, but this defensive approach only served to highlight how extreme he was.

LIBERAL LANDSLIDE

The election was a Democratic triumph. Johnson won 43,129,484 popular votes and 486 electoral votes to Goldwater's 27,178,188 popular votes and 52 electoral votes. Johnson won the biggest popular vote, 61 percent, in American history, better than FDR in 1936, and registered the largest margin of victory. Goldwater's extreme right-wing candidacy, as well as the excitement over Johnson's legislation and the positive memories in the electorate of John Kennedy, drove the size of Democratic majorities to historic levels. The composition of Congress, which the *New York Times* columnist James Reston would later term the "Goldwater Congress,"[56] changed dramatically. With huge majorities in the House (295–140) and the Senate (68–32), Democrats would have more seats than at any time since 1936. Thirty-nine out of forty Democratic incumbents supported by the DSG were reelected, while forty of the sixty-six nonincumbents who received assistance were victorious.[57] The conservative coalition in Congress had been reduced to its smallest size since it had formed.

The Senate Democratic majority was the biggest since 1940. The thirteen liberal Democrats elected to the Senate in 1958 all retained their seats. In addition, Democrats won three Republican seats, including Robert Kennedy's victory over Kenneth Keating in New York. Robert Taft Jr., the son of "Mr. Republican," lost to Stephen Young in a stunning upset. Conservatives were dismayed because many hoped that Taft could become a future leader.[58]

Democrats were disappointed that the Republicans carried the Deep South—Georgia, South Carolina, Alabama, Mississippi, and Louisiana—though the Democratic South had started to crack before Goldwater came on the scene, and there were compensations to the Democrats for the loss of these states. African American voting, though still limited, increased and was almost entirely Democratic.[59] Johnson had started to build a strong coalition in the coastal states and in the Republican Midwest, including in North Dakota, Missouri, Michigan, Iowa, Wisconsin, and Minnesota. The "frontlash," as Johnson had predicted, kept Republican voters away from the polls or impelled them to vote Democratic. Johnson won Kansas with 54.1 percent of the vote, the first time the state had not gone Republican since 1936. Maine went for the Democratic candidate for just the second time in the state's history—and gave him close to 69 percent of the vote. Johnson also won in Vermont, which had not gone Democratic since the 1820s.[60] Goldwater won only sixteen non-southern congressional districts.[61] Democrats did extremely well among women, college-educated voters, and the elderly, and in the big cities and the suburbs.[62]

A study by the *Christian Science Monitor* found no evidence of a white backlash in seven cities where lower- and middle-income white Democrats had been expected to vote Republican in higher numbers as a result of Johnson's push for civil rights. In three Polish districts in New York, the Democratic margin increased from 75 percent in 1960 to 82 percent in 1964. In Chicago, Johnson won in key ethnic communities by margins that were bigger than Kennedy's. Johnson won an overwhelming victory in a ward in Cleveland, Ohio, where African American schoolchildren were being bused into schools with white children. He did extremely well in the state of Indiana, where many observers had wondered, after George Wallace's unexpected victory in the Democratic primary, whether the population of white steelworkers would migrate toward the Republicans.[63] They didn't. The entire Iowa delegation in the House flipped to the Democratic side of the ledger, a dramatic reversal for one of the most conservative Republican factions in Congress. The most successful Republicans were those who had distanced themselves from Goldwater and his conservative politics. The NAACP reported that one senator and thirteen congressmen were defeated mainly because of their votes against civil rights.[64]

There was plenty of evidence from polling data that voters had favored liberal ideas in the election, had confidence in the federal government, and supported, broadly speaking, many of the key Johnson initiatives. According to the National Election Study, one of the most sophisticated analyses of the electorate, Americans had voted in favor of liberalism, tended to favor civil rights legislation, and wanted the government to do more to help people obtain health insurance.

Many Republicans saw their losses as a sign that the decision to shift to the right, notwithstanding their gains in the South, had been devastating to the Republican Party. In New York, one upstate Republican commented, "After this election, the conservatives simply are not entitled to be heard any more. They have had their chance and almost killed the party in the process. The election proves we must appeal to independents and Democrats if we're to win, and that means a far less conservative tack."[65]

With the election behind him, Johnson immediately prepared to ask for more legislation. He was not satisfied with the Civil Rights

Act and the Economic Opportunity Act of 1964. He wanted more from Congress: he wanted everything he had told Bill Moyers and his other advisers he wanted on the night Kennedy was killed; and it seemed to him, or at least he would proclaim, that the American people had just told Congress they wanted exactly what their president wanted.

CHAPTER SIX

THE FABULOUS
EIGHTY-NINTH CONGRESS

The election of 1964 produced the most liberal Congress since the Democratic landslide of 1936. "There were so many Democrats," noted the young Illinois representative Donald Rumsfeld upon surveying the landscape after Lyndon Johnson's victory, "that they had to sit on the Republican side of the aisle."[1] Liberal and moderate Democrats now so outnumbered conservatives that for the first time in decades the conservative southern Democrats were seriously worried about retaining their power. Nor could the southerners depend any longer on the other half of their coalition; not only were there fewer Republicans in Congress, but those who survived were profoundly shaken by the election returns and believed they could no longer afford to obstruct Johnson's proposals. A growing number concluded that if they continued to just say no, as they had to the War on Poverty, the next presidential election would be as disastrous as the last one had been. One New York Republican admitted in the press, "People think of us Republicans as negative, unimaginative with no true feeling for the wants and needs of the 'little people.'"[2] Republicans tended to accept that the election had been both a rebuke to Goldwater's conservatism and an endorsement of Johnson's policies.

In a frightening development for the GOP, Democrats had won even traditionally Republican constituencies in the Midwest.[3]

A few blocks up Pennsylvania Avenue, administration officials were looking at legislative prospects so rosy they stopped talking about the "Southern Democratic-Republican coalition,"[4] a term that had loomed large since FDR's second term. "I can't remember when Southern influence in Congress was at this low point," noted one observer.[5] The administration had scored victories before the election—the tax cut, the Civil Rights Act, and the Economic Opportunity Act—but now the possibilities for passing bills seemed almost limitless. Johnson believed he had the best opportunity he would ever have to flood Congress with ideas, new and old, and to persuade legislators to send those proposals back to the White House as bills for his signature. He had plenty of proposals to send.

Back in the spring of 1964, after an impromptu but mandatory skinny-dip with the president in the White House pool, the speechwriter Richard Goodwin had come up with the trademark Johnson wanted for his domestic agenda. By "the Great Society," the president intended not just a package of programs but a broad, new vision of how the federal government could help every citizen get better access to the fruits of America's economic growth. The Great Society was not a radical idea. Nothing in it was meant to change the basic operations of the capitalist economy or to intervene aggressively in class relations. It was still, however, a very ambitious agenda. As the president had explained when he introduced the concept in his May 1964 address at the University of Michigan, the Great Society "rests on abundance and liberty for all. It demands an end to poverty and racial injustice, to which we are totally committed in our time. But that is just the beginning. The Great Society is a place where every child can find knowledge to enrich his mind and to enlarge his talents. It is a place where leisure is a welcome chance to build and reflect, not a feared cause of boredom and restlessness . . . The Great

Society is not a safe harbor, a resting place, a final objective, a finished work. It is a challenge constantly renewed." The specific proposals Johnson conceived as part of his Great Society were what he
now planned to submit to a Congress newly swollen with liberal support for his aims: voting rights for African Americans, economic
assistance to schools, health insurance for the elderly and the poor,
fair housing laws, government protection for the environment, funding for the arts, an end to discriminatory immigration policies, and
more.

For all the talk then and now about Johnson's skill as a legislative
tactician, by far his most significant advantage in 1965 was the huge
liberal majorities he had just won in the House and the Senate. He
had done what he could with the Eighty-eighth Congress—he had
benefited in this effort from the power of the civil rights movement
and the exigencies of the 1964 election campaign—but the conservative coalition had significantly restrained his accomplishments. The
Eighty-ninth Congress was potentially more fertile ground for the
broad range of controversial programs on his dream agenda.

Johnson knew, however, that despite the political advantages he
now enjoyed, his big election victory did not guarantee he would get
everything he wanted in the time he was likely to have. He had
entered the House of Representatives in 1937, when his hero Franklin Roosevelt was encountering fierce resistance in Congress as he
tried to take advantage of what had seemed like an overwhelming
mandate for the New Deal in the 1936 election. Johnson knew that
the proposals he was going to send to the Hill would be divisive.
Some of them would open up deep splits in core Democratic constituencies. Urban Catholics and liberal Protestants, for example, were
at odds over how programs for federal aid to education should be
designed. With Medicare, Johnson was attempting to resolve a conflict that had devastated Harry Truman's presidency after his big
election victory in 1948, when doctors and insurers, who had immense

influence in the districts and states where Democratic legislators and voters predominated, had fought any extension of the federal government into their industry. Voting rights legislation was certain to spark a forceful negative response from southerners who understood that the legislation would hand to African Americans who had been beaten by southern police the political power to challenge the entire governing structure of the region. Johnson knew he would have to fight hard to make sure southerners did not find ways to sabotage voting rights legislation, and at the same time contain liberals who, by demanding the boldest possible measures, might undermine support among moderates in both parties.

Eager to avoid the strategic mistakes that had stifled his predecessors' efforts, Johnson wanted to move his legislation as soon as he could. He believed that continuous pressure and constant negotiations would maximize his chances for success. In February, he convened all the legislative liaisons of the major cabinet offices and the entire staff of Larry O'Brien, his man in the White House who was responsible for relations with Congress. He told everyone in the meeting, "I want you to work for my legislative program and get as much passed in the next 90 days and in 1965 as is humanly possible. I want you to take out all proposals and do everything to get the elementary and secondary act, educational legislation, Medicare and all this other [legislation]." After listing all the programs he wanted, he told the group, "You may wonder why I am putting such pressure on it, but let's go back and look over what's happened to the Presidents of the United States who are elected." Johnson analyzed Woodrow Wilson's presidency for a half hour, as well as how FDR had overreached with the court-packing plan. "Look," he said, "I've just been elected by an overwhelming vote, but every day that I will be in office, I will be losing some of my ability to convert that victory into legislative reality."[6] To counteract the debilitating trend, he would spend every waking minute on the phones, wheeling and dealing, trying to get legislators to fall in line. He instructed cabinet leaders to return the calls of all representatives and senators within ten minutes.

Johnson's approach to legislating included far more than his famous Treatment. He tailored the approach to the specific political dynamics of each issue. For his education program, he would depend on the sheer partisan power of Democrats on the Hill to muscle his bill through the House and the Senate. For health care, he intended to allow a southern committee chairman, who had concluded that the election rendered obstruction no longer politically viable, to fundamentally reshape the legislation and claim part of the credit for the final bipartisan victory. For voting rights, he did as he had done for civil rights in 1957 and 1964: he aimed to build on the momentum created by civil rights activists and strike a bipartisan deal to close down a Senate filibuster.

He decided it was important to avoid talking about funding for his programs. He was riding the wave of an economy entering its fifth year of expansion, and he would count on continued economic growth and rising incomes to generate tax revenues. The GNP was $47 billion higher in 1965 than it had been one year earlier (it had been $675.6 billion), with unemployment down to 4.1 percent and businesses having to spend a record $51.8 billion for new investment. With corporate profits up and personal consumption higher, Johnson constantly boasted how the tax cut in 1964 had paved the way for phenomenal rates of economic growth. He made certain that his plans for funding his domestic programs stayed murky. He would count on savings that might possibly come in the future from proposed cuts to the military budget. At his command, Secretary of Defense Robert McNamara hid the projected costs of American involvement in Vietnam.[7]

Johnson tabled legislation that would directly benefit unions. Organized labor was at the peak of its power in the 1960s—more than 30 percent of the workforce belonged to unions—but since the passage of the Taft-Hartley Act in 1947, the right-to-work laws (section 14B) had hindered the ability of unions to organize workers in many states, particularly in the South. Union leaders had put the repeal of 14B at the top of their agenda since President Truman's election in 1948, and they were hopeful that their moment had finally arrived with the liberal ascendancy after the 1964 elections.

But the unions were disappointed. A clear-eyed look at Congress convinced Johnson that any effort to make union dreams come true could reenergize the conservative coalition in opposition—just as FDR had done in 1937 when he attempted to pack the Supreme Court after an earlier epic election victory for liberalism.[8] Worse, an attempt to repeal 14B would anger Senator Dirksen, who was under immense pressure from the business community to oppose labor law reform and who was promising to filibuster any repeal effort. Although a majority of the Senate favored repeal of 14B, Dirksen maintained the support of approximately twenty-eight Republicans and southern Democrats.[9] Johnson made it clear to Walter Reuther, the president of the United Automobile Workers and one of his most loyal allies, that he would support legislation to repeal 14B within the year, but not yet. Johnson asked Reuther to help him quiet the growing discontent of labor leaders; he argued, successfully, that pushing too soon for repeal would cause him to lose the support of the Republican legislators he needed for issues that were at the top of his agenda—education, medical care for the elderly, and voting rights.[10]

PUTTING SOUTHERN DEMOCRATS ON NOTICE

Johnson's many years in Congress had taught him that when you had the power, the best move was to maximize your advantages. On the day after he beat Goldwater, LBJ was on the phone, making sure congressional Democrats took every possible step, without going overboard and getting tied up in divisive wrangling, to capitalize on the election. "The 1964 election gave us the legislative machinery to pass it [the Great Society]," one Democrat said, "if we know how to use it."[11] That meant changing some of the rules and procedures upon which conservatives had depended to sustain their power.

Liberal Democrats in the House set out to make a number of reforms that would bolster the effectiveness of their majority, primarily by weakening the power of committee chairmen to obstruct legislation. These changes were spearheaded by the Democratic Study Group, which had grown from 125 to 165 committed liberal members and was now the dominant liberal faction in the House Democratic caucus.

The liberals were undertaking a difficult balancing act. Given the nature of the election, they saw that this was a highly unusual, even historic, opportunity to pass wide-ranging domestic legislation, so they didn't want to get Congress tied up in debates about procedural reform that would delay addressing substantive matters of social policy. While the number of liberals on Capitol Hill had vastly increased, many senior northern, urban Democrats, among them Emanuel Celler and Adam Clayton Powell Jr., didn't want to tamper with the committee process through which they had laid claim to substantial power. The newest Democrats, even those from northern states, also hoped at some point to get a piece of the power seniority could grant them. So any kind of proposed congressional reform could easily open up divisions among Democratic factions, energize the demoralized southern Democrats, and steal valuable time away from debates over domestic policy.

DSG members wanted to send a message to southern Democrats not to stand in the way of Lyndon Johnson's proposals. They began by proposing that the Democratic caucus discipline two southern conservative Democrats, Mississippi's John Bell Williams and South Carolina's Albert Watson, who had publicly endorsed Barry Goldwater in the election. Neither man was the biggest fish in the congressional sea, but taking action against either of them would send a clear message to more prominent southerners that the Democratic caucus was prepared to sanction any colleague who didn't go along with the majority. Watson was a freshman, a protégé of Strom Thurmond's, who had headed "Democrats for Goldwater." Williams was a bigger fish, an eighteen-year veteran of the House, a lifelong segregationist who was next in line to become chair of the powerful House Interstate Commerce Committee. Williams's support for Goldwater had been only the latest in what the liberals saw as a string of despicable acts. He—and the rest of the Mississippi House delegation—had voted against Johnson's tax cut, civil rights, and food stamps. The liberals wanted to strip both men of their committee assignments and kick them out of the Democratic caucus, with the result that they could no longer enjoy "the same privileges, committee assignments, seniority and other prerogatives reserved for loyal members of the Democratic Party."[12] In light of their transgressions, these harsh sanctions would be a highly unusual move—the caucus had not disciplined any member since 1911—but even some southerners agreed with the liberals' plan. Majority Whip Hale Boggs of Louisiana, who had little in common ideologically with the northern liberals, wanted to discipline the two men. As he told the president, "I don't want to put up with these traitorous bastards anymore."[13]

House Speaker John McCormack also endorsed punitive action against Williams and Watson.[14] The Speaker's support was essential for the liberals; it gave the leadership's imprimatur to their initiative. The cigar-chomping, backroom-dealing Speaker was a loyal New Deal Democrat who looked forward to legislating an expanded role for the federal government. He was also eager to step out of the shadow of Sam Rayburn, his legendary predecessor as Speaker. McCormack respected the committee process and had developed strong working relationships with the southerners, but he firmly believed they had no right to stand in the way of President Johnson after the dramatic election results. He resented southern Democrats who had disloyally endorsed the GOP candidate. When the House had reformed the Rules Committee in 1961 by adding three members to the panel so that more liberals could be assigned, McCormack, who was then the House majority leader, had been one of only a few top Democrats who supported a bolder alternative that would have purged Howard Smith's main ally, William Colmer, from the committee for having failed to support Kennedy in 1960. McCormack's outlook was at the center of Democratic Party thinking; he wanted to sanction the recusant members, a decision that the Democratic caucus clearly had the right to make, but he didn't want to boot them out of the caucus, a move that could easily be interpreted as overstepping his power and overturning the democratic decisions of voters.

On January 2, the Democratic caucus met and stripped Williams and Watson of their seniority rights by a strong vote of 157 to 115.

Next the liberal Democrats took direct aim at Howard Smith by asking the Democratic caucus to reinstate the "twenty-one-day rule," which had first been adopted after the 1948 election but was struck down by conservatives two years later. The rule permitted a committee chairman or members of a committee whose bill had been held up by the Rules Committee for twenty-one days to force the legislation out of the committee and onto the House floor.[15] One House liberal, Henry Reuss of Wisconsin, recalled that when the rule had been in effect for the brief period from 1949 through 1950, "It broke open a stopped dike for legislation. But the 88nd [*sic*] Congress threw it out. We need it back now."[16]

President Johnson, honoring the long-standing tradition of presidents' refraining from making public statements about the internal matters of the legislative branch, left no doubt on the phones that he supported bringing back the twenty-one-day rule. He explained to Speaker McCormack that the rule was desperately needed because, despite voters' decisive rejection of Goldwater and his brand of

right-wing conservatism, the most reactionary southern conservatives still chaired the key committees. "These people in these 45
states—44 states and the District of Columbia—they didn't vote for
Howard Smith . . . He's representing another century and Goldwater
represented his viewpoint and they got six states and the people, 15
million of them, say they want to move ahead. And if we don't move
with them they're going to move over us." Democrats needed to
make changes so that "you're the boss up there and not Howard
Smith," the president told McCormack.[17]

Because passage of the twenty-one-day rule would be a reform to
the procedures of the House, a majority of the entire chamber—not
just of the Democratic caucus—had to endorse the change. On the
same day the Democrats voted to punish the turncoats Williams and
Watson, the House considered all the reforms that had been proposed by the DSG. Despite the mood of the postelection period, the
outcome of the vote on the twenty-one-day rule was in doubt. Howard Smith argued that the rule was "unworkable" and would grant
excessive power to the Speaker. But times had changed. The Democratic Study Group was now a significant force in the House, and the
House was more receptive to its proposals than in the past. Howard
Smith no longer seemed as formidable to members as he had in previous years. The House passed the twenty-one-day rule by a close
vote of 224 to 201. Sixteen Republicans, taking the position that (in
the wake of Goldwater's candidacy) it was best to avoid being seen
as the party of obstruction, joined 208 Democrats to provide liberals
the margin of victory.[18] The message had been delivered to Howard
Smith that if he tried to stop a bill from reaching the floor of the
House for a vote, a committee chairman whose panel had passed the
bill could humiliate him by getting the bill forced out of Rules. The
message would also be understood by every other committee chairman who might ever contemplate defying the will of the liberals.

The other major reform proposed by the DSG was to alter the

party ratios on every major committee to reflect the new balance of the parties. Traditionally, when such adjustments had been made after big elections, the leadership tended not to alter party ratios on the Ways and Means Committee. But now McCormack and Carl Albert, with the support of the newly elected Republican minority leader, Gerald Ford, who had successfully challenged Charles Halleck in the leadership election, agreed with the DSG that the changes should be more sweeping, given the size of the Democratic majority. Ford had promised to transform the image of his party, to "promote and communicate the image of a fighting, forward looking party." The change in party ratios would be an effective way for Ford to signal that he was willing to work constructively with the Democrats on their agenda, though House Republicans would not have had much leverage to prevent the change even if they hadn't been searching for a new image.

So the House voted to adjust the committee ratios from three Democrats to two Republicans to two Democrats to one Republican. The members also voted to alter the composition of the Ways and Means Committee from fifteen Democrats and ten Republicans to seventeen Democrats and eight Republicans. Although liberals had not undertaken more drastic reforms—one such reform would have been to strip Ways and Means of its power to make committee assignments for the Democratic caucus—they had changed the vote count in the panel that would take up President Johnson's Medicare proposal for 1965. The southern Democrats and the Republicans no longer constituted a majority on the committee, as they had since Medicare was first proposed in the committee in 1957, because the three new Democrats assigned to the committee all favored Medicare. "This change means half the battle of enacting the Johnson program is over," Larry O'Brien commented.[19] With the reforms, Albert added, it wouldn't matter to the leadership if Wilbur Mills was "for Medicare or not."[20] O'Brien and Albert were clearly exaggerating; Mills continued to have immense power, and his colleagues still feared him, assuming that he would regain all or most of his power within a few years, but the change in ratios would vastly diminish his ability to hold back Medicare in the coming months.

The possibilities for reform were far more limited in the Senate. It would be extraordinarily difficult to reform the filibuster. As they had done at the opening of every new Congress since 1949, a bipartisan group of liberals proposed reducing the number of senators required to end a filibuster to a mere majority rather than two-thirds of the Senate, but the reform never gained much traction, particularly after Johnson, who believed there was little chance of passing it, refrained from advocating for it. Southerners had successfully argued in the past that because only one-third of the chamber was elected in any given election, the Senate was a "continuing body," so that the rules of the previous session always applied at the start of every new session. Hence, any proposed change in filibuster rules could be filibustered. Many western senators were adamantly opposed to filibuster reform, and a number of liberal northerners were dubious about it. Every senator could see how someday he might have a critical need for the filibuster. Johnson knew a fight over the filibuster would be quixotic and would draw Democrats into an internal debate, something the president didn't want as he set about launching his legislative initiatives. The liberal Democrats who supported the reform agreed to postpone debate on their proposal, which meant that effectively it was dead.

BRINGING WASHINGTON INTO THE CLASSROOM

Federal assistance to schools was high among Johnson's priorities. Over the previous decade, the nation's school systems had been struggling to keep up with the influx of baby boom children who were reaching school age. In poorer communities, overcrowded school buildings were crumbling. In many districts, to create more space in elementary school buildings, administrators moved fifth and sixth graders into middle schools and ninth graders into high schools. New York City educational administrators used libraries, cafeterias, and storage spaces as temporary classrooms. Some schools constructed cheap prefab trailer annexes. Desperate administrators put students on shifts. Some children reported at 7:50 a.m. and departed at noon; others came in for the noon to 4:00 p.m. shift.[21] Students lacked supplies; library shelves were sparsely inhabited by books; there were insufficient resources for foreign language studies, art and music classes, and other enrichment programs.

Johnson had long taken a serious interest in education. His experience teaching impoverished children in Texas had given him an appreciation of education as a tool young people could use to lift themselves out of poor economic circumstances; this is what he thought his own education had done for him. Johnson also envied people in Washington who were better educated than he was—some of President Kennedy's advisers and staff, for example, who disparaged Johnson's intelligence and the extent of his education. "He was a nut on education," explained Vice President Humphrey. "He felt that education was the greatest thing he could give to the people; he just believed in it, just like some people believe in miracle cures."[22]

During his time in Congress, Johnson had come to believe that federal money could strengthen educational institutions. In 1944, as a congressman, he had been a strong supporter of the GI Bill of Rights, which helped returning World War II veterans go to college. During the 1950s, when he was Senate majority leader, he headed a bipartisan coalition of legislators who championed federal spending on education. In 1958, a year after the Soviet launch of the Sputnik satellite embarrassed the United States by creating the impression that the communists were more advanced in scientific research and technology,[23] Congress passed legislation that authorized more than $800 million in federal funding for colleges and universities. Public opinion supported Johnson's view of education: people generally believed it was a good idea for the federal government to be involved.[24]

Since the mid-1950s, Congress had considered several bills that would have provided federal financing for public school teachers' salary increases and the construction of school buildings. All had been defeated. Most recently, President Kennedy had proposed $2.5 billion in grants that states could allocate at their discretion to teachers' salaries and school construction as well as some other kinds of expenditures. Congress rejected this proposal.

There were four main reasons why Congress had never passed federal aid to elementary and secondary schools. The first was that a lot of people believed in an American tradition dating from the nineteenth century that public schools should be under local control. The second reason was that federal aid to education was a wedge that divided the parties. Republicans tended to oppose using federal money to help teachers, whose unions generally leaned toward the Democrats. They also defended the localist tradition in primary and secondary education. The third reason was that Catholic Democrats, who were very influential among urban politicians in New York, Philadelphia, Chicago, and other big cities, opposed these proposals because their parochial schools would not receive any funds. Protestant and Jewish Democrats—and the generally Democratic-leaning teachers' unions—resisted Catholic demands for federal grants to parochial schools. The final reason had to do with race. Before Congress passed the Civil Rights Act of 1964, education legislation proposals were opposed by southern Democrats who feared the funds would create an opening for the federal government to integrate first schools and then other public institutions.[25]

Johnson was confident that he could find a way through this political minefield. The election had provided him with more support on Capitol Hill for all his domestic initiatives. The passage of the Civil Rights Act, by guaranteeing a strong federal presence in the states to eradicate segregation, had dampened southern opposition to education legislation. There was a long tradition of southerners' looking to Washington for funds, and now, as segregation in schools was illegal, there was no reason for them not to climb onto the federal gravy train for their schools, just as they had done for their military bases, dams, and highways. "The Civil Rights Act of 1964 is passed anyway," one administration official told a group of southern congressmen. "If you now vote to deny federal aid to education, you are not helping yourself, you are just making it worse, because you might comply in some places and might as well pick up the money."[26]

Johnson believed he had restructured his education proposal to avoid the traditional Democratic infighting over parochial schools. Unlike Kennedy's proposal, which provided grants for school construction and teachers' salaries, Johnson's bill focused on federal assistance to impoverished children regardless of where they went to school. Under his plan, education became an extension of the War on Poverty. This shift in design—from funding buildings and teachers for all public school kids to providing money and services targeted for poor students—had many authors. In Congress, the so-called pupil-centered approach to education policy had been the brainchild of Senator Wayne Morse and two Senate staffers, Stewart McClure and Charles Lee, on the Labor and Public Welfare Committee. Morse, the Oregon maverick and ex-Republican, known as the Tiger of the Senate, was a former law school dean and was chairman of the Subcommittee on Education of the Senate Labor and Public Welfare Committee. Morse's insight was that shifting the target of aid from all children to a particular category of children would diminish some of the opposition that had traditionally hamstrung this issue. The federal government would distribute funds for services that aided poor students regardless of whether they were in public or parochial schools.[27]

Johnson called on civil rights and labor leaders to help him make sure this legislation made it smoothly through the Eighty-ninth Congress. He spoke by phone to Martin Luther King on January 15 and told him, "We've got to try with every force at our command—and I mean every force—to get these education bills that go to those people under two thousand dollars a year income . . . We've got to get them passed before the vicious forces concentrate and get them a coalition that can block them . . . Your people ought to be very, very diligent in looking at those committee members that come from urban areas that are friendly to you to see that those bills get reported right out."[28]

In the bill that was introduced in the House by the Kentucky Democrat Carl Perkins, chairman of the General Education Subcommittee of the House Education and Labor Committee, over $1 billion would be allocated to school districts where 3 percent or more of the student body belonged to families that earned less than $40 a week, which included roughly five million of the nation's forty-eight million students. Local school districts were required to submit to the state their plans to provide services to these children, which could include everything from new after-school programs to new facilities earmarked for the kids of poor families. The state education departments would then make decisions about which plans to approve. School districts applying for these funds would be required to include in their design certain services that would be made available to students of similar income brackets who were enrolled in private schools, most of which would be urban parochial schools often attended by kids from poor ethnic families. The proposal allocated $100 million in grants to subsidize the purchase of books in libraries and other related materials. Parochial schools could receive these funds as long as the books that were purchased would be acceptable in a public school, that is, devoid of religious content. Finally, the proposal authorized about $100 million to establish supplementary education centers that would offer curricula not included in the schools, including instruction in foreign languages, music and art, and science labs. The programs would be run in independent institutions within school districts so that qualified children who were enrolled in parochial schools would have access to them.

The early responses to Johnson's pupil-centered proposal were positive. Catholic organizations expressed cautious support for the legislation. A spokesman for the Roman Catholic Church said, "This emphasis on the child, the student, I applaud." Officials from the National Education Association, who were usually at odds with church officials whenever education legislation was being discussed, stated that the bill did not violate the separation of church and state even though parochial school children would benefit from the funds.[29]

The legislative strategy for aid to education was in the hands of liberal committee chairmen, who would use their muscle to push a bill rapidly through the House before any internal party disagreements developed into conflicts. Carl Perkins was first in line because his General Education Subcommittee was where the bill entered into the legislative process. His constituency, primarily unionized coal miners, ranked toward the bottom of the income ladder and at the top of the charts for unemployment, so the district stood to benefit from the proposed funds.[30] Perkins conducted open hearings on the education program to limit the opportunity for opponents to attack the legislation behind closed doors, where they could avoid the political fallout.

Perkins ran his committee, which was one of the most liberal in the House, with great skill and ruthlessness. He didn't allow opponents time to speak in committee meetings. He stacked the hearings with people who supported the measure so that the hearings didn't become a forum for opponents to voice their criticisms of the legislation for reporters. The subcommittee worked with great speed, accepting Johnson's principle that delay was usually a bad thing because it gave opponents time to cause trouble; there were hearings and deliberations for ten straight days. As Larry O'Brien told the president, Perkins "pushed the committee night and day and did a tremendous job of achieving" a markup of the legislation for the full committee.[31] The markup was the work the subcommittee or committee did in reviewing each section of the bill, rewriting language, and voting on amendments before sending the bill to the next stage of the legislative process.

On February 5, the subcommittee reported out the bill to the full committee by a vote of 6 to 0. Only the six Democrats voted for the bill. The three Republicans on the subcommittee had boycotted the final meeting and refused to vote on the bill, to protest how Perkins had decided to manhandle them on such an important matter. Charles Goodell charged that the subcommittee had considered the legislation in a "hasty and superficial" manner.[32] "This isn't going to be an education act," Goodell said, "it's going to be the 'railroad act of 1965.'"[33] This was characteristic of the focus of Republicans' complaints about committees in the wake of the 1964 election; they tended to criticize as overly partisan the way every proposal was handled by every liberal majority during the legislative process. The abstaining Republicans also suggested that the federal expenditures for education wouldn't help needy kids as much as they would fatten the wallets of politicians and activists in Democratic constituencies.

When the full committee met, Adam Clayton Powell was at the top of his form.[34] He rushed the deliberations so that his opponents wouldn't have time to organize a forceful response. He blocked proposals that would have raised the cost of the legislation or provided funding for school building construction, which, according to O'Brien, would have "completely unzipped the religious consensus" by bringing back old tensions.[35] On March 2, the committee approved the $1.3 billion bill by a vote of 23 to 8.

Even before debate began on the House floor, the whip counts were positive.[36] The legislative committee of the National Education

Association estimated that as of March 2 there were at least 242 positive commitments in the House.[37]

Gerald Ford's promise of a "constructive" approach seemed to be an instant nonstarter. Republicans attacked Johnson as a big-spending liberal. They called him the "wildest spending economizer" in history and ridiculed his claims that he would keep the budget under $100 billion. They charged that he was using "bookkeeping gimmicks" and masking the long-term costs of the program. The Great Society, they said, was an "empire-building scheme with ever bigger government as its central goal." Education, Gerald Ford said, was the great example: "Federalized schools, text books, and teachers, federalized libraries, laboratories, auditoriums, and theaters . . . are now in prospect for our states and local communities."[38]

With the twenty-one-day rule menacing him, Howard Smith had no hope of holding up the bill. It moved swiftly to the floor, where it carried by 263 to 153. There were 41 southern Democrats who voted in favor, 54 in opposition, while Republicans voted against the bill by 96 to 35. There were 187 northern Democrats who supported the bill, with only 3 voting no. Thirty members who had voted against an education bill in the Eighty-seventh Congress voted in favor of this one, based on their understanding of the election as a mandate for President Johnson.[39]

When the bill reached the Senate, Johnson reminded Senator Morse, whose Subcommittee on Education would take up the bill first, that for "fifteen years you've been raising hell with me and every time I go to my telephone you call me about education. Every time I go to the floor I hear Wayne Morse talk about education." Now, Johnson said, the time had come to pass the bill. Morse didn't need the reminder. He told the president he would "take on the opposition" and that the president should not worry about the bill's passage.[40] The centerpiece of their strategy was to pass the House bill without any amendments. If the Senate did that, the rules stipulated that the bill would not have to go to a conference committee, and there would be no requirement to send the final version of the bill back to the House Rules Committee, where Howard Smith would have one last chance to cause problems for Johnson.[41] Despite the twenty-one-day rule, Johnson was not in the mood to take any chances that could "endanger the whole bill."[42]

The Republican attitude toward the education bill was entirely different in the Senate, where reelection required winning votes from a statewide constituency, from what it was in the House, where many Republican members had to court voters only in relatively small, homogeneous districts. House Republicans elected from those districts could afford to remain more rigidly conservative than could senators who had to appeal to a broader base. Republican senators were also more desperate to avoid any association with Goldwater's stands against federal aid to education that would surely hurt them among the moderate voters to whom they had to appeal.

Morse's Subcommittee on Education voted unanimously in favor of the bill: 10 to 0. The full committee followed with a unanimous vote of its own. The bill was reported to the Senate floor without any amendments, where, after Morse warded off over ten proposed amendments, it passed by a decisive vote of 73 to 18. Fifty-five Democrats and 18 Republicans voted in favor of the legislation. Because the Senate had passed exactly the same bill as the House, there would be no conference committee, and the bill would go directly to the president for his signature.

Title I of the Elementary and Secondary Education Act accomplished what Johnson had most desired—federal assistance to "educationally deprived" children. As a result of the law, federal aid for grades K–12 increased from 3 percent of total education spending in 1958 to 10 percent ten years later.[43] The legislation authorized the federal government to provide financial aid to local school districts with high concentrations of low-income families. State education agencies could dispense the money they received from the U.S. commissioner of education as grants to districts. A local district could be eligible for funds only if it had a minimum of one hundred students in families that made $2,000 a year or less in income or relief money. To receive the money, a local district would send an application to the state's education agency that explained how funds would help low-income kids in public, private, and parochial schools. Title II provided $100 million in grants for library materials and textbooks. Title III authorized $100 million for supplementary educational services, including labs, language programs, vocational classes, artistic construction, mobile libraries, and other educational technology. Title IV provided money for educational research and training. Title V provided $25 million to the states to improve the operations of their departments of education.

The new law was unlike any previous legislation in the way it provided federal aid to local school districts, but what it could accomplish had been vastly oversold. Schooling was only one challenge for children living in low-income communities. Educational enhancements would have only limited effects on their lives. There would also have to be changes in homes and communities and the promise of good jobs after a young person's schooling was finished. The formula the legislation used to dispense funds, as Republicans had warned during debates, often neglected some of the poorest children, and weak guidelines for allocation of the funds created room for school administrators to use money for purposes other than those for which it was intended.[44]

Despite these limitations and others that would become clear over time, the legislation was still historic. It provided the biggest injection to that time of federal funds into the educational system, and it established a strong precedent for federal engagement in improving education for the poorest young people in America. Republicans would later find it difficult to roll back these gains, and over the coming decade there would be bipartisan agreement to expand the government's commitment to education.[45]

The Elementary and Secondary Education Act was not the only education legislation passed in 1965. In a separate bill, Congress approved Johnson's request to use $150 million of poverty funds to provide grants to preschool programs for poor children. The programs, established on an experimental basis in the summer of 1965 and known as Head Start, were based on the theory, supported by social science research, that poor children were about a year behind other kids by third grade and three years behind other kids by eighth grade, in part because their school districts did not have nursery schools or kindergartens. The other major victory on education occurred with the passage of the Higher Education Act. This ambitious legislation provided federal funding for university libraries, African American colleges, and community service programs. It also provided low-interest loans to students.

On April 11, Johnson signed the Elementary and Secondary Education Act at a schoolhouse next to the Pedernales River in Stonewall, Texas, where he had once been a student. One of his former teachers, Kate Deadrich Loney, sat beside the president as he signed the legislation, and so did some of the Mexican American students he had taught in Cotulla, Texas. "By passing this bill," Johnson said, "we bridge the gap between helplessness and hope for more than 5 million educationally deprived children."

THE TRIUMPH OF MEDICARE

On January 4, 1965, the same day Johnson called on Congress to pass a health-care bill for the elderly in his State of the Union address, the House Democrat Cecil King of California and the Senate Democrat

Clinton Anderson of New Mexico, whose longtime advocacy of government health care had stemmed from his brush with tuberculosis in his early twenties, introduced a Medicare bill that would cover sixty days of hospital care, sixty days of posthospital care, 240 home health-care visits, and outpatient X-rays and other hospital diagnostic services. The benefits would be paid for by an increase in the Social Security tax, from 3.6 percent to 4.25 percent in 1966–1967 and up to 5 percent in 1968–1970. According to the best estimates, the program would cost a little over $2 billion in the first full year of operation. The Social Security Administration would administer the program.

When this legislation was introduced in Congress, the battle for federal health insurance had been ongoing for more than fifteen years. In fact, the Medicare legislation of 1965 was the latest in a series of bills that had been introduced and tabled in one way or another throughout the period, while the battle raged from the grass roots to the halls of Congress over the very idea of government involvement in health care.

At the start of his second term in 1949, President Truman called for a national health insurance plan for all Americans. Under his proposal, the federal government would offer health insurance for medical, dental, and hospital costs to every American. Although Truman's proposal did not address the question of how the program would be funded, the bill's supporters said they would use a payroll tax on employers and employees just like Social Security. Truman's proposal was attacked by the American Medical Association (AMA), the professional association of physicians; by the insurance industry; and by congressional conservatives who blasted it as "socialized medicine." The AMA spent a reported $1,225,208 lobbying against the bill in the first nine months of 1949, the highest amount spent until that time by any interest group on lobbying in a single year. The opponents of national health care warned that the provision of health insurance would be the first step in a gradual federal government takeover of the entire health industry and the establishment of a system like the National Health Service, which had just gotten under way in the United Kingdom in 1948. Although Truman's proposal was far from government-controlled health care, opponents used exaggerated rhetoric to conjure up the worst fears that Americans had in the cold war era. They warned that a national health-care system would destroy the integrity of the doctor-patient relationship that had been so central in American health care since the late nineteenth century.[46] Under a system of "socialized medicine," the doctors and insurers said, the federal government, not doctors, would make decisions about patient care. For many years after the success of the AMA's lobbying campaign, most liberals shied away from proposing any legislation to provide federal health insurance for all Americans.

In 1957, however, a group of congressional Democrats decided to push for a much narrower plan that would provide insurance to cover the costs of hospital visits only for older Americans through Social Security. The plan had first been discussed at the end of the Truman administration, when it became clear that health insurance for people of all ages stood no chance of passage. The AFL-CIO took the lead in putting the plan together, and the Social Security Administration provided assistance, though the Eisenhower administration never endorsed the plan. Many health-care experts commended the proposal, even though it was much more limited than Truman's proposal.

Most data confirmed that a huge portion of the elderly population in the United States lacked access to health insurance to cover the cost of hospital stays, doctor visits, and prescription drugs. "I am eighty years old and for 10 years I have been living on a bare nothing," one retired schoolteacher explained to Congress. "Two meals a day, one egg, a soup, because I want to be independent . . . I worked

so hard that I have pernicious anemia, $9.95 for a little bottle of
liquid for shots, wholesale, I couldn't pay for it."[47] The burden for
their care often fell on their families, welfare programs, and charitable organizations. Otherwise, they simply survived as long as they
could without any care at all. The situation worsened as health-care
costs for the elderly escalated as a result of the advent of antibiotics,
revolutionary surgical procedures to alleviate heart disease, and
other medical breakthroughs. Doctors were devoting much more of
their time to elderly patients.[48] Hospitals expanded in size as the population of elderly people grew, and there were more ways to treat
their illnesses. There were also good political reasons for Democrats
to support government health insurance for the elderly despite Truman's experience. The elderly were seen by a large majority of Americans as a "deserving" group who were not being well served by
private insurance. By placing benefits for the elderly under Social
Security and paying for them with the Social Security tax, the sponsors of the bill hoped to capitalize on the popularity of the existing
program.

The sponsors believed that the way they had packaged their proposal, along with the support of organized labor, would soften the
opposition. They were wrong. The more limited Medicare proposal
came under the same attacks as had President Truman's proposal for
national health insurance for all Americans. The AMA resuscitated
the charge of "socialized medicine" and conducted a fierce lobbying
campaign in Washington and congressional districts to demonize
the bill.

Organized labor was a driving force in the campaign for Medicare in the late 1950s, primarily through the National Council of
Senior Citizens, an organization with more than 500,000 active
members that was a creation of the AFL-CIO. In the 1950s, a small
cohort of labor leaders had taken an interest in the health-care problems of the elderly, and in 1960 they formed a small group called the

Senior Citizens for Kennedy that persuaded the future president to pay attention to the issue. Nelson Cruikshank, a former Methodist minister who had worked for the Farm Security Administration and the War Manpower Commission and had served as director of the AFL-CIO's Department of Social Security, was one of the major players. The Democratic National Committee and the AFL-CIO worked with this group to launch the National Council of Senior Citizens in July 1961, with the help of Walter Reuther and the UAW. The first president was Aime Forand, the original congressional sponsor of Medicare in 1957. The executive director of the organization was the former director of public relations for the AFL-CIO. The National Council of Senior Citizens lobbied members of Congress, convened rallies, spread its message in the media, and ran letter-writing campaigns.

In early 1962, President Kennedy called on Congress to pass Medicare legislation that would provide hospital insurance to the elderly. In 1961 and 1962, AMPAC—the political arm of the AMA—"educated" voters by sending speakers and pamphlets about the dangers of Medicare to approximately fifty key congressional districts. The AMA sent posters and pamphlets to doctors to be displayed in their waiting rooms; the topic "socialized medicine and you" was addressed in terms of the dangers patients faced from Medicare, primarily the inevitable restrictions on their freedom to choose their own doctors.[49] In Operation Coffee Cup, the AMA's women's auxiliary—the wives of doctors—gathered groups of women in their homes to discuss the perils in the bill. The coffee klatches were advertised as informal events, but they were carefully orchestrated, and the hosts had very specific instructions about what to say. Women who attended were taught how to write to legislators and generate petition drives against the legislation. The women who ran this operation liked to play a record that featured Ronald Reagan, a former Hollywood actor and spokesman for GE, attacking the proposal. "One of the traditional methods of imposing statism or socialism on a people," Reagan said, "has been by way of medicine."[50] Admiral Ben Moreell, one of the founders of the Americans for Constitutional Action, warned, "We should now be aware that we are threatened by total state socialism, an ancient tyranny under modern disguise."[51]

Fiscal conservatives in Congress also went after the bill by raising concerns—stemming from the connection of Medicare to Social Security—that the cost of health-care benefits under Medicare would force the government to raise Social Security taxes on workers and employees to intolerable levels (then considered to be anything above 10 percent). The chief opponent in the House in 1962 and 1963 was Wilbur Mills, the fiscally conservative chairman of the Ways and Means Committee, which had jurisdiction over both Social Security and the Medicare bill. Mills had been holding up the bill since it was first proposed in 1957. In 1960, he had tried to take some of the steam out of Medicare when he and the Oklahoma senator Robert Kerr proposed Medical Assistance for the Aged (known as the Kerr-Mills Act), which provided means-tested assistance to elderly Americans who had too much money to receive welfare but too little to purchase any kind of health insurance. The benefits were funded by states and the federal government and administered by the states. The Kerr-Mills Act was limited, and a number of states didn't even adopt the program, so demands for Medicare continued despite its passage.

Ways and Means debated Kennedy's Medicare proposal, but it never left the committee. Mills had reported to the White House that he didn't have the votes necessary to pass Medicare in his committee, nor did the bill have the support of a majority of the House. President Kennedy's legislative team, though it pushed for Medicare, agreed with Mills in his assessment of the dimensions of the support they could expect for the bill.[52] Mills's primary objection to the bill was the risk Medicare posed to Social Security, though he subscribed to some of the arguments of the AMA, perhaps motivated by threats from the organization that it might make trouble for him in his normally safe district in Arkansas. Based on all the polling data, Mills anticipated that older people would be disappointed when they discovered that the administration's program covered only hospital bills. He predicted they would insist that Congress expand the health-care benefits to include doctors' costs, which would require increases in Social Security taxes. When he assumed the presidency, Johnson had pleaded with Mills to change his position and had his staff rework the proposal to satisfy some of Mills's budgetary concerns, but still the chairman wouldn't budge.

Despite the opposition, the pressure for reform kept mounting. With average hospital costs rising from $29 a day in 1960 to $40 a day in 1964, health insurance providers were continually raising their premiums. These companies charged the highest rates to the elderly because they were considered "bad risks." Only about one in four elderly people had adequate hospital insurance. The American Hospital Association, whose members were overburdened with caring for the elderly, indicated that it supported some kind of federal insurance. Approximately two-thirds of the electorate supported Medicare by 1964.[53]

In the spring of 1964, the AMA heard that the conservative Ways and Means Democrat John Watts from Kentucky, who had been one of the main opponents of Medicare on the committee, unexpectedly started telling colleagues that he might be willing to support a compromise version of the legislation. AMA representatives mobilized to make it clear that they would respond with a show of force in his home state if Watts switched from a no to a yes on the legislation. The association sent word to local government and business officials in the state that it might formally endorse the surgeon general's 1964 landmark report that smoking caused cancer—a report that would certainly deal a crippling blow to the economy of Watts's tobacco-producing district. This was enough to make Watts reconsider. Once the congressman announced that he could not vote for the Medicare legislation under any circumstances, the AMA informed Kentucky's local leaders it was backing off its threat.[54] In 1964, when the Senate added a version of Medicare as an amendment to Social Security legislation that the House had passed, Mills killed the amendment in conference committee.

The election of 1964 changed the situation in Congress. The National Council of Senior Citizens boasted that the election had been a "magnificent mandate" for Medicare. While exaggerated rhetoric was commonplace after elections, in this case the argument happened to be true. The Democratic caucus in the House finally reflected national opinion on the issue. Approximately thirty-seven legislators who had been considered "friends" of the AMA were defeated.[55] Many Republicans felt that Goldwater's opposition to the proposal had been one of the biggest factors in their poor showing in the election. "Social Security and medical care were primary issues in 1964," the Ohio Republican Frank Bow acknowledged, "and the Republican response on these issues was a major factor in the disaster that befell us."[56] There had been a sizable expansion in the number of members who wanted to vote for Medicare. Somewhere between forty-two and forty-four new members of the House were Medicare supporters, and they all were prepared to fight for it. The Ways and Means Committee now had a majority in favor of the bill, which meant that Wilbur Mills could no longer prevent his committee from voting on a bill. If Mills managed to change the minds of his members, a strong majority in the House would probably be willing to force the bill out of his committee anyway, and out of Rules too. Mills, according to Larry O'Brien, had mellowed in his opposition to Medicare; he "wasn't going to take on a crusade that was doomed to failure."[57]

On January 5, 1965, the day after the president's State of the Union address, Mills announced to the administration that his committee's first order of business would be Medicare. He had already given a speech in Little Rock in which he announced his support for Medicare—though he didn't specify his support for every detail of the proposed legislation—but the biggest threat to Medicare was no longer Wilbur Mills. It was the Republicans who would siphon off votes from the administration's proposal to build coalitions behind their own plans. No longer were any Republicans arguing against the federal government's providing help for the elderly. Now the Republicans had legislation they claimed would do a better job than what the administration was proposing. Republicans were hoping they could persuade Democrats on the Ways and Means Committee and in the House to compromise on a bill that would have greater bipartisan support—and would give the federal government less power over the health-care industry than the administration's proposal did. Muting some of its rhetoric about socialized medicine, the AMA focused on pursuing the cheapest alternative. On January 27, two Ways and Means opponents to the White House measure, the Missouri Republican Thomas Curtis and Sydney Herlong, a Florida Democrat, sponsored a proposal written by AMA staffers and informally called Eldercare, which offered voluntary medical insurance to the elderly on the basis of need; it was an expanded version of Medical Assistance for the Aged (Kerr-Mills). States would have to choose to participate in the program, and each would have the power to set its own rules, at an estimated total cost of up to $2.1 billion per year to the federal government. People over sixty-five who qualified could purchase Blue Cross and Blue Shield or commercial insurance and receive subsidies depending on their income. The states, drawing on federal and state general revenues, would supplement the government funds with contributions from the participants. This plan gained little traction in Congress, even among Republicans.

Other Republicans decided to offer a bolder plan. On February 4, the ranking Republican on Ways and Means, John Byrnes of Wisconsin, introduced his own plan, nicknamed Bettercare. The claim here was that the plan differed fundamentally from the administration's proposal, in that it offered more generous benefits to the elderly, particularly the coverage of physicians' costs, that it was an entirely voluntary plan, and that it would have no impact on the Social Security tax. Retirees who chose to participate in Bettercare would be covered for hospital bills, doctor bills, and selected patient services. The projected cost to the government would be $3.4 billion per year. The payroll tax would not finance any of the benefits in the Byrnes bill; the federal government would pay two-thirds of the cost through income tax revenues, while participants would match the federal contribution with what Byrnes called a "premium," but what might just as accurately have been called a tax.

Byrnes's proposal did not come out of left field. The Wisconsin Republican was a business-friendly Republican who represented a largely middle-class constituency in the rural Eighth District, though his constituency did include the cities of Green Bay and Appleton. Many considered Byrnes to be one of the smartest and most honest legislators in Congress, a fitting complement to Wilbur Mills. On social policy, he was relatively liberal, having been deeply influenced by his college course work with liberal labor economists at the University of Wisconsin, from which he graduated in 1936. Byrnes was also extremely proud of his state's progressive heritage.

Like Mills, Byrnes wanted to protect Social Security from the costs of health care. His bill was an effort to keep Republicans in the game when passage of some legislation seemed inevitable. It was also a genuine attempt to promote legislation that he thought was superior to King-Anderson, more generous than what Johnson had proposed. And in many ways, his proposal was more *liberal* than King-Anderson. His proposal, for instance, covered doctor's services inside and outside of hospitals, as well as outpatient services. His program would be funded by the progressive income tax system rather than the regressive Social Security tax.[58]

The tide had turned since November. The issue was no longer whether there would be a health-care program but which health-care program there would be. Wilbur Cohen, the assistant secretary of health, education, and welfare, acknowledged that John Byrnes's Bettercare proposal provided generous benefits under a voluntary program that did not depend on Social Security taxes. The bill had real support in Ways and Means, enough to threaten the passage of King-Anderson. President Johnson remained focused on pushing Medicare through the Ways and Means Committee. He mulled over with his advisers and some legislators the idea of a combination of programs, and he always recognized that he would have to give Mills credit for any change.[59] As he had told Wilbur Cohen, "You get him [Mills] something, though . . . if labor will buy, that he can call a Mills bill, that's what it amounts to, and you're smart enough to do that."[60] Most important, Mills himself had been talking with Johnson's team for more than a year about the potential for some kind of combination that included physicians' costs and an expansion of Kerr-Mills.[61]

Wilbur Mills knew there was enough support in his committee and in the House to pass the administration's Medicare proposal, and rather than try to block the train, he decided to climb on board. On March 2, after weeks of closed-door sessions, the chairman surprised most of the participants in the committee room with a bold move that reframed the entire debate. They had spent the afternoon reviewing Byrnes's plan, which Wilbur Cohen and the Social Security actuary Robert Myers admitted was financially sound. Other Democrats who backed Medicare, among them Representative Eugene Keogh of New York and Senator Jennings Randolph of West Virginia, observed the interaction with growing interest in the

Republican alternative. Mills too grasped that Byrnes's program was sound. "You could see the light bulb flash on his mind," recounted one participant in the room.[62]

Just moments into the session, after a year of discussions about this idea and that one, this bill and that one, this way of funding and that one, the chairman leaned back in his chair, looked at Wilbur Cohen, and said, "Well, now let's see. Maybe it would be a good idea if we put all three of these bills together. You go back and work this out overnight and see what there is to this." At a stroke, Mills had created a "three-layer-cake" that combined Medicare, Eldercare, and Bettercare into one big bill. "It was all over," one committee member said. "The rest would be details. In thirty seconds, a $2 billion bill was launched, and the greatest departure in the social security laws in thirty years was brought about."[63] "The effect of this ingenious plan is, as Mr. Mills told me, to make it almost certain that nobody will vote against the bill when it comes on the floor of the House," Cohen reported to the president. "It should be clear that Mr. Mills would retain all the basic elements of the King-Anderson program financed through social security but add to the bill a supplemental health insurance benefit which many aged people would be willing to purchase because the Government would subsidize out of general revenues some portion of its cost . . . I feel reasonably sure that now after these several weeks of Committee sessions Mills now feels he has developed a combined package approach which is unassailable politically from any serious Republican attack."[64] All that remained to be achieved was a final version, the approval of both chambers of Congress, and the signature of Lyndon Johnson.

Over a period of three months, Wilbur Mills had transformed himself from the chief opponent to the architect of the new law. Combining the three bills had resolved the fiscal and political concerns that had prevented Mills from signing on. The new plan kept the costs of physicians separate from the portion of the program that was funded by Social Security taxes. Hospital stays would be covered by Social Security taxes. All seniors would have to enroll in the hospital program, but insurance for doctor bills would be voluntary; it would be covered by income tax revenue and monthly payments from participants. The bill seemed politically invincible. Cohen explained, "In effect, Mills had taken the AMA's ammunition, put it in the Republicans' gun, and blown both of them off the map."[65]

Mills and the administration had evidence that public opinion was on their side. According to Louis Harris, a majority of Americans supported health-care insurance for the elderly. When given a choice between a program that was funded by the federal government and one that was privately financed, the public supported a government plan by four to three.[66]

Mills knew he needed to move swiftly to prevent opposition from coalescing. His staff and the administration staff would have to finish the final legislation in time for the committee vote he announced for March 15. The schedule offered staffs only thirteen days to draft what would be an enormous bill.[67] Ironically, Mills could speed up the drafting because he had slowed it down for so long. All the key players from the Social Security Administration and the Ways and Means Committee staff were so familiar with every detail of the various bills, after years of negotiations, that they were prepared to work at great speed to finish a new version in executive session.

Johnson was surprised by what Mills had wrought. In a revealing phone conversation with Wilbur Cohen after the announcement of the three-layer cake, Johnson asked many questions about the details of the legislation. Cohen walked him through a number of key provisions.[68]

The legislation carried in the committee on a straight party vote, 17 to 8, with Republicans voting in favor of John Byrnes's proposal, which they were still not ready to abandon, even though it seemed to most observers that Mills's version would win the day. Mills was the hero. When he walked down to the well of the House to introduce the bill, his colleagues stood and applauded. On April 8, the House of Representatives passed the Social Security Amendments of 1965 by 313 to 115. Fifty-nine southern Democrats and 65 Republicans— who joined 189 northern Democrats in the majority—had broken from the conservative coalition. The minority was the remainder of the conservative coalition; it included 40 southern Democrats and 73 Republicans as well as two northern Democrats. The actual vote was not as bipartisan as it appeared in the end. Before the final vote, Republicans had used a technical procedure to allow the House to get a vote on an alternative based on the Byrnes bill. Although that vote failed, it did so narrowly, by 236 to 191, with 128 out of 138 Republicans in favor of the Byrnes substitute.[69]

Part A of the Social Security Amendments offered federal health insurance for hospitalization costs to people sixty-five and over, paid for by Social Security taxes. Part B provided voluntary insurance for the cost of physicians' services, paid for by a combination of monthly contributions from participants and federal contributions from general revenue. Part C of the legislation, Medicaid, expanded Kerr-Mills with a larger means-tested program for people in the existing welfare categories—aid to the elderly, aid to the permanently and totally disabled, aid to families with dependent children, and aid to the blind— that was administered by the states and paid for by state and federal money.

The American Medical Association was resigned to defeat. The tempered mood in the physicians' community was clear when, while the Senate deliberated, twenty-four thousand or so doctors arrived in New York City to attend the association's 114th annual convention. The House of Delegates, its decision-making body, ignored calls by some state chapters that the AMA tell its doctors they should refuse to accept patients whose bills would be covered by the program. Instead, the House of Delegates took the position that individual physicians had the ultimate right to determine whether a program was good for the quality of health care. The new president of the association, James Appel, a fifty-eight-year-old surgeon from rural Pennsylvania who staunchly opposed Medicare, made an appeal in his inaugural address to fellow physicians to reject boycott proposals, which he said would set poor examples of citizenship. He warned that "unethical tactics"—boycotts or strikes against Medicare—would result in Congress's passing even more stringent federal regulations. "We do not have the right, either as physicians or citizens, to deliberately violate a law, or to violate the spirit of the law or its intent."[70]

Now all that stood between America and Medicare were fifty-one votes the White House needed to get in the Senate. The administration did not anticipate a filibuster.[71] Conservatives were in no shape to mount one, and Republicans had little interest in joining one. Mills, one of the most powerful southern Democrats, had designed the legislation, and it was likely that others from the region would support his bill.

The real risk for Johnson came from liberals. He needed to make certain that liberal Democrats in the Senate did not undo Mills's compromise by increasing the cost of the bill in any significant way. Mills would not accept any additional strains on the Social Security tax. He had a winning bill in hand and did not want to give the bill's flailing opponents an argument they could use to weaken support on the floor. President Johnson also wanted a bipartisan vote of confidence in this historic expansion of the role of government so that it couldn't be attacked down the line as a "Democratic bill."

There were efforts to liberalize the bill in the Senate. Though every Democrat understood the risks of adding amendments, in the post-1964 atmosphere some senators refused to be constrained by the traditional pragmatic warnings from their colleagues. A substantial number of amendments from liberal Democrats made it into the final package.

The total cost of the Senate bill was approximately $800 million more than the House bill, enough to raise serious concerns in the White House about what Mills's response would be and whether this cost inflation would jeopardize bipartisan support in the House. On July 9, the Senate passed the legislation, 68 to 21.

During the conference committee, Mills came to the rescue of the version he had crafted in the House. His power as the chairman of Ways and Means enabled him to dominate the conference committee deliberations in a ruthless fashion. Legislators were not about to challenge him, nor were administration officials, who would need Mills on other measures and didn't want to give any hint of a desire to try rolling over the chairman. When senators in the committee saw that Wilbur Cohen, Johnson's point man on Social Security and Medicare and the administration's representative in the conference committee deliberations, was standing behind Mills, they realized there was no point in pushing for the liberalizations that had been included in the Senate version. Senators Russell Long, the majority whip, and Florida's George Smathers, one of Johnson's closest friends in the Senate, also allied with Mills to push back against their colleagues at this point. In the closed room of the committee, shrouded by secrecy, without interest groups or reporters present, a hallmark of this insular era in congressional politics, and with most members deferring to his expertise, Mills systematically knocked out almost every Senate amendment that increased costs, and he shifted specialist services from the mandatory to the voluntary section of the program, thus protecting the Social Security tax and reducing the number of doctors who could complain that they were included in the mandatory program. Larry O'Brien said, "There was nobody in that conference who was going to buck Wilbur Mills on the House side and probably there was little appetite to buck him on the Senate side either."[72]

Medicare did not pose any genuine threat to the private health-care system, despite all the overblown rhetoric of the AMA,[73] but in an effort to design the program in such a way that physicians would buy into it and to further undercut lingering claims that the program would "control" the medical industry, Mills made one decision that would eventually result in exploding costs for the program. He demanded that the law authorize hospitals and doctors, rather than the federal government, to determine what "reasonable charges" should be for their services. He made this move based on the mistaken assumption that it would not result in any huge increases in the costs. Johnson accepted Mills's proposal on the same grounds.

On July 27, the Senate passed the conference committee measure by 70 to 24 and the House by 307 to 116.

Before signing the bill, Johnson wanted to make sure that doctors were fully on board. In late June, he had invited AMA representatives to attend a meeting at the White House. He began by asking if they would agree to send volunteers to help care for soldiers in Vietnam. The delegation said yes. After expressing his appreciation to the group, the president then asked the White House press corps to question the delegates about their Vietnam commitment. When one reporter asked a question many suspected had been planted by the White House—Was the AMA going to boycott Medicare?—Lyndon Johnson interrupted to say, "These men are going to get doctors to go to Vietnam where they might be killed. Medicare is the law of the land. Of course, they'll support the law of the land." Looking at the president of the AMA, James Appel, Johnson said, "Tell him." Appel, realizing that he had been put on the spot, said, "We are, after all, law abiding citizens, and we have every intention of obeying the new law."[74]

On July 30, the president traveled to Independence, Missouri, to sign the legislation at the library of Harry Truman's presidential museum. Truman, eighty-one years of age and still scarred from the hell the AMA had given him over his health-care plan in 1949 and

1950—it slammed the proposal as a "monstrosity of Bolshevik bu-reaucracy"—sat proudly by Johnson's side during the ceremony. More than two hundred people, including thirty-one members of Congress and Vice President Humphrey, were packed into the room to watch. The legislation was a key moment for the Great Society and for American health-care policy. For decades, politicians had unsuccessfully fought to have the federal government provide health insurance. As a result, the federal government had remained a minor, usually inconsequential player in the health-care system. But now, after what had happened in the closed rooms of Ways and Means, things would be different. The federal government would be the insurer of first resort for the nation's elderly and indigent citizens. The right to health care for the elderly and the poor had been enshrined through the Great Society.

There was plenty for liberals to be disappointed about. The legislation was a far cry from the program President Truman had proposed. It created a two-tiered structure that provided federal support only to a segment of the population. Congress had also rejected any cost controls for hospitals and doctors.[75]

Yet most liberals were extremely pleased with the outcome. They understood that the program was a huge step forward in creating a social safety net. It would guarantee that most elderly citizens no longer had to fear they would be unable to pay for hospitals and doctors. Liberals also believed that more was coming. They saw Medicare as an opening wedge for the government to expand its role in the health-care system, eventually bring more groups under its coverage, and ultimately establish a universal program. As Robert Ball, another key figure in the Social Security Administration, later said, "We all saw insurance for the elderly as a fallback position, which we advocated solely because it seemed to have the best chance politically . . . We expected Medicare to be the first step toward universal national health insurance."[76]

201

ENSURING THE RIGHT TO VOTE

The dramatic passage of the Civil Rights Act of 1964 had given civil rights leaders greater clout in Congress, and the liberal gains in the 1964 election, in which approximately 94 percent of registered African Americans voted for Johnson, had demonstrated that the movement could deliver votes. The activists were energized by their triumphs, and they pushed for a new civil rights bill that would give the federal government greater authority to enforce the Fifteenth Amendment, which made it illegal to deny anyone the right to vote based on "race, color, or previous condition of servitude."

After Reconstruction, the federal government did nothing to counteract the malicious effects of literacy tests, residency tests, and poll taxes that southern states passed to make voting extraordinarily difficult, if not impossible, for African Americans—and poor whites too, unless they were exempted by grandfather clauses. The number of African Americans registered to vote in southern states, where the great majority of the African American population lived, remained small throughout the first half of the twentieth century. A mere 3 percent of the five million eligible southern African Americans were registered to vote when World War II began. For almost ninety years, Congress did little to rectify the situation. The Civil Rights Act of 1957 had been so watered down that it relied on local juries, on which only whites could serve, to enforce the voting rights of African Americans in the South. The civil rights legislation of 1960 granted local judges more power to register voters, but they were generally white segregationists who did little or nothing to expand the franchise.

There had been some progress by the early 1960s, but it owed little to Congress. A coalition of civil rights organizations that included SNCC, SCLC, CORE, and the NAACP had established the Voter Registration Project, which provided money to grassroots activists who worked frenetically in southern states to help African Americans circumvent Jim Crow barriers and get registered. In 1964, there had been a higher turnout of African American voters in the South than in any previous presidential election, although almost 57 percent of the African American population there were still not registered to vote.

The Supreme Court was also influential. Under the leadership of Chief Justice Earl Warren, the Court made a series of important rulings between 1962 and 1964 that established the one-man-one-vote rule for state and federal legislative elections. For decades, state legislatures had avoided redrawing voting district lines for U.S. House and state legislature seats, even though rural districts generally had declining or stagnant populations and urban districts were experiencing huge population growth. Many of the urban districts had heavy concentrations of African Americans and young liberal whites, while the rural districts were often all white and politically conservative. In their decisions, the Supreme Court required states to redraw legislative districts so that every voter had equal representation in legislatures.

But the Court rulings and the Civil Rights Act of 1964 were not enough. Registration rates for African Americans in the Deep South remained extremely low. In Louisiana, 32 percent of African American voters were registered; in Alabama, 19 percent; and in Mississippi, 6 percent.[77] Johnson wanted Congress to empower the federal government to supersede state and local laws that prevented African Americans from voting. As he told Martin Luther King, voting rights "will be the greatest breakthrough of anything not even excepting this '64 act, I think the greatest achievement of my administration."[78]

Johnson was confident that when he sent his proposal to Congress, most Republicans, all of whom had seen Goldwater vote against the Civil Rights Act and get buried under an electoral landslide, would support it. As one liberal Republican explained, "Republicans have nothing to gain from being *for* a civil rights bill, but they have everything to *lose* by being against one."[79] A month after the election, without any public fanfare, Johnson had instructed Nicholas Katzenbach, who was slated to become the next attorney general, to move forward with drafting a voting rights proposal. Johnson told Katzenbach he wanted to have a "simple, effective" method of getting African Americans registered to vote.[80]

Johnson had told civil rights leaders he wanted to pass voting rights legislation—but not right away. He was confident the Eighty-ninth Congress would pass a strong law, but first he wanted to use his huge new congressional majorities to pass education and health-care bills, and he wanted to do this in January, before initiating what he expected to be a lengthy congressional debate over voting rights.

The leaders of the civil rights movement were not happy with this approach. They didn't want to wait any longer and risk losing the opportunity they felt they had earned. The desegregation of public facilities had been a major victory, but if they somehow failed to secure basic voting rights, their legislative gains could be reversed, as they had been after Reconstruction. For civil rights leaders, waiting meant that the civil rights movement could lose the momentum it had gained from the Civil Rights Act and from the election. Roy Wilkins, executive director of the NAACP, called on Democrats and Republicans to support the idea that the "Federal Government must assume an expanded and even more vigorous role in removing the unconstitutional barriers to Negro voting."[81] Martin Luther King Jr. appealed to Johnson's self-interest by emphasizing the electoral rewards that could accrue to the president and the Democratic Party from a voting rights bill. "The only states that you didn't carry in the South, the five Southern states, have less than 40 percent of the Negroes registered to vote," he told the president. "It's very interesting to notice. And I think a professor at the University of Texas in a recent article, brought this out very clearly. So it demonstrates that it's so important to get Negroes registered to vote in large numbers in the South. And it would be this coalition of the Negro vote and the moderate white vote that will really make the new South."[82]

Sensing Johnson's intransigence on scheduling an early push for voting rights, King switched his strategy from pressuring the executive to pressuring Congress. The civil rights movement mobilized the grass roots to issue what King believed was the most effective threat: there would be a "march on the ballot boxes by the thousands" if Congress did not act on legislation. "We are not asking," King warned. "We are demanding the ballot."[83]

He was not bluffing. King and other members of the SCLC traveled to Selma, Alabama, in January to draw national attention to local protesters organized by SNCC who had been conducting marches to demand full voting rights. Selma, which had served as a center for Confederate manufacturing during the Civil War, was a natural place to highlight the issue of voting rights. "Selma is a city that's had the most oppressive history against Negroes in the South," said King's assistant Andrew Young.[84] More than half the population was black, but only 2.1 percent of eligible African Americans were registered to vote.

Selma's sheriff, James Clark, was another Bull Connor—a perfect foil for the civil rights movement. He inspired fear in almost everyone he confronted, and he delighted in bullying his opponents. He liked to say that civil rights activists needed to "overcome me." He had a preference for military-style garb, and he wore mirrored sunglasses and a button that said, "NEVER!" King anticipated that attacks on unarmed marchers in Selma would win national sympathy for their cause, and that was exactly what happened. When Clark violently jabbed his billy club right in the neck of Annie Lee Cooper, who had been waiting in line for hours to register to vote, the fifty-four-year-old woman turned around and punched him. The sheriff fell to the ground. As Clark's men held her down to the ground, the embarrassed sheriff got back on his feet and brutally beat her with his nightstick, leaving wounds on her face. Photographs of the attack and the victim appeared in newspapers across the country.[85]

Congress felt the pressure. Clarence Mitchell, the lobbyist for the Leadership Conference on Civil Rights, and the Illinois senator Paul Douglas, who was threatening to propose his own bill, met with the Senate majority whip, Russell Long of Louisiana, to hear his thoughts on voting rights legislation, and they were pleasantly surprised to find that Long, who had participated in the 1964 filibuster, was in an affable mood and indicated he would support the use of federal examiners to enroll voters in states where 40 percent of African Americans were not registered to vote.[86]

President Johnson was outraged by the violence against African Americans in Selma and saw the growing sentiment in Congress to act. He knew the Eighty-ninth Congress favored voting rights, and now he understood that he could reconstitute the bipartisan coalition that had ended the filibuster against the Civil Rights Act and also stop a filibuster before it began. Before sending a proposal to Congress, he instructed Katzenbach to contact Everett Dirksen secretly and see if they could work out an agreement on the framework of legislation. It was clear that the bill would easily pass in the House. Johnson predicted that Dirksen would get on board, and if he did, the legislation would also sail through the Senate.

Dirksen had supported the civil rights legislation of 1957, which was primarily a voting rights bill, and he was prepared to support a voting rights bill again. He had watched the dramatic struggles of the civil rights movement, had played a pivotal role in passing the 1964 legislation, and believed the time had come for the federal government to ensure that African Americans got real voting rights. "The right to vote," Dirksen said in a television and radio address in Illinois, "is still an issue in this free country. There has to be a real remedy. There has to be something durable and worthwhile. This cannot go on forever, this denial of the right to vote by ruses and devices and tests and whatever the mind can contrive to either make it very difficult or to make it impossible to vote."[87] Dirksen understood that after Goldwater, Republicans were in an extremely vulnerable position, and he was determined to keep the party relevant. This meant, in Dirksen's mind, staying out front on important issues. Voting rights was an important issue.

The negotiations in Dirksen's office proceeded, accompanied by the familiar rituals of deliberating, drafting, smoking, and drinking. Dirksen never lost an opportunity to stress his growing importance as a power broker; he often mentioned his most recent telephone conversation with Johnson and stressed his close collaboration with Katzenbach, next to whom he sat at the head of the conference table, to the consternation of Senator Mansfield, who sat on one side. While Dirksen postured and boasted, Katzenbach set the terms of the discussion. Johnson, Katzenbach said, wanted the legislation to have a trigger that would automatically suspend literacy and any other racially discriminatory tests in states where less than 50 percent of the population had registered or voted in the 1964 election. If there were at least twenty complaints in a specific political subdivision that voting rights had been violated, the attorney general could instruct the U.S. Civil Service Commission to send federal examiners into those areas to replace local examiners registering voters and supervising federal, state, or local elections. The attorney general could also move forward if there were other indications that local officials were violating the Fifteenth Amendment. The final recommendation from the administration was that southern states be required to submit any changes they wanted to make in voting procedures, including locations of polling stations and the composition of districts, to the Department of Justice for preclearance. The states would have to prove that any change would not have a discriminatory effect. This rule would apply to any state, or any counties within a state, that had less than 50 percent of its population registered to vote in 1960 and 1964; Alabama, Georgia, Louisiana, Mississippi, South Carolina, and Virginia were states in this category, as were some counties in North Carolina.[88]

Where Dirksen and the administration disagreed was over the degree of power that should be delegated to the attorney general.[89] In addition to the traditional aversion of the GOP to strengthening the attorney general, there were fears among Republicans that federal power over voting rights could be used for partisan purposes. Dirksen's preference was to empower federal judges to appoint examiners to investigate accusations.

On March 2, with the negotiations still secret, Dirksen publicly announced to reporters that he favored voting rights legislation. He predicted there would not be much of a filibuster. "There might be some talk on the floor," he said, "but I wouldn't put the filibuster tag on it."[90]

As the administration and Dirksen negotiated the remaining details, the protests in Alabama intensified. On March 7, approximately six hundred protesters gathered to march from Selma to Montgomery for voting rights. The protesters began their march by kneeling and praying for God to guide them "through a wilderness of state troopers." They marched in double file across the Edmund Pettus Bridge over the Alabama River. When they reached the edge of the city's business district, fifty helmeted troopers awaited them. "Turn around and go back to your church," shouted one officer.

The marchers couldn't have turned around even if they'd wanted to. Sheriff Clark had stationed some possemen on horseback to surround them. When the activists knelt down to pray, the police and state troopers attacked them with nightsticks and electric cattle prods, fired tear gas at them, and, as the protesters scrambled to escape the chaos, charged at them a second time. "Get the Niggers off the streets!" one of the possemen yelled. Police horses trampled some of the wounded activists who were lying bloodied on the ground. "I've never seen anything like it in my life," the SNCC chairman, John Lewis, whose skull was fractured in the melee, told fellow activists.[91] White spectators cheered the police as if they had just scored a touchdown.[92]

The activists insisted they would not be deterred. Speaking at Brown Chapel AME Church before a group of about six hundred protesters, many of them covered with bandages and blood, one of Dr. King's aides warned, "If we stop now, we go back to yesterday, but yesterday is too miserable to live. We can't go back now."[93]

Americans watched these scenes on their television sets, most of them still black and white. ABC *Nightly News* interrupted its evening film, *Judgment at Nuremberg,* to cover the event live.[94] The vivid television images of the protests and violence on "Bloody Sunday" brought the reality of racial violence into American living rooms with an immediacy words or still images in newspapers never had. Viewers saw the horrendous violence being inflicted on African Americans who were simply demanding what many considered a basic right in any democracy—the right to cast a ballot to choose their leaders. With each film clip broadcast on the nightly news, the anger and disbelief outside the Deep South grew.

The shock in Washington was equally intense. Members of Congress, like other Americans, knew something had to be done about what they were witnessing. Speaker McCormack called the attacks a "disgraceful exercise of arbitrary power." Michigan's James O'Hara condemned the police action as "a savage action, storm trooper style, under direction of a reckless demagogue." Unaware of how close the administration and Dirksen were to finishing a deal on legislation, Senator Joseph Clark, an advocate of voting rights since the 1950s, proclaimed that a bill was urgently needed and that he and other Democrats would sponsor their own bills if the president didn't send them something soon. The House Judiciary chairman, Celler, said that if he didn't receive word from the president "shortly," then "I'm going to offer my own bill."[95]

"What the public felt on Monday," said Johnson's special assistant and counsel Harry McPherson, "in my opinion, was the deepest sense of outrage it has ever felt on the civil rights question."[96] Many southerners demonstrated their support for the protesters, outraged as well by what they had seen from the authorities in their region.[97] The president denounced the "brutality" that had taken place when "Negro citizens of Alabama" simply tried to "dramatize their deep and sincere interest in attaining the precious right to vote."

The activists were not finished. James Forman of SNCC, who criticized King for having become too willing to compromise, planned a second march from Selma to Montgomery on March 9. The federal district judge Frank Johnson issued a temporary restraining order to stop the march, on the grounds that terrible violence might ensue and he needed some time to figure out a solution that would keep the marchers safe. Judge Johnson, an Eisenhower appointee who had made a number of important pro-civil-rights rulings and whom Governor Wallace derided as an "intigratin', carpetbaggin', scallawagin', baldfaced liar," was now presenting King with the choice whether or not to participate in a march that had been enjoined by a judge sympathetic to his cause.

Johnson contacted Buford Ellington, the former governor of Tennessee, urging him to persuade Wallace to allow the march to take place.[98] The president didn't want to send in federal troops, concerned that he would trigger a fierce response from southerners who saw this as excessive federal intervention in their racist affairs. Privately, King was uncertain about having another march; he was fearful for his own life and the lives of the people he was leading. But the protesters would not stop; they moved forward. Bill Moyers told Johnson that King said he was under intense pressure from "left-wingers" who "will not let the day go by without some symbol, of a march" to establish the principle "to march."[99]

To prevent more bloodshed, King negotiated a deal with the administration and state police that the civil rights activists could walk across the Edmund Pettus Bridge over the Alabama River, where the road to Montgomery began, say prayers, and then turn around and march back into Selma.

On March 9, two thousand protesters crossed the bridge. King directed them through songs and prayer. After they had sung the anthem of the movement, "We Shall Overcome," King headed back into Selma. Many in the crowd were furious when they realized that a deal had been cut, and this exacerbated the growing divisions inside the movement between the "established leadership" and younger activists who wanted more aggressive actions against racism. In Washington, Justice officials watched the events and "breathed a sigh of relief."[100]

The fragile situation took a bad turn later that day when one of the protesters, James Reeb, a white Unitarian minister from Boston, dined with some friends at Walker's Café, an African American restaurant. After leaving the café, they got lost in an all-white neighborhood. Trying to find their way out, the men passed the Silver Moon Café, an all-white eatery that was popular with members of the Ku Klux Klan and filled with customers who didn't like what they saw through the windows, ministers who had clearly been part of the protests. Reeb was grabbed by four white men yelling, "Hey, niggers. Hey, you niggers!"[101] They beat him with a club and cracked his skull, hoping to let the white minister know what it actually felt like to be an African American living in the South. They succeeded in their goal. Reeb died two days later. Upon hearing the news, administration officials worried there would be total chaos on the streets in Selma and elsewhere.[102]

With each report about the events in Selma, another member of Congress stepped forward to demand that Johnson send a bill to Congress. In the House, the Republican congressman William McCulloch claimed that had the administration acted earlier in proposing legislation, the protests, and the bloodshed, could have been averted. Now he and a group of House Republicans threatened to introduce their own bill. The president privately welcomed their threats and criticism because he believed their demands demonstrated to voters that voting rights was a bipartisan issue. At the same time, a bipartisan group of liberal senators, including the Democrats Paul Douglas, Philip Hart, William Proxmire, and Robert Kennedy and the Republicans Jacob Javits, Clifford Case, and Hugh Scott, announced that they would introduce their own bills in the Senate if Johnson continued to stall on sending legislation to Congress. There were still a few issues to work out with Dirksen. More important, the president was hoping he could hold off on sending the bill, even if for just a few weeks; the House was wrapping up its debate on the education bill, and the Ways and Means Committee was finishing its draft of Wilbur Mills's proposed revision of the Medicare program.

But Johnson's timetable for legislation had been overtaken by events; the pressure from the civil rights protests and from inside Congress could not be resisted; he had to act. In the morning hours of March 11, after an arduous two-hour meeting, Katzenbach and Dirksen finally reached a deal. Dirksen, who felt compelled not to delay until the situation spun out of control, relented on the proposal to authorize the Justice Department to send federal registrars to enroll African Americans whose rights had been violated and agreed to the preclearance provision.[103] Katzenbach agreed to a few minor technical adjustments, including calling the registrars "examiners," to avoid a term that had been used during Reconstruction.[104]

The next day, Mansfield and Dirksen informed reporters there was a deal. Dirksen acknowledged that the legislation included a trigger that would automatically prohibit discriminatory tests in states where registration was low.

Everyone told the president he had to make a public statement about the need for voting rights legislation. "The public knows you are for the enforcement of civil rights. The Deep South knows it; that is why it went for Goldwater," Harry McPherson wrote to the president. The public, he added, had the "deepest sense of outrage" it had ever felt on civil rights. Even the White House counsel Abe Fortas, he said, who was a "reasonable man," now supported sending troops into Selma. McPherson felt that the "public wants you to express your own, present, sense of outrage."[105]

The president set up a meeting with the congressional leadership to discuss the situation. He had persuaded Speaker McCormack to extend him an "impromptu" invitation to appear before a joint session of Congress, the first of its kind since 1946. His personal appearance before Congress would indicate this was a national emergency, which was the only other time such speeches were made, except for the State of the Union address. Though Dirksen warned that they should not create a situation where opponents could say that the president "scared" Congress into passing a bill, the Senate minority leader concurred that the public needed to hear about what the government was going to do about the situation they were seeing.[106]

On March 15, Johnson appeared before a joint session of Congress to deliver a historic speech on voting rights. The chamber was filled with an overflow crowd of members lined up in the aisles. The speech began at 9:00 p.m. The legislators listened attentively to every single word, waiting to hear how the president would rally the nation behind this bill. Their first applause would not come until five minutes into the speech, after which they would not stop cheering as they interrupted him with thirty-nine ovations.[107]

Johnson placed Selma within a long struggle for freedom that began with the American Revolution. He spoke about "man's unending search for freedom" that had been on display in Lexington and Concord, at Appomattox, and now in Selma, Alabama. Johnson said that the time had come to act. "This time, on this issue, there must be no delay, no hesitation and no compromise with our purpose." The president argued that no "constitutional issue" was involved, because "the command of the Constitution is plain. There is no moral issue. It is wrong—deadly wrong—to deny any of your fellow Americans the right to vote in this country. There is no issue of States rights or national rights. There is only the struggle for human rights."

Johnson, who called African Americans the heroes of this struggle, ended with a dramatic proclamation. Embracing the rhetoric of the civil rights movement, he declared, "Their cause must be our cause, too. Because it is not just Negroes, but really it is all of us who must overcome the crippling legacy of bigotry and injustice. And, we shall overcome."

As Johnson uttered the rallying cry of a civil rights movement that was still seen as radical in the eyes of many white Americans living in the South, Richard Goodwin recalled, "There was an instant of silence, the gradually apprehended realization that the president has proclaimed, adopted as his own rallying cry, the anthem of black protest, the hymn of a hundred embattled black marchers. Seventy-seven-year-old Congressman Manny Celler—a lifetime of vigorous, often futile, fights for freedom behind him—leaped to his feet, cheering as wildly as a schoolboy at his first high school football game. Others quickly followed. In seconds almost the entire chamber—floor and gallery together—was standing; applauding . . . some stamping their feet. Tears rolled down the cheeks of Senator Mansfield of Montana. Senator Ellender of Louisiana slumped in his seat."[108]

The president sent his proposal to Congress on March 17 based on what Dirksen, Katzenbach, and Mansfield had agreed upon.

Predicting eighty votes in the Senate, Katzenbach assured the president that the trio would be able to push back against liberals who sought to expand the scope of the bill.[109] Dirksen made it clear to his colleagues and to voters that he favored the bill, so there was little doubt that southern Democrats would be unsuccessful if they attempted to mount a filibuster. Polls showed that 76 percent of the nation supported a bill. Even 49 percent of the white southerners polled between March 18 and March 25 stated that they were in favor of legislation.[110]

The pressure from the grass roots did not abate. The same day Johnson sent his proposal to Congress, Judge Johnson issued a decision stipulating that another march in Selma could move forward and that state and local police authorities had a responsibility to protect the marchers. On March 21, a small group that included King and John Lewis started another march from Selma to Montgomery that lasted four days. President Johnson, who didn't trust Wallace to keep the peace, federalized the Alabama National Guard and sent in federal marshals to maintain order. By the time the protesters gathered for a rally on their final day in Montgomery, there were almost twenty-five thousand of them, including numerous celebrities. The media captured in vivid detail the entire dramatic event.

Back in Washington, the floor debate in the Senate took some unexpected turns. Whereas the biggest challenge for Johnson with civil rights in 1964 had been the conservative coalition, now the main challenge emanated from liberals who wanted more, believing this would be their best opportunity ever to obtain a sweeping measure (just as with Medicare). Massachusetts's senator Edward "Ted" Kennedy, the youngest brother of the deceased president, pushed for an amendment that would create a national prohibition on the use of poll taxes in federal, state, and local elections. On January 23, 1964, the states had already ratified the Twenty-fourth Amendment, passed by Congress in 1962, which banned the poll tax in *federal* elections. Only

THE FIERCE URGENCY OF NOW

four states—Alabama, Mississippi, Texas, and Virginia—still collected a poll tax, though provisions allowing poll taxes remained on the books of twenty-seven state and local governments.[111] But liberals now wanted Congress to ban the use of poll taxes in state and local elections as well. The reason the poll tax angered activists, besides the fact that it symbolized the era when southerners had overturned Reconstruction, was that it was still imposed in local elections; Sheriff Clark was elected by voters who paid a poll tax. Congress, said Roy Wilkins, needed to "sweep the last vestiges of voting discrimination into the sea."[112]

The Justice Department strongly opposed Kennedy's proposal. Katzenbach argued that including a federal ban on poll taxes, which could not be easily categorized as a device that was explicitly meant to discriminate on the basis of race—poor whites were also affected, and poll taxes were imposed in states where very few African Americans lived—could open the legislation up to constitutional challenge down the road. Johnson told liberals in numerous conversations that he didn't like the poll tax either but that every lawyer had agreed that prohibiting these mechanisms through legislation was unconstitutional.

Senator Ted Kennedy, considered a lightweight compared with his brothers, directed an unexpectedly effective campaign push for the poll tax amendment, with the support of his brother Robert, the recently elected New York senator, and almost succeeded. Ted Kennedy felt it was essential to eliminate the "oldest and most infamous of the barriers to voting in the South."[113] The Kennedy brothers proved to be an effective team. Ted tried to persuade colleagues by bombarding them with legal arguments from some top Harvard scholars who disagreed with Katzenbach. Robert relied on tougher tactics, directly warning wavering liberal senators that he would consider their vote on the poll tax amendment to be a statement as to how they felt about him and that if he was ever in the White

House—which seemed quite possible to many Democrats who believed he would challenge Johnson in the 1968 primaries and stood a good chance of winning—he would not forget how they voted.[114]

In the end, senators rejected the amendment by a narrow vote of 49 to 45. Kennedy signed on to the legislation, into which a compromise provision, designed by Mansfield and Dirksen, had been added, which allowed the attorney general to investigate the use of poll taxes in state and local elections if a specified number of complaints were made.

A few southern Democrats and conservative Republicans—led by Bourke Hickenlooper, who was still aiming to supplant the ailing Dirksen as leader of the Senate Republicans—also chimed in with proposed amendments that aimed to weaken the legislation. But they didn't have much fuel in their tank. Senator Russell, the mastermind of the southern caucus, was absent for most of the discussion, himself in treatment in the Walter Reed Hospital for a severe attack of emphysema. As E. W. Kenworthy wrote in the *New York Times,* "Southerners themselves have always recognized that, of all discriminations practiced against the Negro, the denial of his right to vote was the least defensible . . . Although the Southerners had protested bitterly through the debate that the bill was unconstitutional and that it was particularized and punitive legislation, many gave the impression they were not reluctant to have the issue settled."[115]

The filibuster against the Voting Rights Act, which went on for twenty-four days, was brief in comparison to the sixty-day filibuster in 1964 and was primarily theater. Mansfield allowed southerners to make their statements, and their dramatic last stand, so they could demonstrate to their constituents that they understood and shared their opposition to the bill. He didn't want to destroy the southerners; he knew that when Congress moved beyond civil rights issues, their votes could be useful to the Democratic Party.

The Senate voted for cloture by 70 to 30 on May 25 and then

passed the Voting Rights Act of 1965 by 77 to 19. Thirty Republicans voted in favor of the bill; the only two GOP dissenters were the southerners Strom Thurmond and John Tower. The conservative Republicans Bourke Hickenlooper, Norris Cotton of New Hampshire, and Wyoming's Milward Simpson, all of whom had voted against the Civil Rights Act of 1964, voted in favor of voting rights. The southern Democrats too were split. Tennessee's Al Gore and Ross Bass and Texas's Ralph Yarborough broke with their colleagues and changed their votes of the previous year. The conservative coalition had finally splintered on the rock of civil rights.

While the Senate was finishing its deliberations, so was the House, where the forces of liberalism were even stronger in their demands. The majority leader, Carl Albert, reported that in the Democratic Study Group, the Leadership Conference on Civil Rights, and the House Judiciary Committee there was a strong consensus that the bill should include a ban on the poll tax.[116] The Judiciary Committee filed its report on the Voting Rights Act on June 1 and included the prohibition the Senate had voted down. Congressman Celler rejected the idea that the poll tax ban threatened the bill and dismissed the constitutional arguments against taking bolder action. Although Judge Smith tried to hold up the bill in the Rules Committee, warning that "many Communists, subversives, fellow travelers, and others of doubtful loyalty to their country have attached themselves to this movement," Celler used the threat of the twenty-one-day rule to force Smith to let the committee vote on the bill.[117] Johnson warned Martin Luther King that time was precious and asked him, Farmer, Young, and others to come to Washington to speak with McCormack and Mansfield and "tell 'em what you want them to do."[118] In this case, the civil rights forces were divided. King didn't think it was worth endangering the bill over the amendment, but there were enough civil rights leaders and liberal Democrats in the House who were saying something very different. As a result, the administration's proposal, with a prohibition on all poll taxes tacked onto it, sailed through the House on July 9 by 333 to 85.

Because there were two versions of the legislation, House and Senate conferees had to meet to reach a deal. "If the . . . [voting rights debate] drags on in Congress, you'll see demonstrations on a level you have never seen before," King warned.[119] But Johnson prevailed. The conference committee eliminated the poll tax ban and retained the provision that provided for federal examiners. In the beginning of August, the House passed the conference report 328 to 74, and the Senate passed the measure 79 to 18.

The final legislation contained almost everything that was in the deal reached by Dirksen and Johnson before the congressional deliberations began, including the automatic trigger that would require certain states to end discriminatory tests for voting and would enforce this by empowering the federal government to send examiners to register voters and monitor the polls. The bill also included the pre-clearance provision that required southern states to gain approval for any changes to their voting processes, with the agreed-to qualification that a three-judge federal district court in Washington had the power to free southern states from the restrictions if there was clear evidence that racial discrimination had not occurred for at least five years. Finally, the legislation created criminal penalties for any officials found to be infringing on voting rights.

On August 6, Johnson signed the Voting Rights Act of 1965. Before the signing ceremony, he spoke to a crowd of colleagues, civil rights leaders, and reporters in the Capitol Rotunda. "Today is a triumph for freedom as huge as any victory that has ever been won on any battlefield . . . Today the Negro story and the American story fuse and blend . . . Under this act," he said, "if any county in the nation does not want Federal intervention, it need only open its polling places to all of its people." He held the actual signing ceremony in the President's Room near the Senate chamber on a green-baize-covered walnut desk in the very place where President Abraham Lincoln, on the same date in 1861, had signed legislation that freed slaves whom the Confederacy had impressed into military service in the Civil War. This was the desk on which Johnson had signed the Civil Rights Acts of 1957 and 1960 when he was the Senate majority leader. Following the ceremony, Johnson handed the first pen to Hubert Humphrey and the second to Senator Dirksen, thanking the Republican leader for his role in getting the Voting Rights Act passed.

The effects of the legislation were immediate. Federal examiners were in place in Alabama, Louisiana, and Mississippi only four days after Johnson signed the law. By the end of August, they had listed 27,463 people who had been prevented from voting. It took only a few months before almost 250,000 new African Americans voters were registered.[120]

THE CONGRESSIONAL TREATMENT

The momentous education, health-care, and voting rights bills were just a few of the laws Congress passed in the first session of the "Fabulous Eighty-ninth Congress," as Johnson liked to call it. The Immigration and Nationality Act ended the stringent quota system that had been instituted during the height of nativist sentiment in the 1920s. The Appalachian Development Act allocated federal funds to build a highway that would provide public jobs and generate economic development in one of the most economically depressed regions in the country. The Maine senator Ed Muskie's pet project, the Water Quality Act, set national standards on water and created the Water

Pollution Control Administration to monitor them. Congress passed 89 of the 115 proposals that the president had sent it.[121] Speaker McCormack boasted, "It is the Congress of accomplished hopes. It is the Congress of realized dreams."[122] Johnson's approval rating fluctuated between a stunning 60 percent and 70 percent throughout the year.

Johnson's insights and actions, his legislative experience, and his tactics had been crucial in getting the legislation passed. According to the reporter Richard Strout, "Rarely has one man so dominated Washington as President Johnson now does . . . Johnson is like an orchestra leader; a beachmaster on an invasion front, a traffic-control superintendent at a busy railroad front."[123]

In a different political environment, however, all Johnson's vaunted methods probably would not have been enough to get so much important legislation passed. It took the huge House and Senate majorities the recent election had created, with their sizable liberal blocs, and the substantial reduction in the strength of the conservative coalition. The evisceration of Barry Goldwater had made Republicans more hesitant to embrace the principles of conservatism and more willing to accede to Johnson's aims. Even without Republican support, many of Johnson's bills had strong majorities in the House and the supermajority of votes required to end filibusters in the Senate. In this environment, conservative committee chairs had little ability or incentive to obstruct bills; rules changes had abridged their power, and there was a good chance they would lose no matter what they tried to do. With so many liberals in both chambers, at least until the next election, Johnson pushed to pass legislation he knew would be impossible in other years. As Senator Ted Kennedy said of immigration reform, "It's really amazing, a year ago I doubt the bill would have had a chance. This time it was easy."[124] The civil rights movement forced voting rights onto Johnson's agenda at the most fertile time in thirty years for harvesting liberal legislation in Congress.

Johnson was well aware that despite his legislative successes, there were serious threats to his Great Society. There was growing civil unrest in the cities—the summer of 1965 saw a bloody six-day riot in the Watts neighborhood of Los Angeles, provoked by residents' frustration with police brutality—that threatened to exacerbate white backlash against civil rights legislation and other programs perceived by some whites as race related. There would be more riots that would nurture a view of the Great Society as a cause of rather than a solution to urban violence. The Community Action Program had been causing problems in solidly Democratic northern cities; some mayors felt that unelected activists were gaining too much control over federal funds from the Economic Opportunity Act, particularly when the activists criticized the Democratic machines for failing to do enough to solve the problems of the poor. In San Francisco, left-wing activists played a prominent role in CAP. In Chicago, the Woodlawn Organization, a branch of the radical activist Saul Alinsky's network, obtained money directly from the OEO when the city's committee, controlled by allies of Mayor Richard Daley, rejected their proposals.[125]

The war in Vietnam was escalating. Operation Rolling Thunder, a massive bombing campaign against the North Vietnamese, was under way starting in March 1965. Johnson had also authorized a surge of U.S. ground troops that month. Even as advisers kept pushing Johnson to withdraw—Vice President Humphrey argued that the election victory had created the first opportunity to "face the Vietnam problem without being preoccupied with the political repercussions from the Republican right"[126]—the president refused to change course; he was still and always terrified of becoming the Democrat who lost Vietnam to the communists. On July 28, one day after the House passed his Medicare and Medicaid programs, and with voting rights legislation seemingly safe, Johnson had announced a major escalation of the war in Vietnam.[127]

But for the time being, these problems were inchoate, and Johnson was on the crest of a wave of legislative victories. His vision of a second New Deal was coming true.

CHAPTER SEVEN

CONGRESSIONAL CONSERVATISM REVIVED

On January 12, 1966, President Johnson, looking confident and commanding, strode to the rostrum of the House of Representatives to deliver his third State of the Union address. His approval rating was 59 percent, and the Gallup poll had reported that for the third year in a row Americans rated him the "Most Admired Man" in the world, ahead of Martin Luther King and Pope Paul VI. Before members of Congress and a national television audience, Johnson brushed off conservative critics who had argued that the increasing cost of the conflict in Vietnam necessitated cuts in nonmilitary spending. He insisted that the American economy could pay for guns *and* butter. "This nation is mighty enough," the president said, "its society is healthy enough, its people are strong enough, to pursue our goals in the rest of the world while still building a Great Society here at home." Johnson reminded Congress and the nation that the economy was still booming. "Workers are making more money than ever—with after-tax income in the past 5 years up 33 percent; in the last year alone, up 8 percent. More people are working than ever before in our history—an increase last year of 2½ million jobs."

Responding to conservative opponents, Johnson said, "There are men who cry out, 'We must sacrifice.' Well, let us. 'Who will they sacrifice? Are they going to sacrifice the children who seek the learning, the sick who need medical care, or the families who dwell in squalor now brightened by the hope of home? Will they sacrifice opportunity for the distressed, the beauty of our land, the hope of our poor?'" The president announced a record-high peacetime budget of $112.8 billion, far beyond the budget he and Harry Byrd had agreed to in the year he took over the presidency, including $58.3 billion for defense, and he presented a list of major initiatives he hoped Congress would tackle in the coming year. He did not ask for an income tax increase, but he did propose restoring certain excise taxes and speeding up the schedule for withholding taxes.

Johnson persisted in Vietnam despite growing public criticism of his war strategy. There were more than 200,000 American combat troops in Southeast Asia; the costs of the war were escalating rapidly; Johnson was carefully hiding these costs from Congress and relying on supplementary budget requests to obtain the money he needed.

Beneath the confidence Johnson projected, he was feeling a great deal of political anxiety. He knew that the good legislative times he had enjoyed over the past year could not last much longer. The midterm elections were just around the corner, and every politician recognized that midterm elections rarely went well for the party that controlled the White House. The sizable liberal majorities that had been producing huge results would not be as large after November. With the exception of the 1934 elections, when Democrats increased the size of their majorities in the House and the Senate, the president's party had shrunk in midterms ever since the contemporary two-party system had been solidified in 1860. The only question was how deep the losses would be, and a clue to the answer was that losses were usually worst after huge landslide victories. In 1938, Democrats lost a net of seventy seats in the House and seven seats in the Senate after FDR's reelection in 1936; in 1958, Republicans lost forty-eight seats in the House and thirteen in the Senate after Dwight Eisenhower's 1956 landslide.

Johnson agreed with the analysis of his legislative liaison Henry Hall Wilson: "It is clear that new programs will be more difficult to pass this year than they were last year and that the differences are: a) the war, b) election year, and c) the feeling among many members that enough was done last year."[1] Johnson himself warned the civil rights leader Roy Wilkins, "Our legislation is over . . . because second session everybody is looking, running for reelection."[2]

But these gloomy predictions didn't hold him back; he was a politician who loved to take big risks in the pursuit of legislative breakthroughs. The election of 1964 had been good to him. For the time being, he had favorable Democratic majorities in the Eighty-ninth Congress; he believed he could squeeze more out of it. He sent a number of proposals to the Hill, many of which would pass in some form over the coming year. In 1966, Congress created the Department of Transportation, which centralized policy that had been chaotically dispersed among thirty-five different agencies. Though it was severely watered down from Johnson's original plan, the Model Cities Program provided about $900 million to help cities design plans for revitalizing their infrastructures. The Endangered Species Preservation Act empowered the secretary of interior to protect fish and wildlife that were threatened by development. The National Traffic and Motor Vehicle Safety Act aimed to reduce highway deaths by requiring the construction of safer vehicles and encouraging the use of seat belts.

Understanding that the liberal moment was fleeting, Johnson had decided to take a huge gamble on passing one more major piece of civil rights legislation—a bill that would prohibit racial discrimination in the sale or rental of homes. He knew that his proposal would upset northern white Democratic constituents who had been supportive of liberalism since the 1930s. He also knew that the debate over housing discrimination would test the endurance of the legislative coalition upon which he had depended and arouse the fierce opposition of the conservative coalition that had been lying low for almost a year. Despite the risks, Johnson was determined to pass legislation to end discrimination in housing.

RACE IN THE HOME FRONT

The effects of the 1964 Civil Rights Act and the 1965 Voting Rights Act had been swift and impressive. The Justice Department, frustrated by how slowly schools were desegregated in the South after the Supreme Court's *Brown v. Board of Education* decision in 1954, had hastened the desegregation of public accommodations by filing lawsuits or merely threatening legal action against establishments that refused to comply. Despite the bitter and violent clashes that preceded the passage of the 1964 law, its implementation proceeded relatively peacefully and without massive resistance, although there were still stories of violent defiance by individual citizens and of businesses that found ways to evade the laws.[3] Largely as a result of voter registration drives and the voting rights legislation, the percentage of African Americans registered to vote in southern states rose from about 41 percent in 1964 to 52.6 percent in 1966 to 60.3 percent in 1968. The changes in the Deep South were the most impressive: the percentage of African Americans registered to vote in Mississippi reached 59.8 percent in 1967; the figure had been 6.7 percent just three years earlier.[4]

But there was much racial injustice that Congress had not yet addressed. When rioting broke out in the Watts neighborhood of Los Angeles in the summer of 1965, people with divergent attitudes and interests joined a national debate about the causes and cures for racial discrimination and its effects in urban America.

The riots began on August 11 in the wake of what might have been a routine traffic stop on a hot and smoggy evening in an African American neighborhood of clean streets lined with beautiful plush green trees and handsome single-family homes. In a city where tensions over police brutality had been mounting for years, a loud argument between the people in the car and the police drew a crowd, and as the traffic stop grew more heated and the interactions became tense, the crowd threw bottles and rocks at the police. After police arrested the people in the car, rioting broke out and spread quickly through the neighborhood. An estimated five thousand African Americans filled the twenty-block area that the police sealed off. There were rumors that the police had beaten a pregnant woman. One African American merchant said that a group of young men ran into his store, looted most of the goods, and set the building on fire. Another resident hid in his apartment and peeked out his window at young men making Molotov cocktails. The comedian and civil rights activist Dick Gregory, who was there trying to calm people down, was shot. One fourteen-year-old African American girl who was trying to escape from the melee was killed in a traffic accident. A five-year-old boy was killed by sniper fire. Some police cars were stopped and officers dragged out into the street. Stones barraged ambulances.[5] After six days of riots, thirty-four people had been killed and hundreds seriously injured; more than three thousand people were arrested; the infrastructure of many communities was devastated. The entire nation was shocked at the eruption of violence.

In private, Lyndon Johnson criticized the Watts rioters for acting like irresponsible and unappreciative children, but he also expressed sensitivity to the social and economic causes of the riots. He saw them as the result of too many people forced to live in a terrible environment. Of the African Americans in Watts, he said, "They got really absolutely nothing to live for. Forty percent of them are unemployed. These youngsters, they live with rats and they've got no place to sleep . . . broken homes and illegitimate families and all the narcotics are circulating around them."[6]

Civil rights leaders had been urging the federal government to address the problems of inner-city African Americans for as long as there had been a civil rights movement. They had targeted segregation and voting rights in 1964 and 1965 because it seemed possible they could get legislation on these issues, but they always believed that racial equality required a solution for the unemployment, housing discrimination, poverty, and inadequate transportation services that afflicted African Americans particularly in urban areas. In response to conservatives' calls for law and order to prevent more riots like Watts, civil rights proponents argued that the focus should be on improving the living conditions of the people who lived in such places.

In January 1966, Martin Luther King rented a third-floor walk-up apartment in the Chicago slums, where he planned to live temporarily to publicize the racial discrimination in the North that might breed further violence. He announced that the Southern Christian Leadership Conference planned to make Chicago an "Open City," a place with integrated schools, improved mass transit systems, jobs for African Americans, and open occupancy laws. King said he had "never seen—even in Mississippi and Alabama—mobs as hostile and hate-filled as I've seen in Chicago."[7] Though King helped to stimulate national interest in urban issues, factions within the civil rights movement had already spent years fighting to improve conditions in metropolitan areas. The National Committee Against Discrimination in Housing, a network of activists founded in 1950, had asserted that "the Great Society could never become a reality until fair housing was effected."[8] They had been able to win support for fair housing laws in fifteen states, though most of the regulations were weakly enforced and ineffective.[9]

Homeownership had become a central aspiration for millions of middle- and working-class American citizens. Since FDR had persuaded Congress to pass a number of housing programs as part of the New Deal and GI benefits had provided economic assistance to World War II veterans, the percentage of Americans living in homes they owned or homes owned by their families increased from 30 percent in 1930 to 60 percent in 1960.[10]

City, state, and local officials in the North had responded to the huge influx of African Americans from the South in the 1930s and 1940s by erecting barriers against residential integration. Poverty and housing discrimination confined African Americans to some of the most blighted areas of the country. Even before the riots of the mid-1960s, the living conditions of African Americans in the inner cities were dire.[11] The riots were a culmination, not a cause, of years of decay. Major cities could be mapped by the color of their neighborhoods. Although a small number of African Americans made it into the suburbs, those neighborhoods too were segregated by race. While some African Americans preferred to live in nonwhite communities, as opponents of civil rights loved to point out, most data indicated that a clear majority of them wanted to reside in racially integrated neighborhoods.[12] Their hope was to live in neighborhoods that had good schools for their children, safe streets, plentiful jobs, and all the well-advertised privileges of the American dream, but by 1966 African Americans suffered from the worst rates of residential isolation of any racial or ethnic group in U.S. history.[13] Without access to housing in the wealthier outposts of the cities or suburbs, African Americans could not obtain a first-rate public education, were denied the residential advantages that helped many white children to thrive, and were very often remote from the quality industrial jobs upon which non-skilled workers depended. Trade unions, usually informally organized around ethnic groups, were unwilling to accept African American members.

Various public policies supported systematic residential segregation, even though that was not always the explicit intention of the officials who designed the policies. In some cities, local government officials used federal money that had been distributed through the Department of Housing and Urban Development to raze African American ghettos—and also the homes of working-class Jews, Irish, Italians, and Hispanics—usually for the stated purpose of highway construction but also to make room for better housing the evicted residents couldn't afford. Sometimes neighborhoods were "upgraded" with such improvements as Dodger Stadium, which the city of Los Angeles built for its baseball team. In the process, African American and Chicano communities were destroyed, and the public housing units built to replace flattened homes, in Los Angeles and in other cities where similar "gentrification" took place, were generally substandard constructions in other blighted inner-city areas.

Between the 1920s and the 1940s, restrictive covenants and deeds—explicit contracts that homeowners would not sell their property to people of another race—had prevented African Americans from purchasing homes in desirable locations. Realtors and buyers who tried to circumvent such restrictions were confronted with intimidation, protest, and sometimes physical violence.[14] The Supreme Court declared restrictive covenants unconstitutional in 1948, but the Federal Housing Administration (FHA) incorporated other racially discriminatory mechanisms into its programs. Through redlining, the FHA rated neighborhoods based on their assessed value. Banks would lend funds to purchase homes located only in the "best" areas on the federal maps, while the FHA and the Veterans Administration would back loans only in the highly rated neighborhoods, which were primarily white. Neither the banks nor the government

232

would provide loans to people who wanted to move into any neighborhood where there was even a sprinkling of African Americans, as those areas were deemed to be economically risky. As a result of simple racism and the restrictive covenants that gave it quasi-legal contractual support, even if an African American was willing to live with constant racial harassment, he couldn't move his family into an all-white neighborhood, because no one would sell or rent him a home there. If he wanted to move into a decent neighborhood that had been even slightly integrated, he couldn't get a loan because of redlining.[15] Suburban communities used zoning laws and land use regulations to exclude affordable housing. While some African Americans were able to move into these prosperous areas, one open-housing activist in Cleveland explained that "the peppering of white suburbia, if it's going to come at all . . . has to come from federal leverage."[16] But federal leverage worked to the opposite effect.

Local neighborhood associations mobilized opposition against anyone who wanted to let African American families move in. They lobbied local officials and pressured realtors to protect the color line. In some cases, they were willing to act violently against property owners who even contemplated selling or renting to an African American. Real estate agents "steered" African Americans away from properties in white neighborhoods.

Another technique predicated on discrimination was blockbusting. Shady real estate agents and building developers would sell African Americans a house in a white neighborhood with the explicit purpose of generating fear among homeowners. Some agents paid African Americans to stroll through white neighborhoods, or gave money to young African American children to knock on doors and hand out pamphlets, to frighten residents into selling their homes at bargain-basement prices. Once the white residents had fled, the real estate developers who purchased the homes sold them at marked-up prices to middle-class African Americans desperate to leave the segregated ghetto.[17] Blockbusting seemed a particularly egregious form of discrimination, but it existed at the edge of a national land-scape in which government, bankers, realtors, and sellers all partici-pated and in which racial segregation was taken for granted.

Early in 1965, Lyndon Johnson had persuaded Congress to pass legislation that empowered local Public Housing Agencies, which the states had been authorized to establish by federal legislation—the United States Housing Act of 1937—to select poor families from a waiting list and place them in private housing; the federal govern-ment would pay the difference between the market rate rent and what the tenants could afford. The legislation, though extremely modest, had been highly controversial because of its potential for creating integrated housing, and Congress blocked operating funds for the program.[18]

So, despite the success of the Civil Rights Act of 1964 and the Voting Rights Act of 1965, Congress had done nothing to end the widespread discrimination in housing. African Americans were still at the mercy of a complex network of real estate agents, property developers, and homeowners who wanted them excluded from most neighborhoods.

President Johnson wanted to pass legislation that would prohibit discrimination against African Americans who had enough money to buy or rent a home, no matter what neighborhood the dwelling was in. The law would ensure that they could make the deal or get the lease regardless of the color of their skin; government and private lending institutions would be required to provide equal financial assistance to African Americans and to eliminate redlining and all other practices that resulted in residential segregation. The president saw this as an essential building block of the Great Society: "Employ-ment is often dependent on education, education on neighborhood schools and housing, housing on income, income on employment. We have learned by now the folly of looking for any single crucial link in the chain that binds the ghetto. All the links—poverty, lack of education, underemployment and now discrimination in housing—must be attacked together."

Given how entrenched residential discrimination was throughout the nation, the prospects for passing President Johnson's third civil rights bill were slim. Unlike the other two civil rights bills Congress had passed, the housing provision directly affected northern Democrats who had been integral to the liberal coalition and midwestern Republicans who had partnered with the president in 1964 and 1965. When Johnson's commitment to racial justice had angered southern Democrats, he was compensated with increased support in northern states. The reverse would not be true. Senator Sam Ervin, who had long been an enemy of civil rights, said, "For the first time we have a bill which proposes that other than Southern oxen to be gored."[19]

Johnson knew that many white working- and middle-class Democrats in northern cities would see an end to segregated housing as a threat to their property values and their local schools. "The phrase open housing is hurling a pack of dynamite with the fuse sizzling," one African American writer said.[20] Polls showed that a majority of Americans did not support legislation that guaranteed the right of African Americans to buy a house in any neighborhood.[21]

Ending housing discrimination, the special assistant Sherwin Markman wrote to the president, was a "loser in Congress."[22] In both the House and the Senate, there was resistance to tackling race relations so close to the midterm elections, especially after members had already been asked to cast many controversial votes. Many representatives who had played key roles in the success of earlier civil rights bills, Attorney General Katzenbach reported, were "very cool" this time around.[23]

Johnson was not deterred by the lack of enthusiasm. On April 28, 1966, he sent Congress his proposal for an omnibus bill that included a provision to end housing discrimination—Title IV, which covered all rentals and sales of new and existing homes and prohibited an owner from refusing to enter into an agreement on the basis of the race of the person seeking to inhabit a property—and also provisions to end discrimination in the selection of juries, to empower the attorney general to initiate desegregation suits in education and public accommodations, and to provide more protection for civil rights workers.

Southerners didn't like the provisions dealing with juries and education, but the bill wasn't going to get their votes anyway. What mattered was how intense the negative response to the housing provisions would be from northerners.

The first indication came from the midwestern Republicans who had reliably partnered with Johnson on civil rights in 1964 and 1965. Republican leaders always began negotiations by expressing skepticism, no matter what the proposal was, with the aim of increasing their leverage over specific provisions in a bill, but this time their staunch objections to Title IV seemed genuine. Senator Dirksen, who was up for reelection in 1968, immediately declared that the proposal was unconstitutional and that it would not pass. "If you can tell me what in interstate commerce is involved about selling a house fixed on soil or what federal jurisdiction there is, I'll eat the chimney on the house," Dirksen said. As members of the southern caucus huddled in their quarters to decide on their strategy, Dirksen made it clear that he would not support cloture.[24] His opposition was a huge problem because, as Bryce Harlow, a veteran political adviser and lobbyist, explained, "the entire apparatus can be summed up in one word—Dirksen."[25] Congressman William McCulloch, the other key player on the Republican civil rights team, announced that the country was not prepared for a third civil rights bill of this magnitude.[26] What McCulloch really meant but could not say explicitly was that the housing provision in the civil rights bill was unacceptable because it directly threatened the material interests of northern constituencies, including his own.

The real estate industry mobilized against the legislation in a lobbying blitz that matched the intensity of the AMA's vicious attacks on Medicare. In the case of Medicare the threat was socialized medicine; in the case of housing the threat was to destroy the financial security of families. Home builders and realtors had no stomach for federal regulations that would alter the property arrangements they had developed to protect white consumers from African Americans who wanted to live among them. The last thing they wanted was legislation that would cause housing prices to fall in forcibly integrated neighborhoods. Testifying before Congress, representatives of the real estate industry said they opposed granting the federal government more power to regulate home contracts and did not think "forcing" African Americans to live in white communities was the best path toward racial integration. "We suggest that this is not cause for rejoicing on the part of more than 30 million home owners," Alan Emlen of the National Association of Real Estate Boards said, "each of whom must have assumed that their right to own property carries with it the right to dispose of it to the persons of their choice."[27] The National Association of Real Estate Brokers (NAREB) flooded local communities throughout the North with propaganda about how the legislation would destroy their most cherished investment and bring crime, and possibly incidents like those in Watts, to their communities. Many suburbanites accepted these principles, that a "man's home is his castle" and individuals have the right to do as they wish with their property. As one California housewife, who was married to a real estate agent, said, "Watts is no concern of mine. It's none of my business and should be none of my Congressman's business. Let the Watts Congressman worry about Watts; my Congressman should worry about me and my neighbors."[28]

The lobby was working well. Congressional mail was arriving in legislators' offices, with about a hundred opponents for every one supporter by the start of summer.[29] The situation was so volatile that even one of the most liberal subcommittees of Judiciary, one of the most liberal committees in the entire House, couldn't make any progress on Title IV. Chairman Celler eventually reported the bill to the full committee without making any recommendations about Title IV. The prospects for the bill in the full committee did not seem good.

The bill might have died there had not Charles McC. Mathias of Maryland proposed a compromise. Mathias was a Republican and a Yale Law School graduate who had been a strong supporter of civil rights since his election to the House in 1960.[30] His proposal was to limit the range of housing and rental stock that the new law would cover in order to ensure that at least some regulations passed. His plan exempted the sale of owner-occupied homes where real estate agents were not used in the sale—this provision became known as the Mrs. Murphy rule—and smaller buildings that were occupied by owners with rooms for rent. Everyone else in the real estate business, including mortgage lenders, builders, realtors, and brokers, would be bound by the law that banned discrimination in the sale or rental of property on the basis of race. If proponents of the legislation could say they were leaving individual owners alone, Mathias believed there was a better chance of moving the bill through the House. McCulloch liked the proposal and urged his colleague to speak with Celler. On June 24, Mathias and McCulloch discussed the proposal with Celler and Katzenbach. All agreed it might work.

As soon as the press started to report on the Mathias compromise, civil rights leaders understood that it would mean that many of the nation's homes, including a majority of those in the suburbs, would not fall under the regulations. They expressed their displeasure with the revision, though they realized that the chances of passing the original proposal were nil.

Meanwhile, Mathias tried to rally other Republicans behind his compromise. He warned that staunch and public Republican opposition would enable Democrats to claim they were once again the party of civil rights. Even if Republicans could win support among white working-class northern voters—which was far from a sure bet, because many of these voters remained deeply appreciative of New Deal and Great Society programs that provided them with economic relief and opportunity—African Americans would continue to defect from the party of Lincoln. If Democrats cobbled together support for a bill, no matter how watered-down it might be, the GOP would supplant the Dixiecrats as the chief opponents of racial progress. Mathias received encouragement from three moderate Republican governors—Nelson Rockefeller of New York, George Romney of Michigan, and Bill Scranton of Pennsylvania—and New York's liberal Republican mayor, John Lindsay.

When the Judiciary Committee first voted on the bill on June 28, a majority rejected the Mathias amendment, though a majority also rejected a proposal to eliminate Title IV from the bill. The following day, the committee voted on a revised version of Mathias's amendment that exempted land that was to be sold for housing development, excluded certain sales by religious and educational institutions, and expanded the original exemption from one- to four-family homes. In the final hours, the Maryland congressman had done a good job selling his plan behind closed doors. The committee passed Mathias's amendment 21 to 13. Four Republicans voted in favor of the final bill; 6 Democrats voted no, including the Michigan Democrat John Conyers, who would become a founder of the Congressional Black Caucus in 1969. Conyers believed the revised Mathias compromise would render the program ineffective.[31]

Sitting in his oversize leather chair, Emanuel Celler, who was usually the person in the room demanding the boldest legislative proposals, told reporters that the compromise was essential because "sometimes you've got to stretch your feet according to the blanket."[32]

Members of the Leadership Conference on Civil Rights gathered to decide whether or not to support the bill. Most of them criticized the Mathias amendment for severely weakening the legislation, but finally most of them said either they would support the compromise, which would help the Democratic leadership capture Republican votes in the Senate, or they would remain silent.[33]

The situation on the House floor was volatile. The National Association of Real Estate Brokers sent out a secret bulletin imploring its members to tell representatives to reject the compromise. The Washington office of the NAREB urged every local branch to "telephone, wire or write [its] Representative in the House to vote to strike Title IV [the housing provision] from the bill."[34]

The political situation in the North continued to deteriorate. President Johnson watched nervously as the tensions within Democratic constituencies worsened throughout the summer, with the midterms just a few months away. Civil rights activists, calling for fair housing and improved conditions in the cities, confronted police and white mobs in the streets. The opposition to fair housing in states outside the South was much more ferocious than Johnson had anticipated it would be, and he had expected ferocious opposition. Many working- and middle-class Democrats saw the urban street clashes as disorganized mob violence, quite different from the scenes they had watched in 1964 and 1965 of orderly, peaceful men, women, and children under attack from police with fire hoses and snarling dogs. It was one thing for liberal northern Democrats to see police clashing with African American demonstrators in Birmingham, quite another thing to see King and other civil rights leaders marching in Chicago and the surrounding suburbs to demand fair housing.

"We will march until every white man in the area votes— Republican," announced the civil rights activist James Bevel.[35] In one of the Chicago marches, white hecklers violently attacked the African American protesters. "I wish I were an Alabama trooper," chanted some of the whites. "Oh, how happy I would be, for if I were an Alabama trooper, then I could kill niggers legally."[36] In Waukegan, Illinois, a city of about forty thousand people located forty miles from Chicago, rioting lasted three nights. In a two-square-mile area, eighty were arrested and many were injured. Six people returning from church were burned after someone threw a gasoline bomb into their car. The rioting took place just five blocks from a residence where the president's daughter Luci Johnson Nugent was visiting for the weekend. The city's pugnacious mayor, Robert Sabonjian, blamed the unrest on "scums, animals, winos, and junkies" whose actions were instigated by radical agitators. The mayor invoked an emergency curfew to reestablish the peace.[37] In Dayton, Ohio, violence erupted after a thirty-nine-year-old African American named Lester Mitchell was killed outside his house by three white men in a pickup truck.

The context of these confrontations had also changed because of a real split in the civil rights leadership. New young leaders, frustrated with the limitations of what Congress had achieved and what King and other senior figures were prepared to ask for, were using much bolder rhetoric about how to achieve racial progress—rhetoric that scared many white Democrats. In June 1966, Stokely Carmichael, the new leader of SNCC, on a march to register African American voters, was arrested in Greenwood, Mississippi. Addressing a crowd after being released, Carmichael warned that he would not return to jail. He said, "We want black power!" His supporters responded that they wanted black power too. The speech, when it was broadcast on all the TV news programs, shocked and stirred Americans who were hearing such rhetoric for the first time. "We have to raise questions about whether or not we do need new types of political institutions in this country," Carmichael later said in a different speech, "and we in SNCC maintain that we need them now.

We need new political institutions in this country. Any time—any time Lyndon Baines Johnson can head a Party which has in it Bobby Kennedy, Wayne Morse, Eastland, Wallace, and all those other supposed-to-be-liberal cats, there's something wrong with that Party." Opponents of the fair housing legislation connected the clashes in the cities to the black power movement; they suggested that radical leaders were encouraging protesters to be extreme in their demands and their tactics.

The housing bill exacerbated racial tension that already existed in some cities over the Community Action Program's funding of so-called radical activists who attacked mayors and Democratic machines. Representative Roman Pucinski warned that civil rights activists were now undermining support for the party and destroying entire neighborhoods.[38] "Go into Chicago today in any home, any bar, any barber shop," said Pucinski, a labor-backed Democrat who had supported the civil rights bills in 1964 and 1965 and who endorsed Mathias's compromises on the housing provision, "and you will find people are not talking about Vietnam or rising prices or prosperity. They are talking about Martin Luther King and how they [African Americans] are moving in on us and what's going to happen to our neighborhoods."[39] Pucinski was a seven-year congressman whose Illinois district was 99.7 percent working-class white ethnic Democrats— the other three-tenths of a percent were mostly Asian Americans. He was facing a challenge from a Republican alderman named John Hoellen, who was making open housing his central campaign theme. Hoellen had become a national poster child for the white backlash against civil rights; he had famously attacked the Wright Junior College in Chicago when some professors had assigned students to read *Another Country* by the African American writer James Baldwin; Hoellen deemed the book's treatment of race relations too radical, and he persuaded the Chicago City Council Committee on Schools to condemn the decision to require that students read the book. That

Speaker of the House John McCormack (right) believed the election had created the best opportunity Democrats would have for decades to enact new domestic policies.

The first major bill Johnson sent to Congress was for a program to provide federal aid to education. The New York congressman Adam Clayton Powell Jr., chairman of the House Education and Labor Committee, here seen at a 1965 press conference, used his authority to move this bill through the House, but his erratic personal behavior frustrated Johnson despite their shared goals.

When the federal education bill reached the Senate, Oregon's Wayne Morse made sure it passed the chamber intact. Morse, a former law school dean, helped the administration design a bill that would avoid the disputes over parochial schools that had bogged down previous proposals.

LBJ signs the Elementary and Secondary Education bill on April 11, 1965, in front of a former school in Stonewall, Texas. Beside him is his first schoolteacher, Kate Deadrich Loney.

Health care was a top priority for the Eighty-ninth Congress. The New Mexico Democratic senator Clinton Anderson, shown here, who almost died from tuberculosis in his twenties, had been sponsoring proposals for Medicare since 1961. Until 1965, the House Ways and Means chairman, Wilbur Mills, a Democrat from Arkansas, had prevented the legislation from being reported out of his committee.

Retired senior citizens rallying in favor of Medicare.

The Wisconsin representative John Byrnes, ranking Republican on the House Ways and Means Committee, proposed an alternative to Medicare that would have covered the cost of physician care (Medicare covered only the cost of hospitals). Administration officials worried that the Byrnes proposal might siphon off votes from their bill.

Assistant Secretary of Health, Education, and Welfare Wilbur Cohen (who became undersecretary in April 1965), the consummate Social Security insider, had only a few days to redraft the entire Medicare bill when Wilbur Mills surprised everyone in closed hearings by announcing he wanted to combine the administration and the Republican proposals into one giant bill.

Secretary of Health, Education, and Welfare John Gardner outlines the steps for implementing Medicare. Johnson was determined to get Medicare running effectively as quickly as possible so that elderly recipients would oppose any legislator who tried to tamper with the program.

During a march from Selma to Montgomery, Alabama, on March 7, 1965, to demand full voting rights for African Americans, the SNCC leader John Lewis (light coat, center) is viciously attacked by a state trooper. This and other images from the march shocked Americans and produced more demands from Republicans and Democrats in Congress to pass a voting rights bill. Few legislators knew that Senator Dirksen had already been negotiating the details of a bill with Nicholas Katzenbach.

President Johnson's special address to Congress on voting rights on March 15, 1965. Toward the end of the speech, thunderous applause filled the chamber and civil rights supporters wept as Johnson uttered the words "We shall overcome."

The Pennsylvania senator Joseph Clark (left) and the Massachusetts senator Ted Kennedy were two of the most passionate advocates of civil rights. Kennedy caused some political problems for Johnson when the senator pushed for a federal ban on the poll tax as part of the Voting Rights Act of 1965.

After the passage of the Voting Rights Act, tensions over race relations escalated. A six-day riot broke out after police arrested a man in the predominantly African American neighborhood of Watts in Los Angeles.

Johnson's decision to propose a fair housing bill caused huge political problems for Democrats. White residents in traditionally Democratic districts in the North reacted violently against this phase of the civil rights struggle. In this photograph, civil rights demonstrators in Chicago duck in an effort to avoid flying rocks and firecrackers hurled at them during a protest march against the housing practices of real estate offices in all-white neighborhoods.

There was growing tension in 1966 between Chicago's mayor, Richard Daley, and the White House over the Economic Opportunity Act. Daley was angered to see federal funds directed to activists and community organizers who were outside the control of his machine.

Vietnam politics were heating up in 1966. Senator William Fulbright (pictured in front of Senator Mike Mansfield) conducted televised hearings during which he grilled administration officials about the war.

President Johnson was less concerned about Senator Fulbright than he was about Republican criticism that he wasn't being hawkish enough in Vietnam. Here, the House minority leader, Gerald Ford (center), expresses this criticism at a White House meeting with Senator Everett Dirksen (left) and Congressman Leslie Arends (right) seated beside him.

Johnson came under growing pressure to raise taxes to contain inflation and pay for Vietnam. Here he meets with his fiscal team to discuss the gloomy budgetary situation.

The Senate majority leader, Mike Mansfield, reviews the 1966 midterm elections. Republicans put together effective campaigns that focused on Vietnam, inflation and deficits, and law and order.

Senator Robert Kennedy (left) campaigning for Senator Paul Douglas (right) in Illinois. Kennedy praised Douglas as a pioneer in the civil rights movement, but Douglas lost to the charismatic Republican businessman Charles Percy, who benefited from the backlash against civil rights among white ethnic Democrats.

African Americans line up to vote at the courthouse in Camden, Alabama. Many of them were voting for the first time as a result of the protections afforded by the Voting Rights Act of 1965. Despite their participation, the conservative coalition regained its strength in the House and the Senate.

By 1967 and 1968, images of Americans in combat in Vietnam were grabbing national attention, and the war was becoming more controversial.

Antiwar activists protest Johnson's policies in Vietnam. Until 1967, the president had ignored the antiwar Left (dismissing its members as "little shits on the campuses"). But he could ignore them no more.

The budgetary concerns about Vietnam mounted. The Federal Reserve chairman, William McChesney Martin Jr., called on the White House and Congress to reduce the federal deficit to prevent an inflationary spiral. Johnson still postponed sending Congress a tax surcharge proposal in the hope that he would be in a stronger position by the summer to obtain the bill he wanted with minimal cuts in his cherished programs.

The riots in Detroit, Michigan (pictured here), and Newark, New Jersey, strengthened the hand of congressional conservatives who wanted to cut spending. In response, they argued that liberal social policies were rewarding lawless behavior and causing domestic chaos.

At an Oval Office meeting on July 24, 1967, to address the Detroit riots, a dejected president Johnson (seated, foreground) confers with (background, left to right) his adviser Marvin Watson, J. Edgar Hoover, Secretary of Defense Robert McNamara, General Harold Johnson, the domestic adviser Joe Califano, and Secretary of the Army Stanley Resor.

On November 17, 1967, a visibly furious Lyndon Johnson reprimands Congress for tying up his proposed tax surcharge at the risk of destabilizing the global financial system. Johnson warned that Wilbur Mills and Gerald Ford would "rue the day" they had blocked his surcharge.

The House Ways and Means Committee chairman, Wilbur Mills, was unmoved by President Johnson's personal attacks on him. As a result of the midterms, congressional conservatives once again held the balance of power in Congress, and Mills was in a position to insist that Johnson choose between guns and butter.

President Johnson (back to the camera) meets with the Minnesota senator Eugene McCarthy—the leader of the antiwar bloc in Congress—on June 11, 1968. In March, McCarthy's strong second-place finish in the New Hampshire Democratic primary had stunned the White House and was a factor in Johnson's decision to withdraw from the race.

Vice President Hubert Humphrey (far left) seemed helpless as Vietnam dragged down his candidacy. The antiwar movement condemned the vice president for supporting Johnson's failed war policies.

Richard Nixon in a motorcade during the 1968 presidential campaign.
His campaign avoided much specific discussion of the Great Society.

The incoming president, Richard
Nixon, meets with Johnson in
the White House on January 20,
1969. Nixon retained most of the
Great Society, expanded some of
its programs, and even added new
domestic initiatives.

was child's play compared with the way he attacked the housing bill.[40] "The major issues for the 11th district voters," Hoellen said, "involve the property rights and the community rights of almost a half-million citizens."[41] The Democrat Cecil King of California pointed out how his state had passed a fair housing law in 1963 and overturned it one year later as a result of a backlash against the policy. "This is about all a politician needs to know—regardless of his own feelings," King explained. "And the conduct of those people in Watts hasn't helped."[42] Freshman Democrats were most vulnerable to white backlash; many of them had been elected by traditionally Republican voters who couldn't bear to pull the lever for Goldwater. "It's just not worth sacrificing my political hide," one midwestern Democrat complained. "And, particularly, since it looks like the Senate might kill it off anyway."[43]

Chicago's mayor, Richard Daley, predicted that the open-housing protests could end up knocking out of Congress the very politicians upon whom civil rights organizations had depended for their landmark victories in 1964 and 1965. He said that Democratic congressmen who had voted for civil rights were now "getting hell at home" while "Republicans are standing on the sidelines laughing at them." As a prime example, he pointed to Senator Paul Douglas, who was falling into a "serious trap" against Charles Percy. Douglas, an icon of liberalism, was facing an unexpectedly strong challenge from the self-made millionaire Republican who looked as if he'd been cast by Hollywood for the Senate. "He was," Douglas recalled, "just the candidate for suburbia and middle-class youth: a kind of Horatio Alger hero in a Brooks Brothers suit."[44] Percy could attract moderate voters who were scared about the turbulence on the streets but not ready to side with right-wing conservatism. He was a liberal Republican who supported civil rights but could still distance himself from Johnson's record. If the civil rights bill enabled a Republican to defeat a Democrat with the impeccable liberal credentials of Douglas, a politician who had carried the flame for civil rights, Daley said, "What do we accomplish?" He felt that the protests were "ruining the Democratic ticket for November."[45] In other states, Daley feared that the backlash could be even worse and could elect conservative Republicans.

The most direct threat to the housing provision came when the conservative West Virginian Arch Moore proposed an amendment to kill it. Faced with Moore's proposal and the ongoing news reports about confrontations between African American protesters and white onlookers, legislative supporters of residential desegregation became even more open to compromise.[46] To save the civil rights legislation from total defeat in the increasingly hostile environment, Mathias pushed for another compromise. His new amendment provided that real estate brokers could ignore antidiscrimination laws if they were directly instructed to do so by the homeowner, as long as they did not solicit the homeowner to place a racial condition on the sale. Though some liberals argued that this provision would make passage of the bill an "empty" victory, they recognized that the amendment could protect eighteen votes that might otherwise go to Moore. The political environment had changed so drastically since the year began that they realized this was the best they could probably get.

The final iteration of the amendment, which exempted 60 percent of the nation's housing stock from the regulations, was extremely controversial. Adam Clayton Powell Jr., who was still supporting the bill, said publicly that at this point it didn't really matter whether it became a law or not. Mathias responded to criticism from liberals to his amendment by saying that even with this revision the legislation would result in twenty-three million new homes and large apartments becoming available to the almost twenty million African Americans living in the United States, in addition to the approximately one million new homes that would be constructed annually. Barely enough liberals agreed with Congressman Celler's conclusion that "the all-or-nothing approach produces nothing except a slogan," and the House passed the Mathias amendment by a vote of 180 to 179.[47] The DSG's leader, Richard Bolling, cast the tiebreaking vote.[48] For Bolling and others in the DSG this compromise was a bitter pill to swallow, but swallow it they did.

The Mathias amendment was crucial to picking off some of Moore's support among Republicans; now even fewer of their constituents would be subject to the law.[49] The Democratic leadership also won over moderate votes by accepting a "law and order" amendment that imposed more stringent penalties for individuals who attempted to instigate riots from across state lines. The Moore amendment was backed by southern Democrats, a sizable contingent of Republicans, and six of the freshman Democrats who had been part of Johnson's reliable voting bloc on domestic policy, but it went down to defeat, 222 to 190. On August 13, the House passed the Civil Rights Act by 259 to 157. The bill received the support of 183 Democrats, including 169 from non-southern states and 14 southerners, and 76 Republicans.

The prospects remained bleak in the Senate. Dirksen had been willing to negotiate a deal on the voting rights bill before the Senate even started debating the legislation, but now the Senate minority leader was publicly insisting on his opposition to the housing bill. No one thought he was bluffing; he had always opposed granting the federal government power over the housing market, and he had been quite disturbed by the racial violence in and around Chicago. Most of it had been white citizens lashing out against African Americans, but Dirksen, like a growing number of Republicans, blamed civil rights activists tied to the black power movement, who he said were stirring up trouble in Illinois by demanding too much and forcing dangerous confrontations on the streets.

When Republicans and southern Democrats started a filibuster on September 8, Dirksen refused to endorse a vote for cloture. Senator Philip Hart told the press, "If Dirksen delivers the votes this year, we'll have a good bill," but Dirksen responded, "I don't think you, you're going to get cloture on any civil rights bill this year."[50] The president said there was a "great revulsion" developing against civil rights that would give the South control of Congress.[51] Polls indicated that 52 percent of white Americans believed the administration was moving too fast on civil rights.[52] The administration's vote counters believed Dirksen would have enough votes to sustain a filibuster. Times had changed. The filibuster was once again a formidable weapon against civil rights.

Johnson reached out to his friend Abe Fortas, whom he had recently appointed to the Supreme Court, to plead that the Court take up "law and order this session and tell these fellas that they've got to quit turning over cars and stuff." Johnson frequently consulted Fortas despite the doctrine of separation of powers. Nor did he see any reason to hide his political motivations. He told his old friend that if the Court tackled these issues, it would be helpful to the Democratic Party; the rioting was shaping the mood of the electorate more than Vietnam or inflation; and "every white man just says by god he don't want his car turned over and don't want some Negro to [be] throwing a brick at him."[53]

On September 19, Senator Hart confirmed Dirksen's prognosis and pronounced the civil rights bill dead. Martin Luther King warned that the action by the Senate "heralds darker days for this social era of discontent. The executioners of the 1966 civil rights bill have given valuable assistance to those forces in the Negro communities who counsel violence."[54] Johnson did not give up on the legislation, but he decided to hold off fighting for it until after the election. Mansfield warned that the "rioting, marches, shootings and inflammatory statements" would have to end before the bill could be passed.[55]

Republicans were ramping up their attacks on the Democrats as the party responsible for urban rioting. They called on the federal government to establish law and order by cracking down on violence and crime. On September 20, one day after Hart's declaration, Gerald Ford, at the Illinois State Fair, called Democrats the party "with the big riots in the streets" and asked voters, "How long are we going to abdicate law and order—the backbone of any civilization—in favor of a soft social theory that the man who heaves a brick through your window or tosses a firebomb into your car is simply the misunderstood and underprivileged product of a broken home?"[56]

THE CONSERVATIVE CAMPAIGN

The bitter conflict that had taken place over the civil rights bill in the spring and summer of 1966 was the backdrop for the midterm elections. The liberal majorities that had spearheaded the Great Society were fracturing under the strain of the backlash against residential integration in the North. The conservative coalition had experienced a boost in confidence; it had a wedge issue that was dividing liberals. Some reliable liberal Democrats were angry at Johnson for pushing them into political hot water right before the difficult midterm elections.

The midterms offered an opportunity for the conservative coalition to reestablish itself as the dominant force in the House and the Senate, even if liberals were to remain a much bigger presence in the chambers than they had been at any time since the 1930s. Republicans—and conservative Democrats—used the campaign to develop and refine themes and strategies they could use in attacks on Johnson now and in the next presidential election.

The Republicans were determined to capitalize on the underlying fragility of the liberal victories in 1964 by exploiting the tensions that had arisen over housing, the War on Poverty, civil rights, and other issues Johnson and the liberals had pushed. They targeted the freshman Democrats from the Midwest who had won seats in Republican districts in 1964. In Wisconsin, for instance, the Republican National Committee poured money into the campaign of William Steiger, a twenty-eight-year-old state legislator who was challenging the Democratic freshman John Race, a former union president, who had barely won the seat from a Republican incumbent in the Sixth District, which included Oshkosh and Sheboygan. Steiger, who was being promoted by Governor Warren Knowles as one of the most exciting new moderate voices in the Republican Party, had won in the primary over a right-wing candidate supported by the John Birch Society. He had co-authored the open-housing law in his state. The incumbent Democrat had been loyal to Johnson on most of his other major bills, including education and Medicare. In 1965, he voted 94 percent of the time with the administration. But the mood of his electorate had changed over the year. Struggling as a Democrat to survive in a district where President Johnson had become highly unpopular, Race opposed the civil rights bill that was stuck in the Senate. Though Steiger had a more liberal record on residential desegregation, the polls indicated that backlash sentiment in his district and elsewhere would hit Democrats harder, because they would be associated with Johnson and his approach to the issue. Race, a fanatic poll watcher, voted with Johnson only 63 percent of the time in 1966.[57]

In Iowa, Republicans made a strong play for five Democratic seats. One of them was in the Seventh District, where the husky farmer William Scherle challenged the Democratic freshman John Hansen. "Two years ago I was on the attack," Hansen admitted. "Now I've got to defend my record."[58]

Besides targeting freshmen who were not conservative enough for their districts, Republicans across the country—in local, state, and national elections—tapped into national themes that seemed to be effective on the campaign trail: a critique of race relations viewed primarily as an issue of law and order, hawkish attacks on how the war in Vietnam was being conducted, and jeremiads on the terrible threat of inflation. The political center, at least rhetorically, had shifted back to the right, and candidates were willing to go where the ill-fated Goldwater had gone—but not as far.

Some Democrats—and Republicans too—tried to capitalize on a white racial backlash against the civil rights movement and civil rights legislation. They did so in different ways.[59] There were conservatives in both parties who directly played to feelings of racial hatred. They blamed urban unrest on the radicalization of the civil rights movement and Johnson's liberal domestic policies.

The Democratic primary for the Maryland governorship, which had started as a debate over government corruption, was transformed by the congressional battles over housing discrimination. The liberal representative Carlton Sickles, a forty-five-year-old lawyer who strongly supported the civil rights bill, lost to the Baltimore contractor George Mahoney, who promised to veto any open-housing bill that his state legislature passed. His slogan was "Your home is your castle—vote to protect it!"

The notorious segregationist Lester Maddox was running against the Republican Bo Callaway for the governorship of Georgia. Callaway was the first Republican nominee for the governorship since 1876. Maddox, who had prevailed in the primaries over more racially moderate candidates, including the state senator Jimmy Carter, had made a name for himself following the passage of the Civil Rights Act of 1964 by brandishing an ax handle and chasing three African Americans away from his whites-only restaurant. When the Supreme Court rejected a challenge to the legislation, Maddox shut down his restaurant and hung a sign out front that read, "Lights Turned Out by LBJ."[60] His opposition to the Civil Rights Act launched his career.

In other cases, moderate Republicans who favored civil rights argued that they could handle the issue better than their Democratic opponents. As Thomas Hauser, manager of Charles Percy's campaign against Senator Douglas, admitted, racial unrest could provide "a general advantage to Republicans, if the people think the Democrats have not been able to deal with the problem effectively."[61]

In Illinois, just as Mayor Daley had predicted, many ethnic white residents were thinking of voting for the GOP as a result of the summer of violence and King's presence in the city. Talk about law and order accelerated after an armed intruder killed Percy's twenty-one-year-old daughter in their lakeside home. Though the murderer was never identified, the racial implications were clear when, drawing on the rhetoric of the realtor lobby in its campaign against open-housing legislation, anonymous Percy supporters circulated a leaflet throughout the Chicago area that proclaimed, "Your home is your castle—Let's keep it that way!"[62] Senator Douglas counseled President Johnson against visiting the state, because the "white backlash" was "very strong in the lower income people,"[63] but Percy, who had reversed his earlier opposition to the housing bill, chose not to appeal to racist sentiment; he adamantly supported a compromise version of the housing bill. His defense of the civil rights accomplishments of the 1960s also represented a strong appeal to African American voters in the city.

A majority of Republican candidates didn't believe that opposing civil rights or even focusing on urban unrest was their best strategy. The GOP had invested so much in shaping the civil rights legislation of 1957, 1964, and 1965 that most Republican candidates did not want to break the promises made by these laws. Irrespective of strategic considerations, most Republicans were uninterested in stoking the flames of racial hatred and generally agreed with the premises of the civil rights movement. Though a racial backlash might have softened the Democratic electorate and exposed areas of weakness, most Republicans decided to steer their campaigns toward issues where they sensed there was much broader opposition to Democrats.

A number of Republican candidates, including Percy, emphasized foreign policy, particularly the war in Vietnam. They blasted the administration for allegedly covering up its plans to escalate the number of ground troops to be sent there in 1967. They argued that Johnson was indecisive, a waffler, unable to commit to a full-scale war against communism, and fearful of the growing body of left-wing antiwar activists on college campuses.[64] The president worried about polls from Virginia and North Carolina that indicated voters wanted the administration to go "all out" militarily to bring the Vietnam conflict to an end.[65] A farmer in Piatt County, Illinois, who had voted for President Johnson in 1964 because he was the "lesser of two evils" was now reconsidering his decision; he asked, "Can't Johnson do more and get it over with?"[66]

For a majority of Republicans, the most popular campaign issues after the Vietnam War were inflation and the budget deficit. They had successfully used the rising cost of living in the 1952 presidential and congressional campaigns, when the GOP won the presidency for the first time in the post–New Deal era.[67] Fiscal policy once again offered a compelling cudgel for them to wield against Democrats.

Americans accorded great importance to balanced budgets; they traditionally compared the federal government's fiscal books unfavorably with the budgets maintained in private homes.[68] Conservatives argued that federal deficits were provoking inflation by injecting excessive amounts of federal money into the economy. There were in fact signs of higher prices in 1966 (though inflation remained low by historical standards). In March, the consumer price index rose by 0.5 percent, the biggest increase for any February since 1951 during the Korean War.[69] Much of the retail price increase was occurring where Americans felt it most, at the supermarket, particularly for meat. Pork chops cost eighty-nine cents a pound in 1966 compared with sixty-five cents a pound one year earlier. The 13.5 percent increase in meat prices drove the 4.5 percent rise in food costs. Other rising costs included transportation, medical fees and hospital services, and household services.[70]

Internal White House polls indicated that voters were worried. In California, 76 percent of those polled gave the president unfavorable performance ratings for keeping down the cost of living.[71] Throughout the country, housewives organized boycotts at supermarkets to demand reductions in food prices. In Denver, thousands of housewives joined a "beans to bacon" boycott of the city's supermarket chains. Lyndon Johnson said that in the 1950s it had been impossible for a politician to visit any home without being asked, "'What do you think about McCarthy?' . . . Now it is, 'What do you think about inflation?'"[72]

Despite the Republican arguments, there were hardly any economists who believed prices were rising primarily because of federal budget deficits. The evidence suggested that the early signs of inflation resulted from the Federal Reserve's expansionary monetary policy, which had kept interest rates low in the early 1960s, and from higher consumer demand that had resulted from generally booming economic conditions.[73]

In fact, the deficit in 1966 was not alarmingly high. It had been $1.4 billion in 1965, but it had been $7.1 billion in 1962, $4.8 billion in 1963, and $5.9 billion in 1964. In 1966, the deficit would rise, but only to $3.7 billion. The federal deficit had been considerably larger in the 1950s, when the Republican Dwight Eisenhower was president; it had reached $12.8 billion in 1959. In 1960, there was a $300 million surplus.

Johnson could not rely on the traditional policy used to control inflation in times of war: mandatory wage and price controls. There was limited congressional support in the 1960s for reimposing such controls. The crisis wasn't severe enough to generate solid majorities in the House or the Senate, and Johnson had made it difficult for himself by not asking Congress to declare war: he was doing everything possible to avoid triggering more controversy about Vietnam than already existed. In his first two years, Johnson had tried to persuade business and labor leaders to abide by voluntary price and wage agreements. By 1966 his appeals, though they had initially had some positive response, were not as effective.[74]

Republicans were eager to focus public discussion on the deficit. Johnson understood the political implications of the voters' uneasiness about federal deficits—they felt as they would feel if they had spent themselves into heavy debt—but he didn't want to talk about the issue until after the midterms.

An effective deficit reduction package that would contain inflation and not be paid for primarily by cuts in services to the poor required a combination of tax increases and spending cuts. Tax increases were essential because they were a progressive way to pull money out of circulation, as opposed to cutting welfare or raising interest rates, both of which were harder on middle- and lower-income people. When Johnson had surveyed legislators about their opinion on the subject, almost every one told him, "No and hell no." Each legislator, he said, felt that his "whole future is in danger if he votes for [a] tax increase" because "the man after him at home is going to welcome him at the station and say here's a man who went up there and voted to raise your taxes." The president concluded, "Republicans and Democrats, liberals and conservatives, reactionaries, and ADA'ers [the liberal organization Americans for Democratic Action] are generally speaking scared to vote for a tax increase four months before an election."[75] So he had decided to wait.

But most Republican candidates viewed deficit reduction not as a macroeconomic tool that could be used to moderate inflation but as the cure for a cancer that was gradually destroying the economy. They tried to sell the idea that there was a genuine fiscal crisis, and they proposed deficit reduction based on cuts in nondefense spending. This approach, which the Republicans labeled "budgetary austerity," liberals labeled "balancing the budget on the backs of the poor and middle class." The Republicans managed to call for deficit

reduction without directly questioning the necessity of specific federal programs—Barry Goldwater had made the political mistake of
doing this in the 1964 campaign—because polls showed that even
though Americans harbored negative views about government spending in general, a majority supported specific programs Johnson had
introduced, Medicare among them.[76]

The Republican Campaign Committee distributed pamphlets
complaining about "Great Society play money" that featured pictures
of Texas longhorns hovering over LBJ, saying, "Progress is a shrink-
ing dollar." Republican candidates staged photo ops at supermarkets
where they pushed shopping carts and lamented the rising prices of
household goods.[77] Senator Dirksen stumped for Republicans by saying, "Every housewife who shops in a grocery store knows this. They
are the living, breathing signs of this destructive burglarizing force."[78]
During one campaign speech, Richard Nixon urged voters to make
the election "a National Price Protest Day."[79] Republicans warned
that the administration was secretly planning to send proposals to
Congress, after the election, that would impose wage and price controls and raise taxes.

The midterm elections took on added significance at the national
level because several Republicans were seeking to use the campaign
to claim the mantle of front-runner in 1968. The most visible was the
former vice president Richard Nixon. The midterm campaigns
marked his full-fledged return to the national political arena. Nixon,
who had a staff of just three people and generally traveled on com-
mercial airlines, was able to raise $6.5 million for the GOP and spoke
in support of over eighty candidates in thirty-five states.[80] Another
Republican who gained national attention was Ronald Reagan, who
sought to unseat Governor Pat Brown of California. A product of the
conservative movement, Reagan railed against the college counterculture and condemned Johnson's policies for having created social
havoc in the cities. He attacked Brown's support of the state's fair

housing bill and the California Supreme Court ruling in 1966 that held that Proposition 14—which overturned the fair housing law—was unconstitutional. Governor George Romney of Michigan used his reelection campaign against Zolton "Zolty" Ferency as an opportunity to establish his national credentials as the most electable person in the GOP.

The Republican campaign issues were a serious concern to Johnson. He didn't want to see the Republican attacks on his domestic proposals and the growing opposition to his policies in Vietnam lead to southern Democratic chairmen and their Republican counterparts regaining all their former power to thwart his legislation. The congressional liaison Charles Roche said, "This is the big ball game of 1966. The results will be reflected in the next two years of legislative activity on the Hill."[81]

Taking a page out of the 1964 campaign playbook, Johnson attempted to portray Republicans as appealing to the worst emotions of the country. In Newark, New Jersey, he said, "The Republican symbol is the elephant and the elephant never forgets. The Republicans remember that they have always been elected by scaring people. Their platform this year is made up of one word, and that word is fear."[82]

Johnson and other Democrats also had a positive message about their legislative productivity. "I am willing to let any objective historian look at my record," Johnson told an aide. "If I can't do more than any[one else] to help my country, I'll quit. FDR passed five major bills in the first one hundred days. We passed 200 in the last two years. It is unbelievable. We must dramatize that."[83] Johnson urged Democrats to highlight the ways in which their programs, those that Republicans would certainly try to cut if they had more power, were helping the country. Johnson could make these claims effectively because he had made certain that his initiatives were up and running within a year. As information that was assembled by White House staffers revealed, Medicare was fully operational by the summer of 1966, one year after Congress had enacted the law. Almost 4.5 million would be receiving benefits by 1967. The Elementary and Secondary Education Act had already benefited 7 million schoolkids through special education projects for disadvantaged children and 49 million kids who were using library books and textbooks.[84] In a motorcade tour in New York City, the president reminded voters that "the war on poverty has helped 9,000,000 Americans, and they are glad that fear struck out. Today 3,000,000 educationally deprived American children are glad that fear struck out."[85] The White House research team also distributed evidence to the media of how essential congressional Democrats were to key votes, if the "legislative process is not to grind to a halt."[86]

The president tried to combat the racial backlash. Two nights before the election, he made a statement toward the end of a press conference in which he said, "I can think of nothing more dangerous, more divisive, or more self-destructive than the effort to prey on what is called 'white backlash.'" He urged "every American to ask himself before he goes to the polls on Tuesday: Do I want to cast my vote on the basis of fear? Do I want to follow the merchants of bigotry? Do I want to repudiate good men—Democrats and Republicans alike—who have given us Medicare, a great education program, a higher minimum wage, new parks and playgrounds, protection for the consumer, the hope for cleaning out our slums and rivers and the air we breathe?"

Four days before the election, Johnson held three ceremonies to sign eight bills that provided support for Great Society programs, including legislation that authorized $6.1 billion in assistance to the elementary and secondary school program. All the signings took place in front of a turquoise backdrop, ideal for broadcasts on color television. The president, who shook the hands of numerous legislators and furiously handed out pens, clearly intended the events for the edification of a national audience. The Marine Corps orchestra played "Hail to the Chief" each time he entered the room for another ceremony.[87]

THE RESULTS

The final efforts were not enough. As Johnson had expected, the elections went poorly for liberals. Although Democrats continued to control Congress, with 64 Democrats in the Senate and 248 Democrats in the House, the size of the conservative coalition had grown substantially.[88] In the House, their numbers grew from approximately 240 members in the Eighty-ninth Congress to 278 in the Ninetieth.[89] Republicans gained 47 seats in the House and 3 seats in the Senate. This was well above the predictions of most pundits, and notably higher than the 33-seat-average opposition party gain in off-year midterm elections since 1934.[90]

Only thirty-eight out of seventy-one Democrats elected in the Johnson landslide—slightly more than half of the 1964 freshman class—were reelected to the House in 1966. Just twenty-three of the forty-seven freshman Democrats who had been elected in Republican districts in 1964—not counting the freshmen who had defeated Democratic incumbents—were victorious.[91] At the state level, Republicans won a net of eight governorships as well as 557 state legislative seats. Richard Nixon, who had watched the returns from a room at the Drake Hotel and gone home to his Fifth Avenue apartment at about midnight, called his staff at 2:30 a.m. to receive an update on the returns. They reported each victory, state by state. "We've beaten the hell out of them," Nixon yelled into the receiver, "and we're going to kill them in '68!"[92]

There was deep disappointment for younger liberal Democrats in Dixie, who had once hoped to replace senior conservatives. Liberal and moderate Democrats had been hoping to appeal to the growing number of southerners who wanted to move beyond racial issues, focus on the economic revitalization of their region, and attract suburbanites who wanted to relocate from the North to the "New South." From the vantage point of 1965, when liberals were still enjoying the afterglow of the 1964 election and Congress was passing major domestic legislation on a regular basis, a positive outcome had seemed plausible if not certain to younger southerners, but political conditions had changed rapidly throughout 1966, as the struggle over the civil rights bill had revealed. Rather than liberal southerners taking control, a new generation of Republicans was replacing the old Dixiecrats. In Virginia's Eighth District, liberal Democrats celebrated Howard Smith's defeat in the primary—the unexpected result of court-ordered redistricting—until his conqueror, the progressive George Rawlings, was defeated in the general election by William Scott, a conservative Republican attorney from Fairfax.

The GOP also rebounded in its traditional stronghold of the Midwest, where the party had been humiliated two years earlier. Republicans regained many of the House seats they had lost in 1964; they won 57 percent of the rural vote.[93] The election of two Republican senators, Percy in Illinois and Robert Griffin in Michigan, was considered a major victory for the GOP. Republicans did extremely well regaining ground in Michigan, where the defeated freshmen Wes Vivian, Paul Todd, John Mackie, Raymond Clevenger, and Billie Farnum were nicknamed the Michigan Five Fluke Freshmen. In Ohio, Republicans beat three Democratic freshmen and two senior members. In Wisconsin, the two freshman Democrats, one of them John Race, were defeated. The only Democratic freshmen to survive in the Midwest were John Culver in Iowa and Indiana's Andrew Jacobs and Lee Hamilton, all of whom had benefited from gerrymandering.[94]

The overall outcome was worse than liberals had hoped for, but it was not a surprise; it was a predictable midterm loss after a huge landslide triumph. It boded ill, however, for the future. The campaigns and the final vote seemed to expose 1964 as more of an aberration than liberals wanted to believe. The number of liberal Democrats in the House and the Senate had significantly declined. Southern committee chairmen would face a diminished threat that the Democratic caucus could force bills out of their committees. Allied with non-liberal Republicans, conservative southern Democrats would have enough votes on the floor to threaten the success of liberal proposals. According to the *Congressional Quarterly*, "The pro civil rights coalition which had operated so effectively in previous years—Republicans and Northern Democrats in Congress and civil rights, labor and church groups outside Congress—fell apart in 1966."[95]

"The nation has voted to restore the two parties to their normal competitive balance," noted the editors of the *New York Times*. "The Republican party has become once again a viable and effective opposition after the Goldwater debacle of 1964."[96] Ray Bliss, the Republican National Committee chairman, told a packed room of reporters in a Washington hotel, "This press conference will be a little different from my first one, when you were asking me if the Republican Party would survive. It looks to me as if we have a very live elephant."[97]

The polls showed that the Republican campaign themes had resonated with the electorate. Many voters were not pleased about the direction of civil rights. Seventy-three percent of those polled in one major study said that activists were moving too fast. Voters were also worried about inflation. Seventy-eight percent of those surveyed thought prices would continue going up, and only 35 percent of respondents thought they would be doing better economically within a year.[98]

Civil rights activists tried to make the best of the outcome; they pointed out that the election resulted in higher numbers of moderate Republicans in the Senate. In Illinois, for instance, the backlash helped defeat Paul Douglas, but the victor, Charles Percy, was a strong supporter of civil rights.[99] Voters in Massachusetts had made Edward Brooke the first African American in the Senate since Reconstruction. Some Democrats who were under fire from opponents of racial integration, like Chicago's congressman Pucinski, survived the election. "Despite appeals to bigotry of an intensity and vulgarity never before witnessed in the north," Martin Luther King said, trying to make the best of the situation, "millions of white voters remained unshaken in their commitment to decency."[100]

In many respects, King and others were right. The elections rolled back the victories from 1964, but they didn't make them disappear. The Democratic caucus remained much more liberal than it had been in the previous decade. Even conservative members of both parties expected that most of the programs enacted by the Eighty-ninth Congress would remain in place for decades to come.

Yet, at some level, King and other civil rights leaders did understand that the election represented the end of this important and historic liberal moment. There was some clear evidence that race mattered in the northern electorate. Percy won by triple the normal Republican margin in the Thirteenth Ward of Chicago, a neighborhood populated by Eastern Europeans and a site of open-housing protests in the summer. Douglas did worse than Democrats had traditionally done in the Democratic hotbed of Chicago, with most of the falloff coming from white Catholic voters.[101]

Vietnam was also causing discontent, and fears of inflation and deficits registered high among voters. The outcome had made the prospects for passing more liberal legislation increasingly bleak. The liberal majorities from 1964 had been deflated, and those liberals who survived were scared by the political trends they were seeing.

Frustrated as he was by the campaign and the election results,

Johnson was not subdued. In fact, the conservative revival seemed to make him even more determined to fight for all he could get for as long as he could. On the last day of the year, the president told Humphrey that when they faced the new Congress in January, he would go after his opponents with "hammer and tongs."[102] Both men knew just how different the Ninetieth Congress would be. The good times for legislating were over, the battles would be more grueling, and the agenda would have to change drastically.

CHAPTER EIGHT

THE TRIUMPH OF
AUSTERITY POLITICS

For three years, Lyndon Johnson had chosen to ignore warnings that Vietnam was not an essential battleground in the cold war and that sending troops would be a mistake. By early 1967, he was paying the price for having chosen to prosecute the war. In 1966, 6,000 Americans had been killed in Vietnam, and 30,000 had been wounded. With approximately 450,000 troops bogged down there and no end of the combat in sight, the antiwar protests at home were intensifying. The Senate Foreign Relations Committee chairman, William Fulbright, the person on whom Johnson had relied to sell the Gulf of Tonkin Resolution to Democrats in the upper chamber, had given mainstream legitimacy to critics of the war by conducting televised hearings in which he grilled high-level administration officials and exposed flaws in their logic for pursuing victory in Vietnam.

In his determination to deprive conservatives of a potent political weapon against him—the argument that he was soft on communism abroad—Johnson had alienated the very people who were naturally the supporters of his domestic policies: the liberals. Martin Luther King Jr. blamed the "ill-considered warfare" for Johnson's "leisurely approach to social change." King told the Senate, "The guns of war become a national obsession."[1] King's statements shattered Johnson, who believed he had done all he could to advance the cause of African American equality in the past two years.

Middle-class students on the left who had once cheered Johnson's work on the Civil Rights Act of 1964 now railed against what they called Johnson's War. They staged dramatic protests around the country, burned their draft cards in front of the national media, and accused politicians of war crimes. On college campuses, protesters blockaded the offices of military recruiters and departments enriched by government grants to develop weapons. One of the most popular antiwar songs of early 1967, from the folksinger Pete Seeger, featured the lyrics "If you love your Uncle Sam, Bring 'em home, bring 'em home. Support our boys in Vietnam, Bring 'em home, bring 'em home. . . . Show those generals their fallacy, Bring 'em home, bring 'em home."

Johnson's idea that by embracing a hawkish stance he could successfully insulate himself from right-wing attacks on his domestic moves had been partially successful. He had divided the GOP: Senator Dirksen, among others, had become, though fitfully, his ally, but other GOP leaders berated the president for being insufficiently aggressive.

Taking flak over the war from both his left and his right flanks, Johnson turned his long-delayed attention to paying for it. At this point he had very few options. Everyone in Washington had noticed the growth in the federal budget and the expansion of the deficit. The anticipated deficit for fiscal year 1967 was $8.64 billion, a significant jump from $3.7 billion the year before. Republicans had successfully made the deficit a big issue in their election campaigns, and the January numbers confirmed that government expenditures were growing at a fast pace. Not surprisingly, domestic spending had surged. Between 1963 and 1966, total expansion of federal social welfare expenditures had been $14.5 billion; the growth in the budget was a total of $35.3 billion in fiscal years 1966 and 1967, when spending on Social Security, Medicare, education, and Medicaid were the biggest items.[2] But domestic programs were not the only driving force behind the deficit; the war was too. According to the Pentagon, spending for Southeast Asia would be $19.4 billion in fiscal 1967 and reach $21.9 billion in fiscal 1968. Johnson's advisers predicted that the overall Pentagon budget would reach $72.3 billion by fiscal 1968, a level not reached since World War II.[3]

By the time Johnson was finally prepared to ask Congress to raise taxes, he faced a much more hostile legislative environment than he had in the recent past. The conservative coalition, revitalized by the midterms, had already demonstrated its renewed strength in the first days of the Ninetieth Congress by mustering enough votes to eliminate the twenty-one-day rule. Emanuel Celler said, "The Republicans and Dixiecrats are going to kill all liberal legislation. They will be utterly reactionary."[4] Johnson told the civil rights leader Roy Wilkins, "Our whole damn program is dead as a doornail. I think the Republicans have taken over. I think they are in control. I think our own people have split up."[5]

Confronting this new Congress, Johnson would have to pay a high price for the tax surcharge he had decided he needed. The conservative coalition was tentatively on board with a surcharge, but it also demanded steep cuts in discretionary spending—money Congress had not already committed to supplementary Vietnam budgets, payments on the federal debt, or Social Security and Medicare. The steep cuts the conservatives wanted would have to come out of money Lyndon Johnson wanted to spend for education and cities, for the poor and the disabled, for all those still struggling in the lower depths of American's Great Society.

THE DRIVE TOWARD AUSTERITY

Zeal for deficit reduction was animating Washington politicians across the political spectrum. All politicians knew that voters generally believed warnings about the dire consequences of federal deficits when they were presented in terms of your family budget but with bigger numbers. In fact, the comparison was misleading precisely because the government, unlike your family, could stimulate the economy by going into debt and could, unlike your family, print more money if necessary to pay the interest. Deficits could result in bad consequences for various groups in the economy, but not always the consequences those who used the comparison intended voters to infer. In fact, budget deficits usually shrank when the economy, as intended, boomed in response to the stimulus they could provide; people and corporations paid higher taxes, social service costs were reduced, other government savings resulted, and deficits diminished. In short, a rising economic tide by itself generally lowered the deficit. Nevertheless, conservatives, and some liberals, persistently compared the federal government to a family, the federal budget to your family budget, and Lyndon Johnson to an irresponsible father. Senator Dirksen said, "Every American family knows that, while it can perhaps for a little while live beyond its means, it cannot do so for very long without finding itself on the short and rocky road to the poor house. A government—any government—is no exception . . . Like a family, a government cannot rely on hoped-for income nor can it endure economically for very long if needless expenditures which it can't afford are permitted."[6]

The president's Council of Economic Advisers, all liberal economists who supported Johnson's domestic agenda, were also looking to reduce the federal deficit, but from an entirely different perspective. Since 1965, they had been imploring the president to raise taxes to get enough money for his domestic programs and to put a brake on inflation. Johnson had refused to do so for more than a year, even though he was concerned about the impact of the growing imbalance between government expenditures and revenues; he believed the popular and political reaction against a tax increase could ruin whatever chances he still had to pass more domestic programs. The tight money policies the Federal Reserve had adopted in 1966 had created a credit crunch and slowed down the economy, and Johnson hoped that would be enough to quell passions for deficit reduction. He also remained concerned that an excessive austerity package could cause a recession. "I've been in this town for 35 years, and I've seen every President put the brakes on too long or too soon," he said. "The result was recession. I am not going to make that mistake."[7]

In January 1967, Johnson's economic advisers said loud and clear that it was too risky to wait any longer. The Federal Reserve had eased its monetary policies, and the economy was booming again; unemployment was low, and wages were high. With the boom came signs of the *potential* for inflation. Consumer prices had risen by 4.5 percent in the past eighteen months, and things might get worse. Johnson and his advisers knew that the deficit would become significantly larger in the next few years because the administration had hidden the projected costs of the Vietnam War; the current deficits were just the tip of the iceberg. Johnson was fully committed to continuing the war, and the size of the troop presence at the start of the year made any immediate end to the conflict impossible. The economists were telling him that if the deficits ballooned as expected, the government would be putting a lot of money into the economy; the effect of that would be upward pressure on consumer prices that would outpace any growth in wages—an inflationary spiral.

Johnson understood that rising deficits were politically dangerous; he had seen it firsthand in the Republican campaigns in 1966. If he didn't do something about the deficit, he would be allowing congressional conservatives to set the terms of the debate, and they would focus entirely on making big domestic spending cuts. Perhaps if he was proactive and persuaded Congress to pass a tax increase while he still had some political muscle left, he could prevent the conservative coalition from building support for an austerity package that decimated domestic spending.

Johnson's economists recommended a temporary 6 percent surcharge on income and corporate taxes. The simple idea was that higher taxes would dampen inflationary pressure by lowering demand; consumers would have less money to spend. The taxes would affect 80 percent of the nation's fifty-five million wage earners—Americans in the lowest income brackets would be exempted—but would be so spread out that the impact on any individual or family would be minimal.

Congressional conservatives in both parties had supported deficit reduction for both economic and political purposes. For decades, they had pointed to rising deficits as evidence that liberals were irresponsible and that their programs damaged private markets. They drew on technical economic arguments to prove how deficits hurt investment, and they claimed that balanced budgets were a sign that elected officials were good managers of the public trust that government represented. In numerous elections, including in 1966, conservatives had found that attacking deficits did not open them up to the same dangers as calling for cuts in specific government programs that often proved far more popular with voters than conservatives expected. Most conservatives accepted that a tax increase was necessary to balance the budget, but they wanted most of the deficit reduction to come from spending cuts.

There was also a business faction—primarily banking, investment, and housing industry interests—that was behind the drive for a tough austerity package.[8] These interests subscribed to the conventional economic wisdom that large U.S. deficits created dynamics that would weaken American and international economies. To begin with, according to this analysis, the Federal Reserve usually responded to an overheated economy by raising interest rates. The housing sector was still trying to climb out of the hole caused by the Federal Reserve's tight monetary actions in 1966. Total housing starts had fallen by 26 percent between September 1965 and September 1966.[9] The Federal Reserve chairman, William McChesney Martin, was prepared to clamp down on the economy again; he believed there was a real danger of inflation, and he didn't trust Congress to take the necessary actions. Higher interest rates meant fewer people could afford to borrow money for housing or any other consumption, and this meant less money in circulation. Higher interest rates also increased the expenses businesses incurred and generally passed on to consumers. Bankers and investors claimed that the expanding federal debt, which was funded through government bonds, diverted money from private investment—the stock market—which had already been suffering for more than a year. They warned that international confidence in the value of the dollar would decline because of the deficit and inflation. If European bankers started selling their dollars for gold, the international monetary system would collapse. That financial system, established in 1944 by forty-four allied nations led by the United States, revolved around the value of gold being fixed at $35 an ounce and the United States keeping enough gold in reserve to pay back governments and private investors overseas who wanted to redeem the dollars they had accumulated. Finally, those in the financial sector didn't like inflation, because they didn't want debtors to be paying them back for their investments in depreciated dollars.

The proposal for a tax surcharge found support in other parts of the business community. Although much more reluctant to support higher corporate and individual taxes, a sizable number of leaders from the manufacturing sector also backed austerity measures, based on the conventional belief that chronic deficits were bad for the economy. The conservative National Association of Manufacturers, an organization that normally had little love for the Johnson White House, agreed that Congress should enact a tax surcharge to reduce an "intolerable" deficit.[10]

Some liberals believed that all these arguments were based as much on mythology as on empirical economics. As the economist Walter Heller had reported to President Kennedy when JFK faced similar problems in 1962, "New York bankers tell the U.S. via the financial press that Europeans will lose confidence in the dollar unless we are good boys, i.e., cut spending, balance the budget, restrict credit, raise interest rates. The fact is that European bankers and financiers, who don't worry about balanced budgets in their own countries, worry about U.S. budget balance only because their New York counterparts tell them they should."[11] But liberals like Heller were generally drowned out by Democratic politicians who were unwilling to let deficits grow indefinitely. Although a number of them had accepted deficits in 1964 as a Keynesian tool to expand economic growth, their embrace of this concept had always been tentative. Most liberals, including Johnson, still assumed that chronic large deficits were a bad thing, even if their fiscal habits were inconsistent with this belief. Regardless, even Keynesians had argued that in periods of inflation the federal government had to use a combination of tax increases and spending cuts to restrain the economy. This combination would also reduce the budget deficit.

THE BUDGET BATTLES BEGIN

It was no surprise that when President Johnson sent his budget proposal to the Ninetieth Congress on January 24, it landed with a thud. He had started his presidency with the frugal budget Harry Byrd demanded, but he had subsequently allowed the costs of Vietnam and domestic policy to expose him to the charges of being a free-spending Democrat he had been so desperate to evade. One year earlier, he had proposed a $112.8 billion budget. At $172.4 billion, his proposed budget for fiscal 1968 was the largest in American history. It was "guns, butter and a lot of fat," in the opinion of the former House minority leader Charles Halleck.[12] Senator Dirksen said that Republicans would accept a "reasonable" deficit to pay for Vietnam but that domestic spending—he emphasized the Great Society—would "get a hard look. That was the signal the people gave in the Nov. 8 election. They said they want reasonably sound financing of Government expenditures and not extravagant outlays on wasteful programs."[13] Johnson didn't have much credibility left when it came to money. In the previous year, the budget had actually turned out to be more than $126 billion, not $112.8 billion, and Vietnam spending ended up at approximately $20 billion, rather than the $10 billion the president had promised it would be.[14]

Johnson announced to Congress he would soon ask it for a temporary 6 percent tax surcharge on individual and corporate income taxes. The tax surcharge was necessary to finance the war and the Great Society and to contain inflation. "While we have this problem [inflation]," Johnson said, "and this emergency in Vietnam, while we are trying to meet the needs of our people at home, your Government asks for slightly more than one-fourth of that tax cut [the tax cut of 1964] each year in order to try to hold our budget deficit in fiscal 1968 within prudent limits and to give our country and to give our fighting men the help they need in this hour of trial." The federal government had traditionally raised taxes as a part of national mobilization during times of war, and liberal Democrats feared that voting for the tax would be equivalent to endorsing the undeclared war in Vietnam. By waiting to ask for revenue until so late in this conflict, Johnson had made things much more difficult for himself; by now, legislators were less motivated by talk about a military emergency and more attuned to the negative political fallout the war was emitting. Southern Democrats and Republicans said they would support a tax surcharge only if the president agreed to accept much deeper cuts in domestic spending, which the liberals argued would place too much of the burden of deficit reduction on the poor. The House Appropriations Committee chairman, George Mahon, a Texas Democrat, supported budget cuts; he said, "When we are in an inflationary period and the budget is in the red, it is especially imperative that we take a critical look at all the phases of the budget and cut everything as much as we can."[15] Public sentiment was on the side of Johnson's opponents. A Harris poll found that to combat inflation, 75 percent polled supported spending cuts, with only 11 percent opposed to them. In the same poll, Harris reported that 65 percent of Americans opposed the 6 percent tax surcharge.[16]

Johnson heard the response to his tax surcharge idea and decided to postpone sending the request to Congress until the summer. He thought that strong economic conditions would lower the federal deficit and that political conditions would improve as the momentum conservatives were currently enjoying from the election faded. When those things happened, he would be in a better position to negotiate spending cuts with Wilbur Mills, whose committee had jurisdiction over income taxation.

THE RIOTS

Over the next few months, conditions on Capitol Hill only got worse. The political opposition to domestic programs grew more vehement when a summer of urban riots fueled conservative arguments for law and order and against the waste, inefficiency, and ineffectiveness they claimed infected the Great Society.

On July 12, two white policemen arrested an African American cabdriver in Newark. Residents of a public housing project across the street from the police station watched the arrest and congregated to protest what the officers had done. At 2:30 a.m., a day after the violence began, Governor Richard Hughes received a hysterical call from the mayor of Newark, who, according to the governor, said his "city was burning down" and that he needed help from the state police and the National Guard.[17] Over the next six days, there were violent clashes between the National Guard, largely white, and the rioters. The situation in Newark was "hell," the president confided to the U.S. ambassador to the United Nations, Arthur Goldberg, and he believed that if he sent in federal troops, or even cooperated with state authorities, it would look to rioters, who he believed were drugged up, like the "big white man on the top of the hill is coming after 'em."[18]

The police action immediately tapped into the long-standing frustration of African American residents with brutal police treatment of people in their community. Residents of Newark had extensive experience with police routinely acting with violence against criminal suspects and randomly harassing law-abiding citizens. Most of the residents of Newark lived in dilapidated housing, traveled on filthy streets, and contended with crime daily in their neighborhoods; living in these conditions only aggravated their anger. When the Newark riots ended on July 17, twenty-six people were dead, and hundreds had been injured.

A week later, in the early hours of a hot and humid night of July 23, undercover police in Detroit raided one of the city's many unlicensed bars, where a large crowd, almost entirely working-class African Americans, had gathered to celebrate the return of several veterans from Vietnam. Such raids were common and usually perfunctory, but this time the police rounded up all eighty-two people in the room. When the vehicles to transport the arrestees were delayed for about half an hour, a crowd of more than two hundred surrounded the police and yelled, "Black power. Don't let them take our people away."[19] After the wagons finally arrived, loaded up, and departed, a small group of men shattered the windows of a clothing store, entered, and began to loot the place. The violence quickly escalated and spread to other neighborhoods, including downtown Detroit.

Lyndon Johnson followed the events from the presidential yacht in the Potomac, where he was finalizing the tax surcharge proposal he was about to submit to Congress.[20] When he returned to the White House in the evening, bleary-eyed and anxious, he faced a situation that was deteriorating by the minute. Governor George Romney of Michigan spoke to Attorney General Ramsey Clark at three in the morning about the possibility that federal troops might be needed but had not requested them; he was reluctant to ask for help controlling his own state from the president he planned to run against the following year. National Republican leaders were making the most of the situation; they released a statement that warned, "The nation is in crisis, and this Administration has failed even to make a proposal to protect our people on the streets and in their homes from riots and violence."[21]

At 10:00 p.m. Cyrus Vance, the former deputy secretary of defense whom Johnson had trusted as an adviser on numerous issues since the 1950s and who was monitoring events on the ground, told Joseph Califano that the president should federalize the Michigan National Guard and move it into Detroit. It would be the first use of federal troops to quell a riot since 1943, when another riot had taken place in the same city. In recent years, though troops had been used to deal with racial desegregation in the South, they had not been used when there were riots in northern urban areas. Johnson desperately wanted a different solution but concluded he had no choice if he wanted to restore peace to the city. "They have lost all control in Detroit," the FBI director, J. Edgar Hoover, said. "Harlem may break loose within thirty minutes. They plan to tear it to pieces."[22]

Slumped forlornly in his chair, Johnson signed a presidential proclamation that ordered federal troops to intervene. On the evening of July 24, in an emotional television address, the president said, "We will not tolerate lawlessness. We will not endure violence. It matters not by whom it is done, or under what slogan or banner. It will not be tolerated." By justifying his actions on law-and-order grounds, Johnson purposefully echoed the themes that Republicans had been using against him and other Democrats for almost a year.

The rioting continued for several terrible days. Forty-three people died; more than a thousand were injured; almost seven thousand people were arrested. More than a thousand buildings were damaged. Massive clouds of black smoke hovered over the city. "It looks like Berlin in 1945," lamented Mayor Jerome P. Cavanagh.[23]

As the rioting was finally calming down in Detroit, Johnson established the National Advisory Commission on Civil Disorders, under the direction of Illinois's governor, Otto Kerner, to investigate the root causes. Some advisers were skeptical. Califano complained to the president, "The cities are aflame, the country's coming apart, LBJ can't get a tax bill, so what does he do? Set up a commission and say a prayer."[24] The commission's report was released in February 1968. It concluded, "Our nation is moving toward two societies, one black, one white—separate and unequal," and endorsed a number of government actions, including programs to end residential segregation and reduce minority unemployment.

The political impact of the riots was immediate on Capitol Hill. The turmoil hardened the conservative resolve to go after domestic programs on the grounds that they were not producing positive results and were, in some cases, making conditions worse than before. The Vermont Republican Winston Prouty released the text of a telegram from a Newark police official, Dominick Spina, to Sargent Shriver in May; Spina had warned that War on Poverty funds were being used to foment riots. "If Mr. Shriver and his colleagues blind themselves to the newer and more serious charges from Newark," noted the editors of the conservative *Chicago Tribune,* "they may soon find themselves in the business of subsidizing local 'wars of liberation' in cities all over the country."[25] The Oklahoma Republican Page Belcher expressed the sentiment of many conservatives when he said, "If you keep telling a man he's downtrodden, sooner or later he'll believe it. Ghetto conditions have nothing to do with it. We've had them for hundreds of years. It wasn't until we started passing civil rights bills that the trouble started."[26]

When the riots began, Congress had been working on legislation to provide $40 million in grants to local governments to subsidize rat extermination programs in urban neighborhoods. The bill had seemed likely to pass by large margins, given that rodents were widely considered a major public health problem. Events in the cities changed the vote count. Conservatives derided the "Civil Rats Bill," which they said would create a "rat bureaucracy" and provide the White House with more funds to distribute to urban machines. Only three days after the Newark riots started, the conservative coalition killed the bill in the House by a vote of 207 to 176.[27] One hundred forty-eight Republicans and 59 Democrats voted no. Every reporter and politician attributed the dramatic turn in legislative sentiment to the riots. President Johnson called the defeat a "cruel blow to the poor children of America." The Leadership Conference on Civil Rights called the vote an "act of shocking irresponsibility." Theodore Kupferman, a liberal Republican from New York City's silk-stocking district, which abutted Harlem, said, "If you were a hardworking father coming home from work to find one of your children bitten by a rat, you might very well start a small riot yourself."[28]

Johnson's real problem wasn't Republicans and southern Democrats. The biggest threat to his legislation was that a growing number of legislators who represented traditionally Democratic northern districts, especially those with white ethnic voting groups—Polish Americans, Italian Americans, and others—were hearing from their constituents that civil rights and the Great Society had gone too far.

The House Education and Labor Committee postponed action on a bill to provide funding for the War on Poverty because members were concerned that the riots were strengthening and broadening the opposition. Legislators and the public were starting to talk about the War on Poverty as primarily urban policy, connected to the unrest, though it had been largely rural from the outset. One liberal House Democrat told a reporter, "We've got to convince the members that poverty workers have not instigated the riots, but rather have been helpful in keeping them from getting worse or even starting in many cities of the nation."[29] Shaking his head in despair, Senator Philip Hart, who had been instrumental in moving the civil rights bills through Congress in 1964 and 1965, admitted, "What people saw a few years ago on television was police dogs jumping on people trying to vote. Now they see Negroes throwing rocks in store windows."[30]

Polls showed that the riots were stimulating intense fears among voters about the potential for more violence. There was a sharp difference along racial lines about causes. According to one poll, 45 percent of whites thought radicals and communist agitators had started the riots, compared with 7 percent of African Americans. Ninety-three percent of African Americans felt that living conditions in African American slums and ghettos fueled the riots, compared with 40 percent of whites.[31] Richard Veith, who headed one of the nation's most profitable guard dog rental agencies, said that since the riots, "My phone hasn't stopped ringing."[32]

The polls taken by Harris and Gallup after the riots showed that President Johnson's approval level had fallen to 39 percent, a decline of thirteen percentage points since June; it was the worst approval rating for a president since Harry Truman in 1952. Gallup reported that 54 percent disapproved of how the president was handling Vietnam. There was weakening support for how he was handling race relations. A thirty-one-year-old woman, the wife of a minister in Rochester, New York, said, "With rioting, inflation, and civil unrest, our society seems to be crumbling around us while Johnson is wasting our resources on Vietnam." Another poll found that Governor Romney was doing better than Johnson in a projected presidential election.[33]

Johnson was acutely aware of the negative political repercussions of what had taken place, in terms of his ability both to defend the Great Society and to win reelection in 1968. The influential political scientist Richard Scammon, the founder of the Elections Research Center and one of the leading analysts of political statistics, reminded Johnson that the key characteristics of the voter who would determine the election in 1968 were that he is "un-young. He is un-black. He is un-poor." This meant that with all the chaos taking place in the cities, the campaign of 1968 would have to target "white, middle-aged, middle class voters." Scammon called these the people who "bowl regularly." Based on his analysis, the depth of "anti-Negro sentiment" was extraordinarily strong among these voters.[34]

LURCHING INTO AN INTERNATIONAL CRISIS

Johnson's bet to delay asking for a tax surcharge had not paid off.

The need for revenue was even more urgent toward the end of the summer than it had been in January, and the political conditions in Congress were worse. Now Johnson needed the tax surcharge immediately, and it would have to be bigger than what he had been planning to request just a few months earlier. The budget situation had deteriorated since January: government spending had increased, and tax revenue was much lower than had been expected. Johnson's economists had been predicting a deficit of $8 billion, but they were now saying, and Johnson was publicly admitting, that the federal deficit might reach $29 billion. The rapid rise in consumer prices during June and July fueled concerns about inflation.

On August 3, Johnson finally delivered a special message to Congress to propose a 10 percent surcharge, rather than the 6 percent discussed in January, on all corporations and on most individuals— the lowest wage earners were excluded—and $2 billion in discretionary spending cuts. For a family of four who earned $10,000 a year and paid $1,100 in taxes, the surcharge would mean an increase of about $9.25 a month. It would raise an estimated $6.3 billion for the federal government; additional revenue from proposed increases in excise taxes would bring the total increase to almost $7.4 billion. If Congress didn't pass the measure immediately, Johnson warned, there would be higher interest rates when the Federal Reserve took the necessary steps to slow runaway inflation. The Fed would tighten the money supply, and this would make it harder for individuals and businesses to get loans. As a result, the overall growth of the economy would be slowed. Johnson insisted there were limits to the cuts he could make in expenditures, especially for the Vietnam War, so he had no option but to raise taxes.

Johnson's sharp warning of the potential for "a ruinous spiral of inflation" and "brutally higher interest rates" if Congress did not endorse his plans satisfied neither the public nor most of the political class. Slightly more measured in their rhetoric were Harvard's John Kenneth Galbraith, Yale's James Tobin, and many others of the nation's most prestigious economists, who did support the president. In a joint statement, they warned that economic restraint was essential to "maintain orderly growth, prevent a resurgence of inflation, and forestall excessive reliance on tight money. With government expenditures rising rapidly, the growth of total demand threatens to exceed the capacity of the economy to increase total output."[35]

Republicans, who were demanding major cuts in spending, were quick to attack the president. He was on the rocks, and they knew it; if they could block his fiscal plans, they believed they would benefit politically. The House minority leader, Gerald Ford, led the chorus of critics when he told reporters, "I will not concede that the present level of Federal spending cannot be cut back sufficiently to avoid a tax increase," while John Byrnes, the ranking Republican on the House Ways and Means Committee, bluntly announced, "Without an austerity program on expenditures, a tax increase is out of the question."[36] A significant number of Republicans and southern Democrats who had voted for the president's domestic programs were now calling for cuts in all domestic spending. It was now their intention—and Johnson knew it—to cripple his programs and to make it impossible for him to create any new ones.

The most important player in the House of Representatives was Wilbur Mills. Upon hearing the president's message, Chairman Mills, in his characteristically elusive fashion, announced to reporters, "I'm uncommitted."[37]

Although Mills said no more in public about the president's surcharge, he didn't agree with Johnson's interpretation of why there was inflation. The chairman subscribed to the "cost-push" theory of inflation, which blamed overly generous wage settlements with unions for driving up the costs that businesses faced. An inflationary cycle ensued, Mills argued, when businesses raised their prices to cover these costs, which then led consumers to demand even higher wages so they could afford to purchase costlier goods. Based on this interpretation of the economic situation, Mills argued that raising taxes could make things worse by creating greater pressure on wage earners to demand raises. In contrast, he believed, federal spending cuts would remove money from the economy without affecting individual and corporate income.[38]

Mills, however, had reluctantly come to the conclusion that there would have to be a tax increase as part of a deal in which the White House and non-southern Democrats would support essential spending cuts. Without a deal, the nation would have to live with skyrocketing deficits. Mills's fellow conservatives, including Senator Dirksen, had reached the same conclusion.

So the outline of a deal was clear. Congressional conservatives would obtain the spending cuts they desired, and the president would get the tax surcharge his advisers were saying was essential. Mills also believed that coupling the surcharge with spending cuts was necessary to make sure the new revenue was not spent on additional programs, thereby negating any anti-inflationary effects. For "those who are concerned with the size of the deficit—and I am certainly in that category," Mills said, "matching expenditure reduction with tax increases should be highly desirable: It doubles the reduction in the deficit."[39]

While the administration was contemplating a deal that included $2 billion in immediate spending cuts, the most Johnson and his advisers thought was possible without damaging his domestic programs, Mills and fellow conservatives had in mind a figure closer to $6 to $8 billion. Mills also pressed for cuts of funds that had been appropriated but not used the previous year, instead of their being incorporated into the new budget for each agency. He also demanded that the next budget include proposed future cuts—about $20 billion—in domestic spending.

Whereas Mills had been virtually powerless to stop Johnson in 1965 when the administration proposed the Medicare bill he had previously opposed, in 1967 the political situation was reversed. The conservative coalition was resurgent, and the president was asking Congress to take things away from Americans rather than give them benefits.

In a private telephone conversation in September, Mills tried to reason with Johnson. He told the president that if he was willing to cut deeper into congressional appropriations, which would only strengthen the impact the package would have on the federal deficit and inflation, they would have enough votes to pass the bill in the House. Administration officials believed Mills had the power to move any bill he wanted to move, but the chairman insisted that if the deal was to include the president's taxes, it would require concessions on spending that could win twenty to twenty-five Republican votes. Mills told Johnson, "I never saw such damned opposition any day in my life as there is to . . . any increase in taxes."[40]

Johnson's closest advisers told him that if he stood firm against spending cuts, Mills would blink first, but Mills didn't blink. In early October, Ways and Means set aside the legislation. "The tax bill is dead unless this is done," Mills said, referring to the inclusion of deeper spending cuts in the package.[41] The conservative coalition was the core of the vote. John Watts, who offered the motion, was joined by Mills, eight other Democrats, and all ten Republicans to shelve the bill; it was a sign of the fragility of the liberal coalition. Congressman Dan Rostenkowski, an Illinois Democrat who was a product of Mayor Daley's machine and who had been a loyal Johnson supporter, agreed to raise taxes but felt that bigger spending cuts would be necessary to win congressional support. The "president was not moving," Rostenkowski observed, defending the committee's decision to shelve the legislation, "and we are not moving . . . We hope this will get the executive branch off dead center."[42]

For the time being, the legislation was going nowhere. Mills told reporters, "Contrary to the impression that is sometimes given by intemperate critics of the Congress, these actions are not irresponsible, bullheaded, or spiteful, nor are they maneuvers for partisan advantage. They are, on the contrary, an expression of the anxiety, which many Members of Congress feel—fortified by the uneasiness they found in their constituencies over the recent Labor Day recess—about the recent sharp rise in federal outlay and the proliferation of federal government activity."[43]

At his press conference on November 17, Lyndon Johnson was uncharacteristically animated and informal. He removed his glasses, stepped away from the podium, and moved around with a portable microphone tucked into his jacket. He answered reporters' questions with the manic bravado he often showed when twisting congressional arms but rarely displayed in his careful, and usually monotonous, public speeches.[44] He expressed his anger and frustration with Congress, and he reprimanded his opponents for their decisions in blunt language. Mills and Ford, he said, would "live to rue the day when they made" the decision to block this legislation, "because it is a dangerous decision. It is an unwise decision."

In January 1968, with the fate of the tax surcharge still uncertain, Johnson's proposed budget for fiscal 1969 hit $186.1 billion. The bulk of the increased spending was once again for Vietnam and for payments, including interest on the debt and Social Security, that were fixed by law. It looked as if the deficit for fiscal 1968 would end up being approximately $20 billion. Naturally, Republicans disputed the number the president had announced and publicly predicted that the deficit would be closer to $35 billion than to $20 billion. With the GNP predicted to grow at a rate of 7.75 percent, which most economists considered unsustainable, and prices rising at 4 percent in the past six months (up from a rate of 3 percent in the past two years), those economists believed an inflationary period had begun.[45] The situation was generating international warnings that the U.S. government was out of control and its economy in a perilous condition.

As the cost of the Vietnam War continued to rise, the situation on the ground deteriorated steadily. The administration sent more and more ground troops, but it was clear that U.S. forces were not making substantial gains against the North Vietnamese and the Vietcong.

The United States had conducted a ruthless bombing campaign—the Republicans complained that Johnson was too timid—but instead of breaking the will of the enemy, the bombing hardened their resolve to endure and to drive out the Americans.

Johnson had utterly lost control of the war. While the United States wielded overwhelming firepower, the North Vietnamese and the Vietcong fought tenaciously; they knew how to use the terrain and were supported by many of the people in South Vietnam. Their strategy was to wear down American troops through constant surprise attacks and stealth warfare. The members of the South Vietnamese military were incompetent and corrupt allies. On the home front, avoidance of and resistance to the military draft fueled widespread dissatisfaction with the war policy and provoked the slogan "Hey, hey, LBJ, how many kids did you kill today?" and the bitter advice that the U.S. government should "declare victory and withdraw."

On January 31, 1968, it became clear that the war and its costs were not about to end anytime soon. The Vietcong launched a surprise attack, the Tet Offensive, on the U.S. embassy in Saigon and on other American targets in South Vietnam, and even though U.S. forces were able to turn back the assaults, their intensity showed that Vietnam was a "quagmire" and that promises by Johnson and General William Westmoreland, the commander of U.S. military forces, that victory was in sight had been foolish if not deceitful. Many Americans were shocked when General Westmoreland requested 206,000 more troops on top of the over half a million who were already there. Controversy over the war overwhelmed all other issues.

Senator Eugene McCarthy, the professorial six-foot-four senator from Minnesota who liked to quote the great poets, was the voice of the antiwar movement in Washington. He was not your ordinary politician. Before entering government, McCarthy had studied to be a monk and had taught courses in several Catholic colleges. He had been elected to the House in 1948 and to the Senate ten years later.

Although McCarthy had originally supported the war—he voted for the Gulf of Tonkin Resolution—by 1968 he had turned vehemently against it. What distinguished the senator more than anything else from others in his party was his willingness to take a forceful stand against the president on this issue. He called the war "diplomatically indefensible" and "morally wrong." On November 30, 1967, his challenge to Johnson's policy became a campaign for the Democratic nomination. Many college students found his campaign compelling and a refreshing alternative to the stalemate that seemed to grip the parties in Washington. These younger Democrats poured into New Hampshire to build support for McCarthy in the first primary of the presidential election season. Johnson did not campaign in New Hampshire, not an unusual strategy in an era when the party leaders still determined who the nominee would be and presidents rarely partook in the few primaries that were held.

Liberal unrest over Vietnam was a powerful factor in the primary, though the younger Democrats who had been politicized by their opposition to the war were also dissatisfied with what they perceived to be the limits of Johnson's efforts on domestic issues since 1966. McCarthy received 42.2 percent of the vote in New Hampshire, surprisingly close to Johnson's 49.4 percent. Suddenly the New Hampshire primary was no longer the minor event it had always been; the results in that rural New England backwater made it crystal clear just how low Johnson's political stock had fallen.

The president seemed very beatable. He had invested all his political capital in legislation he knew would anger core Democratic constituencies—southern conservatives and urban ethnic liberals. He understood clearly that legislative victories did not automatically translate into political strength. In fact, he had moved legislation that was sure to take a toll on his standing. Now he was paying the price. Johnson had also pushed the nation deeper and deeper into the unpopular war in Vietnam, in a misguided effort to appease hawks and protect his congressional coalition from right-wing attacks. The fiscal and political reckoning for these choices had been a long time in the making.

Richard Goodwin, who as a speechwriter for Johnson had coined the term "the Great Society," was now serving on McCarthy's campaign. He believed that McCarthy's strong showing had "unmasked the subterranean discontent with the president and his policies, revealed how intense and widespread was the desire for change, and transformed a Minnesota senator into a national political leader, a hero."[46]

Just a few days after the New Hampshire primary, on March 16, Senator Robert Kennedy announced he would be running for the Democratic nomination himself. Like McCarthy, he defined himself by attacking Lyndon Johnson from the left; he promised to do more to fulfill the objectives the president had promised to accomplish on the domestic front and assured supporters he would end the disastrous war in Vietnam. McCarthy's followers were furious with Kennedy, who they felt had avoided the primaries until their candidate had demonstrated how Johnson could be defeated. Still, RFK's entrance was exciting to a large number of Democrats who were lukewarm, at best, about President Johnson and nervous that Senator McCarthy would not be able to defeat any of the Republicans who could be nominated. During the press conference to announce his candidacy, Kennedy explained he would "seek new policies—policies to end the bloodshed in Vietnam and in our cities, policies to close the gap that now exists between black and white, between rich and poor, between young and old, in this country and around the rest of the world . . . the reality of recent events in Vietnam has been glossed over with illusions. The report of the Riot Commission has been largely ignored. The crisis in gold, the crisis in our cities, the crisis in our farms and in our ghettos have all been met with too little and too late."

The gold crisis to which Kennedy referred was greatly increasing pressure on Johnson and Mills to reach a deal on taxes and spending. U.S. policy makers, European bankers, and Wall Street genuinely feared that the international system of finance was in danger of collapse. As more investors outside and inside the United States were coming to believe the dollar would fall in value as a result of the stalemate over fiscal policy, there was a rapid outflow of gold from the United States as investors traded their paper currency for bullion. Speculators took advantage of these fears and made the situation even more acute. This was the kind of crisis that deficit hawks had been warning about for more than a year. In the *New Republic*, the economics reporter Edwin Dale agreed that the collapse of the finance system "could bring a world-wide depression."[47]

For a generation that had lived through the Great Depression in the 1930s, the possibility of a global financial meltdown had an almost palpable effect. "If the monetary crisis was not handled with skill by all concerned," Johnson later wrote in his memoirs, "it could easily throw the world economy into the kind of vicious cycle that had been so disastrous between 1929 and 1933. We were dealing not simply with money and exchange rates but with trade and jobs and the livelihood of millions of families."[48] "Americans have been hearing warnings for a long time about an impending 'gold crisis,'" noted the editors of the *Los Angeles Times*. "That crisis is now upon us, and this country simply has to make some hard decisions if we are to dampen the shock waves which threaten the very foundations of the U.S. economy."[49] The undersecretary of the Treasury, Joseph Barr, recalled, "It was a hair-raising period in which we literally had to watch the gold markets day by day and hour by hour."[50] Richard Nixon described the international crisis as a "vote of no confidence" in Johnson's fiscal policies.[51]

On March 13, Vice President Humphrey had warned, "We literally have to frighten people by telling them the sorry facts—the danger to the dollar, the possibility of severe budget cuts, the necessity of financing the war, and the danger of inflation."[52]

On a long and tense weekend in the middle of the month, Johnson and a group of international finance officials from Western European governments produced an agreement that temporarily stopped the outflow of gold. When the foreign exchange markets reopened on March 18, one day after the agreement, the exchange of dollars for gold slowed down dramatically.

This was not, however, in the opinion of most policy makers, a long-term solution. The key was to reestablish confidence in the dollar so that international government officials and investors would no longer be interested in trading the currency in for gold. The key in their minds was for the president and Congress to show that they were taking control of the deficit.

The crisis pushed members of both parties closer to a compromise. Senate Republicans announced they would support a tax increase, though less than the 10 percent sought by President Johnson, in order to avert a catastrophic gold crisis.[53] Chairman Mills announced that Congress would have to take action through a tax surcharge to stabilize the dollar. Secretary of the Treasury Henry Fowler told Johnson that Mills was "persuaded now of the key relationship of the tax bill, real or psychological, to the international monetary system."[54] Johnson's congressional vote counters were reporting that there was much greater support on the House floor to pass a tax surcharge if an agreement could be reached on spending.

In an effort to get the legislative process moving, Senators George Smathers of Florida and John Williams of Delaware, a well-known zealot for budgetary frugality, decided to circumvent the House, where Mills had shelved the bill in the Ways and Means Committee, and start pushing this bill in the upper chamber. The senators attached an amendment that included the 10 percent surcharge and $6 billion in discretionary spending cuts to excise tax legislation that the House had already passed. Although the amendment did not specify where the spending cuts should be made, most assumed that the president and Congress would fulfill their obligation with domestic programs that benefited the least powerful constituencies and avoid cuts that impacted the military. Indeed, the amendment exempted spending on Vietnam, debt interest payments, veterans' benefits, and Social Security and Medicare, all of which were considered "precommitted." Given that most legislators were scared to cut Pentagon funds or close military bases, this meant that domestic programs would suffer the most. The Smathers and Williams amendment also proposed cutting unspent agency funding from previous years and previously promised increases to various programs.

Johnson worried that by supporting the Senate amendment, he would anger Mills, because the Smathers and Williams amendment had been expressly designed to get around him.[55] Mills, however, expressed no opposition to the amendment; he believed it would help him move a package he wanted through the House. Mills was worried that his committee didn't have the authority to report a tax bill that included spending cuts; spending was properly the province of the Appropriations Committee. He feared that the House would vote for the tax surcharge and not the spending cuts if they were handled separately. But if the Senate combined them through an amendment, he would be able to ensure in conference committee that the entire package survived intact and obtain a rule from the Rules Committee prohibiting any amendments to the bill when it came out of the conference committee and onto the House floor. During their conversation on March 24, Mills told Johnson that Senate passage of an amendment could be useful to him by showing his colleagues in the House that there was strong bipartisan support for combining the two forms of deficit reduction.[56]

Liberal Democrats in the Senate were under immense pressure to vote against the amendment. Most of the major liberal organizations, including the AFL-CIO, the National School Boards Association, the National Education Association, the National League of Cities, the Catholic Conference, the National Council of Churches, and the Urban League, said that the Smathers and Williams amendment was unacceptable because of the size of the spending cuts. All of these organizations argued that any spending cuts above $2 billion would do irreparable damage to domestic programs. They also took the position that support for the tax surcharge would give implicit support to a continuation of the war in Vietnam and expressed a belief that taking so much money out of the economy would trigger a recession. Johnson responded by telling liberal Democrats that accepting this package was the best way to prevent conservatives from making much steeper cuts that would "murder" his domestic programs.[57]

In this fraught moment, facing a much more conservative Congress than the one with which he had worked a year earlier, Johnson believed he had no option but to accept the deal. Legislators on both sides of the debate were still expecting Johnson to apply the Treatment to Congress—and get himself out of the bind he was in. When Johnson heard of talk that he could deliver the spending cuts even if liberals were unhappy, because he was still "Master of the Senate," he said, "I'm not master of a damn thing . . . I'm not master of nothing . . . We cannot make this Congress do one damn thing that I know of."[58]

On the matter of spending cuts, Johnson felt he was at the mercy of the Ways and Means Committee chairman. "I don't believe that I've got a bit of influence with him," Johnson said of Mills. When Secretary of the Treasury Fowler said they might possibly get a better deal on spending cuts if they stood firm with the Senate, Johnson reminded him that the legislation would eventually have to pass through the conference committee, which Wilbur Mills would chair. And if Wilbur Mills didn't like the deal, Johnson reminded the secretary, "Wilbur Mills cuts your peter off."[59]

Privately, Johnson was ready to accept the spending cuts the congressional conservatives were demanding. All he had to do was persuade liberals to support his decision and conservatives to honor the deal.

GOOD-BYE WITHOUT LEAVING

The debate over the tax surcharge was consuming most of the president's time. He complained to Walter Reuther in March that he didn't have the energy to hit the campaign trail. "I don't have much time to make calls like this," Johnson said. "I am just fighting my heart out by god on the monetary question. I'm doing my best to keep 'em from cutting my budget 20 billion . . . if I let it come to a vote, that's exactly what the Republicans and the Southerners will do to me while the liberals are cutting at me. I've got the problem of Vietnam."[60]

In mid-March, Johnson was feeling worn down and pessimistic. Everything seemed to be going wrong. He had "lost" the New Hampshire primary to Eugene McCarthy and was facing, in Robert Kennedy, an even more serious challenger for renomination. His approval ratings were a miserable 36 percent. More than 60 percent of Americans disapproved of how he was handling Vietnam. Antiwar sentiment was sweeping the country. The Tet Offensive had killed any hope the war would end soon. The Left was causing turmoil on college campuses; protesters called the war unjust and immoral. The Right was blasting Johnson for his refusal to use greater force against the enemy. Even the liberal internationalist wing of the party, led by Senator Fulbright, was openly critical of the administration's policy in Southeast Asia. Johnson's domestic policies were not faring much better. The Great Society, his signature achievement and the cudgel with which he had battered Goldwater, had become a political weakness. The riots and the black power movement had produced opponents from within the Democratic coalition and awakened conservative critics who had been in hibernation since the 1964 election. The inflationary trends in the economy, now dominating the news as a result of the tax debate, ended the period in which Johnson could boast to voters about impressive economic conditions.

Johnson wasn't sure he could even win the nomination, let alone the general election. He saw how younger Democrats were drawn to McCarthy and Kennedy. Even if he pulled out a victory, he could foresee a disastrous second term. He saw how he might have a better chance of negotiating an end to the Vietnam War as a lame duck and how an end to the war might revitalize support for his Great Society. Johnson also had serious health concerns; he was physically and emotionally worn down, had suffered from chest pains, a benign polyp, and surgery to remove his gallbladder. He and Lady Bird worried about the physical toll a second term would take on his body.

In the final week of March, Johnson decided not to run for reelection. Johnson had been seriously considering retiring after his term was over since the fall of 1967 when Vietnam was taking a toll on his approval ratings. He had privately contemplated announcing that he would not seek reelection several times before, but he had changed his mind at the last minute. This time was different. He wasn't going to back down. He planned to announce his decision during a speech from the White House about a temporary bombing halt in Vietnam.

On Sunday, March 31, he attended church services with Lady Bird. He asked the Secret Service to retrieve the text of a speech from his nightstand. After the services, Johnson stopped at the home of Vice President Humphrey, who was about to take a trip overseas, and showed him a draft. Humphrey read through the beginning of the text and affirmed that it was very good. Then Humphrey reached the statement announcing that Johnson would not run for reelection. Humphrey was stunned; he felt on the verge of an anxiety attack.[61]

Eyes watering, he told the president he could not step down and said, "There's no way I can beat the Kennedys."[62]

The president went on television at 9:00 p.m. On this day, Gallup had released a poll showing that approval of his policies in Vietnam had reached a new low. The White House circulated the text of the remarks one hour before Johnson went on the air, without including the portion about his decision not to run.

With an air of confidence and resolve Johnson outlined to television viewers a shift in his war policy. There would be a temporary bombing halt if the North Vietnamese agreed to accelerate negotiations. Richard Goodwin was "stunned" as he watched the president; he "seemed not subdued but drained, as if the life force had been dissolved, his face pallid, lined, aged."[63]

Then came the bombshell. Johnson said, "With America's sons in the fields far away, with America's future under challenge right here at home, with our hopes and the world's hopes for peace in the balance every day, I do not believe that I should devote an hour or a day of my time to any personal partisan causes or to any duties other than the awesome duties of this office—the presidency of your country. Accordingly, I shall not seek, and I will not accept, the nomination of my party for another term as your president." As soon as the cameras were off, Johnson smiled at the people standing in the room. Lady Bird, dressed in an elegant red suit with blue trim, dashed over to her husband and gave him a big hug. Their two daughters, Lynda and Luci, who had sat beside their mother as Johnson delivered the historic news to the nation, came over to embrace and kiss their father as well.[64] Surrounded by his family, the president stood up and walked away to his private residence.

Johnson's announcement surprised almost everybody. Few had anticipated that his decision not to run for reelection was even a remote possibility. He was, after all, the incumbent and still the dominant force in the Democratic Party. Senator Kennedy was on a plane just returned from the first leg of his campaign in Phoenix when the Democratic state chairman John Burns stormed up the aisle of the American Airlines plane to tell him, "Johnson isn't running." "Fantastic," said William vanden Heuvel, a close adviser of the senator's. "This sure solves a lot of our troubles."[65]

Congressman Clement Zablocki, who was organizing the Johnson effort in the upcoming Wisconsin primary, learned about the news while working at a campaign dinner. Just a few days earlier he had been at an event in the White House where the president had told him to move forward in Wisconsin at full speed.[66]

Senator Eugene McCarthy's supporters were thrilled. Volunteers at Milwaukee hotels, where their campaign was preparing for the Wisconsin primary, chanted, "The wicked witch is dead."[67] In New York City's Greenwich Village, where counterculture figures like Bob Dylan commanded much more respect than the commander in chief, a small group marched on Eighth Street chanting, "Good-by, Lyndon. Good-by, Lyndon. Good-by, Lyndon. We're glad to see you go." Said one demonstrator, "It's a magnificent gesture on Johnson's part. It's a good thing for him to do."[68]

The president's announcement had an immediate impact on the tax debate. It motivated the Senate leadership to finish up work on the tax legislation that included the Smathers and Williams amendment, with its 10 percent tax surcharge and $6 billion in discretionary spending cuts. There was a very brief moment of good feeling for the president in Congress. He was no longer merely a "self-seeking politician"; he was a "self-sacrificing statesman," one columnist wrote.[69] He had sacrificed himself for the national good; the bill was sold as the sacrifice for citizens to make—through tax hikes and spending cuts—for the good of the nation. Now that Johnson was freed from immediate political considerations, most of his opponents in Congress expected that he would be more willing to make a deal on spending in order to obtain the tax revenue, even if the cuts angered liberals and the tax surcharge alienated moderate voters and conservatives.

The Democratic leadership seized the opportunity to obtain a vote, and on April 2 the Senate passed the revenue legislation that included the 10 percent tax surcharge. The vote on the amendment was 53 to 35, with strong support from the conservative coalition and a lukewarm response from liberals. Republicans were strongly in favor of the austerity package, with only 3 voting no; 31 in the GOP voted in favor. Democrats were more divided. Thirty-two Democrats voted against the amendment, with only 22 voting yes. Southern Democrats voted 10 to 8 in favor of the amendment.

Seventeen of the 29 senators running for reelection, well aware that no voter liked higher taxes and cuts in domestic benefits, voted against the bill, but the full Senate passed the bill, with substantial support from both parties, 30 Republicans and 27 Democrats.

"Only last week," wrote the *Washington Post* reporter Frank Porter, "before President Johnson's dramatic announcement of an initiative for Vietnam deescalation and his unavailability for reelection—prospects for the omnibus revenue and economy measure were dubious."[70]

AN AUSTERITY BUDGET

On April 4, Martin Luther King Jr. was shot and killed as he stood on the balcony of his motel room in Memphis, Tennessee, where King had just given a speech in support of striking sanitation workers. Memphis, with a population that was 40 percent African American, was a tinderbox in which news of the shooting spread like a flame. Tennessee's governor, Buford Ellington, immediately announced a curfew and ordered four thousand National Guard troops into the city.

The administration expected that the murder would spark more rioting in the cities and knee-jerk law-and-order rhetoric from conservative Democrats and Republicans. Another round of devastating riots would likely set back the progress that had been made on civil rights since 1964. Robert Kennedy, who had decided to enter the Democratic primaries a few weeks before Johnson withdrew from the race, was about to deliver a speech on a street corner in an African American neighborhood in Indianapolis when he learned about what had happened. He broke the news to the crowd and asked them to act not with violence but with "love and wisdom, and compassion toward one another, and a feeling of justice toward those who still suffer within our country, whether they be white or whether they be black."[71] The people cheered and applauded the senator, and they remained calm.

Although conditions remained stable in Indianapolis, riots erupted in more than a hundred cities, including New York, Boston, Washington, and Trenton, New Jersey. Johnson sent the National Guard to establish calm. Forty-six people were killed and approximately two thousand injured, according to reports. More than thirteen thousand troops were stationed in Washington by the time the riots simmered down, some patrolling on foot and others by jeep.[72]

It was something of a surprise that the fury over King's murder led to one of the few legislative breakthroughs of the year for liberals—the Civil Rights Act of 1968 and its prohibition of racial discrimination in the sale or rental of *some* housing. Twenty-one House Republicans announced they would support the housing proposal that had stalled the civil rights bill in the House Rules Committee.[73] The real estate lobby was caught off guard by the sudden change in the legislative climate,[74] and on April 10 the House passed the bill by a vote of 229 to 195. The following day, Johnson signed the legislation.

Supporters of the legislation had been debating and redrafting the bill for more than a year, compromising and narrowing the scope of the proposal, hoping that an opportunity would arise to bring back the idea that had caused so much controversy in 1966. Ironically, though it was rioting that had made passage of the legislation almost impossible in 1966, the assassination of Dr. King in 1968 and the rioting that followed propelled Congress to adopt a measure that would demonstrate its concern to African American voters. Senator Joseph Clark called on his colleagues to pass the bill and said that by doing so, his colleagues could "build for him [King] a lasting monument of law."[75] In an unpredictable turn of events, some of the Republicans who had been elected with the help of the racial backlash in 1966, Charles Percy among them, were instrumental in moving the bill toward passage in the Senate. The fact that the civil rights movement—black power advocates and mainstream leaders, King among them—had been presenting more radical demands for economic equality made open housing seem a much milder demand than it had just two years earlier. The good news for civil rights activists was that the Civil Rights Act of 1968 firmly established the principle of nondiscrimination in housing and rental markets, including a ban on the notorious practice of blockbusting.[76] But the final legislation was in fact a watered-down compromise of a watered-down compromise. It would not cost the federal government any substantial amount of money to implement—there were virtually no enforcement mechanisms in it—a good thing given how the budget was shaping up.[77]

Johnson sent a different message to the electorate in the wake of the King assassination when he pushed for the Omnibus Crime Control and Safe Streets Act, which Congress passed in June. The legislation offered a Democratic response to demands for law and order—among them were restrictions on the sale of handguns and a federal grant for research on the social and environmental factors that caused crime. The centerpiece of the bill was the establishment of the Law Enforcement Assistance Administration to coordinate crime-fighting operations.

The King assassination also led to further polarization of the budget battles that had been taking place since January. Both sides of the legislative debate were even more certain now of the correctness of their positions. Congressional conservatives pointed to the riots that followed the assassination as further evidence of the breakdown of law and order and proof that Johnson's social experiments were not working. Liberals, shattered by the death of one of the most influential people of the decade, were doubly determined to protect their most treasured social policies from the depredations of legislative conservatives.

The closer the president and Mills got to an agreement, the more desperate some liberal officials in the administration became to persuade Johnson to stand his ground on an absolute maximum of $4 billion in discretionary spending cuts—a definite retreat from their previous ceiling of $2 billion. Even as a lame-duck president, Johnson had some leverage. For all the trouble the conservatives were giving him, they were equally intent on passing the bill; they were sincerely concerned lest the growth of deficits rattle international financial markets. They needed Johnson to signal his support to non-southern Democrats who were skittish about the bill, and they needed to make sure there was no possibility of his vetoing it. Joseph Califano believed the outcome of the budget fight would be decisive in shaping the political dynamics for the remainder of Johnson's term.[78] If the president agreed to spending cuts that were too deep, conservatives would be confident enough to ignore him on everything else. If he stood his ground and won, he would demonstrate the strength he still had. "If you get stuck either with no tax bill or with provisions of the kind Mills is now peddling," Califano wrote to Johnson, "I think the ball game may well be over on the Hill for the rest of the year."[79]

The passage of the Senate amendment had shifted the terms of debate. While Johnson was still hoping he would be able to reduce the size of the spending cuts in conference committee by going along with the Senate he had allowed himself to be placed in a position where he was publicly fighting to reduce spending cuts already passed in the Senate rather than putting the burden on Mills and the conservatives to fight for more reductions.[80]

The president was in fact resigned to accepting the deal on Mills's terms. At a meeting with his cabinet, Johnson had shared a memo from the Council of Economic Advisers that emphasized the urgency of passing the tax hike. Arthur Okun, the chairman of the council, had told Johnson that if the "political realities" meant they had to accept a $6 billion budget cut, then they should go ahead and do it, because "by a definite margin . . . our economy is much better off with this overdose of fiscal restraint than none at all." Secretary of the Treasury Henry Fowler agreed with Okun; he pointed out that after nine months "we are only able to get 150 House Democrats willing to vote for a tax bill," which was clearly not enough to win support for legislation that included smaller spending cuts. Secretary of State Dean Rusk supported Johnson by warning his cabinet colleagues that the "international consequences will be very grave indeed if there is no tax bill. It is just absolutely essential."[81]

At a May 1 meeting, Johnson pondered with his advisers the possibility of accepting $6 billion in discretionary spending cuts, though he continued to believe that Congress would not insist on that number. He had concluded that the White House might need to "take the bull by the tail and get the tax bill now" and explained that they should make the reductions in the least painful way possible. Johnson continued to work toward a smaller reduction in spending, but by the end of the month he had resigned himself to the necessity of the congressional cuts. Speaking to the "liberals and progressives" in the cabinet meeting of May 29, Johnson said, "I can take this $6 billion and walk and breathe and live if I get a $10 billion Tax Bill. I want to tell you that you are going to hurt more if I have to take $6 billion and no Tax Bill." Reminding them of the stakes of this battle, he looked around the room and said, "We'll look like [Herbert] Hoover if we don't use all the horsepower we've got. This is a question of survival. It is not Democratic or Republican."[82]

The president met with House and Senate leaders in an atmosphere of considerable tension about what to do next. The House majority leader, Carl Albert, warned him that passage of a tax bill through conference committee and then again on the floor of each chamber would still not be an "easy proposition," because House liberals would not be happy with the $6 billion in spending cuts that had been accepted in the Senate.[83]

In an effort to placate liberals, the Democratic leadership, with Johnson's consent, allowed the House to vote on an amendment by the Massachusetts Democrat James Burke that would instruct the conferees to include $4 billion in spending cuts rather than $6 billion. The amendment had no chance of passing, but liberal Democrats could vote for it and get credit from their constituents for their effort.

The day after the House rejected the Burke amendment, President Johnson publicly announced for the first time that he would support the $6 billion in spending cuts. A few days later, Carl Albert announced his support as well.

Wilbur Mills scheduled the final vote for June 20 so that members would have sufficient time to review the entire package. In the intervening weeks, there was more tragedy, when Robert Kennedy was shot in Los Angeles on June 5 and died the following day. Kennedy had lost to McCarthy in Oregon but won in California, and he had been celebrating the revival of his candidacy when he was shot.

Kennedy's campaign had stalled McCarthy, and Kennedy's death left Vice President Hubert Humphrey the inevitable nominee. If there was any candidate who could heal the rifts that had emerged in the Democratic coalition and move liberals beyond the horrendous losses of King and Kennedy, Humphrey was not that candidate. Once one of the most exciting voices in the party, when he had challenged the southern conservative barons of Capitol Hill in the 1940s and 1950s, Humphrey was seen in 1968 by the left wing of his party as the embodiment of the broken status quo. He was the heir, they feared, to Lyndon Johnson's failed presidency, a politician who would stubbornly continue with the Vietnam War and not do much more on domestic policy.

With liberals totally deflated about the direction of Washington politics, on June 20, after more than a year of brutal legislative debate, the final budget bill sailed through the House (268–150) and the Senate (64–16). The legislation received opposition only from a small coalition of ardent liberals, unhappy with the cuts, and from staunch conservatives who refused to go along with any kind of tax hike. Much of the opposition from both wings was minimal, intended to please constituents, with full realization that the legislation would pass.[84]

The Revenue and Expenditure Control Act of 1968 increased revenue by $15.5 billion in 1969. The bill included $6 billion in immediate cuts to the fiscal 1969 budget (exempting spending on Vietnam, debt interest payments, veterans' benefits, Medicare, and Social Security). The bill also cut $8 billion from cabinet budgets that had not been spent in the previous fiscal year, rather than allow agencies to carry the money over. The final legislation specified that the following year's budget would have to recommend additional cuts—beyond the $6 billion to be implemented immediately—that would amount to a total of $10 billion over about two years. The deficit would fall by an estimated $22.5 billion, down to $7.5 billion.[85]

Johnson normally signed a bill in a public ceremony in the East Room, surrounded by legislators and supporters, but this time he quietly signed in his office. In his statement on the new law, the president explained, "Now we can attack decisively—at the roots—the threats to our prosperity: accelerating inflation, soaring interest rates and deteriorating world trade performance." The president jabbed Congress for having forced a "deep reduction" in the budget but said he had to accept this, given how important the bill was to the vitality of the economy.

The legislation and the debate that led to its passage had shifted liberals from the politics of expansion to the politics of protection.[86] "What was left," the historian Robert Collins wrote, "was not the powerful reform surge of mid-decade but only its inertia."[87] Congress had shifted the debate from liberal growth to austerity, where talk about the creation of big new programs that required more spending would be difficult. Republicans continued to attack the president for his fiscal record. Richard Nixon warned of the "grave and permanent damage to the economy" that had been administered by the "Johnson-Humphrey Administration." Once the president had acknowledged the criticism of his spending record by signing into law a policy of restraint, there was little room for him to transform the government any further along liberal lines. His window for legislating had closed. Now all he could do was use his remaining power to protect his legacy from further destruction and come up with a way to get out of Vietnam.

CHAPTER NINE

THE ENDURANCE
OF THE GREAT SOCIETY

After the midterm elections and the austerity battles, President Johnson could no longer pass important legislation. The tax surcharge and spending cuts in the summer of 1968 were his last achievements. He had managed the liberal ascendancy and made the Eighty-ninth Congress historically productive, but the midterm elections, the budget debates, and the Vietnam War had eroded all his advantages. In the Ninetieth Congress, he could control very little, and he could dominate nothing. The political landscape in which he could twist arms to achieve legislative victories had vanished; even if he had twisted every arm in Congress, he could not have moved any more important legislation. He spent most of his final months in the White House fruitlessly trying to find a way to close out the war in Vietnam and to withstand fierce attacks from liberals who were condemning his presidency. Republicans continued to rail against what they characterized as chaos in the streets and on college campuses; they demanded the restoration of law and order and depicted Johnson's America as a country coming unglued.

Hubert Humphrey, the unfortunate heir to Johnson's political legacy, seemed the candidate of last resort. Committed as he was to the president's disastrous Vietnam policy, he struggled to regain the moral high ground he had staked out in his early political career. As intra-party conflict demoralized the Democrats, the third-party candidate George Wallace, the former Alabama governor, appealed to voters who opposed any further legislation for civil rights and any social programs that aimed for racial justice. The Republican Richard Nixon rebounded from his devastating defeat in the 1962 California gubernatorial election to take advantage of the damaged state of Democratic politics. He vowed to avoid Barry Goldwater's disastrous southern strategy in 1964 and developed a message tailored for conservative Democrats, moderate and progressive Republicans, the business and financial community, and the party stalwarts in the Midwest.

THE SUMMER CONVENTIONS

The Republican delegates who streamed into sunny Miami Beach for their nominating convention displayed an air of controlled confidence. They were a clean-cut cross section of Middle America, small business, and middle-class values, a self-conscious counterexample to the plague of protests, violence, and chaos Americans had become accustomed to watching on their television sets. Inside the Miami Beach Convention Center they prepared to align themselves with Richard Nixon and his careful politics, in which passion was limited to two issues—ending the war in Vietnam and upholding law and order. "From the convention hall," wrote the campaign chronicler Theodore White, "boredom spread all up and down the Beach."[1]

The Republican selection process promised to be straightforward. Governor George Romney of Michigan had been knocked out of the race a year earlier after telling reporters he had been "brainwashed" by the U.S. military during a visit to Vietnam. The New York governor Nelson Rockefeller's flip-flopping on whether or not to run had damaged his image as badly as had his 1962 divorce, which always haunted him on the campaign trail. The GOP rank and file showed more enthusiasm for Ronald Reagan than for the liberal Rockefeller as an alternative to Nixon but not enough enthusiasm to block the former vice president, who had campaigned around the country for Republican candidates in 1966, reintroduced himself to a national audience, and picked up many IOUs from those he had supported in a big Republican year. In the 1968 primaries, he skillfully outmaneuvered his competitors by finding a center-right position that eluded all of them.

Nixon's resurgence shocked those who hoped the political exile that followed his electoral defeats would be permanent; he had positioned himself as a coalition builder who could appeal to the right wing and to moderates in both parties. He had transformed himself from the rabid anticommunist attack dog he had been in the 1940s and 1950s into the new statesman of his party.

Ever cognizant of Barry Goldwater's 1964 campaign as a paradigm for what not to do, the new Nixon held to the center, as Democrats had done for most of the time since the New Deal and as Dwight Eisenhower had done during his two terms in the White House. His campaign team calculated there were twenty-one solidly Republican states, from which Nixon could get 117 of the 270 electoral votes he would need to win. His campaign targets included the battleground states Michigan, Pennsylvania, Ohio, Illinois, Missouri, Wisconsin, Texas, and California and the peripheral southern states Florida, Virginia, Tennessee, North Carolina (some campaign staffers felt that South Carolina was up for grabs too).[2] With polls indicating that Nixon might carry New York and New Jersey, his campaign manager, John Mitchell, predicted that because of discontent among many Democrats "the time is ripe for a great movement of Democrats and independents to active Nixon support."[3]

The candidate and his advisers believed that the immense turmoil of the last few years had created the possibility for them to build a new governing coalition by grafting onto the Republican Party some detached parts of the coalition FDR had built and Lyndon Johnson had expanded until it fractured under the stresses of the Vietnam War and urban riots. Southerners and working-class northern Democrats were his obvious targets. His acceptance speech in Miami Beach was addressed to them. "The long dark night for America is about to end," he said. He urged Americans to listen to "the quiet voice in the tumult and the shouting. It is the voice of the great majority of Americans, the forgotten Americans, the non shouters, the non demonstrators. They are not racists or sick; they are not guilty of the crime that plagues the land. They are black and they are white—they're native born and foreign born—they're young and they're old . . . They give drive to the spirit of America. They give lift to the American dream. They give steel to the backbone of America. They are good people. They are decent people; they work and they save and they pay their taxes and they care."

Nixon's choice of Spiro Agnew as his running mate was meant to appeal to disaffected Democrats and encourage Republicans who had abandoned the party in 1964 to return to the fold. On many policies, the Maryland governor had a moderate record. He had proposed the first fair housing law for Maryland; its prohibitions on racial discrimination in the sale or rental of housing were weakly enforced but nevertheless a symbolic milestone, the first such law in a southern state. Vice President Humphrey admitted that Governor Agnew represented a "significant compromise in the Republican Party."[4]

But the tough-talking Agnew also appealed to hard-line conservative, working-class Democrats Nixon wanted to steal away from their party. Following a riot in Baltimore in the wake of Dr. King's assassination, Agnew blamed civil rights leaders for stirring up trouble.

Later he said, "It is deplorable and a sign of sickness in our society that the lunatic fringes of the black and white communities speak with wide publicity while we, the moderates, remain continuously mute. I cannot believe that the only alternative to white racism is black racism."[5] His presentation of himself—as a supporter of civil rights who had become a tough proponent of law and order in response to urban rioting—was intended to resonate with the experience of many white Democrats who had been dissatisfied since Watts with certain of their party's positions.

The Republican convention was an image of law and order. The Democratic convention, later in the summer in Chicago, was the spectacle of a coalition disintegrating.

Angry activists gathered in Lincoln Park, a lakeside park three miles from the convention center where the city permitted protests to take place. In the three days leading up to the convention, a series of violent confrontations ensued between the protesters and the Chicago police, who had been instructed to maintain order at all costs. Most of the activists had traveled to Chicago to protest the party's support of the Vietnam War and its refusal to include in its platform a plank calling for an immediate and unconditional cessation of the bombing against the North Vietnamese, a mutual withdrawal of military forces from South Vietnam, and the establishment of a unified national coalitional government. On August 28, several hundred protesters marched to Grant Park, which was located across the street from the Hilton hotel, the main headquarters for delegates and politicians. At the convention, delegates voted for a party platform that reiterated the official policy of the White House—a bombing halt only if it would "not endanger the lives of our troops in the field," a withdrawal of forces only after the war ended, and free and open elections in South Vietnam. These positions made it clear to the protesters that the Democratic leadership had no determination whatsoever to end the war anytime soon.

Chicago's mayor, Richard Daley, believed the protesters in the park and in the streets were embarrassing the party at a moment when it was trying to sell its presidential candidate to the nation. He ordered the Chicago police to be tough with the protesters. What followed was shocking violence at a level Daley might not have intended. Hundreds of officers brutally attacked the unarmed protesters. They sprayed the protesters with tear gas, charged at them, and beat them with their nightsticks. Images of the violence were broadcast on national television. When Hubert Humphrey opened his hotel window to see what was happening on the streets, he could smell the tear gas. Senator Abraham Ribicoff, in his nominating speech for the antiwar South Dakota senator George McGovern, addressed Mayor Daley directly and decried the "Gestapo tactics on the streets of Chicago."[6]

Inside the convention hall, chants of "Stop the War!" continually interrupted the proceedings. In agreeing to the hawkish Vietnam platform plank, Humphrey was defending a position he had always warned Johnson was disastrous. He told a reporter, "I think the policies the President has pursued are basically sound." The candidate, who had been privately criticizing the Vietnam War since 1964 and warning Johnson that it would tarnish all the Democrats' important domestic accomplishments, now refused to separate himself from the president's policies, an act of personal loyalty that seemed certain to kill his chances of winning in November. At the moment Humphrey secured the nomination, police were battering protesters just outside the convention hall; some inside the hall believed that Humphrey lost the election at the moment he was nominated.

The wild card in the election campaign was George Wallace, the Alabama governor who had become famous for his racist opposition to civil rights. As the candidate of the right-wing American Independent Party, he aimed to take enough support away from both major-party candidates to block either from getting the 270 Electoral

College votes necessary for election. The decision would then be made by the House of Representatives, where each state would have one vote.[7] Such an outcome would demonstrate to the nation that Wallace was a formidable political force, and it would place pressure on the two mainstream candidates to court southern legislators by promising to back down on civil rights.

Wallace sought to create a narrow coalition of southern Democrats and disaffected northern Democrats who detested the counterculture and felt that African Americans were threatening their jobs, homes, safety, schools, and communities. He was less interested than Nixon in winning over the moderate Republicans or business leaders who were usually sympathetic to the GOP. They were not his crowd. He spoke about law and order with a much tougher tone than Nixon or any other Republican. "The first anarchist who picks up a brick should get a bullet in the head," Wallace snarled.[8] He said his campaign would appeal to "the man in the textile mill, this man in the steel mill, this barber, this beautician, the policeman on the beat."[9] He questioned whether there was any real difference between Democrats and Republicans, and because he raised more than $9 million, he was a threat to both parties. Democrats feared he would capture northern votes in traditional Democratic territory; Nixon saw him undercutting his appeal to the restless white base of the Democratic Party.

THE FALL CAMPAIGNS

Nixon believed the best way to build a broad electoral coalition of essentially incompatible constituencies was to run a campaign vague on everything but the urgency of not having another Lyndon Johnson in the White House. Throughout the fall, he intentionally avoided any issue that could alienate any faction he might conceivably attract.

The 1966 midterms provided him with a useful template for this kind of campaign.

On Vietnam, Nixon's primary message was that Johnson had gotten the nation into a huge military mess. He assured voters that he had a plan that would end the war and also preserve America's strength overseas, but he gave no details of how he would accomplish either goal. To win over working-class northern white voters, he ridiculed those hippies who protested the war, got high on drugs, wore beads and headbands, and practiced free love. He called for a restoration of law and order in the cities and promised to provide federal support to the valiant police who went after the drug dealers and the rioters. He accused Johnson of initiating an inflationary spiral by his pursuit of reckless budgetary policies and by his deception about the costs of the war in Vietnam. Nixon connected these budgetary themes to his discovery of the "forgotten Americans," who were struggling to support their families while irresponsible college students protested and disorderly city residents rioted. "In the last two years," he pointed out, "the average American worker has been on a Government-operated treadmill. New taxes and rising prices have more than wiped out all the pay raises he has won since 1965." He said, "The new taxes on income, requested publicly by this Administration, and the hidden tax of inflation, imposed clandestinely by this Administration, have together left the purchasing power of the American worker below what it was in December of 1965."[10]

Democrats, perfectly capable of understanding what they were hearing with their own ears, accused Nixon of running a campaign on empty platitudes. Humphrey taunted him: "Come out, wherever you are." Nixon came out by supporting the idea that government could solve some domestic problems—in ways just a little bit different from the ways in which Democrats would solve them.

Johnson, consumed by his travails in Vietnam, could still find one reason to smile: Nixon rarely targeted the Great Society in his campaign. His message was reorganization and reform rather than elimination. He voiced his support for Medicaid and suggested studies to find ways of putting the program on a sounder financial foundation; in New York and some other states, the costs were rising rapidly as state governments liberalized eligibility rules. He criticized the War on Poverty as wasteful, but he endorsed tax benefits for private businesses that developed plans for training the unemployed, creating new jobs, or participating in efforts to rebuild the cities. On a few occasions, Nixon even called for a bigger federal government. He said he would continue the Head Start program and perhaps even expand it. He said, "Compensatory education is the first step toward bringing equality of education to slum schools. Without it, the children of poverty will never catch up with the children of abundance."[11] He supported Medicare and proposed that seniors be allowed to take a full income tax deduction for their drug and medical expenses. On Social Security, Nixon tried to get ahead of Democrats, who had relied on Congress to raise benefits every two years to keep up with the rising cost of living, by proposing that the program be indexed to inflation so that benefits would rise automatically with consumer prices.

Humphrey, the former "Happy Warrior," had nothing at all to be happy about. Nixon's campaign rolled smoothly through September, and his polls continued to rise. Humphrey's rallies drew mostly hecklers who attended only to publicly condemn the candidate's commitment to continue fighting in Vietnam. Shadowed relentlessly by the war, Humphrey could find little time to talk about the bread-and-butter domestic issues that had motivated him for most of his career.

On September 30, with his campaign almost completely out of gas—and money—Humphrey made a dramatic move to save his candidacy. He announced on a paid national television broadcast that he supported an end to the bombing of North Vietnam, but hedged by adding that if the "government of North Vietnam were to show bad faith, [he] would reserve the right to resume the bombing."

Lyndon Johnson now viewed Hubert Humphrey as one more Democrat who didn't appreciate everything he had done for the party and blamed him for undermining his chances of getting a peace deal in the final months of his presidency, but Johnson's hurt feelings notwithstanding, the speech seemed to give the campaign some bounce and renewed spirit. When the candidate arrived at a Boston hotel, he recalled, "I found myself surrounded by hundreds of students carrying signs that read, 'We're for you, Hubert,' or simply, 'Hubert for President.' This was the same Boston that only a few weeks earlier had been the scene of noisy demonstrators who heckled . . . me."[12] The speech had snatched away from the Republicans their biggest issue, and this enabled Humphrey to turn back to domestic issues, where he was most comfortable. Praising the civil rights accomplishments of the Johnson administration, Humphrey told one crowd in Detroit, "We are the only country on the face of the earth that has ever dared to try to make what we call a biracial, a pluralistic society work. We are going to see whether we can do it in a spirit of community, whether we can do it in a spirit of unity . . . or whether or not it has to be apartheid."[13]

Unions had mobilized against Wallace in battleground states; as the racist dropped precipitously in the polls, Humphrey picked up steam. As Wallace talked louder about law and order, the unions reminded voters of Alabama's horrible record toward organized labor and of the many benefits already coming to workers through Great Society programs.[14] Wallace also stumbled among Democrats and many moderate Republicans on October 3 by naming as his running mate the retired air force general Curtis LeMay, a former commander of the Strategic Air Command, whose view on the war was that the United States should bomb the North Vietnamese "back to the Stone Age." Even for Democrats who were still on board with the war, this was a bridge too far when it came to winning at any cost.

Meanwhile, Nixon was having trouble holding his coalition together. Wallace had considerable support in the South, where unions had little influence and open appeals to racist sentiment were received with more enthusiasm. Nixon tried to counteract Wallace by being more vocal in his opposition to busing schoolchildren as a way to integrate schools, but the shift in tone didn't work. When it came to appealing to racist sentiment in the electorate, Nixon couldn't compete with Wallace.

By the end of October, Humphrey had caught up to Nixon in the polls. According to Harris, the gap between them had narrowed; Gallup had reported it down from fifteen points in September to ten in the middle of October to eight points at the end of the month going into the election.[15] Many of Nixon's operatives feared that if Johnson announced a peace agreement in Vietnam, the election would belong to the Democrats.

On October 31, Johnson announced that he was temporarily halting the bombing as part of ongoing peace negotiations with the North Vietnamese, but on November 2, the South Vietnamese announced they would not participate in any further negotiations. Johnson heard from his intelligence sources that Nixon's foreign policy advisers, working through third-party channels, had contacted the South Vietnamese and assured them they would get a better deal with Nixon in office. Johnson called Nixon's actions "despicable" and told Senator Dirksen that it would "rock the nation" if he revealed what had taken place.[16] In the end, the president did not reveal what Nixon had done, in large measure because he thought it would dangerously subvert Nixon if he won.

Nixon won the election by a narrow margin: 43.4 percent of the popular vote to 42.7 percent for Humphrey and 13.5 percent for

Wallace. Nixon won 301 Electoral College votes to Humphrey's 191 and Wallace's 46. Wallace won almost ten million popular votes; he carried five southern states—Alabama, Arkansas, Georgia, Louisiana, and Mississippi—and got some working-class votes in the North and the Midwest. Overall, his appeal proved much weaker than he had expected; he did not do well with working-class and lower-middle-class voters in the North, who had generally benefited from Democratic programs ever since the New Deal and remained loyal to the Democratic Party. His tally suggested that the New Deal coalition was unbroken outside the Deep South. Democrats retained control of Congress, though the conservative coalition had grown slightly larger in both houses. In the Senate, Democrats controlled the chamber by a margin of 57 to 43, a loss of five seats for the majority. In the House, the party balance was 243 to 192.

It was clear to all that the election awarded Nixon no mandate to dismantle the Great Society. He had criticized Johnson on Vietnam and law and order, but he had steered clear of criticizing domestic legislation and even suggested that he would strengthen certain Great Society programs. Wallace's poor showing in the North gave Republicans pause about how unhappy northern Democrats really were with Johnson's domestic programs. Humphrey might well have won had he sooner and more definitively distanced himself from Lyndon Johnson on Vietnam and more assiduously reminded voters of the benefits civil rights laws and Great Society programs had delivered to the nation.

"Dick Nixon is going to be taking over a government one hell of a lot different than the one he left in January, 1961," Joseph Califano said. "There were about 45 domestic social programs when the Eisenhower administration ended. Now there are no less than 435."[17] Robert Finch, the incoming secretary of health, education, and welfare, was a pragmatic Republican who had served as the lieutenant governor for Ronald Reagan in California and had helped the governor scale down his antigovernment objectives when dealing with a Democratic legislature. Finch announced right away that under his direction the Department of Health, Education, and Welfare would focus on rationalizing existing programs rather than on expanding or contracting them.[18]

The New Deal had generated new expectations about what the federal government could do, and so did the Great Society. Johnson's programs had energized conservatives, but they had also energized liberals, who were unhappy about Vietnam but proudly stood behind civil rights, Medicare, and federal education assistance. Liberals who came of age during the creation of the Great Society were everywhere in Washington after 1969, much to Nixon's chagrin. They filled the federal bureaucracies and fought to make sure Great Society programs received sufficient budgetary support and ran effectively even with Nixon in the White House. A robust network of interest groups and activists lobbied to extend federal benefits to more Americans in need and to promote federal actions to protect consumers and the environment. Liberals went to the courts to fight for more expansive definitions of who had the right to receive benefits. A sizable contingent of the liberal Democrats who had entered Congress in the 1960s fought Nixon on those few occasions when he did attack Great Society programs, and they continued to push against the conservative coalition for liberal legislation in the House and the Senate.

Johnson's ability as president to get legislation passed has often been exaggerated and the depth of support for liberalism during his presidency overstated, but when grassroots activists and voters had created conditions that were favorable to producing bills on Capitol Hill, the president and his legislative allies had been able to enact profoundly significant laws within a short period of time. The programs themselves proved to be sustainable even after Johnson was gone. The pressure from civil rights activists and voters had been so intense in 1964 and 1965 that many Republicans and moderate

Democrats had signed onto the bills, and conservatives had grasped that these bills had somehow been written not just into law but into the American social contract. The bipartisan imprimatur Johnson secured for his programs steeled them against future efforts to reverse them.

During the worst moments of the budget battles in 1967 and 1968, Johnson had hoped that Congress would not impose the spending cuts after the deal was done. Although the budget deal had killed any chances he had for passing more legislation and had given momentum to Republicans in the 1968 election, the zeal for austerity was short-lived. In the end, legislators always have strong political incentives to spend once programs are in place. While many Americans don't like government in principle, they often like the specific programs government delivers, and this was the case with much of the Great Society. People, constituents, voters, soon came to depend on the effective government programs Johnson and his allies had created. With Johnson out of the White House, Congress continued to push hard for spending on the programs that had quickly become popular with constituents all over the country.

President Nixon, with a politically astute eye toward reelection in 1972, worked with Congress to spend more on domestic programs. He decided to fight the worsening inflationary spiral by instituting wage and price controls, rather than by cutting spending. To prevent future gold crises, he simply abrogated the entire international finance system that was based on the convertibility of gold into dollars at a fixed price.

Federal spending increased throughout Nixon's first term. He signed, for example, Social Security legislation that indexed benefits so they would rise automatically with inflation—he also raised benefits substantially—and centralized and federalized the existing state programs that provided federal assistance to the aged, blind, and disabled under a new program called Supplemental Security Income.

The same legislation also expanded Medicare coverage to include two million more people.

Nixon also signed legislation that bolstered the school lunch and food stamps programs, two of the most popular policies of the welfare state. He signed amendments that reauthorized the Elementary and Secondary Education Act at a cost of $24.6 billion over three years, increased funding for children who lived in public housing, and offered educational assistance to kids with disabilities. Federal expenditures for Americans living in poverty were increased by 50 percent between 1969 and 1973.[19]

In a few instances, Nixon's political interests led him to support new expansions of government that would probably have been impossible for a liberal Democratic president to accomplish. In 1969, the Department of Labor under Secretary George Shultz launched the "Philadelphia Plan," which required unions that received over $500,000 in federal funds in the City of Brotherly Love to hire a certain percentage of African American workers. The plan had originally been put into place by the Department of Labor in 1967, but it had been dismantled when the comptroller general deemed that the existing structure was not legal on the basis that it violated the Civil Rights Act of 1964. The plan was revised, and Shultz brought it back in 1969; the following year it was extended to all federal contracting.[20] There is substantial evidence that Nixon's motivation for supporting this first affirmative action plan was to divide Democrats by pitting white working-class Americans against African Americans over jobs. He and some of his advisers assumed white workers would associate this program with Johnson's civil rights laws rather than blame Nixon, especially because the plan was the quiet result of administrative changes rather than loud, public congressional debates. Whatever Nixon's intentions, affirmative action was born.

In 1969, an oil spill in the Pacific Ocean off Santa Barbara, California, brought Nixon under bipartisan pressure to take action.

Environmental concerns had become a priority for a growing segment of voters, among them moderate suburbanites who had been a part of Nixon's electoral support. He saw the oil spill as an opportunity to improve his reelection chances by expanding the role of the federal government in protecting the environment. Johnson had worked with Congress on clean air and clean water legislation, but Nixon now moved to establish the Environmental Protection Agency to develop and enforce regulations to preserve the environment. He never devoted many resources to the agency, but in future years it became a powerful force. Nixon also signed a bill intended to appeal to working-class voters; the bill established the Occupational Safety and Health Administration to enforce stricter workplace safety standards.

In the few instances when Nixon directly attacked the Great Society, he lost. In 1970, he proposed revising the Voting Rights Act to eliminate the preclearance and triggering provisions southerners had always disliked—the provisions in the legislation that required states with low levels of registered African American voters to clear any changes in their election rules with the Department of Justice. The elimination of the triggering provisions would make the law apply to the entire nation instead of only to the South. While in principle liberals would have been happy to expand the scope of the law, they believed that in practice requiring the Department of Justice to cover the entire country would strain its resources for addressing problems in places where they were most significant. Without the preclearance requirement, the burden of proof for showing that voting plans would be racially discriminatory would fall on the federal government rather than on the local voting units seeking to gain approval for new plans. Liberals in Congress led by Emanuel Celler warned that the changes would threaten the law. Nixon backed down and ended up signing a five-year extension of the Voting Rights Act without any major changes to the law.

When Johnson died of a heart attack on January 22, 1973, just two days after Nixon's second inauguration, the Great Society was still in good health. Any intention Nixon might have had, after his landslide reelection victory in 1972, to make a hard shift to the right was thwarted by the Watergate scandal, which brought him down from what had been the summit of his political power. His resignation in August 1974 left his successor, Gerald Ford, in a weak position from which to accomplish anything during his brief time in the White House.

By then, Great Society programs had become even more securely entrenched politically. Legislators could see that their constituents accepted desegregation and voting rights for African Americans as normal aspects of daily life. They saw that growing numbers of their constituents enjoyed and depended on Great Society benefits. By the time the nation elected the conservative Republican Ronald Reagan and a majority Republican Senate in 1980, the Great Society was so firmly established that any conservatives wanting to attack it would face a monumental challenge.

PERSISTENT POLICIES

Over the next four and a half decades, conservatism was resurgent. In the wake of the determined expansion of the federal government through the Great Society and frustration over the Vietnam War, public debate and the range of political options shifted back to the right, and conservatives won support for income tax cuts and economic deregulation. For all their victories, however, conservatives in the age of Reagan never succeeded in reversing the gains of the Great Society. The programs Lyndon Johnson initiated and Congress enacted into law proved to be more enduring than the political coalition that built them.

When Johnson delivered his Great Society speech in May 1964 at the University of Michigan, he had called on the nation to do more than simply move toward being a rich and powerful society. Rather, he posed the challenge to move "upward to the Great Society." In many respects, Congress met the challenge.

For almost a decade after 1964, War on Poverty programs reduced the incidence and severity of poverty in America. Though conditions have deteriorated for the poor since the 1980s, the programs remain part of the fabric of benefits upon which the disadvantaged depend.[21] According to one of the best studies that we have on poverty, conducted by economists at Columbia University, poverty declined from 26 percent to 16 percent between 1967 and 2012, a significant drop that largely resulted from the government programs created in the 1960s.[22] By the end of the twentieth century, almost thirty million preschoolers had benefited from Head Start. Over forty-seven million Americans counted on food stamps in 2013.

Medicare and Medicaid guaranteed health-care coverage to the elderly and the medically indigent. The historian Michael Katz writes, "Medicare and Medicaid improved health care dramatically. In 1963, one of every five Americans who lived below the poverty line never had been examined by a physician, and poor people used medical facilities far less than others. By 1970, the proportion never examined had dipped to 8 percent, and the proportion visiting a physician annually was about the same as for everyone else."[23] Medicaid vastly expanded over the 1980s to include pregnant women, children, and other categories of people who had had only limited access to care. During the heyday of conservative politics, Medicaid expanded the number of beneficiaries to thirty-six million people by 1996, a substantial increase from the period between 1973 and 1989 when the average was twenty to twenty-three million.[24] By 2011, close to one-third of all Americans, not just the elderly, were covered by Medicare or Medicaid.[25] The programs were a massive federal intervention into health-care markets. Hospital administrators and physicians, who had once derided the Medicare program as "socialized medicine," came to depend on the federal dollars that came from it. States relied on Medicaid funds to keep hospitals open, health-care workers employed, and poor patients cared for. When the possibility of program cuts came up in Congress, the various segments of the health-care industry were the first in line to protest any moves toward retrenchment.

Civil rights legislation secured rights African Americans had been deprived of since the end of Reconstruction. The laws eliminated segregation in public facilities and dramatically increased the number of African American voters. "It used to be Southern politics was just 'nigger' politics—a question of which candidate could 'out-nigger' the other," the civil rights activist and congressman Andrew Young said in 1976. "Then you registered 10% to 15% in the community, and folks would start saying 'Nigra.' Later you got 35% to 40% registered, and it was amazing how quick they learned how to say 'Nee-grow.' And now that we've got 50%, 60%, 70% of the black votes registered in the South, everybody's proud to be associated with their black brothers and sisters."[26] The civil rights legislation of 1964 was also a stepping-stone for women on the path to gender equality.

Civil rights laws also worked in conjunction with the health-care and education programs that were established in this period. Because local institutions could not receive federal money if they were segregated, hospitals and schools hastened to end segregation. Six months after Medicare was put in place, there were no more segregated hospitals in the South.[27]

Education reforms resulted in vastly greater educational opportunities for millions of Americans. Higher education grants and loans made it possible for more young Americans to enter colleges and universities. Funds for educational institutions were also a tool the federal government used to speed up the desegregation of schools and to pressure local districts to implement other reforms.[28]

The programs were far from perfect. Local school districts notoriously used federal funds for purposes other than helping poor children. Medicare played a significant role in the growth of health-care expenditures during the latter half of the twentieth century; federal funding gave hospitals a strong incentive to increase their costs. Civil rights laws did not end racism in American society. None of the programs could counteract the bad effects of spiraling inflation and high unemployment on the economy in the 1970s. African American families continued to suffer from horrible economic devastation, and African American men were incarcerated and jobless at shockingly high rates.

Imperfect as they were, the programs were important contributions to American society. Taken in their totality, they constituted nothing short of a dramatic transformation of American government that provided a new foundation of security for all Americans. The Great Society improved the lives of millions of citizens by creating a robust social safety net, and it affirmed the principle that intervention by the federal government was a good way, perhaps the best way, to guarantee rights, to help the disadvantaged, and to improve the quality of life for all Americans.

During the mid-1980s, at the height of Ronald Reagan's power, shortly after his landslide reelection victory over the Democrat Walter Mondale, the budget bureau spokesman Edwin Dale admitted, "I wouldn't quarrel that Medicare's been a success. In fact, much of the social safety net was accomplished during the Great Society, and whatever gets trimmed, the safety net will remain intact."[29] Many conservatives were shocked when President George W. Bush worked with Democrats in 2001 to expand the role of the federal government in education and allied with the Republican Congress in 2003 to add prescription drug benefits to Medicare. Even George W. Bush was governing in Lyndon Johnson's shadow.

So embedded are Great Society policies in the nation's fabric that many citizens can no longer conceive of life without them. When one senior citizen, a Tea Party conservative, confronted the South Carolina Republican congressman Robert Inglis in a 2009 town hall meeting about President Obama's health-care proposal, which included cuts to Medicare, he warned, "Keep your government hands off my Medicare!"

In a way, the statement made sense. It perfectly captured the changes that have been produced by the Great Society. Within a few months, Johnson's legislation produced a vast policy infrastructure that no ideological onslaught could displace. In 2009, a conservative could oppose a new proposal for universal government-sponsored health insurance with a defense of what Lyndon Johnson and Congress had built. Grassroots activists and voters had given Johnson a tremendous opportunity in 1964 and 1965 to remake domestic policy. He took advantage of that moment, fully aware it would not last very long, and Americans in the twenty-first century are still living with the domestic policies born out of that transformative moment.

Because of all the legislative breakthroughs Lyndon Johnson engineered, he has become an iconic figure for students of American history. His successors in office and their advisers—even those who hated what he achieved—have sought to figure out how the shrewd Texan was able to get so much legislation passed.

But we must understand that the Great Society wasn't all about one man's political talents or gifts or magic. Nor was it a result of a Congress that naturally worked, where members got along and just knew how to legislate. The political acumen Johnson and his colleagues on Capitol Hill possessed was essential, but what made the difference was the forces that temporarily reshaped Congress and broke the hold of conservatives on that notoriously inertial institution. A grassroots movement and a sea change election were critical to the liberal ascendancy that overwhelmed, if briefly, the forces of conservatism that had been, and are today, so strong. Critical too were the controversial and costly compromises Johnson made to hold off rightward pressure on Capitol Hill.

We as citizens and as politicians must study not only the great personalities who have inhabited the White House but also the full history of the political landscapes in which they operated and which made their achievements possible. Only if we understand how political landscapes change and can be changed will we ever have a chance of breaking the current gridlock in Washington.

ACKNOWLEDGMENTS

I would like to thank all the institutions and people who made the writing of this book possible. Princeton University has continued to provide a wonderful intellectual home. The Russell Sage Foundation offered me an enriching year to devote my time to this project and to engage with a fascinating community of social scientists, all of whom asked tough questions about the analytical framework of the book. Galo Falchettore and Claire Gabriel at the Russell Sage Foundation provided useful polling data from the period and tracked down important material.

Many individuals have also helped me in the process of writing this book. Joseph Parrott at the University of Texas offered essential assistance helping to gather archival material that I needed at the LBJ Presidential Library. At the same time that he was working on his doctoral dissertation, he has helped me check key material when I needed clarification on what was contained in certain documents. At Princeton University, Steven Server found some detail and color that made it into the book.

The staff at the LBJ Presidential Library were outstanding, as they have been for every project that has involved their collections. Tina Houston, Claudia Anderson, Margaret Harman, and Allen Fisher never tired of my e-mails and offered all the assistance I needed.

A number of scholars read earlier versions of the manuscript, or chapters of the manuscript, and provided helpful commentary. They include Ed Berkowitz, Margot Canaday, Dorothy Sue Cobble, Gareth Davies, Michael Katz, Kevin Kruse, Don Ritchie, Dan Rodgers, and Bruce Schulman. In addition, Daniel Zitin offered unbelievable editorial commentary that helped me refine the narrative and improve the writing. Jake Blumgart provided his excellent fact-checking skills at the final stages of the editing process. Participants at the seminars of the Russell Sage Foundation, Princeton University's Davis Center, Columbia's Congress and History Conference, and Yale's Institution for Social and Policy Studies gave me critical feedback to the arguments.

My editor at Penguin, and former agent, Scott Moyers, has been superb. He has been confident and enthusiastic about this project from the start. He constantly pushed me to write the book that he believed I was capable of writing. Throughout, he had a strong vision of the contribution that this work could make to the national dialogue about Washington and American history. Mally Anderson has been very helpful in the final stages of the project. My agent, Andrew Wylie, has also offered shrewd advice and great representation at every stage of the project. He is a rare person who can combine the intellect of an academic with the acumen of the best businessperson.

My whole family has been great throughout the process of writing this book, and I would like to offer my thanks. My parents, Viviana and Jerry, were great as always and constantly enthusiastic about what I was doing. My mother-in-law, Ellie, has been wonderful and loving, and I've enjoyed our many conversations.

Back on the home front, my wife, Meg, offered phenomenal support and unending love. Her readings were invaluable. Because of her, I was able to bring out the story line of a complex and tumultuous period. She helped me to see what this book could become. More important, she's built a warm, loving, and lively home that is magical each time I step through the door. Our walks in the streets of New

York City provide a permanent oasis that reenergizes and inspires. Each step of building our life together has been a treasure. Our friendship and our marriage is the ultimate collaboration, one that comes from the heart. Abigail, Sophia, Nathan, and Claire are the best children that a man could hope for. Each a star in his or her own right, they make each day superb, fun, and filled with the kind of noise that brings the world alive. Although they primarily know Lyndon as our four-pound Maltese dog, named after the former president, I hope that one day they can enjoy the findings in this book.

NOTES

I do not include endnotes for public presidential statements (made at press conferences, speeches, etc.) because they are easily available at the University of California, Santa Barbara, American Presidency Project, www.presidency.ucsb.edu/index _docs.php.

CHAPTER 1: THE CHALLENGES OF A LIBERAL PRESIDENCY

1. Robert A. Caro, *The Years of Lyndon Johnson,* vol. 4, *The Passage of Power* (New York: Knopf, 2012), 179–80.
2. Jack Valenti, "Lyndon Johnson: An Awesome Engine of a Man," in *Lyndon Johnson Remembered: An Intimate Portrait of a Presidency,* ed. Thomas W. Cowger and Sherwin J. Markman (Oxford, U.K.: Rowman & Littlefield, 2003), 37.
3. Ira Katznelson, *Fear Itself: The New Deal and the Origins of Our Time* (New York: Norton, 2013).
4. For a recent book emphasizing and praising the functional nature of Congress in this period, see Todd S. Purdum, *An Idea Whose Time Has Come: Two Presidents, Two Parties, and the Battle for the Civil Rights Act of 1964* (New York: Henry Holt, 2014).
5. Bruce J. Schulman, *Lyndon B. Johnson and American Liberalism: A Brief Biography with Documents,* 2nd ed. (Boston: Bedford, 2007), 3. See also Caro, *Passage of Power,* xiv. For an alternative view, focusing on the Civil Rights Act of 1964, see Clay Risen, *The Bill of the Century: The Epic Battle for the Civil Rights Act* (New York: Bloomsbury, 2014).
6. Rowland Evans and Robert Novak, *Lyndon B. Johnson: The Exercise of Power* (New York: New American Library, 1966), 104.
7. Ronald Suskind, *Confidence Men: Wall Street, Washington, and the Education of a President* (New York: Harper, 2011), 370.
8. Nolan McCarty, Keith T. Poole, and Howard Rosenthal, *Political Bubbles: Financial Crises and the Failure of American Democracy* (Princeton, N.J.: Princeton University Press, 2013), 8.
9. Stephen Skowronek, *The Politics Presidents Make: Leadership from John Adams to George Bush* (Cambridge, Mass.: Belknap Press of Harvard University Press, 1993), 341.

CHAPTER 2: DEADLOCKED DEMOCRACY

1. "The Torch Has Been Passed," *New York Times,* Jan. 21, 1961.
2. Susan Dunn, *Roosevelt's Purge: How FDR Fought to Change the Democratic Party* (Cambridge, Mass.: Belknap Press of Harvard University Press, 2012).
3. A. James Reichley, *The Life of the Parties: A History of American Political Parties* (New York: Free Press, 1992), 279.
4. There is a voluminous literature in political science about the committee system and southern politics. For a review of the findings, see Julian E. Zelizer, *On Capitol Hill: The Struggle to Reform Congress and Its Consequences, 1948–2000* (New York: Cambridge University Press, 2004), 14–32.
5. Judd Choate, *Torn and Frayed: Congressional Norms and Party Switching in an Era of Reform* (Westport, Conn.: Greenwood Press, 2003), 54.
6. Timothy Thurber, "The Second Reconstruction," in *The American Congress: The Building of Democracy,* ed. Julian E. Zelizer (Boston: Houghton Mifflin, 2004), 531.
7. "Southern Democrats-GOP Won 71% of Test Votes," *1959 Congressional Quarterly Almanac,* 141–46; "'Conservative Coalition' Appeared in 22% of Roll Calls," *1960 Congressional Quarterly Almanac,* 117–25; "'Conservative Coalition' Appeared on 28% of Roll Calls," *1961 Congressional Quarterly Almanac,* 642–52.
8. Zelizer, *On Capitol Hill,* 31.
9. Martin B. Gold and Dimple Gupta, "The Constitutional Option to Change Senate Rules and Procedures: A Majoritarian Means to Overcome the Filibuster," *Harvard Journal of Law and Public Policy* 28, no. 1 (Fall 2004): 216.
10. Neil MacNeil and Richard A. Baker, *The American Senate: An Insider's History* (New York: Oxford University Press, 2013), 302–34.
11. David M. Kennedy, *Freedom from Fear: The American People in Depression and War, 1929–1945* (New York: Oxford University Press, 1999), 343.
12. Zelizer, *On Capitol Hill,* 33–62.
13. Carl Solberg, *Hubert Humphrey: A Biography* (New York: Norton, 1984), 76.
14. Timothy N. Thurber, *The Politics of Equality: Hubert H. Humphrey and the African American Freedom Struggle, 1945–1978* (New York: Columbia University Press, 1999), 62.
15. Zelizer, *On Capitol Hill,* 38.
16. Ibid.
17. Nelson Lichtenstein, *The Most Dangerous Man in Detroit: Walter Reuther and the Fate of American Labor* (New York: Basic Books, 1995), 389; Taylor E. Dark, *The Unions and the Democrats,* updated ed. (Ithaca, N.Y.: Cornell University Press, 1999), 51–56; J. David Greenstone, *Labor in American Politics,* 2nd ed. (Chicago: University of Chicago Press, 1977); Kevin Boyle, *The UAW and the Heyday of American Liberalism, 1945–1968* (Ithaca, N.Y.: Cornell University Press, 1999).
18. Alan Draper, *A Rope of Sand: The AFL-CIO Committee on Education, 1955–1967* (New York: Praeger, 1988).
19. Eric Pace, "Clarence M. Mitchell Is Dead; N.A.A.C.P. Lobbyist Till '78," *New York Times,* March 20, 1984.

20. Mary Dudziak, *Cold War, Civil Rights: Race and the Image of American Democracy* (Princeton, N.J.: Princeton University Press, 2000).

21. Raymond Arsenault, *Freedom Riders: 1961 and the Struggle for Social Justice* (New York: Oxford University Press, 2007).

22. Robert Dallek, *An Unfinished Life: John F. Kennedy, 1917–1963* (Boston: Little, Brown, 2003), 384.

23. Robert A. Caro, *The Years of Lyndon Johnson*, vol. 3, *Master of the Senate* (New York: Knopf, 2002).

24. Ibid., 895–909.

25. Ibid., 1003.

26. Zelizer, *On Capitol Hill*, 51.

27. Irving Bernstein, *Promises Kept: John F. Kennedy's New Frontier* (New York: Oxford University Press, 1991), 48.

28. Evan Thomas, *Robert Kennedy: His Life* (New York: Touchstone, 2000), 132.

29. Dallek, *Unfinished Life*, 381.

30. Arthur M. Schlesinger Jr., *Robert Kennedy and His Times,* 2nd ed. (New York: First Mariner, 2002), 317.

31. Taylor Branch, *Parting the Waters: America in the King Years, 1954–1963* (New York: Simon & Schuster, 1988), 518.

32. Geoffrey Kabaservice, *Rule and Ruin: The Downfall of Moderation and the Destruction of the Republican Party from Eisenhower to the Tea Party* (New York: Oxford University Press, 2012), 98.

33. "Kennedy Scored on Civil Rights," *Baltimore Sun,* Feb. 13, 1963; Peter J. Kumpa, "House Gets Rights Bill," *Baltimore Sun,* Feb. 1, 1963.

34. "GOP in National Drive to Regain Colored Vote," *Chicago Daily Defender,* Feb. 9, 1963.

35. Risen, *Bill of the Century,* 63–64, 72.

36. Rodney Crowther, "GOP Assails Rights Views," *Baltimore Sun,* March 3, 1963.

37. "Kennedy's Civil Rights Plan Hit by Rockefeller," *Los Angeles Times,* March 6, 1963.

38. Robert Albright, "GOP Challenges Administration, Offers Broad 'Rights' Program," *Washington Post,* March 29, 1963.

39. "Republicans Propose Civil Rights Bills," *Atlanta Daily World,* March 29, 1963.

40. "Kennedy Administration Missing Boat on Rights: CORE Chiefs," *Chicago Daily Defender,* April 22, 1963.

41. Richard Reeves, *President Kennedy: Profile of Power* (New York: Simon & Schuster, 1994), 468.

42. James T. Patterson, *Grand Expectations: The United States, 1945–1974* (New York: Oxford University Press, 1996), 478.

43. Robert J. Donovan and Ray Scherer, *Unsilent Revolution: Television News and American Public Life, 1948–1991* (Washington, D.C.: Woodrow Wilson International Center for Scholars; New York: Cambridge University Press, 1992), 3–22.

44. Branch, *Parting the Waters,* 709–10.

45. Ibid., 744–45.

46. Reeves, *President Kennedy,* 488.

47. Byron C. Hulsey, *Everett Dirksen and His Presidents: How a Senate Giant Shaped American Politics* (Lawrence: University Press of Kansas, 2000), 174.

48. Dan T. Carter, *The Politics of Rage: George Wallace, the Origins of the New Conservatism, and the Transformation of American Politics* (New York: Simon & Schuster, 1995), 151.
49. Ibid., 151–52.
50. Jonathan Rosenberg and Zachary Karabell, *Kennedy, Johnson, and the Quest for Justice: The Civil Rights Tapes* (New York: Norton, 2003), 128.
51. Ibid., 136–39; Reeves, *President Kennedy*, 585; Charles Whalen and Barbara Whalen, *The Longest Debate: A Legislative History of the Civil Rights Act of 1964* (Cabin John, Md.: Seven Locks, 1984), 27.
52. Richard L. Lyons, "Mr. Civil Rights Recalls 'Hard, Grueling Fight,'" *Washington Post*, Oct. 26, 1972; Kabaservice, *Rule and Ruin*, 99.
53. Kabaservice, *Rule and Ruin*, 99.
54. Whalen and Whalen, *Longest Debate*, 13–14.
55. Ibid., 35.
56. Reeves, *President Kennedy*, 629.
57. Whalen and Whalen, *Longest Debate*, 39–40.
58. Caro, *Passage of Power*, 266–67.
59. Whalen and Whalen, *Longest Debate*, 46.
60. Rosenberg and Karabell, *Kennedy, Johnson, and the Quest for Justice*, 187.
61. Reeves, *President Kennedy*, 630.
62. "House Unit Votes Bipartisan Plan for Civil Rights," *New York Times*, Oct. 30, 1963.
63. Rosenberg and Karabell, *Kennedy, Johnson, and the Quest for Justice*, 178.

CHAPTER 3: NEW PRESIDENT, SAME OLD CONGRESS

1. This account of the assassination and transfer comes from Steven M. Gillon, *The Kennedy Assassination—24 Hours After: Lyndon B. Johnson's Pivotal First Day as President* (New York: Basic Books, 2009).
2. Randall Woods, *LBJ: Architect of Ambition* (New York: Free Press, 2006), 561.
3. Gillon, *Kennedy Assassination*, 183.
4. Ibid., 188; Robert Dallek, *Flawed Giant: Lyndon B. Johnson and His Times, 1961–1973* (New York: Oxford University Press, 1998).
5. Larry L. King, "Bringing Up Lyndon," *Texas Monthly*, Jan. 1976, 83.
6. Robert Dallek, *Lyndon B. Johnson: Portrait of a President* (New York: Oxford University Press, 2004), 30.
7. Charles Peters, *Lyndon Johnson* (New York: Times Books, 2010), 7.
8. Schulman, *Lyndon B. Johnson and American Liberalism*, 17.
9. Ibid., 24.
10. Caro, *Master of the Senate*, 720.
11. Ibid., 685–1040.
12. Irving Bernstein, *Guns or Butter: The Presidency of Lyndon Johnson* (New York: Oxford University Press, 1996), 31.
13. Johnson, Moyers, and Sorensen, telephone conversation, Nov. 25, 1963, White House presidential tapes, Lyndon Baines Johnson Presidential Library, Austin, Tex. (hereafter cited as LBJL).
14. Caro, *Passage of Power*, 422.

15. Dallek, *Flawed Giant,* 72.
16. Bernstein, *Guns or Butter,* 32.
17. Nicholas Kotz, *Judgment Days: Lyndon Baines Johnson, Martin Luther King Jr., and the Laws That Changed America* (Boston: Houghton Mifflin, 2005), 37; "Congress: The Full Treatment," *Time,* Dec. 13, 1963, 31; Caro, *Passage of Power,* 475.
18. Walter Heller, interview by David McComb, Dec. 21, 1971, White House Oral History Collection, 19–21, LBJL.
19. Johnson and Albert, telephone conversation, Jan. 9, 1964, White House presidential tapes, LBJL.
20. Reeves, *President Kennedy,* 434.
21. Frank C. Porter, "Tax Bill Unfair, Union Leader Says," *Washington Post,* Feb. 24, 1964.
22. Alan L. Otten, "President Sets Budget at $97.9 Billion, Tips His Election Strategy," *Wall Street Journal,* Jan. 9, 1964.
23. Caro, *Passage of Power,* 553.
24. John D. Morris, "Byrd Steps Aside in Tax Bill Fight," *New York Times,* Jan. 27, 1964.
25. Dallek, *Lyndon B. Johnson,* 191.

CHAPTER 4: LEGISLATING CIVIL RIGHTS

1. Risen, *Bill of the Century,* 168.
2. Keith M. Finley, *Delaying the Dream: Southern Senators and the Fight Against Civil Rights, 1938–1965* (Baton Rouge: Louisiana State University Press, 2008), 266–67. For a comprehensive look at the legislative battle behind the Civil Rights Act of 1964 that also pays close attention to the role of Congress, see Purdum, *Idea Whose Time Has Come;* Risen, *Bill of the Century;* and Robert Mann, *The Walls of Jericho: Lyndon Johnson, Hubert Humphrey, Richard Russell, and the Struggle for Civil Rights* (New York: Harcourt Brace, 1996).
3. Mann, *Walls of Jericho,* 402.
4. Roscoe Drummond, "Can Power of Senate Filibuster Be Broken? It's Up to Democrats," *Los Angeles Times,* Feb. 4, 1964.
5. G. Calvin MacKenzie and Robert Weisbrot, *The Liberal Hour: Washington and the Politics of Change in the 1960s* (New York: Penguin, 2008), 55–56.
6. "The Gut Fighter," *Time,* June 8, 1959.
7. James L. Sundquist, *The Decline and Resurgence of Congress* (Washington, D.C.: Brookings Institution, 1981), 374.
8. Richard S. Beth, "The Discharge Rule in the House: Recent Use in Historical Context," Congressional Research Service, 2003.
9. Anthony Lewis, "President Spurs Drive for House to Act on Rights," *New York Times,* Dec. 4, 1963.
10. Johnson and McDonald, telephone conversation, Nov. 29, 1963, White House presidential tapes, LBJL.
11. Caro, *Passage of Power,* 498.
12. Richard L. Lyons, "Liberal Democrats Aim for Reforms in House," *Washington Post,* Dec. 15, 1963.
13. Caro, *Passage of Power,* 495–500.

14. Johnson and Anderson, telephone conversation, Nov. 30, 1963, White House presidential tapes, LBJL.

15. Johnson and Graham, telephone conversation, Dec. 2, 1963, White House presidential tapes, LBJL.

16. "Tyrant in the House," *Washington Post,* Dec. 6, 1963.

17. "'Work on' Congressmen During Holidays, Rights Group Urges," *Atlanta Daily World,* Dec. 26, 1963; "Clergy Backs Discharge Petition on Rights Bill," *Chicago Daily Defender,* Dec. 24, 1963.

18. "Mass Protests Resuming," *Afro-American,* Dec. 28, 1963.

19. Caro, *Passage of Power,* 496–97.

20. Don Oberdorfer, "'Judge' Smith Moves with Deliberate Drag," *New York Times,* Jan. 12, 1964.

21. Bernstein, *Guns or Butter,* 44.

22. E. W. Kenworthy, "Quips Mark Start of Rights Hearing," *New York Times,* Jan. 10, 1964.

23. Kotz, *Judgment Days,* 92; William Knighton Jr., "Johnson Asks Negroes' Aid," *Baltimore Sun,* Jan. 19, 1964.

24. Thomas Jackson, *From Civil Rights to Human Rights* (Philadelphia: University of Pennsylvania Press, 2006).

25. "LBJ Meets with Negro Leaders; All Five Worry About Poverty," *Chicago Daily Defender,* Jan. 20, 1964.

26. Bruce J. Dierenfield, *Keeper of the Rules: Congressman Howard W. Smith of Virginia* (Charlottesville: University Press of Virginia, 1987), 192–93.

27. Joseph W. Sullivan, "Civil Rights Coup? Tough Bill Likely Will Zip Through Congress as Opposition Crumbles," *Wall Street Journal,* Feb. 3, 1964.

28. Denton L. Watson, *Lion in the Lobby: Clarence Mitchell Jr.'s Struggle for the Passage of Civil Rights Laws* (New York: William Morrow, 1990), 592–93.

29. James F. Findlay, "Religion and Politics in the Sixties: The Churches and the Civil Rights Act of 1964," *Journal of American History* 77, no. 1 (1990): 79–86.

30. JV to the President, Jan. 21, 1964, Presidential Files, Legislative Background, Civil Rights Act 1964, box 1, file: Legislative Relations, LBJL; Taylor Branch, *Pillar of Fire: America in the King Years, 1963–65* (New York: Simon & Schuster 1998), 592.

31. Caro, *Passage of Power,* 559–60.

32. Gerald Griffin, "Rights Push Bipartisan," *Baltimore Sun,* Feb. 9, 1964.

33. Branch, *Pillar of Fire,* 231.

34. Jo Freeman, "How 'Sex' Got into Title VII; Persistent Opportunism as a Maker of Public Policy," *Law and Inequality: A Journal of Theory and Practice* 9, no. 2 (March 1991): 163–84.

35. Dorothy Sue Cobble, *The Other Women's Movement: Workplace Justice and Social Rights in Modern America* (Princeton, N.J.: Princeton University Press, 2003), 168–71.

36. E. W. Kenworthy, "Jobs Issue Blocks Attempt in House to Vote on Rights," *New York Times,* Feb. 9, 1964.

37. Dennis Hevesi, "Ex-rep. Edith Green, 77, Is Dead; Early Opponent of Vietnam War," *New York Times,* April 23, 1987.

38. Branch, *Pillar of Fire,* 233.

39. Jerry Landauer, "Southern Senators Fight to Divide Forces Backing Rights Bill, Block Passage Intact," *Wall Street Journal,* March 24, 1964.
40. Robert C. Albright, "A Rights Bill 'If It Takes All Summer,'" *Washington Post,* March 8, 1964.
41. Donald A. Ritchie, *Reporting from Washington: The History of the Washington Press Corps* (New York: Oxford University Press, 2005), 200–201.
42. "Debate in the Senate; a Meeting in Birmingham," *Time,* April 10, 1964.
43. Mann, *Walls of Jericho,* 400.
44. John H. Averill, "Dixie Foes to Renew Fight on Rights Bill," *Los Angeles Times,* Feb. 20, 1964.
45. "The Filibuster Before the Filibuster," *Time,* April 3, 1964.
46. E. W. Kenworthy, "Pressures Mount for Civil Rights Bill," *New York Times,* April 5, 1964.
47. Finley, *Delaying the Dream,* 257–58.
48. Mann, *Walls of Jericho,* 403–4.
49. Arthur Krock, "A Pilot Ruling on Equal Employment Opportunity," *New York Times,* March 13, 1964.
50. Hugh Davis Graham, *The Civil Rights Era: Origins and Development of National Policy, 1960–1972* (New York: Oxford University Press, 1990), 150.
51. Joseph Hearst, "Senators Eye Wallace Vote," *Chicago Tribune,* April 9, 1964.
52. Nicholas deB. Katzenbach, *Some of It Was Fun: Working with RFK and LBJ* (New York: Norton, 2008), 142.
53. Tom Wicker, "Johnson, in Debut, Lasts Nine Innings of Baseball and Two of Politics," *New York Times,* April 14, 1964; John H. Averill, "Senators Rush from Ball Game," *Los Angeles Times,* April 14, 1964.
54. Maire McNair, "The Real Senators Lost Game First," *Washington Post,* April 15, 1964.
55. Wicker, "Johnson, in Debut, Lasts Nine Innings of Baseball and Two of Politics."
56. William Moore, "Dirksen Defies Civil Rights Picket Threat," *Chicago Tribune,* Feb. 18, 1964.
57. Nicholas Chriss, "St. Augustine 'Hot Place': Mother of Mass. Gov. in Florida Rights Battle," *New Journal and Guide,* April 4, 1964; Fred Powledge, "88 More Seized in St. Augustine," *New York Times,* April 2, 1964; "Debate in the Senate; a Meeting in Birmingham."
58. Baker E. Morten, "King Warns Senate Dixiecrats," *Afro-American,* April 4, 1964.
59. E. W. Kenworthy, "Churches Termed Key to Rights Bill," *New York Times,* March 21, 1964.
60. Mann, *Walls of Jericho,* 412.
61. Findlay, "Religion and Politics in the Sixties," 79–80.
62. Mann, *Walls of Jericho,* 413.
63. Whalen and Whalen, *Longest Debate,* 165.
64. Risen, *Bill of the Century,* 195.
65. Whalen and Whalen, *Longest Debate,* 164; Jerry Doolittle, "Rain Fails to Deter Start of Prayer Vigil on Rights," *Washington Post,* April 20, 1964.
66. Caro, *Passage of Power,* 565–66.

67. Louis Harris, "South Joins Opposition to Rights Bill Filibuster," *Washington Post,* April 27, 1964.

68. Dallek, *Flawed Giant,* 114.

69. Joseph A. Califano Jr., *The Triumph and Tragedy of Lyndon Johnson: The White House Years* (New York: Simon & Schuster, 1991), 54.

70. Woods, *LBJ,* 477.

71. Risen, *Bill of the Century,* 204.

72. Roscoe Drummond, "Johnson's Leadership," *Washington Post,* May 13, 1964.

73. Woods, *LBJ,* 476.

74. Marjorie Hunter, "President Hailed on 5-State Tour of Poverty Areas," *New York Times,* April 25, 1964.

75. Branch, *Pillar of Fire,* 304; "The Whirlwind President," *Time,* April 1964.

76. Jack Valenti, *A Very Human President* (New York: Norton, 1975), 182–83.

77. Bernstein, *Guns or Butter,* 67.

78. Hubert Humphrey, interview by Michael Gillette, June 21, 1977, interview 3, 6, White House Oral History Collection, LBJL.

79. Dallek, *Flawed Giant,* 118–19.

80. Hulsey, *Everett Dirksen and His Presidents,* 188.

81. Robert Mann, *When Freedom Would Triumph: The Civil Rights Struggle in Congress, 1954–1968* (Baton Rouge: Louisiana State University Press, 2007), 195.

82. Humphrey, interview by Gillette, 6.

83. Katzenbach, *Some of It Was Fun,* 141.

84. Ibid., 142–43.

85. Mann, *Walls of Jericho,* 419–20; Timothy N. Thurber, *The Politics of Equality: Hubert H. Humphrey and the African American Freedom Struggle* (New York: Columbia University Press, 1999), 141. I also discussed this with Nicholas Katzenbach in 2012 during a visit to Princeton.

86. Johnson and Kennedy, telephone conversation, May 13, 1964, White House presidential tapes, LBJL.

87. Johnson and Dirksen, telephone conversation, May 13, 1964, White House presidential tapes, LBJL.

88. John G. Stewart, "Tactics II," in *The Civil Rights Act of 1964: The Passage of the Law That Ended Racial Segregation,* ed. Robert D. Loevy (Albany: State University of New York Press, 1997), 279.

89. Ibid., 280.

90. Johnson and Humphrey, telephone conversation, May 13, 1964, White House presidential tapes, LBJL.

91. Richard B. Stolley, "Eve and Hubert, Heroes of the Historic Session," *Life,* June 19, 1964, 36–37.

92. "Everett McKinley Dirksen's Finest Hour," *Peoria Journal Star,* June 10, 1964.

93. Marjorie Hunter, "Packed Senate Galleries Tense; 10-Minute Vote Makes History," *New York Times,* June 11, 1964.

94. Elmer Lammi, "Senate Spectators Gasp in Relief," *Washington Post,* June 11, 1964.

95. Ernest B. Furguson, "Quiet Drama Quickly Over," *Baltimore Sun,* June 11, 1964.

96. "The Covenant," *Time,* June 19, 1964.
97. Edward G. McGrath, "Johnson Tells Holy Cross End of Racial Injustice in Sight," *Boston Globe,* June 11, 1964.
98. "The Final Vote," *Time,* June 26, 1964.
99. Branch, *Pillar of Fire,* 359.

CHAPTER 5: HOW BARRY GOLDWATER BUILT THE GREAT SOCIETY

1. "Johnson Sights 'Creative Period,'" *Christian Science Monitor,* July 7, 1964.
2. Nicholas Lemann, *The Promised Land: The Great Black Migration and How It Changed America* (New York: Vintage, 1991), 142.
3. For the best history of this issue, see Michael B. Katz, *The Undeserving Poor: From the War on Poverty to the War on Welfare* (New York: Pantheon, 1990).
4. Michael Gillette, *Launching the War on Poverty: An Oral History* (New York: Oxford University Press, 2010), 15.
5. Allen J. Matusow, *The Unraveling of America: A History of Liberalism in the 1960s* (New York: Harper, 1984), 97–127.
6. Johnson and Mahon, telephone conversation, Aug. 1, 1964, White House presidential tapes, LBJL.
7. Lewis L. Gould, *Grand Old Party: A History of the Republicans* (New York: Random House, 2003), 365.
8. Rick Perlstein, *Before the Storm: Barry Goldwater and the Unmaking of the American Consensus* (New York: Hill and Wang, 2001).
9. Laurence H. Burd, "Outlook for '64: A War on Poverty," *Washington Post,* Jan. 1, 1964. (Emphasis in original.)
10. "Barry Assails 'Madison Av.' Poverty Bill," *Chicago Tribune,* July 22, 1964.
11. Robert S. Allen and Paul Scott, "Anti-poverty Plan Under Attack," *Los Angeles Times,* July 30, 1964.
12. "Hits Centralized Rule: Eisenhower Explains Why He's Republican," *Los Angeles Times,* April 5, 1964.
13. Johnson and Larry O'Brien, telephone conversation, July 31, 1964, White House presidential tapes, LBJL.
14. Daley and Johnson, telephone conversation, Jan. 20, 1964, White House presidential tapes, LBJL.
15. Michael D. Brown, *Race, Money, and the Welfare State* (Ithaca, N.Y.: Cornell University Press, 1999), 224–32.
16. Gareth Davies, *From Opportunity to Entitlement: The Transformation and Decline of Great Society Liberalism* (Lawrence: University Press of Kansas, 1996).
17. Johnson and George Meany, telephone conversation, July 28, 1964, White House presidential tapes, LBJL.
18. Johnson and Mahon, telephone conversation, July 29, 1964, White House presidential tapes, LBJL.
19. Nichole Mellow, *The State of Disunion: Regional Sources of Modern American Partisanship* (Baltimore: Johns Hopkins University Press, 2008), 93.

20. Deborah Ward, *The White Welfare State: The Racialization of U.S. Welfare Policy* (Ann Arbor: University of Michigan Press, 2005), 135.
21. David Torstensson, "Beyond the City: Lyndon Johnson's War on Poverty in Rural America," *Journal of Policy History* 25, no. 4 (2013): 593.
22. Robert C. Albright, "Goldwater Hits Poverty Legislation as Worthless," *Los Angeles Times,* July 22, 1964.
23. Sargent Shriver, interview by Michael Gillette, in *Launching the War on Poverty,* 170–71.
24. For some examples of his tactics, see Andrée E. Reeves, *Congressional Committee Chairmen: Three Who Made an Evolution* (Lexington: University Press of Kentucky, 1993), 126.
25. O'Brien and Johnson, telephone conversation, Feb. 10, 1964, White House presidential tapes, LBJL.
26. Marjorie Hunter, "Landrum Defies G.O.P. on Poverty," *New York Times,* April 10, 1964.
27. Gillette, *Launching the War on Poverty,* 150–65.
28. Johnson and Teague, telephone conversation, Aug. 5, 1964, White House presidential tapes, LBJL.
29. Johnson and O'Brien, telephone conversation, July 29, 1964, and Johnson and Joseph Barr, telephone conversation, July 30, 1964, White House presidential tapes, LBJL.
30. Scott Stossel, *Sarge: The Life and Times of Sargent Shriver* (Washington, D.C.: Smithsonian Books, 2004), 385–87.
31. Ibid.; James Adler, interview by Michael Gillette, Feb. 23, 1983, 30, 38, White House Oral History Collection, LBJL; Norbert Schlei, interview by Michael Gillette, May 15, 1980, interview 1, 38, White House Oral History Collection, LBJL.
32. The following account about the meeting comes from Stossel, *Sarge,* 386–91.
33. Dallek, *Flawed Giant,* 110.
34. Julian E. Zelizer, *Arsenal of Democracy: The Politics of National Security from World War II to the War on Terrorism* (New York: Basic Books, 2010), 178.
35. Dallek, *Flawed Giant,* 149.
36. Joseph R. L. Sterne, "Attackers 'Destroyed'; Goldwater Questions Policy," *Baltimore Sun,* Aug. 4, 1964.
37. Johnson and McNamara, telephone conversation, Aug. 3, 1964, White House presidential tapes, LBJL.
38. George Ball, *The Past Has Another Pattern* (New York: Norton, 1978), 379.
39. Woods, *LBJ,* 516.
40. Dallek, *Flawed Giant,* 150.
41. Woods, *LBJ,* 516–17.
42. Don Oberdorfer, *Senator Mansfield: The Extraordinary Life of a Great American Statesman and Diplomat* (Washington, D.C.: Smithsonian Books, 2003), 247.
43. Gary Stone, *Elites for Peace: The Senate and the Vietnam War, 1964–1968* (Knoxville: University of Tennessee Press, 2007), 39–40.
44. David Farber, *The Age of Great Dreams: America in the 1960s* (New York: Hill and Wang, 1994).

45. "Pastore Hits G.O.P. in Keynote Talk," *Chicago Tribune,* Aug. 25, 1964; "Text of Pastore Keynote Speech," *Los Angeles Times,* Aug. 25, 1964; "Keynoter Pastore Heaps Scorn on 'Captive' GOP," *Hartford Courant,* Aug. 25, 1964.

46. "LBJ Says GOP Faces 'Frontlash,'" *Hartford Courant,* Aug. 28, 1964. See also Johnson and Richard Daley, telephone conversation, Aug. 17, 1964, White House presidential tapes, LBJL.

47. Robert David Johnson, *All the Way with LBJ: The 1964 Presidential Election* (New York: Cambridge University Press, 2009), 191–99.

48. "Polls Show Huge Johnson Lead," *Los Angeles Times,* Aug. 28, 1964; "27% GOP 'Frontlash' Hits Barry," *Boston Globe,* Sept. 6, 1964.

49. Valenti to Johnson, Sept. 7, 1964, White House Central File (WHCF) Ex PL2, box 84, file: PL 2 9/6/64–9/14/64, LBJL.

50. Johnson, *All the Way with LBJ,* 203.

51. For a detailed account of the ad, see Robert Mann, *Daisy Petals and Mushroom Clouds: LBJ, Goldwater, and the Ad That Changed American Politics* (Baton Rouge: Louisiana State University Press, 2011).

52. Valenti to Johnson, Sept. 7, 1964.

53. These ads can be seen on the Web site www.livingroomcandidate.org.

54. E. W. Kenworthy, "Johnson Exhorts South on Rights," *New York Times,* Oct. 10, 1964. See also Carroll Kirkpatrick, "Miller Criticizes Medicare Program," *Washington Post,* Sept. 12, 1964; William Knighton, "Midwest Throngs Hear Johnson Stress Prosperity," *Baltimore Sun,* Oct. 8, 1965.

55. "Goldwater Mocks 'War' on Poverty," *Baltimore Sun,* Sept. 19, 1964.

56. Bernstein, *Guns or Butter,* 155.

57. Roger H. Davidson, David M. Kovenock, and Michael K. O'Leary, *Congress in Crisis: Politics and Congressional Reform* (New York: Hawthorn, 1966), 131.

58. "Results of the 1964 Election," *1964 Congressional Quarterly Almanac,* 23–24.

59. Philip E. Converse, Aage R. Clausen, and Warren E. Miller, "Electoral Myth and Reality: The 1964 Election," *American Political Science Review* 59, no. 2 (June 1965): 327–30.

60. Johnson, *All the Way with LBJ,* 293.

61. Kabaservice, *Rule and Ruin,* 121.

62. Fred Panzer to Hayes Redmon, Jan. 21, 1966, Aides, Office Files of Frederick Panzer, box 407, file: Memos to Hayes Redmon (2 of 2), LBJL.

63. "Johnson Landslide Buries Slightest Trace of 'White Backlash': Cities Report," *Christian Science Monitor,* Nov. 7, 1964.

64. "'Frontlash' Defeats 14 Congressmen," *New Journal and Guide,* Nov. 14, 1964.

65. Alan L. Otten, "Whither the GOP?," *Wall Street Journal,* Nov. 5, 1964.

CHAPTER 6: THE FABULOUS EIGHTY-NINTH CONGRESS

1. Robert Remini, *The House: The History of the House of Representatives* (New York: Harper, 2006), 403.

2. Gallup Poll, press release, Jan. 22, 1965, DNC, ser. 1, box 50, file: Republican Party—Future of the GOP, 1965, LBJL.

3. Patterson, *Grand Expectations,* 564.

4. Lawrence O'Brien, interview by Michael Gillette, July 24, 1986, 1, 6, White House Oral History Collection, LBJL; "Congress—Mathematics of the 89th," *New York Times,* Jan. 3, 1965.

5. David Kraslow, "Southern Power Fades in Current Congress," *Los Angeles Times,* Jan. 6, 1965.

6. Wilbur Cohen, interview by James Sargent, March 18, 1974, 130–31, Columbia University Oral History Project.

7. Woods, *LBJ,* 559.

8. Johnson and Reuther, telephone conversation, Nov. 24, 1964, White House presidential tapes, LBJL.

9. George Meany, interview by Paige Mulhollan, Aug. 4, 1969, 14–15, White House Oral History Collection, LBJL; *1965 Congressional Quarterly Almanac.*

10. Johnson and Reuther, telephone conversation, Jan. 14, 1965, White House presidential tapes, LBJL.

11. Robert C. Albright, "89th Congress Will Open in Fighting Mood," *Washington Post,* Jan. 3, 1965.

12. "Study Group Hits Demo 'Turncoats,'" *Spokesman Review,* Jan. 2, 1965.

13. Johnson and Boggs, telephone conversation, Nov. 4, 1964, White House presidential tapes, LBJL.

14. Johnson and McCormack, telephone conversation, Nov. 5, 1964, White House presidential tapes, LBJL.

15. Davidson, Kovenock, and O'Leary, *Congress in Crisis,* 134.

16. Richard L. Strout, "Liberals to Push for Congressional Rule Reforms," *Christian Science Monitor,* Nov. 12, 1964.

17. Johnson and McCormack, telephone conversation, Nov. 5, 1964, White House presidential tapes, LBJL.

18. "An Adequate Number of Democrats," *Time,* Jan. 15, 1965.

19. Dallek, *Flawed Giant,* 194.

20. Johnson and Albert, telephone conversation, Nov. 9, 1964, White House presidential tapes, LBJL.

21. Fred M. Hechinger, "Schools Reopen; Rolls Up 19,618," *New York Times,* Sept. 11, 1962.

22. Dallek, *Flawed Giant,* 196.

23. "The Head of the Class," *Time,* Oct. 15, 1965.

24. Hugh Davis Graham, *The Uncertain Triumph: Federal Education Policy in the Kennedy and Johnson Years* (Chapel Hill: University of North Carolina Press, 1984), xvii.

25. Gareth Davies, *See Government Grow: Education Politics from Johnson to Reagan* (Lawrence: University Press of Kansas, 2007), 9–13.

26. Edward Berkowitz, "The Great Society," in *The American Congress,* ed. Julian E. Zelizer (Boston: Houghton Mifflin, 2004), 573.

27. Francis Keppell, interview by John Singerhoff, July 18, 1968, Administrative History, Department of Health, Education, and Welfare, box 3A, file: Appendices: The History of the Office of Education, 14, LBJL; James L. Sundquist, *Politics and Policy: The Eisenhower, Kennedy, and Johnson Years*

(Washington, D.C.: Brookings Institution, 1968), 210–11; Davies, *See Government Grow*, 36–37.

28. Johnson and King, telephone conversation, Jan. 15, 1965, White House presidential tapes, LBJL.
29. Marjorie Hunter, "Catholics Favor Education Plans," *New York Times,* Jan. 13, 1965.
30. Carl Perkins, interview by Michael Gillette, May 12, 1983, interview 1, 2, White House Oral History Collection, LBJL; Reeves, *Congressional Committee Chairmen*, 180–81.
31. Bernstein, *Guns or Butter*, 194.
32. Elsie Carper, "School Aid Bill Passes House Unit," *Washington Post*, February 6, 1965.
33. "House Okays Contested $1.3 Billion Education Bill," *Garden City Telegram*, March 27, 1965.
34. Samuel Halperin, interview by Steve Trachtenberg, July 24, 1968, Administrative History, Department of Health, Education, and Welfare, box 3A, file: Appendices: The History of the Office of Education, 4, LBJL.
35. O'Brien to Johnson, March 3, 1965, Office Files of White House Aides, Henry H. Wilson, box 7, file: Education (2 of 2), LBJL.
36. Harry McPherson to Mr. Watson, March 22, 1965, Office Files of White House Aides, Harry McPherson, box 7, file: Education Bill 1965, LBJL.
37. Douglas Cater to Johnson, March 2, 1965, Office Files of White House Aides, Bill Moyers, box 1, file: Education (2 of 2), LBJL.
38. "LBJ: History's Wildest Spending Economizer," *Republican Congressional Committee Newsletter,* Feb. 1, 1965; "GOP Leaders Rap LBJ Grab for Federal Power," *Republican Congressional Committee Newsletter,* March 22, 1965, DNC series 1, box 52, file: Republican Party Publication Congressional Committee Newsletters, LBJL.
39. Barbara Sinclair, "Can a Polarized Congress Legislate Responsibly?" (paper presented to the Congress and History Conference, Columbia University, June 2013).
40. Johnson and Morse, telephone conversation, Jan. 12, 1965, White House presidential tapes, LBJL.
41. Davies, *See Government Grow*, 44.
42. Johnson and George Meany, telephone conversation, April 1, 1965, White House presidential tapes, LBJL.
43. Jonathan Zimmerman, "Uncle Sam at the Blackboard: The Federal Government and American Education," in *To Promote the General Welfare: The Case for Big Government*, ed. Steven Conn (New York: Oxford University Press, 2012), 54–55.
44. James T. Patterson, *The Eve of Destruction: How 1965 Transformed America* (New York: Basic Books, 2012), 61–63; Matusow, *Unraveling of America*, 224–26.
45. Davies, *See Government Grow*.
46. Paul Starr, *The Social Transformation of American Medicine: The Rise of a Sovereign Profession and the Making of a Vast Industry* (New York: Basic Books, 1983).

47. Robert Stevens and Rosemary Stevens, *Welfare Medicine in America: A Case Study in Medicaid,* 2nd ed. (New Brunswick, N.J.: Transaction Books, 2003), 38.

48. John N. Wilford, "More Doctors Devote Full Time to the Aged; Research Outlays Rise," *Wall Street Journal,* Jan. 12, 1961.

49. Sundquist, *Politics and Policy,* 309.

50. David Leonhardt, "When Medicare Was Defeated (Again and Again)," *New York Times,* Sept. 2, 2009; Larry Dewitt, "Operation Coffeecup: Ronald Reagan's Effort to Prevent the Enactment of Medicare" (unpublished paper).

51. "AMA President Elect Asks All to Fight Medicare," *Atlanta Daily World,* Jan. 18, 1963.

52. Henry Wilson to Larry O'Brien, June 8 and April 20, 1964, Office Files of White House Aides, Henry H. Wilson, box 3, file: Medicare, LBJL.

53. Social Security History online, www.ssa.gov/history/.

54. Nelson Cruikshank, interview by Peter A. Corning, Feb. 15, 1966, interview 2, 96–97, Columbia University Oral History Project.

55. Herbert Black, "Did A.M.A. Lose the Election?" *Boston Globe,* Nov. 7, 1964.

56. Bernstein, *Guns or Butter,* 170.

57. Larry O'Brien, interview by Michael Gillette, July 24, 1986, White House Oral History Collection, LBJL.

58. Peter Swenson, "From Medicare to Obamacare: Business Interests and the Building of the Health Care State," *Clio,* forthcoming.

59. David Blumenthal and James A. Morone, *The Heart of Power: Health and Politics in the Oval Office* (Berkeley: University of California Press, 2009), 188–90.

60. Johnson and Cohen, telephone conversation, March 21, 1964, White House presidential tapes, LBJL. See also Blumenthal and Morone, *Heart of Power.*

61. Blumenthal and Morone, *Heart of Power,* 179–81.

62. Arlen J. Large, "Mills and Medicare," *Wall Street Journal,* Aug. 2, 1965.

63. Julian E. Zelizer, *Taxing America: Wilbur D. Mills, Congress, and the State, 1945–1975* (New York: Cambridge University Press, 1998), 241. Notwithstanding speculative conversations that had taken place between Mills and Johnson about the possibility of combining the various programs, there is not much evidence that Johnson actually foresaw, let alone coordinated, the combination package that Mills proposed. For an alternative view, see Blumenthal and Morone, *Heart of Power.*

64. Cohen to Johnson, March 2, 1965, WHCF, Legislation, box 75, file: LE/IS 1 3/1/65–5/31/65 (2 of 2), LBJL.

65. Zelizer, *Taxing America,* 242. See also Cohen to Johnson, March 2, 1965.

66. Louis Harris, "Public Feels Deeply About Need to Get Health Plan Started," *Washington Post,* March 8, 1965.

67. Bernstein, *Guns or Butter,* 172.

68. Johnson and McCormack, Mills, and Cohen, telephone conversation, March 23, 1965, White House presidential tapes, LBJL.

69. Sinclair, "Can a Polarized Congress Legislate Responsibly?"

70. Carl M. Cobb, "Accept Medicare, New AMA Head Says," *Boston Globe,* June 21, 1965.

71. Ezra Klein, "This Is Not Lyndon Johnson's Senate," *Washington Post,* May 8, 2012.

72. Larry O'Brien, interview by Michael Gillette, July 24, 1986, XI, 28, White House Oral History Collection, LBJL.

73. Patterson, *Eve of Destruction,* 52–54; Paul Starr, *Remedy and Reaction: The Peculiar American Struggle over Health Care Reform* (New Haven, Conn.: Yale University Press, 2011), 46–48.

74. Woods, *LBJ,* 573.

75. Starr, *Remedy and Reaction,* 46–48.

76. Jonathan Oberlander, *The Political Life of Medicare* (Chicago: University of Chicago Press, 2003), 33.

77. U.S. Commission on Civil Rights, *The Voting Rights Act: The First Months* (Nov. 1965); Michal R. Belknap, *The Supreme Court Under Earl Warren, 1953–1969* (Columbia: University of South Carolina Press, 2005), 110.

78. Johnson and King, telephone conversation, Jan. 15, 1965, White House presidential tapes, LBJL.

79. "Birth of a Bill," *New Republic,* May 15, 1965, 13.

80. Johnson and Katzenbach, telephone conversation, Dec. 14, 1964, White House presidential tapes, LBJL.

81. Roy Wilkins, "Excerpt from Annual Report at Annual Meeting of the National Association for the Advancement of Colored People," Jan. 4, 1965, President Legislative Background, Voting Rights Act of 1965, box 1, file: Preparation of Voting Rights Bill, LBJL.

82. Johnson and King, telephone conversation, Jan. 15, 1965.

83. John Herbers, "Alabama Vote Drive Opened by Dr. King," *New York Times,* Jan. 3, 1965.

84. Paul Good, "Dr. King to Open 1965 Rights Drive with Speech in Selma, Ala., Today," *Washington Post,* Jan. 2, 1965.

85. David J. Garrow, *Protest at Selma: Martin Luther King Jr. and the Voting Rights Act of 1965* (New Haven, Conn.: Yale University Press, 1979), 45.

86. Denton L. Watson, *Lion in the Lobby: Clarence Mitchell Jr.'s Struggle for the Passage of Civil Rights Laws* (New York: Morrow, 1990), 643.

87. Everett Dirksen, "The Old Problem of Voting Rights," March 15, 1965, Radio-TV Weekly Reports, Dirksen Papers, Dirksen Congressional Center, Pekin, Ill.

88. Graham, *Civil Rights Era,* 166–70.

89. Hulsey, *Everett Dirksen and His Presidents,* 212.

90. Adam Clymer, "Dirksen Asks Vote Rights Legislation," *Baltimore Sun,* March 3, 1965.

91. Taylor Branch, *At Canaan's Edge: America in the King Years, 1965–1968* (New York: Simon & Schuster, 2006), 53.

92. "Negro Marchers Gassed, Beaten," *Boston Globe,* March 8, 1965; "Negroes Routed by Tear Gas," *Chicago Tribune,* March 8, 1965; "Negro Marchers Clubbed: Melee in Selma," *Los Angeles Times,* March 8, 1965; Roy Reed, "Alabama Police Use Gas and Clubs to Rout Negroes," *New York Times,* March 8, 1965.

93. "Negro Marchers Gassed, Beaten."

94. Woods, *LBJ*, 581; Patterson, *Eve of Destruction*, 79.

95. Nan Robertson, "Johnson Pressed for a Voting Law," *New York Times*, March 9, 1965; E. W. Kenworthy, "House G.O.P. Unit Says Johnson Lags on Selma," *New York Times*, March 10, 1965.

96. Woods, *LBJ*, 582.

97. Patterson, *Eve of Destruction*, 79–80.

98. Johnson and Ellington, telephone conversation, March 8, 1965, White House presidential tapes, LBJL.

99. Johnson and Moyers, telephone conversation, March 9, 1965, White House presidential tapes, LBJL.

100. Katzenbach, *Some of It Was Fun*, 164.

101. Wilbur Cohen to Johnson, March 2, 1965, WHCF, Legislation, box 75, file: LE/IS 1 3/1/65–5/31/65 (2 of 2), LBJL.

102. Bernstein, *Guns or Butter*, 235.

103. "Accord Is Reached on Voting Rights," *New York Times*, March 12, 1965.

104. Gary May, *Bending Toward Justice: The Voting Rights Act and the Transformation of American Democracy* (New York: Basic Books, 2013).

105. McPherson to Johnson, March 12, 1965, Legislative Background, Voting Rights Act of 1965, box 2, file: March 12, 1965-Fauntroy et al., LBJL.

106. Jack Valenti, Notes from White House meeting with congressional leaders, March 14, 1965, President's Appointment File (Diary Backup), box 15, file: March 14, 1965, LBJL.

107. Richard B. Stolley, "Inside the White House: Pressures Build Up to the Momentous Speech," *Life*, March 26, 1965.

108. Richard Goodwin, *Remembering America: A Voice from the Sixties* (Boston: Little, Brown, 1988), 334.

109. Johnson and Katzenbach, telephone conversation, March 25, 1965, White House presidential tapes, LBJL.

110. Patterson, *Eve of Destruction*, 84.

111. Graham, *Civil Rights Era*, 172.

112. Dan Day, "Wilkins Calls for Stronger Voting Rights Legislation," *Call and Post*, April 3, 1965.

113. Adam Clymer, *Edward M. Kennedy: A Biography* (New York: Morrow, 1999), 66.

114. Johnson and Vance Hartke, telephone conversation, May 7, 1965, and Johnson and Katzenbach, telephone conversation, May 7, 1965, White House presidential tapes, LBJL.

115. E. W. Kenworthy, "Senate, 70 to 30, Invokes Closure on Voting Rights," *New York Times*, May 26, 1965.

116. Johnson and Albert, telephone conversation, May 18, 1965, White House presidential tapes, LBJL.

117. Dierenfield, *Keeper of the Rules*, 204.

118. Johnson and King, telephone conversation, July 7, 1965, White House presidential tapes, LBJL.

119. Jack Nelson, "Massive Rights Rallies Predicted If Bills Fails," *Los Angeles Times*, July 24, 1965.

120. U.S. Commission on Civil Rights, *Voting Rights Act*.

121. Mark K. Updegrove, *Indomitable Will: LBJ in the Presidency* (New York: Crown, 2012), 170.
122. Sundquist, *Politics and Policy,* 3.
123. Richard L. Strout, "Johnson's Treadmill Spins," *Christian Science Monitor,* April 5, 1965.
124. Dan Cordtz, "Immigration Reform," *Wall Street Journal,* Oct. 4, 1965.
125. John Morton Blum, *Years of Discord: American Politics and Society, 1961–1972* (New York: Norton, 1992), 172; Matusow, *Unraveling of America,* 243–71.
126. Humphrey to Johnson, Feb. 17, 1965, University of California, Santa Barbara, The American Presidency Project online.
127. Patterson, *Eve of Destruction,* 171.

CHAPTER 7: CONGRESSIONAL CONSERVATISM REVIVED

1. Wilson to Johnson, Feb. 24, 1966, Legislative Background: Tax Increase, box 1, file: Tax Increase—January–August 1966, LBJL.
2. Johnson and Wilkins, telephone conversation, Oct. 30, 1965, White House presidential tapes, LBJL.
3. Timothy Minchin and John A. Salmond, *After the Dream: Black and White Southerners Since 1965* (Lexington: University Press of Kentucky, 2011), 23.
4. Ibid., 26–27.
5. Dave Smith, "Los Angeles Area Tense After Riot," *Washington Post,* Aug. 13, 1965; Peter Bart, "2,000 Troops Enter Los Angeles on Third Day of Negro Rioting; 4 Die as Fires and Looting Grow," *New York Times,* Aug. 14, 1965; Gladwin Hill, "Los Angeles Rioting Is Checked; Troops Hunt Snipers; 31 Are Dead; Policeman Is Slain in Long Beach," *New York Times,* Aug. 16, 1965.
6. Johnson and John McCone, telephone conversation, Aug. 18, 1965, White House presidential tapes, LBJL.
7. David Reynolds, *America, Empire of Liberty: A New History of the United States* (New York: Basic Books, 2009), 347.
8. Thomas J. Sugrue, *Sweet Land of Liberty: The Forgotten Struggle for Civil Rights in the North* (New York: Random House, 2009), 422.
9. Barefoot Sanders to Charles Roche, July 26, 1966, Aides, WHCF, Office Files of Charles Roche, box 1, file: Civil Rights, LBJL.
10. Sugrue, *Sweet Land of Liberty,* 204.
11. Thomas J. Sugrue, *The Origins of the Urban Crisis* (Princeton, N.J.: Princeton University Press, 1996).
12. Douglas S. Massey and Nancy A. Denton, "Trends in the Residential Segregation of Blacks, Hispanics, and Asians, 1970–1980," *American Sociological Review* 6 (Dec. 1987): 802–25.
13. Douglas S. Massey and Nancy A. Denton, *American Apartheid: Segregation and the Making of the Underclass* (Cambridge, Mass.: Harvard University Press, 1993), 57.
14. Ibid., 56–57.
15. Paul S. Rothenberg, *Race, Class, and Gender in the United States,* 7th ed. (New York: St. Martin's, 2007), 49.

16. Sugrue, *Sweet Land of Liberty*, 424.
17. Sugrue, *Origins of the Urban Crisis*, 194–97.
18. Alexander von Hoffman, "Let Us Continue: Housing Policy in the Great Society, Part One" (paper published for the Joint Center for Housing Studies, Harvard University, April 2009), 13–24.
19. Bernstein, *Guns or Butter*, 368.
20. Sugrue, *Sweet Land of Liberty*, 420.
21. Ibid.; Charles Johnson to George Reedy, April 22, 1964, Confidential File, box 80, file: Public Opinion Polls (April 1964–June 1965) (4 of 4), LBJL.
22. Markman to Larry O'Brien, March 11, 1966, Aides, Office Files of Charles Roche, box 1, file: Civil Rights, LBJL.
23. Katzenbach to Joseph Califano, March 12, 1966, "Summary of the Congressional Contacts," 1966, and Katzenbach to Califano, March 9, 1966, Aides, WHCF, Office Files of Charles Roche, box 1, file: Civil Rights, LBJL.
24. Russell Freeburg, "Dirksen Hits Bid for Fair Housing Law," *Chicago Tribune*, May 3, 1966; Robert C. Albright, "Rights Bill's Housing Attacked by Dirksen," *Washington Post*, May 3, 1966.
25. Hulsey, *Everett Dirksen and His Presidents*, 223.
26. Henry Wilson to Johnson, March 11, 1966, and Katzenbach to Califano, March 9, 1966, Aides, Office Files of Charles Roche, box 1, file: Civil Rights, LBJL; Wilson to Johnson, March 11, 1966, Office Files of White House Aides, Henry H. Wilson, box 11, file: Civil Rights, LBJL.
27. Joseph Hearst, "Open Housing Called Bar to Race Harmony," *Chicago Tribune*, May 25, 1966.
28. "The Voters' Mood," *Wall Street Journal*, Nov. 7, 1966.
29. Beryl Satter, *Family Properties: Race, Real Estate, and the Exploitation of Black America* (New York: Metropolitan, 2009), 194.
30. The following account of the Mathias amendment is from Charles McC. Mathias and Marion Morris, "Fair Housing Legislation: Not an Easy Row to Hoe," *Cityscape: A Journal of Policy Development and Research* 4 (1999): 21–24. See also Watson, *Lion in the Lobby*, 673–77.
31. Graham, *Civil Rights Era*, 261.
32. Bruce Winters, "House Unit Approves Rights Bills," *Baltimore Sun*, June 30, 1966.
33. Ben A. Franklin, "Wilkins Presses for Open Housing," *New York Times*, July 27, 1966.
34. Ben A. Franklin, "Realtors' Lobby Calls for Fight on Open Housing," *New York Times*, July 29, 1966.
35. Paul H. Douglas, *In the Fullness of Time* (New York: Harcourt Brace Jovanovich, 1972), 585.
36. Gene Roberts, "Attack by Whites Foiled in Chicago," *New York Times*, Aug. 4, 1966.
37. "Passes Law Requiring Marchers' Names, Addresses," *Jet*, Sept. 29, 1966, 4; "Youth Killed, Score Hurt In," *Jet*, Sept. 15, 1966; "Waukegan Invokes Emergency Curfew," *Washington Post*, Aug. 30, 1966; "Seize 64 in Waukegan Riot," *Chicago Tribune*, Aug. 29, 1966.

38. Davies, *From Opportunity to Entitlement*, 148–49.
39. John Herbers, "Rights Backers Fear a Backlash," *New York Times*, Sept. 21, 1966.
40. Henry W. De Zutter, "The Coattails of Bigotry," *New Republic*, Nov. 5, 1966, 8–9.
41. John Dreiske, "Hoellen, Pucinski Court 'Backlash,'" *Washington Post*, Sept. 25, 1966.
42. Lyn Shepard, "Congress Wary of Title IV," *Christian Science Monitor*, Aug. 2, 1966.
43. Marjorie Hunter, "Democrats Split on Open Housing," *New York Times*, Aug. 1, 1966.
44. Douglas, *In the Fullness of Time*, 580.
45. Johnson and Daley, telephone conversation, Aug. 16, 1966, White House presidential tapes, LBJL.
46. Watson, *Lion in the Lobby*, 676.
47. Richard Lyons, "House Softens Rights Housing by 1 Vote Margin," *Washington Post*, Aug. 4, 1966.
48. John Herbers, "Exemption of 60% in Open Housing Voted by House," *New York Times*, Aug. 4, 1966.
49. Henry H. Wilson to Johnson, Aug. 5, 1966, WHCF Legislation, box 65, file: LE/HU 2 8/1/64–12/31/66, LBJL.
50. Bruce Winters, "Rights Group Presses for Housing Bill," *Baltimore Sun*, Sept. 9, 1966; Andrew J. Glass, "Dirksen Turns Back on Rights Movement," *Washington Post*, Sept. 9, 1966.
51. Johnson and McNamara, telephone conversation, Sept. 29, 1966, White House presidential tapes, LBJL.
52. "1966 Civil Rights Act Dies in Senate," *1966 Congressional Quarterly Almanac*.
53. Johnson and Fortas, telephone conversation, Oct. 3, 1966, White House presidential tapes, LBJL.
54. "1966 Civil Rights Act Dies in Senate."
55. "Time Yet to Come," *Christian Science Monitor*, Sept. 22, 1966.
56. Rick Perlstein, *Nixonland: The Rise of a President and the Fracturing of America* (New York: Scribner, 2008), 146. See also Michael Flamm, *Law and Order: Street Crime, Civil Unrest, and the Crisis of Liberalism in the 1960s* (New York: Columbia University Press, 2005).
57. D. J. R. Bruckner, "Wisconsin GOP Fights to Regain House Seats," *Los Angeles Times*, Oct. 24, 1966; Donald Janson, "G.O.P. in Wisconsin Has Uphill Battle," *New York Times*, Oct. 25, 1966.
58. Howard James, "Congressional Targets in Iowa for GOP," *Christian Science Monitor*, Oct. 7, 1966.
59. This aspect of the election has been chronicled in Perlstein's *Nixonland*.
60. Kevin Kruse, *White Flight: Atlanta and the Making of Modern Conservatism* (Princeton, N.J.: Princeton University Press, 2007), 226.
61. D. J. R. Bruckner, "Illinois Backlash Vote for Percy Not Seen," *Los Angeles Times*, Sept. 18, 1966.
62. Donald Janson, "Backlash Issue Boils in Illinois," *New York Times*, Nov. 5, 1966.

63. Johnson and Douglas, telephone conversation, Oct. 16, 1966, White House presidential tapes, LBJL.

64. Zelizer, *Arsenal of Democracy,* 197.

65. Oliver, Quayle, and Company, *A Survey of the Political Climate in Virginia,* April 1966, Confidential File, box 81, file: PR 16 Public Opinion Polls (1966) (3 of 9), LBJL.

66. William M. Blair, "Republican Gains Expected in the Farm Belt as Vietnam and Spending Stir Discontent," *New York Times,* Oct. 30, 1966.

67. Meg Jacobs, *Pocketbook Politics: Economic Citizenship in Twentieth-Century America* (Princeton, N.J.: Princeton University Press, 2005), 246–61.

68. James D. Savage, *Balanced Budgets and American Politics* (Ithaca, N.Y.: Cornell University Press, 1988), 1–8.

69. Tom Wicker, "The Inflation Debate," *New York Times,* March 30, 1966.

70. Albert T. Kraus, "Inflation Today a Two-Sided Coin," *New York Times,* March 27, 1966.

71. Oliver, Quayle, and Company, *A Survey of the Political Climate in the 22nd Congressional District of California,* March 1966, Confidential File, box 81, file: PR 16 Public Opinion Polls (1966) (3 of 9), LBJL.

72. Matusow, *Unraveling of America,* 161.

73. Savage, *Balanced Budgets and American Politics,* 179–81.

74. For an analysis that stresses some of the continued success of this strategy, see David Shreve, "Lyndon Johnson and the Keynesian Revolution: The Struggle for Full Employment and Price Stability," in *Looking Back at LBJ: White House Politics in a New Light,* ed. Mitchell B. Lerner (Lawrence: University Press of Kansas, 2005), 190–201.

75. Johnson and Don Cook, telephone conversation, May 14, 1966, White House presidential tapes, LBJL.

76. Research Council, *Popular Support for the "Welfare State,"* Jan. 11, 1966, Confidential File, box 81, file: Public Opinion Polls (1966) (3 of 9), LBJL.

77. Perlstein, *Nixonland,* 149–50.

78. Hulsey, *Everett Dirksen and His Presidents,* 223.

79. "Make Election a Price Protest Day, Nixon Says," *Los Angeles Times,* Nov. 8, 1966.

80. Don Irwin, "Nixon Comeback Had Its Start in Ashes of 1964 GOP Debacle," *Los Angeles Times,* Aug. 8, 1968; J. William Middendorf II, *A Glorious Disaster: Barry Goldwater's Presidential Campaign and the Origins of the Conservative Movement* (New York: Basic Books, 2006), 247.

81. Roche to Johnson, May 20, 1966, Aides, Office Files of Charles Roche, box 3, file: Memos to the President 1966, LBJL.

82. "Lyndon Says G.O.P. Tries to Scare Voter," *Chicago Tribune,* Oct. 8, 1966.

83. Joseph A. Califano Jr., *The Triumph and Tragedy of Lyndon Johnson: The White House Years,* rev. ed. (New York: Simon & Schuster, 2000), 151–52.

84. "Estimates of the Number of Persons Who Have Benefited from Selected Legislative Actions of the 89th Congress," Oct. 11, 1966, Office Files of Frederick Panzer, box 334, file: Congress (Great), LBJL. See also Fred Panzer to Johnson, Oct. 4, 1966, Office Files of Frederick Panzer, box 398, file: Memos for the President 4/67 10/66–4/67, LBJL.

85. Philip Potter, "Johnson Lays 'Fear' Tactic to GOP Again," *Baltimore Sun*, Oct. 13, 1966.

86. Roche to Johnson, Oct. 5, 1966, Aides, Office Files of Charles Roche, box 3, file: Memos to the President 1966, LBJL.

87. "Johnson Signs 8 Bills Supporting Great Society," *New York Times*, Nov. 4, 1966.

88. "A Close Look at the Results over the Country," *U.S. News and World Report*, Nov. 21, 1966, 37–45; "GOP '66: Back on the Map," *Newsweek*, Nov. 21, 1966, 31–32.

89. "Republicans Score Net Gain of 47 House Seats," *1966 Congressional Quarterly Almanac*.

90. "The 91st: A House That Will Be Less Than Homey," *Time*, Oct. 25, 1968; "Republicans Score Net Gain of 47 House Seats."

91. John Tierney and David Yalof, "First-Term Presidents and Their Party's House Freshmen: Crafting a Strategic Alliance," *Presidential Studies Quarterly* 28 (Winter 1998): 23.

92. Lewis L. Gould, *Grand Old Party: A History of the Republicans*, rev. ed. (New York: Oxford University Press, 2012), 382.

93. Tom Wicker, "House Seats Shift," *New York Times*, Nov. 9, 1966.

94. "Heartland Recaptured," *Time*, Nov. 18, 1966.

95. Graham, *Civil Rights Era*, 203.

96. "Republican Renascence," *New York Times*, Nov. 13, 1966.

97. "A Party for All," *Time*, Nov. 18, 1966.

98. American National Election Studies, 1966.

99. "The Elusive White Backlash," *Afro-American*, Nov. 5, 1966.

100. "White Backlash No Big Factor in Vote, Says King," *Chicago Tribune*, Nov. 10, 1966.

101. Donald Janson, "Percy Calls War a Victory Factor," *New York Times*, Nov. 10, 1966; "Percy Unseats Douglas as Senator from Illinois," *Washington Post*, Nov. 9, 1966.

102. Johnson and Humphrey, telephone conversation, Dec. 31, 1966, White House presidential tapes, LBJL.

CHAPTER 8: THE TRIUMPH OF AUSTERITY POLITICS

1. Martin F. Nolan, "Dr. King Hits 'Ill-Considered' Vietnam War," *Boston Globe*, Dec. 16, 1966.

2. Ida Merriam, Alfred M. Skolnik, and Sophie R. Dales, "Social Welfare Expenditures, 1967–1968," *Social Security Bulletin*, Dec. 1968.

3. MacKenzie and Weisbrot, *The Liberal Hour*, 318.

4. John Herbers, "Coalition Takes Control in House," *New York Times*, Jan. 11, 1967.

5. Johnson and Wilkins, telephone conversation, Jan. 11, 1967, White House presidential tapes, LBJL.

6. Everett Dirksen, statement to the press, Feb. 2, 1967, U.S. Congress, House of Representatives, 90th Cong., 1st sess., *A Record of Press Conference Statements Made by Senator Everett McKinley Dirksen and Representative Gerald R. Ford*, Dec. 13, 1967, 1, Dirksen Congressional Center.

7. Dallek, *Flawed Giant,* 309.
8. Cathie J. Martin, *Shifting the Burden: The Struggle over Growth and Corporate Taxation* (Chicago: University of Chicago Press, 1991), 82, 87–88.
9. "FHA Housing Starts Fell 26% in September from 1965," *Wall Street Journal,* Oct. 21, 1966.
10. Eileen Shanahan, "N.A.M. Endorses Tax Rise but Says 10% Is Too Much," *New York Times,* Aug. 22, 1967.
11. Martin, *Shifting the Burden,* 59.
12. "Congressmen Ask Cuts in Domestic Plans," *Los Angeles Times,* Jan. 25, 1967.
13. "Budget Deficit for War Is Backed by Dirksen," *Washington Post,* Jan. 2, 1967.
14. Matusow, *Unraveling of America,* 160.
15. "Congress Vows a 'Hard Look,'" *Boston Globe,* Jan. 25, 1967.
16. Fred Panzer to Johnson, Feb. 24, 1967, Office Files of Frederick Panzer, box 398, file: February, LBJL; "People Not Willing to Accept Tax Boost," *Boston Globe,* February 27, 1967.
17. Governor and Mrs. Richard Hughes, interview by Joe Frantz, Aug. 6, 1969, interview 1, 82, White House Oral History Collection, LBJL; Perlstein, *Nixonland,* 191.
18. Johnson and Goldberg, telephone conversation, July 15, 1967, White House presidential tapes, LBJL.
19. Joshua Bloom and Waldo E. Martin, *Black Against Empire: The History and Politics of the Black Panther Party* (Berkeley: University of California Press, 2013), 88.
20. Califano, *Triumph and Tragedy of Lyndon Johnson* (1991), 213.
21. Philip Potter, "GOP Charges 'Total Failure' in Proposals to Curb Riots," *Baltimore Sun,* July 25, 1967.
22. Curt Gentry, *J. Edgar Hoover: The Man and His Secrets* (New York: Norton, 2001), 601.
23. Gene Roberts, "U.S. Troops Sent into Detroit: 19 Dead; Johnson Decries Riots: New Outbreak in East Harlem," *New York Times,* July 25, 1967.
24. Califano, *Triumph and Tragedy of Lyndon Johnson,* 219.
25. "Subsidized Riots," *Chicago Tribune,* July 20, 1967.
26. William C. Selover and Lyn Shepard, "Opposition to Great Society Hardens," *Christian Science Monitor,* Aug. 5, 1967.
27. Woods, *LBJ,* 791.
28. Richard L. Lyons, "House Rejects Funds to Kill Rats," *Boston Globe,* July 21, 1967; James Macnies, "Clarence Mitchell Assails House for Rat Bill Failure," *Baltimore Sun,* July 25, 1967.
29. "Riots May Set Back Poverty War," *Chicago Daily Defender,* July 27, 1967.
30. Selover and Shepard, "Opposition to Great Society Hardens."
31. Fred Panzer to Johnson, Aug. 11, 1967, Office Files of Frederick Panzer, box 398, file: August, LBJL.
32. "Guard Dog Rentals Are Booming," *Washington Post,* July 29, 1967.
33. George Gallup, "Romney Takes Lead over Sagging Johnson in Ratings," *Los Angeles Times,* Aug. 20, 1967; "Public Confidence in President Johnson at Lowest Point," *Boston Globe,* Aug. 12, 1967.

34. Douglas Cater, Ben Wattenberg, and Ervin Duggan to Johnson, Aug. 19, 1967, Aides, Files of Douglas Cater, box 17, file: Memos to the President, August 1967, LBJL.

35. Hobart Rowen, "Economists Back LBJ on Tax Rise," *Washington Post,* Sept. 11, 1967.

36. Richard L. Lyons, "Tax Increase Plan Faces Stiff Battle in Both Houses," *Washington Post,* Aug. 4, 1967.

37. Ibid.

38. Zelizer, *Taxing America,* 268–69.

39. "Texts of Announcement and Address by Representative Mills on Taxes and Expenditures," *New York Times,* Nov. 21, 1967.

40. Johnson and Mills, Sept. 19, 1967, White House presidential tapes, LBJL.

41. Norman C. Miller, "Johnson's Tax-Boost Bill Appears Doomed; Cuts Likely in Anti-poverty, Aid Programs," *Wall Street Journal,* Oct. 9, 1967.

42. Philip Warden, "LBJ Surtax Bill Shelved," *Chicago Tribune,* Oct. 4, 1967.

43. "Text of Mills Statement on Federal Spending and Growth of Government," *New York Times,* Oct. 7, 1967.

44. Robert Schlesinger, *White House Ghosts: From FDR to George W. Bush* (New York: Simon & Schuster, 2008), 180–81.

45. *Economic Report of the President, February 1968* (Washington, D.C.: U.S. Government Printing Office, 1968), 11.

46. Goodwin, *Remembering America,* 512.

47. Edwin L. Dale, "The Gold Rush," *New Republic,* March 23, 1968, 10.

48. Lyndon Baines Johnson, *The Vantage Point: Perspectives on the Presidency, 1963–1969* (New York: Popular Library, 1971), 316.

49. "The Gold Crisis Is Here," *Los Angeles Times,* March 14, 1968.

50. Robert M. Collins, *More: The Politics of Economic Growth in Postwar America* (New York: Oxford University Press, 2000), 69.

51. Don Irwin, "Nixon Lays Gold Crisis to U.S. Deficit Spending," *Los Angeles Times,* March 16, 1968.

52. Humphrey to Barefoot Sanders, March 13, 1968, Papers of Barefoot Sanders, box 29, file: Tax Bill 1/68–3/68, LBJL.

53. Larry Levinson, minutes, "Meeting in the Cabinet Room to Discuss the Tax-Increase-Expenditure Reduction Situation," Nov. 21, 1967, Aides, Files of Joseph Califano, box 16, file: Memos to the President, 11/1/67–12/7/1967, LBJL; Tom Johnson, notes on meeting, Nov. 20, 1967, Tom Johnson's Notes on Meeting, box 1, file: November 20, 1967, 5:05 p.m., Bipartisan Congressional Leadership, LBJL.

54. Fowler to Johnson, March 8, 1968, Confidential File, box 63, file: Legislation LE/FI 11-4, LBJL; Barefoot Sanders to Johnson, March 15, 1968, White House Central Files, box 53, file: LE/FI 11-4 2/1/68–4/30/68, LBJL.

55. Johnson and Dirksen, telephone conversation, March 12, 1968, White House presidential tapes, LBJL.

56. Johnson and Mills, telephone conversation, March 24, 1968, White House presidential tapes, LBJL.

57. Johnson and Willard Wirtz, telephone conversation, March 23, 1968, White House presidential tapes, LBJL.

58. Johnson and Fowler, telephone conversation, March 24, 1968, White House presidential tapes, LBJL.

59. Ibid.

60. Johnson and Reuther, telephone conversation, March 20, 1968, White House presidential tapes, LBJL.

61. Zelizer, *Arsenal of Democracy*, 214–15; James R. Jones, "Why LBJ Bowed Out," *Los Angeles Times*, March 30, 2008.

62. Woods, *LBJ*, 836.

63. Goodwin, *Remembering America*, 522–23.

64. Robert J. Donovan, "Withdrawal Announcement Catches Nation by Surprise," *Los Angeles Times*, April 1, 1968.

65. Homer Bigart, "Kennedy, Told News on Plane, Sits in Silence amid the Hubbub," *New York Times*, April 1, 1968.

66. Clement J. Zablocki, interview by Paige Mulhollan, Jan. 16, 1969, interview 1, 8, White House Oral History Collection, LBJL.

67. Goodwin, *Remembering America*, 523.

68. "Johnson's Announcement Spurs Increase in Long-Distance Calls," *New York Times*, April 1, 1968.

69. Henry Gemmill, "Outlook for LBJ," *Wall Street Journal*, April 2, 1968.

70. Frank C. Porter, "Package Passes 57 to 31," *Washington Post*, April 3, 1968.

71. Thomas, *Robert Kennedy*, 367.

72. Richard Scott, "Rioting Improves Prospects of Civil Rights Bill," *Guardian*, April 9, 1968.

73. Massey and Denton, *American Apartheid*, 194.

74. Graham, *Civil Rights Era*, 271–72.

75. David L. Chappell, *Waking from the Dream: The Struggle for Civil Rights in the Shadow of Martin Luther King Jr.* (New York: Random House, 2014), 17.

76. Ibid.

77. Denton and Massey, *American Apartheid*, 195–96.

78. Califano to Johnson, April 10, 1968, Aides, Office Files of Joseph Califano, box 16, file: Memos for the President—March, LBJL.

79. Califano, *Triumph and Tragedy of Lyndon Johnson*, 285.

80. Barefoot Sanders to Johnson, April 27, 1968, WHCF, EX FI 11-4 7/16/67, box 61, file: FI 11-4 3/28/68–5/20/68, LBJL.

81. Okun to Johnson, May 13, 1968, and minutes, cabinet meeting, May 14, 1968, Cabinet Papers, box 13, file: Cabinet Meeting 5/14/68 (2 of 3), LBJL.

82. Transcript, "Cabinet Meeting of May 1, 1968," Cabinet Papers, box 13, file: Cabinet Meeting 5/1/68 (1 of 4); transcript, "Cabinet Meeting of May 29, 1968," Cabinet Papers, box 13, file: Cabinet Meeting 5/29/68 (1 of 3), LBJL.

83. Tom Johnson, notes on meeting in Cabinet Room with leaders of House and Senate, April 3, 1969, Tom Johnson Notes of Meetings, box 3, file: April 2—Tuesday Luncheon: April 3, 1968-Cabinet Meeting Luncheon Meeting with the House and Senate Committee, LBJL.

84. Barefoot Sanders to Johnson, May 9, 1968, Aides, Office Files of Joseph Califano, box 54, file: Taxes—1967–1968, LBJL.

85. "Effects of the Tax Hike," *Time*, June 28, 1968.

86. Collins, *More,* 96–97.
87. Ibid., 97.

CHAPTER 9: THE ENDURANCE OF THE GREAT SOCIETY

1. Theodore White, *The Making of the President: 1968* (New York: Atheneum, 1969), 243.
2. Matusow, *The Unraveling of America,* 427.
3. "Nixon Will Wage 2-Pronged Strategy," *News and Courier,* Sept. 1, 1968.
4. "Hubert Calls Agnew Choice Compromise," *Chicago Tribune,* Aug. 9, 1968.
5. Steven F. Hayward, *The Age of Reagan: The Fall of the Old Liberal Order, 1964–1980* (New York: Crown, 1984), 200.
6. David Farber, *Chicago '68* (Chicago: University of Chicago Press, 1988), 201.
7. Carter, *Politics of Rage,* 338–39.
8. Walter Pincus, "The Public and the Private George Wallace," *Washington Post,* Aug. 10, 1968.
9. Lewis L. Gould, *1968: The Election That Changed America,* 2nd ed. (Chicago: Ivan Dee, 2010), 29.
10. "Nixon Scores 'Tax of Inflation'; Says Worker Is on Treadmill," *New York Times,* Sept. 2, 1968.
11. "Where Nixon Stands on the Issues," *Los Angeles Times,* Oct. 27, 1968.
12. Woods, *LBJ,* 868.
13. Matusow, *Unraveling of America,* 432.
14. Ibid., 432–33.
15. Louis Harris, "Nixon Leads by Questionable 3 Points," *Boston Globe,* Nov. 1, 1968; "Humphrey Gains in Polls, but Time Is Running Out," *Newsday,* Oct. 28, 1968; "Humphrey Gaining; Wallace Dropping," *Boston Globe,* Oct. 27, 1968; George Gallup, "Humphrey Gains: Wallace Declines," *Los Angeles Times,* Oct. 27, 1968.
16. Johnson and Dirksen, telephone conversation, Oct. 31, 1968, White House presidential tapes, LBJL.
17. Clayton Knowles, "Great Society: What It Was, Where It Is," *New York Times,* Dec. 9, 1968.
18. Stephen E. Nordlinger, "Finch to Retain Most Programs," *Baltimore Sun,* Dec. 17, 1968.
19. Patterson, *Grand Expectations,* 720.
20. Paul Marcus, "The Philadelphia Plan and Strict Racial Quotas in Federal Contracts," Faculty Publications, William & Mary Law School Scholarship Repository, 1970, 817.
21. Katz, *Undeserving Poor,* 113.
22. Christopher Wimer, Liana Fox, Irv Garfinkel, Neeraj Kaushal, and Jane Waldfogel, "Trends in Poverty with an Anchored Supplemental Poverty Measure" (Dec. 5, 2013).
23. Katz, *Undeserving Poor,* 113.
24. Colleen Grogan and Eric M. Patashnik, "Between Welfare Medicine and Mainstream Entitlement: Medicaid at the Political Crossroads," *Journal of Health, Policy, Politics, and Law* 28, no. 5 (2003): 831.

25. Martha J. Bailey and Sheldon Danzinger, "Legacies of the War on Poverty," in *Legacies of the War on Poverty*, ed. Martha J. Bailey and Sheldon Danzinger (New York: Russell Sage, 2013), 23.

26. David R. Goldfield, *Still Fighting the Civil War: The American South and Southern History* (Baton Rouge: Louisiana State University Press, 2004), 257.

27. Katherine Swartz, "Medicare and Medicaid," in Bailey and Danzinger, *Legacies of the War on Poverty,* 269.

28. Elizabeth Cascio and Sarah Reber, "The K–12 Education Battle," in ibid., 85.

29. David E. Rosenbaum, "20 Years Later, the Great Society Flourishes," *New York Times,* April 17, 1985.

ILLUSTRATION CREDITS

INSERT 1

Page 1: Above: Lyndon B. Johnson Presidential Library, photo by Yoichi Okamoto. Below: U.S. Senate Historical Office.

Page 2: Above: The University of Virginia Library. Below: AP Photo/Bill Hudson.

Page 3: Above: William M. McCulloch Papers, Ohio State University. Below: Lyndon B. Johnson Presidential Library.

Page 4: Above: © Bettmann/Corbis. Below: Photograph © AFL-CIO, used with permission.

Page 5: Above: Smithsonian Institution Archives, Image #SIA2011-2223, photo by James Wallace. Below: Abbie Rowe, White House Photographs, John F. Kennedy Presidential Library and Museum, Boston.

Page 6: Above: White House Photo Office, Lyndon B. Johnson Presidential Library. Below: Lyndon B. Johnson Presidential Library, photo by Yoichi Okamoto.

Page 7: Above: Lyndon B. Johnson Presidential Library, photo by Yoichi Okamoto. Below: Lyndon B. Johnson Presidential Library, photo by Yoichi Okamoto.

Page 8: Above: William M. McCulloch Papers, Ohio State University. Below: © Bettmann/Corbis.

Page 9: © Library of Congress/Science Faction/Corbis.

Page 10: Above: Lyndon B. Johnson Presidential Library, photo by Cecil Stoughton. Middle: Lyndon B. Johnson Presidential Library, photo by Yoichi Okamoto. Below: AP Photo/Bill Allen.

Page 11: Above: Lyndon B. Johnson Presidential Library, photo by Cecil Stoughton. Below: Lyndon B. Johnson Presidential Library, photo by Yoichi Okamoto.

Page 12: Above: © David J. & Janice L. Frent Collection/Corbis. Below: Photograph of William Fulbright and Lyndon B. Johnson, The J. William Fulbright Papers, University of Arkansas Libraries, Fayetteville.

Page 13: Above: © Bettmann/Corbis/AP Images. Below: Lyndon B. Johnson Presidential Library, photo by Cecil Stoughton.

Page 14: Above: AP Photo. Below: AP Photo.

Page 15: Above: Lyndon B. Johnson Presidential Library, photo by Cecil Stoughton. Below: Lyndon B. Johnson Presidential Library, photo by Yoichi Okamoto.

Page 16: Above: Lyndon B. Johnson Presidential Library. Below: Used by permission of University of Missouri–Kansas City Libraries, Dr. Kenneth J. LaBudde Department of Special Collections, photo by Nate Fine Photo.

ILLUSTRATION CREDITS

INSERT 2

Page 1: Above: Lyndon B. Johnson Presidential Library, photo by Yoichi Okamoto. Below: AP Photo/Charles Gorry.

Page 2: Above: U.S. Senate Historical Office. Below: Lyndon B. Johnson Presidential Library, photo by Yoichi Okamoto.

Page 3: Above: U.S. Senate Historical Office. Below: © Bettmann/Corbis.

Page 4: Above: Wisconsin Historical Society. Middle: Lyndon B. Johnson Presidential Library. Below: © Corbis.

Page 5: © Bettmann/Corbis.

Page 6: Above: Lyndon B. Johnson Presidential Library, photo by Cecil Stoughton. Below: © Bettmann/Corbis.

Page 7: Above: © Bettmann/Corbis. Below: © Bettmann/Corbis.

Page 8: Above: Lyndon B. Johnson Presidential Library, photo by Yoichi Okamoto. Below: Lyndon B. Johnson Presidential Library, photo by Yoichi Okamoto.

Page 9: Above: Lyndon B. Johnson Presidential Library, photo by Yoichi Okamoto. Below: Lyndon B. Johnson Presidential Library, photo by Yoichi Okamoto.

Page 10: Above: Lyndon B. Johnson Presidential Library, photo by Yoichi Okamoto. Below: © Bettmann/Corbis.

Page 11: © Bob Adelman/Corbis.

Page 12: Above: National Archives, photo no. 127-N-A704884. Below: Lyndon B. Johnson Presidential Library, photo by Frank Wolfe.

Page 13: Above: © Bettmann/Corbis. Below: © Bettmann/Corbis.

Page 14: Above: Lyndon B. Johnson Presidential Library, photo by Yoichi Okamoto. Middle: Lyndon B. Johnson Presidential Library, photo by Yoichi Okamoto. Below: © Bettmann/Corbis.

Page 15: Above: Lyndon B. Johnson Presidential Library, photo by Yoichi Okamoto. Below: National Archives, photo no. 192616.

Page 16: Above: Nixon Presidential Library. Below: Lyndon B. Johnson Presidential Library, photo by Frank Wolfe.

INDEX

and Medicare, 186, 187–88
and the nonunion South, 3, 70
Philadelphia Plan, 317
power of, 167
and racial discrimination, 50, 70, 232
right-to-work laws, 4, 70, 167–68
and Section 14B, 168
and Taft-Hartley Act, 4, 70, 167–68
teachers' unions, 176
and Wagner Act, 4
and War on Poverty, 143–44
Landon, Alf, 14
Landrum, Philip M., 142–43
Law Enforcement Assistance
Administration, 298
Leadership Conference on Civil Rights, 27,
57, 60, 90, 96, 97, 110, 114, 121, 206,
218, 276
Lee, Charles, 177
Lehman, Herbert H., 23, 25
LeMay, Curtis, 312
Levison, Stanley, 38
Lewis, John (SNCC chairman), 209, 215
liberalism:
and attacks on LBJ, 303
campaign about conservatism vs., 151–59
in Congress, 22–28, 163–68, 169, 202, 221
congressional opposition to, 12, 13–22
grassroots activism of, 22, 28
and Great Society, 3–5, 165, 169, 247
and hawkish foreign policy, 9
"Liberal Manifesto," 26
myth about, 3–5
and New Deal, 22, 64–65, 158
and 1964 election, 8–9, 159–62,
163–64, 259
political aims of, 27
and racial equality, 4–5; *see also various*
Civil Rights Acts; civil rights bills
and social problems, 4, 27, 133, 165,
201, 239
and voting rights, 215–18
Lincoln, Abraham, 39, 119, 123, 220, 239
Lindsay, John V., 40, 239
Little Rock Central School, 29, 32
Lodge, Henry Cabot, 136
Loney, Kate Deadrich, 184
Long, Edward V., 108
Long, Russell B., 199, 206

MacArthur, Douglas, 69–70
McCarthy, Eugene J., 26, 284–86, 292, 294

McClure, Stewart, 177
McCormack, John W., 88, 144–45, 170–72,
173, 209, 213, 218, 221
McCulloch, William M., 40, 42, 54–56, 57,
58, 59, 97–98, 101, 212, 236
McDonald, David, 88
McGovern, George, 308
Mackie, John C., 258
McNamara, Pat, 139
McNamara, Robert S., 144, 145, 149,
167, 291
McPherson, Harry C. Jr., 210, 213
Maddox, Lester, 249
Magnuson, Warren G., 108, 120
Mahon, George H., 135, 138, 272
Mahoney, George P., 249
Malone, Vivian, 48
Manatos, Mike, 109
Mansfield, Mike:
and civil rights, 102, 104, 105, 107–8, 110,
115, 118, 120, 127, 246
and Vietnam, 150
and voting rights, 207, 212, 214, 217, 218
Markman, Sherman, 235
Marshall, Burke, 46, 50, 54, 55, 56, 109,
119, 120
Marshall, Thurgood, 37
Martin, Joseph W., Jr., 15–16
Martin, William McChesney, 269
Mathias, Charles McC., 238–40, 242,
244–45
Maverick, Maury, 67
Meany, George, 26
Medicaid, 197, 222, 265, 311, 320, 321
Medicare, 184–201, 222, 254, 256, 265
expansion of, 317, 320
and JFK, 188–90
and Mills, 189–92, 193, 194–97,
198–200, 281
opponents of, 159, 165–66, 237
and Social Security, 185, 186, 189–99,
311, 317
support for, 173, 190, 201
midterm elections:
1934, 226
1938, 226
1958, 20, 227
1966, 9–10, 226, 247–61, 265, 271, 310
Miller, William, 158
Mills, Wilbur, 74, 76, 81, 173–74
and the economy, 272, 280–83, 287,
288–90, 298–300